ETHNOGRAPHIC NOTES

ETHNOGRAPHIC NOTES

IN

SOUTHERN INDIA

EDGAR THURSTON

With 40 Plates

GYAN

Published by

GYAN

Gyan Publishing House
5, Ansari Road
Daryaganj, New Delhi-110002
Phone: 011-47034999, 9811692060
E-mail: books@gyanbooks.com

Distribution Network
gyanbooks.com
India, USA, Canada, UK, Australia, France

ISBN : 978-81-212-9636-6 (PB)
First Published, 1906

2nd Impression 2023

Printed at: Gyan Press, Delhi.

ETHNOGRAPHIC NOTES
Author: EDGAR THURSTON

Frontispiece.

Badaga Funeral Car.

ETHNOGRAPHIC NOTES

IN

SOUTHERN INDIA.

With 40 Plates.

BY

EDGAR THURSTON,

SUPERINTENDENT, MADRAS GOVERNMENT MUSEUM;
SUPERINTENDENT OF ETHNOGRAPHY, MADRAS;
CORRESPONDENT ÉTRANGER, SOCIÉTÉ D'ANTHROPOLOGIE DE PARIS.

1906.

PREFACE.

IT has been well said that "there will be plenty of money and people available for anthropological research, when there are no more aborigines. And it behoves our museums to waste no time in completing their anthropological collections." Under the scheme for a systematic ethnographic survey of the whole of India, a superintendent for each Presidency and Province was appointed in 1901, to carry out the work of the survey in addition to his other duties. The other duty, in my particular case—the direction of a large local museum—luckily makes an excellent blend with the survey operations, as the work of collection for the ethnological section goes on synchronously with that of investigation.

For many years I have been engaged in bringing together the scattered information bearing on 'Manners and Customs' in South India, surviving, moribund, or deceased, which lies buried in official reports, manuals, journals of societies, and other publications. The information thus collected has been supplemented by correspondence with district officers and private individuals, and by the personal wanderings of myself and my assistants, Mr. K. Rangachari (from whose negatives most of the illustrations have been made), Mr. V. Govindan and Mr. C. Hayavadana Rao, in various parts of the Madras Presidency, Mysore, and Travancore, in connection with the work of the survey, which demands the writing of a book on lines similar to Risley's 'Tribes and Castes of

Bengal.' For the issue of this book the time is not yet ripe, and, as an *ad interim* measure, I send forth the present farrago in the hope that it may be of some little use and interest to those who are engaged in the study of ethnological and sociological questions in the arm-chair or the field. For such, rather than for the general public, it is intended.

To the many friends and correspondents, European and Native, who have helped me in the accumulation of facts, or whose published writings I have made liberal use of, I would express collectively, and with all sincerity, my great sense of indebtedness. And I would further express a hope that readers will draw my attention to the errors, such as must inevitably arise when one is dealing with a mass of evidence derived from a variety of sources, and provide me with material for a possible future edition.

"Let those now send who never sent before;
And those who have sent, kindly send me more."

Some of the articles, originally published in my Museum Bulletins, are now reproduced with additions.

I may add that the chapter devoted to omens, evil eye, etc., is intended only as a mere outline sketch of a group of subjects, which, if worked up in detail, would furnish material for a very bulky volume.

E. T.

CONTENTS.

PLATES.

SOME MARRIAGE CUSTOMS IN SOUTHERN INDIA.

At the outset I may appropriately quote the account of the Brāhman marriage ceremony as given in the Census report, 1891, to show how the Brāhman ritual has been grafted on the non-Brāhman community. "On the marriage day the bridegroom, dressed in true Vaidiki * fashion with cadjan (palm leaf) books and a bundle of rice on his shoulder, pretends to be setting out for Benares,† there to lead an ascetic life, and the girl's father, meeting him, begs that he will accept the hand of his daughter. He is then taken to the marriage booth (pandal), and is formally entrusted with the girl. The sacred fire (hōmam) is prepared, and worshipped with oblations of ghī (clarified butter), the blessings of the gods are invoked, and the tāli or bottu (marriage badge) ‡ is tied round the neck of the girl by the bridegroom. The couple then go round the sacred fire, and the bridegroom takes up in his hands the right foot of the bride, and places it on a mill-stone seven times. This is known as saptapadi (seven feet), and is the essential and binding portion of the marriage ceremony. The bride is exhorted to be as fixed in constancy as the stone, on which her foot has been thus placed. The bridegroom, holding the

---

* The Vaidikis are the first class of Brāhmans, whose occupation is teaching the Vēdas, performing and superintending sacrifices, and preserving the moral principles of the people.

† The mock flight to Benares is known as Kāsiyātra.

‡ The tāli or bottu corresponds to the ring of European Christendom.

bride's right hand,* repeats the mantrams (prayers) recited by the family priest, and announces, in the presence of the sacred fire, the gods invoked, and the Brāhmans assembled, that he will have her as his inseparable companion, be faithful and so forth. And lastly the bride and bridegroom exchange garlands of flowers. Seed-grains of five or nine kinds are mixed up, and sown in small earthern vessels specially made for the purpose, and filled with earth. The couple water these both morning and evening for four days. On the fifth day the seedlings are thrown into a tank (pond) or river. The boy and girl play every evening with balls of flowers, when women sing songs, and much merriment prevails. On the second night the girl takes her husband to an open place, and points out to him the star Arūndati, (pole star) implying that she will remain as chaste and faithful as that goddess." The earth, in which the seed-grains are sown, is generally obtained from a white-ant hill.

Among some sections of the Brāhmans, especially the Tamil sections, prominence is given to the maternal uncles of the bride and bridegroom on the fourth day after marriage, and at the ceremony called mālaimāththal (exchange of garlands). At this ceremonial both bride and bridegroom should be carried astride on the shoulders of their maternal uncles. Outside the wedding booth the uncles, bearing their nephew and niece, dance to the strains of a band, and, when they meet, the bride and bridegroom exchange garlands. On the fourth

* The marriage is sometimes called, for this reason, pāni grahanam, or grasping the hand.

day a procession is got up at the expense of the maternal uncle of the bride, and is hence named Ammān kōlam. The bride is dressed up as a boy, and another girl is dressed up to represent the bride. They are taken in procession through the street, and, on returning, the pseudo-bridegroom is made to speak to the real bridegroom in somewhat insolent tones, and some mock play is indulged in. The real bridegroom is addressed as if he was the syce (groom) or gumasta (clerk) of the pseudo-bridegroom, and is sometimes treated as a thief, and judgment passed on him by the latter.

It is said that, on the dhiksha visarjana (shaving) day, six months after marriage, in cases where the Brāhman bridegroom is a young boy, he is dressed up as a girl, and the bride's party, when they detect the fraud, jeer at him and his relations for having deceived them. Brāhmans may not shave for six months after marriage, for a year after the death of a parent, and till the birth of the child when their wives are pregnant.

The Mādhva Brāhmans commence the marriage ceremony by asking the ancestors of the bridal couple to bless them, and be present throughout the performance of the rite. To represent the ancestors, a ravike (bodice) and dhotra (man's cloth) are tied to a stick, which is placed near the box containing the sālagrāma stone * and household gods. In consequence of these ancestors being represented, orthodox Vaidiki Brāhmans refuse to take food prepared in the marriage house. When the

* The Sālagrāma stone is a fossil ammonite, found in certain rivers, *e.g.* Gandak, Son, etc., which is worshipped by Brāhmans. "The Sālagrāma is often adopted as the representative of some god, and the worship of any god may be performed before it."—YULE and BURNELL, HOBSON-JOBSON.

bridegroom is conducted to the marriage booth by his future father-in-law, all those who have taken part in the Kāsiyātra ceremony throw rice over him. A quaint ceremony, called rangavriksha (drawing), is performed on the morning of the second day. After the usual playing with balls of flowers (nalagu or ñalangu), the boy takes hold of the right hand of the bride, and, after dipping her right forefinger in turmeric and lime paste, traces on a white wall the outline of a plantain tree, of which a sketch has previously been made by a married woman. The tracing goes on for three days. First the base of the plant is drawn, and, on the evening of the third day, it is completed by putting in the flower spikes. On the third night the bridegroom is served with sweets and other refreshments by his mother-in-law, from whose hands he snatches the vessels containing them. He picks out what he likes best, and scatters the remainder about the room. The pollution caused thereby is removed by sprinkling water and cow-dung, which is done by the cook engaged for the marriage by the bridegroom's family. After washing his hands, the bridegroom goes home, taking with him a silver vessel, which he surreptitiously removes from near the gods. Along with this vessel he is supposed to steal a rope for drawing water, and a rice-pounding stone. But in practice he only steals the vessel, and the other articles are claimed by his people on their return home. On the fourth morning the bridegroom once more returns to the booth, where he ties a tāli of black glass beads and a small gold disc round the bride's neck in the presence of 33 crores (33 millions) of gods, who are represented by a number of variously coloured large and small pots. Close to the pots are the figures of two elephants, designed in rice grains and salt respectively. After going round the pots, the bridal couple separate, and the groom stands by the salt elephant, and the bride by the other. They then begin to talk about the money value of the two animals, and an altercation takes place, during which they again go round the pots, and stand, the bridegroom near the rice elephant, and the bride by the salt one. The bargaining as to the price of the animals is renewed, and the bride and bridegroom again go round the pots. This ceremonial is succeeded by a burlesque of domestic life. The bride is presented with two wooden dolls from Tirupati, and told to make a cradle out of the bridegroom's turmeric-coloured turban, which he wore on the tāli-tying day (muhurtham). The contracting couple are made to converse with each other on domestic matters, and the bridegroom asks the bride to attend to her household affairs, so that he may go to his duties. She pleads her inability to do so because of the children, and asks him to take charge of them. She then shows the babies (dolls) to all those who are present, and a good deal of fun is made out of the incident. The bride, with her mother standing by her side near two empty chairs, is then introduced to her new relations by marriage, who sit in pairs on the chairs, and make presents of pān-supāri (betel leaves and nuts), and turmeric. She is then formally handed over to her husband.

At a wedding among Srī Vaishnava Brāhmans, at an auspicious hour on the fourth day, the bridal pair are seated in the wedding booth, and made to roll a cocoanut to and fro across the dais. The assembled Brāhmans keep on chanting some ten stanzas in Tamil, composed by a Vaishnava lady, named Āndāl, (an avātar of Lakshmi) who dedicated herself to Vishnu. She narrates to her attendants, in the stanzas, the dream in which she went through the marriage ceremony after her dedication to the god. Pān-supāri, of which a little, together with some money, is set apart for Āndāl, is then distributed to all who are present. Generally a large crowd is assembled, as they believe that the chanting of Āndāl's srisukthi (praise of Lakshmi) brings a general blessing. The family priest then calls out the names and gōtras (house names) of those who have become related to the bridegroom and the bride through their marriage, and, as each person's name is called out, he or she is supposed to make a present of cloths, money, etc., to the bride or bridegroom.

Reference has been made (page 4) to the nalagu or nalangu ceremony. This, among Telugu non-Brāhman castes, consists of the anointing of the bride and bridegroom with oil, and smearing the shoulders and arms with turmeric or flour paste, or a paste made with the pods of *Acacia concinna*, or *Phaseolus Mungo*. With some castes it consists of the rolling of a cocoanut, or ball made of flowers, between the bridal couple. By Brāhmans nalangu is restricted to the painting of the feet of the couple with a mixture of turmeric paste and chunām (lime) called nalangu māvu. But the smearing with sandal, turmeric paste, etc., is also carried out.

The Rāzus (Telugu agriculturists), who are settled in Tinnevelly, claim to be Kshatriyas, and to belong to the second of Manu's four castes, Brāhman, Kshatriya,

Plate I.

Rāzu Bridegroom.

Vaisya, and Sūdra. Some of their women are gōsha (kept in seclusion). Men may not shave the face, and wear a beard until their marriage. Nor are they, so long as they remain bachelors, invested with the sacred thread. At the marriage the bridegroom goes through the birth, naming, tonsure, and thread investiture ceremonies on the tāli-tying day. These ceremonies are performed as with Brāhmans, except that, in lieu of passages from the Vēdas, slokas specially prepared for the classes below the Brāhmans are chanted. When the bride is with the bridegroom on the dais, a wide-meshed green curtain is thrown over her shoulders, and her hands are pressed over her eyes, and held there by one of her brothers, so that she cannot see. Generally two brothers sit by her side, and, when one is tired, the other relieves him. At the moment when the tāli is tied, the bride's hands are removed from her face, and she is permitted to see her husband. On the third day the bride is brought to the marriage booth in a closed palanquin, and she is once more blind-folded while an elaborate ceremonial with pots is gone through. "In the Godāvari district," the Rev. J. Cain writes, "there are several families of the Sūryavamsapu Rāzus who are called Basava Rāzulu, in consequence, it is said, of one of their ancestors having accidentally killed a basava or sacred bull. As a penalty for this crime, before a marriage takes place in these families, they are bound to select a young bull and a young cow, and cause these two to be duly married, and then they are at liberty to proceed with their own ceremony."*

* Ind. Ant.. VIII. 1879.

"The Hindus," Sir Walter Elliot writes, "recognise eight descriptions of marriage, two of which, the most ancient, are characterised as accomplished by force. That called irākkadan is thus described. When bold men, becoming enamoured of a damsel, adorned with large ornaments of gold, resolve to seize her by force: this is the marriage rite peculiar to the broad and high-shouldered giants, who wander over the earth, exhibiting their prowess.* Still more applicable to the Australian mode is the paisācha union, in which the possession of the persons of females is obtained, while under the protection of their non-consenting relations, by violence, and in a state of insensibility."†

In savage societies, it has been said, sexual unions were generally effected by the violent capture of the woman. By degrees these captures have become friendly ones, and have ended in a peaceful exogamy, retaining the ancient custom only in the ceremonial form. Whereof an excellent example is afforded by the Khonds (hill tribe) of Ganjam, concerning whom the author of the Ganjam Manual writes as follows. "The parents arrange the marriages of their children. The bride is looked upon as a commercial speculation, and is paid for in gontis. A gonti is one of anything, such as a buffalo, a pig, or a brass pot; for instance, a hundred gontis might consist of ten bullocks, ten buffaloes, ten sacks of corn, ten sets of brass, twenty sheep, ten pigs, and thirty fowls. The usual price, however, paid by the bridegroom's father for

* According to the Hindu Shastras, marriage after forcible abduction is known as rākshasa, which becomes in Tamil irrākkadhan.

† Ind. Ant., XVI., 1887; Ellis. Kural.

the bride is twenty or thirty gontis.* A Khond finds his wife from among the women of any mutāh (village) than his own. On the day fixed for the bride being taken home to her husband's house, the pieces of broom in her ears are removed, and are replaced by brass rings. The bride is covered over with a red blanket, and carried astride on her uncle's back towards the husband's village, accompanied by the young women of her own village. Music is played, and in the rear are carried brass play-things, such as horses, etc., for the bridegroom, and cloths and brass pins as presents for the bridegroom from the bride's father. On the road, at the village boundary, the procession is met by the bridegroom and the young men of his village, with their heads and bodies wrapped up in blankets and cloths. Each is armed with a bundle of long thin bamboo sticks. The young women of the bride's village at once attack the bridegroom's party with sticks, stones, and clods of earth, which the young men ward off with the bamboo sticks. A running fight is in this manner kept up until the village is reached, when the stone-throwing invariably ceases, and the bridegroom's uncle, snatching up the bride, carries her off to her husband's house. This fighting is by no means child's play, and the men are sometimes seriously injured. The whole party is then entertained by the bridegroom as lavishly as his means will permit. On the day after the bride's arrival, a

* Money being till recently unknown in Khondistan, the value of all property is estimated in lives; a bullock, goat, pig or fowl, a bag of grain or a set of brass pots being each, with anything else that may be agreed upon, a life.—Vizagapatam Manual.

buffalo and a pig are slaughtered and eaten, and, upon the bride's attendants returning home on the evening of the second day, a male and female buffalo, or some less valuable present is given to them. On the third day all the Khonds of the village have a grand dance or tamâsha (festivity) and on the fourth day there is another grand assembly at the house of the bridegroom. The bride and bridegroom are then made to sit down on a cot, and the bridegroom's brother, pointing upwards to the roof of the house, says: "As long as this girl stays with us, may her children be as men and tigers; but, if she goes astray, may her children be as snakes and monkeys, and die and be destroyed!" In his report upon the Khonds (1842) Macpherson tells us that "they hold a feast at the bride's house. Far into the night the principals in the scene are raised by an uncle of each upon his shoulders, and borne through the dance. The burdens are suddenly exchanged, and the uncle of the youth disappears with the bride. The assembly divides itself into two parties. The friends of the bride endeavour to arrest, those of the bridegroom to cover her flight, and men, women, and children mingle in mock conflict. I saw a man bearing away upon his back something enveloped in an ample covering of scarlet cloth. He was surrounded by twenty or thirty young fellows, and by them protected from the desperate attacks made upon him by a party of young women. The man was just married, and the burden was his blooming bride, whom he was conveying to his own village. Her youthful friends were, according to custom, seeking to regain possession of her, and hurled stones and bamboos at the head of the devoted bridegroom, until he reached the confines of his own village. Then the tables were turned, and the bride was fairly won; and off her young friends scampered, screaming and laughing, but not relaxing their speed till they reached their own village." Among the Khonds of Gūmsūr, the friends and relations of the bride and bridegroom collect at an appointed spot. The people of the female convoy call out to the others to come and take the bride, and then a mock fight with stones and thorny brambles is begun by the female convoy against the parties composing the other one. In the midst of the tumult the assaulted party take possession of the bride, and all the furniture brought with her, and carry all off together.* According to another account, the bride, as soon as she enters the bridegroom's house, has two enormous bracelets, or rather handcuffs of brass, each weighing from twenty to thirty pounds, attached to each wrist. The unfortunate girl has to sit with her two wrists resting on her shoulders, so as to support these enormous weights. This is to prevent her from running away to her old home. On the third day the bangles are removed, as it is supposed that by then the girl has become reconciled to her fate. These marriage bangles are made on the hills, and are curiously carved in fluted and zigzag lines, and kept as heir-looms in the family, to be used at the next marriage in the house.† Among the Kutiya Khonds chastity is said not to be known, or at least practised by the girls. They

* J. A. R. Stevenson, Madras Journ. Lit. Science, VI, 1837.

† Madras Mail, 1894.

go naked till marriage, and the unmarried men and girls sleep together in a house set apart for the purpose in some villages. In others, by invitation of the girl, any man she fancies visits her at her parent's house. When a man proposes marriage to a girl, he offers to buy her a new cloth, and, after that, she is expected to remain virtuous.* According to a still more recent account of marriage among the Khonds,† an old woman suddenly rushes forward, seizes the bride, flings her on her back, and carries her off. A man comes to the front similarly, catches the groom, and places him astride on his shoulder. The human horses neigh and prance abont like the live quadruped, and finally rush away to the outskirts of the village. This is a signal for the bride's girl friends to chase the couple, and pelt them with clods of earth, stones, mud, cowdung, and rice. When the mock assault is at an end, the older people come up, and all accompany the bridal pair to the groom's village.

A correspondent informs me that he once saw a Khond bride going to her new home, riding on her uncle's shoulders, and wrapped in a red blanket. She was followed by a bevy of girls and relations, and preceded by drums and horns. He was told that the uncle had to carry her the whole way, and that, if he had to put her down, a fine in the shape of a buffalo was inflicted, the animal being killed and eaten on the spot. It is recorded that a European magistrate once mistook a Khond marriage for a riot, but, on enquiry, discovered

* Manual of the Ganjam district.

† J. E. F. Pereira, Journ. As. Soc., Bengal, LXXI, 1902.

his mistake. At the ceremonial for settling the preliminaries of a Khond marriage, a knotted string is put into the hands of the sēridāh'pa gātāru (searchers for the bride), and a similar string is kept by the girl's people. The reckoning of the date of the betrothal ceremony is kept by undoing a knot in the string every morning.

Some years ago, a young Khond was betrothed to the daughter of another Khond, and, after a few years, managed to pay up the necessary number of gifts. He then applied to the girl's father to name the day of the marriage. Before the wedding took place, however, a Pāno (hill weaver) went to the girl's father, and said that she was his daughter (she had been born before her parents were married), and that he was the man to whom the gifts should have been paid. The case was referred to a panchayat (council), which decided in favour of the Pāno.

Among the hill Muduvans, who are said to have migrated from the Tamil country to Travancore, after a marriage has been settled, the bridegroom forcibly takes away the maiden from her mother's house, when she goes for water or firewood, and lives with her for a few days or weeks in a secluded part of the forest. They then return, unless in the meanwhile they have been found by their relations.*

"The Kois (cultivating hill tribe) of the Godāvari district," the Rev. J. Cain writes,† "generally marry when of fair age, but infant marriages are not unknown. If the would-be bridegroom is comparatively wealthy, he can easily secure a bride by a peaceable arrangement

* Travancore Census Report, 1901. † Ind. Ant., V, 1876.

with her parents; but, if too poor to do this, he consults with his parents, and friends, and, having fixed upon a suitable young girl, he sends his father and friends to take counsel with the headman of the village where his future partner resides. A judicious and liberal bestowal of a few rupees and arak (liquor) secure the consent of the guardian of the village to the proposed marriage. This done, the party watch for a favourable opportunity to carry off the bride, which is sure to occur when she comes outside her village to fetch water or wood, or it may be when her parents and friends are away, and she is left alone in the house. [The head-man is generally consulted, but not always, as in 1876 a wealthy widow was forcibly carried off from the house of the chief Koi of a village, and, when the master of the house opposed the proceedings, he was knocked down by the invading party.] The bridegroom generally anxiously awaits the return home of his friends with their captive, and the ceremony is proceeded with that evening, notice having been sent to the bereaved parents. Some of the Kois are polygamists, and it not unfrequently happens that a widow is chosen and carried off, it may be a day or two after the death of her husband. Bride and bridegroom are not always married in the same way. The more simple ceremony is that of causing the woman to bend her head down, and then, having made the man lean over her, the friends pour water on his head, and, when the water has run off his head on to that of the woman, they are regarded as man and wife. The water is generally poured out of a bottle-gourd. But usually, on this all-important occasion, the two are brought together, and, having promised to be faithful to each other, drink some milk. Some rice is then placed before them, and, having again renewed their promises, they eat the rice. Then they go outside the house, and march round a low heap of earth which has been thrown up under a small pandal (booth), singing a simple song as they proceed. Afterwards they pay their respects to the elders present, and beg for their blessing, which is generally bestowed in the form of 'May you be happy'! 'May you not fight and quarrel!' etc. This over, all present fall to the task of devouring the quantity of provisions provided for the occasion. If the happy couple and their friends are comparatively wealthy, the festival lasts several days . . . . Even at the present day more disputes arise from bride-stealing than from any other cause."

In a recent case, two Mālas (Telugu Pariahs) of the Godāvari district seized a girl, who had just reached maturity, by the shoulders when she went to a stream to fetch water, and carried her off to their house, where she was locked in. At night she was either married, or an attempt made to marry her to one of the men. In one statement the girl said that she was married, but she subsequently stated that she was unwilling, and broke the string of the tāli. The accused man stated that he married her with her consent, and that it was a custom of his caste to carry off a girl by force and marry her, and that he was related through her ancestors. Three witnesses stated that a man might carry off a girl who was his paternal aunt's daughter or maternal uncle's daughter. But the accused did not allege that the girl was so related to him. The Judge ruled that the girl was kidnapped and abducted, and the men were sent to prison.

At a wedding among the hill Urālis of Coimbatore, when the bridegroom's procession arrives at the home of the bride, entrance into the marriage booth is prevented by a stick held across it by people of the bride's village. A mock struggle takes place, during which turmeric water is thrown by both sides, and an entrance into the house is finally effected. At a Jōgi (Telugu beggars and pig-breeders) wedding, when the bridegroom and his party proceed to the bride's hut for the ceremony of tying the bottu (marriage badge), they are stopped by a rope or bamboo screen, which is held by the relations of the bride and others. After a short struggle, money is paid to the men who hold the rope or screen, and the ceremonial is proceeded with. The rope is called vallepu thadu or relationship rope, and is made to imply legitimate connection, as distinguished from incest. In the marriage ceremony of the Toreyas (Canarese fishermen) of Coimbatore, the bridegroom's sister meets the newly-married couple as they approach the bride's home, and prevents them from entering till she has extracted a promise from them that their child shall marry her child. In like manner, on the last day of the marriage ceremonies among the Telugu Balijas and Kammas, during the mock ploughing and sowing rite, the sister of the bridegroom puts a cloth over the basket containing earth, wherein seeds are to be sown by the bridegroom, and will not allow him to go on with the ceremony till she has extracted a promise that his first-born daughter shall marry her son. When a Tangalān Paraiyan bridegroom brings his bride to her house a few days after the marriage ceremony, he is met at the entrance by his brother-in-law, who puts rings on his second toe, and keeps on pinching his feet till he has received a promise that the bridegroom will give his daughter, if one is born to him, in marriage to the son of his brother-in-law. At the first menstrual ceremony among the Tangalān Paraiyans, the girl is sometimes beaten with a flour-cake (puttu) tied in a cloth by her mother-in-law or paternal aunt, and the latter repeatedly asks the girl to promise that, if a female child is born to her, she shall marry her son. At an Odde or Wudder (navvy class) wedding, at Coimbatore, when the bridegroom and his party try to enter the bride's house, they are met on the threshold by some of the relatives of the bride, who ask them to sing at least one song before going in.

A Coorg bridegroom, mounted on a pony, dismounts at the gate of the bride's residence, which he approaches bare-footed, and advances like a traveller of old on a long journey, with an alpine staff in his hand. When he has advanced within the gate, men hold upright the stems of a plantain tree with the leaves on them. A large broad Coorg war-knife is put into his hand, and he has to cut through a plantain stem with one blow. Three chances are allowed him. It is clear that the possession of physical strength has always been regarded by this race as an essential requisite in a suitor, and the survival of this custom is a safeguard against the premature marriage of children, which prevails elsewhere. The shooting of a tiger is a glorious event in a Coorg man's life. The hero goes through a formal ceremony of marriage with the dead monster.* At the Mattupongal festival "towards evening festoons of aloe fibre and cloths containing coins are tied to the horns of bullocks and cows, and the animals are driven through the streets with tom-tom and music. In the villages, especially those inhabited by the Kallans (thief caste) in Madura and Tinnevelly, the maiden chooses as her husband the man who has safely untied and brought to her the cloth tied to the horn of the fiercest bull. The animals are let loose, with their horns containing valuables, amidst the din of tom-tom (native drum) and harsh music, which terrifies and bewilders them. They run madly about, and are purposely excited by the crowd. A young Kallan will declare that he will run after such and such a bull—and this is sometimes a risky pursuit—and recover the valuables tied to its horn. The Kallan considers it a great disgrace to be injured while chasing the bull.†"

The custom of carrying off the bride with some show of resistance is still observed by the Savaras (hill tribe) of Ganjam. In a case which occurred a few years ago, the bridegroom did not comply with the usual custom of giving a feast to the bride's people, and her mother objected to the marriage on that account. The bridegroom's party, however, managed to carry off the bride.

* T. C. Rice, Malabar Quart. Review, 1902.

† S. M. Natesa Sastri, Hindu Feasts, Fasts, and Ceremonies, 1903.

Her mother raised an alarm, on which a number of people ran up, and tried to stop the bridegroom's party. They were outnumbered, and one man was knocked down, and died immediately from rupture of the spleen.

A detailed account of a form of wedding ceremony among the Savaras or Sauras of Ganjam has been published by Mr. F. Fawcett.* A young man, who wished to marry a girl, went to her house with a pot of liquor, an arrow, and a brass bangle for her mother. The liquor and arrow were placed on the floor, and the young man and two of his relations drank the liquor. The father of the girl suggested that, if more liquor was brought, they would talk over the matter. The young man then struck the arrow in the thatch of the roof, and went off with the empty pot. On the next occasion, the father of the girl smashed the pot of liquor, and beat the young man. Again he went to the house, and stuck an arrow in the thatch by the side of the first one. The father and the girl's nearest male relative each took one of the arrows, and, holding them in their left hands, drank some of the liquor. More presentations of arrows and liquor followed, and eventually the young man, with about ten men of his village, went to watch for the girl going to the stream for water, and, when they saw her, caught her, and ran off with her. She cried out, and the people of the village came out, and fought for her, but she was got away to the young man's village, and remained with him as his wife. The object of the arrow is probably to keep off evil spirits. At a marriage among

* Journ. Anth. Soc., Bombay, I, 1888.

the Khonds of Balliguda, after the heads of the bride and bridegroom have been brought together, an arrow is discharged from a bow by the younger brother of the bridegroom into the grass roof of the hut. In like manner, among the Bechuanas, the bridegroom throws an arrow into the hut before he enters to take up his bride. At a wedding among the Krishnavakkars of Travancore, the brides' party go, on the third day, to the house of the bridegroom, with an air of burning indignation, and every effort is made to appease them. They finally depart without partaking of the proferred hospitality. On the seventh day the newly-married couple return to the bride's house. The practice is said to be carried out as symbolising the act of bride-capture resorted to by their divine ancestor Krishna in securing an alliance with Rukmani.

At a Māppilla (class of Muhammadans) wedding in Malabar, the bridegroom, after the tāli has been tied round the bride's neck, takes her up, and runs away with her to the adjoining bridal chamber. This custom is very rigorously observed by the Labbai Muhammadans of the east coast for three consecutive days after marriage.*

At a wedding among the Mala (hill) Arayans of Travancore, the bride and bridegroom sit and eat from the same plantain leaf, after which the tāli is tied. The bride then seizes any ornament or cooking vessel in the house, saying that it is her father's. The bridegroom snatches

* P. V. Ramuni, Madras Christ. Col. Mag., 1896.

it from her, and the marriage rite is concluded.* The mother of a Pulayan (agrestic serf) bride in Travancore, is, by a curious custom, not permitted to approach the bridegroom on the wedding day or after, lest she should cause ceremonial pollution.†

A young Badaga of the Nīlgiri hills, who cannot obtain the girl of his choice, makes known that he will have her or kill himself. Understanding which, some friends place him at their head, go, if need be, to seek reinforcements among the Todas, and return with a band of sturdy fellows. Generally the abduction is successful.‡ When a Golla (Telugu shepherd) bridegroom sets out for the house of his mother-in-law, he is seized on the way by his companions, who will not release him until he has paid a piece of gold.§ The same custom is recorded as occurring among the Idaiyans (Tamil shepherds) of the Madura district. At their weddings, on the third day, when the favourite amusement of sprinkling turmeric-water over the guests is concluded, the whole party betake themselves to the village tank (pond). A friend of the bridegroom brings a hoe and a basket, and the young husband fills three baskets with earth from the bottom of the tank while the wife takes them away, and throws the earth behind. They then say "We have dug a ditch for charity." This practice may be probably explained by remembering that, in arid districts, where the Idaiyans often tend their cattle, the tank is of the greatest importance.||

* Travancore Census Report, 1901. † *Ibid.*

‡ Reclus, Primitive Folk. § Manual of the Nellore district.

|| Manual of the Madura district.

A Palli or Vanniyan (Tamil agriculturist) bridegroom, at the close of the marriage ceremony, goes to a plot of ground outside the village near a tank, carrying a toy yoke, crowbar and spade. He is followed by his wife carrying some rice gruel in an old pot. On reaching the tank, the man turns up some soil with the spade, and, after pretending to plough with the yoke, feigns fatigue, and sits down. The bride offers him some rice gruel, which he accepts, and throws it into the tank. Mixed grains sown in earthen vessels are then worshipped, and also thrown into the tank. The bride fills her pot with water, and carries it home, to be used on the following day for cooking purposes.

The Parenga Gadabas of Vizagapatam have two forms of marriage, one of which (bibā) is accompanied by much feasting, gifts of bullocks, toddy, rice, etc. The most interesting feature is the fight with fists for the bride. All the men on each side fight, and the bridegroom has to carry off the bride by force. Then they all sit down, and feast together. In the other form (lethulia) the couple go off together to the jungle, and, when they return, pay twenty rupees, or whatever they can afford, to the girl's father. Among the Bonda Gadabas, a young man and a maid retire to the jungle, and light a fire. Then the maid, taking a burning stick, applies it to the man's gluteal region. If he cries out Am! Am! Am! he is unworthy of her, and she remains a maid. If he does not, the marriage is at once consummated. The application of the brand is probably light or severe according to the girl's feelings towards the young man. According to another version, the girl goes off to the jungle with several men, and the scene has been described as being like a figure in the cotillion, as they come up to be switched with the brand.

At a wedding among the Bagatas (fishing caste) of Vizagapatam, the bridegroom is struck by his brother-in-law, who is then presented with a pair of new cloths.* In like manner, part of the marriage ceremony of the Oriya Haddis (cultivators) consists in the bride's striking the bridegroom.† At a wedding among the Ghāsis (scavengers) of Ganjam, an earthen pot filled with water is suspended from the marriage booth. On the last day but one of the protracted ceremony, the bridegroom breaks the vessel. The bride's brother then strikes him on the back, and he leaves the house in mock anger. Next day the bride goes to his house, and invites him back.‡ At a wedding among the Muhammadan Marakayars of the east coast, the Hindu custom of tying a tāli round the neck of the bride is observed. On the fourth day the bride is dressed like a Brāhman woman, and holds a small brass vessel in one hand, and a stick in the other. Approaching the bridegroom, she strikes him gently, and says: "Did not I give you butter-milk and curds? Pay me for them." The bridegroom then places a few tamarind seeds in the brass vessel, but the bride objects to this, and demands money, accompanying the demand by strokes of the stick. The man then places copper, silver and gold coins in the vessel, and the bride

* Madras Census Report, 1901. † *Ibid.*

‡ S. P. Rice, Occasional Essays on Native South Indian Life.

retires in triumph to her chamber.* The Dūdēkulas (cotton cleaners), though Muhammadans, have adopted or retained many of the customs of the Hindus around them, tying a tāli (a bead necklace) to the neck of the bride at marriage, being very ignorant of the Muhammadan religion, and even joining in Hindu worship as far as allowable. They pray in mosques, and circumcise their boys before the age of ten, and yet some of them observe the Hindu festivals.† The Sirukudi Kallans (Tamil thief caste) use a tāli, on which, curiously enough, the Muhammadan badge of a crescent and a star is engraved. The Puramalai-nādu sub-division also follow the Muhammadan practice of circumcision.‡

A singular custom called alaka or offence is said to be common at weddings among many classes in the Nellore district. In the middle of the celebrations on the fourth night, the bridegroom and his party make a pretence to take offence at something done by the bride's people. They stop the proceedings, and withdraw in affected anger. Whereupon the bride's relations and friends follow them with presents, seeking a reconciliation, which is speedily effected, and then both parties return together to the bride's house with much show of rejoicing.§

At a marriage among the Badhoyis, (carpenters and blacksmiths) and various other castes in Ganjam, two pith crowns are placed on the forehead of the bridegroom. On his way to the bride's house he is met by her purōhit

* Madras Mail, 1900.

† Manual of the North Arcot district; Census Report, 1901.

‡ Madras Census Report, 1901.

§ Manual of the Nellore district.

(priest) and relations, and the barber washes his feet, and presents him with a new yellow cloth, flowers, and kusa grass (*Eragrostis cynosuroides*). When he arrives at the house, amid the recitations of stanzas by the priest, the blowing of conch-shells and other music, the women of the bride's party make a noise called huluhuli, and shower kusa grass over him. At the marriage booth the bridegroom sits upon a raised 'altar,' and the bride, who arrives accompanied by her maternal uncle, pours salt, yellow-coloured rice, and parched paddy over the head of the bridegroom, by whose side she seats herself. Various Brāhmanical rites are then performed, and the bride's father places her hand in that of the bridegroom. A bundle of straw is now placed on the altar, on which the contracting parties sit, the bridegroom facing east and the bride west. The purōhit rubs a little jaggery (molasses) over the bridegroom's right palm, joins it to the palm of the bride, and ties their two hands together with a rope made of kusa grass. A yellow cloth is tied to the cloths which the bridal pair are wearing, and stretched over their shoulders. One of the pith crowns is next removed from the bridegroom's forehead, and placed on that of the bride. The hands are then untied by a married woman. Srādh (memorial service for the dead) is performed for the propitiation of ancestors, and the purōhit, repeating some mantrams, blesses the pair by throwing yellow rice over them. On the sixth day of the ceremony the bridegroom runs away from the house of his father-in-law, as if he was displeased, and goes to the house of a relation in the same or an adjacent village. His brother-in-law, or other male relation of the bride, goes in search of him, and, when he has found him, rubs some jaggery over his face, and brings him back.* .

The Relli (gardener) bridegroom of Ganjam, with the permission of the village magistrate, marches straight into the bride's house, and ties a wedding necklace round her neck. A gift of seven and-a-half rupees and a pig to the caste-men, and of five rupees to the bride's father, completes this very primitive ceremony.† The usual bride price among the Jōgis (Telugu beggar caste) is a pig and Rs. 19–4–0, and on the wedding day the pig is killed, and its head is taken by the bride's party, while its body is reserved for a general feast.‡ At the betrothal ceremony of some Khonds, a buffalo and pig are killed, and some of the viscera eaten. Various parts are distributed according to an abiding rule, viz., the head to the bridegroom's maternal uncle, the flesh of the sides to his sisters, and of the back among other relations and friends.

At a Pallan (Tamil agriculturist) wedding, before the wedding is actually performed, the bridegroom suddenly leaves his house and starts for some distant place, as if he had suddenly abandoned his intention of marrying, in spite of the preparations that had been made for the wedding. His intended father-in-law intercepts the young man on his way, and persuades him to

* D. Mahanty. MS.

† S. P. Rice, Occasional Essays on Native South Indian Life.

‡ Madras Census Report, 1901.

Plate II.

Kāpu Bride and Bridegroom.

return, promising to give his daughter as a wife. To this the bridegroom consents.* A Kamsala (artisan) bridegroom, in the course of the marriage ceremony, ties a pilgrim's cloth upon him, places a brass water-pot on his head, holds a torn umbrella in his hands, and starts off from the booth, saying that he is going on a pilgrimage to Benares, when the bride's brother runs after him, and promises that he will give him his sister in marriage. The bridegroom, satisfied with this promise, abandons his pretended journey, takes off his pilgrim's clothes, and gives them, together with the umbrella, to the officiating Brāhman.† According to the shāstras, after the Brāhmachārya asramam (bachelorhood or studentship), all the twice-born are expected to enter grahastha asramam, or married life. Immediately on the close of the student stage, they are expected to travel to Benares, and bathe in the river Ganges. The qualifications for a bridegroom are such a bath, and a knowledge of the Vēdas. So fathers who have marriageable daughters are expected to go in search of young men who are learned in the Vēdas, and are snathakas (men who have bathed in the Ganges). Even the mere thought or proposal of a pilgrimage to Benares is said to be sufficient to obtain some pūnyam (good as opposed to sin). Consequently the mock pilgrimage to Benares is resorted to.

The Tiyan (toddy tapping caste) bridegroom of Malabar sets out with his relations and friends for the

* G. Oppert, Madras Journ. Lit. and Science, 1888.

† Manual of the Nellore district.

bride's house, accompanied by two other youths dressed exactly like himself. Some of his male relations and friends, armed with swords and targets, play in front of him. The bridegroom, and two other youths dressed alike, sit together, and have rice thrown over them in common. The tāli-tying ceremony is carried out, and, as the bride and bridegroom, with the two groomsmen, leave the wedding pavilion, they are met by the machchūnan* or uncle's son prepared to contest with them for the bride as a prize, he having, according to marumakkatāyam † ideas, a better claim to her than any one else. It is on this account that the two groomsmen are dressed up like the groom himself, in order to puzzle the machchūnan as to his identity. The machchūnan's claims are bought off with two fanams (a small sum of money), and he in turn presents betel-leaf in token of conciliation. On reaching the bridegroom's house, the bride and groom must enter the door placing their right feet simultaneously on the door-step.‡

On the second day of a Heggade (Canarese cultivator) marriage, a pretence of stealing a jewel from the person of the bride is made. The bridegroom makes away with the jewel before dawn, and, in the evening, the bride's party proceeds to the house where the bridegroom is to be found. The owner of the house is told that a theft has occurred in the bride's house, and is asked whether the thief has taken shelter in his house.

* Machunan = mother's brother's, or father's sister's son.

† Marumakkatāyam: the law of inheritance through the female line.

‡ Manual of Malabar.

A negative answer is given, but the bride's party conducts a regular search. In the meantime a boy has been dressed up to represent the bridegroom. The searching party mistake this boy for the bridegroom, arrest him, and produce him before the audience as the culprit. This disguised bridegroom, who is proclaimed to be the thief, throws his mask at the bride, when it is found to the amusement of all that he is not the bridegroom. The bride's party then, confessing their inability to find the bridegroom, request the owner of the house to produce him. He is then produced, and conducted in procession to the bride's house.*

A custom prevails among the Kaikōḷans (weavers) by which one woman in each family becomes a prostitute, while retaining her caste. The girl chosen is taken to the temple, where a sword is placed beside her with a tāli (marriage badge) under it. The tāli is then tied round her neck by any woman present, and she returns to her own house, where she is permitted to carry on any amours she chooses. She receives her share of the family property, just as if no such ceremony had taken place.†

Among the Kaikōlan musicians of Coimbatore, at least one girl in every family should be set apart for the temple service, and she is instructed in music and dancing. At the tāli-tying ceremony she is decoṛated with jewels, and made to stand on a heap of paddy (unhusked rice). A folded cloth is held before her by two Dāsis (dancing girls), who also stand on heaps of

* Manual of South Canara. † Manual of the Salem district.

paddy. The girl catches hold of the cloth, and her dancing master, who is seated behind her, grasping her legs, moves them up and down in time with the music which is played. In the evening she is taken, seated astride a pony, to the temple, where a new cloth for the idol, the tāli, and other articles required for doing pūja have been got ready. The girl is seated facing the idol, and the officiating Brāhman gives sandal and flowers to her, and ties the tāli, which has been lying at the feet of the idol, round her neck. The tāli consists of a golden disc and black beads. She continues to learn music and dancing, and the *ars amoris*, and eventually goes through the form of a nuptial ceremony. The relations are invited for an auspicious day, and the maternal uncle, or his representative, ties a golden band on the girl's forehead, and, carrying her, places her on a plank before the assembled guests. A Brāhman priest recites mantrams, and prepares the sacred fire (hōmam). For the actual nuptials a rich Brāhman if possible, and, if not, a Brāhman of more lowly status is invited. A Brāhman is called in as he is next in importance to, and the representative of the idol. It is said that, when the man who is to receive the first favours of a Kaikōlan Dāsi joins her, a sword must be placed, at least for a few minutes, by the side of the girl. A peculiar method of selecting a bride, called siru tāli-kattu (tying the small tāli) is said to be in vogue among some Kaikōlans. A man, who wishes to marry his maternal uncle's or paternal aunt's daughter, has to tie a tāli, or simply a bit of cloth torn from her clothing, round her neck, and report the fact to his parents and the headman. If the girl eludes him, he cannot claim her, but, should he succeed, she belongs to him.

As a Dāsi can never become a widow, the beads in her tāli are considered to bring good luck to women who wear them. Some people send the tāli required for a marriage to a Dāsi, who prepares the string for it, and attaches to it black beads from her own tāli.

The Jakkulas are, in the Census report, 1901, returned as an inferior class of prostitutes, mostly of the Balija (Telugu trader) caste. At Tenali, in the Kistna district, it was customary for each Jakkula family to give up one girl for prostitution. She was "married" to any chance comer for one night with the usual ceremonies. Under the influence of social reform, the members of the caste entered into a written agreement to give up the practice. A family went back on this, so the head of the caste prosecuted them and the "husband" for disposing of a minor for the purpose of prostitution.

Among a certain tribe of the Jeypore hill-tracts, it is the custom, at the feast of the green mango, when the fruit is about three-quarters grown, for all the men of the village to go out hunting. If they come back without any spoil, the women will not let them into the village, but pelt them with cow-dung, and anything else which is at hand. If the hunt has been successful, a great feast is held, whereat the older men and women get intoxicated. At night all the marriageable young men and maidens go into a large house, generally situated in the centre of the village, and lie together in a crowd. If, as the result of the orgy, any of the girls becomes pregnant, she names the father of the child, and he has to marry her.

The father of a would-be bride among the Malaiālis (hill people) of the Yelagiri hills, in the Salem district, when he hears of the existence of a suitable bride, repairs to her village with some of his relations, and seeks out the Ur-Goundan, or headman, between whom and the visitors mutual embraces are exchanged. The object of the visit is explained, and the father says that he will abide by the "voice of four" in the matter. If the match is fixed up, he gives a feast in honour of the event. When the visitors enter the future bride's house, the eldest daughter-in-law of the house appears on the threshold, and takes charge of the walking-stick of each person who goes in. She then, with some specially prepared sandal paste, makes a circular mark on the foreheads of the guests, and retires. The feast then takes place, and, before the parties retire, the daughter-in-law again appears, and returns the walking-sticks.* It is said that, even if the number thereof is more than fifty, she, like an American lift-boy, who remembers the numbers of all those staying in a hotel, always hands over the sticks to their owners. When a stranger of the caste approaches a Malaiāli village, the first man who sees him, salutes him and relieves him of the bamboo stick, which all carry. He then conducts him to his house, and places the stick in a corner as a sign that the visitor shall receive hospitality in that house alone.†

* C. Hayavadana Rao, MS.

† Manual of the North Arcot district.

A Malaiāli of the North Arcot district has to serve for a year in the house of the bride in order to receive the consent of her parents, in the same way that some Paniyans of Malabar have to serve for six months. A Kādir (jungle man of the Cochin hills) goes out of his own village, and lives in another for a whole year, during which period he makes a choice of a wife. At the end of the year he returns to his own village, and obtains permission from the villagers to effect the contemplated union. Then he goes away again to the village of his bride-elect, and gives her a dowry by working there for another year. He then makes presents of cloths and iron tools to the girl's mother, after which follows a feast, which completes the ceremony. Among the Badagas of the Nīlgiris, it is said to be common for one who is in want of labourers to promise his daughter in marriage to the son or other relative of a neighbour not in circumstances so flourishing as himself, and, these engagements being entered into, the intended bridegroom serves the father of his betrothed as one of his own family till the girl comes of age, when the marriage is consummated, and he becomes a partner in the general property of the family of his father-in-law.* Formerly the prospective Gadaba (hunting and agricultural tribe) bridegroom in Vizagapatam used to work in his father-in-law's house for one year before marriage, but a cash payment is now substituted for service.† Now and then a Malaiāli bride is carried off by force, but this custom

* Harkness. Description of a singular Aboriginal Race inhabiting the Neilgherry hills, 1832.

† Madras Census Report, 1901.

is viewed with much disfavour, and the bridegroom who resorts to it must paint his face with black and white dots, and carry an old basket filled with broken pots and other rubbish, holding a torn sieve over him as an umbrella before the celebration of the marriage. At the wedding, the bridegroom gives the girl's father a present of money, and a pile of firewood sufficient for the cooking of the two days' feast. On the first day the food consists of rice and dhāl (*Cajanus indicus*), and on the second day pork curry is consumed. At sunrise on the third day the bridegroom produces the tāli, and ties it. A sword is then laid upon the laps of the bridal pair, and the Nāttan (headman), or an elderly man blesses the tāli, and gives it to the bridegroom, who ties it round the bride's neck.* Among the Alias (cultivators) of Ganjam, if a girl cannot find a proper match before puberty, a nominal marriage, called gaudo bibāho, is performed with a bow in the place of a husband. The Chenchus, who inhabit the jungles of the Nallamalai hills, stick three or four arrows in a row, or arranged in the form of a square, between the bridal couple. This is done with the object of finding out the auspicious hour for throwing rice over their heads. Midday, when the arrow casts no shadow, is believed to be the most auspicious time. The Yānādis, who are allied to the Chenchus, believe that noon is the proper time for tying the tāli, and, as they do not possess bows and arrows, they use a straight stick for determining the proper moment for the ceremony.

* Manual of the North Arcot district.

As soon as a Coorg boy is born, a little bow made of a castor-oil plant stick, with an arrow made of a leaf stalk of the same plant, is put into his little hands. He is thus, at taking his first breath, introduced into the world as a future huntsman and warrior.*

I am informed that, among all the Oriya castes, except Brāhmans, which follow the rule of infant marriage, a girl is married to an arrow, if a suitable husband has not been found for her before she reaches puberty. The actual marriage may take place at any time afterwards.

A Nāyar girl of Travancore must get married with the tāli before the age of eleven, to avoid reproach from friends and neighbours. In case of need, a sword may be made to represent the bridegroom.† Among the Dhōbis (washermen) of Mysore, pre-puberty marriage is the rule, but puberty is no bar. The girl must, however, be first married to a tree or a sword, before being married to the bridegroom.‡

At an Idiga (Telugu toddy-drawer) wedding the maternal uncle of the bride bathes, and, going to the place where kalli (*Euphorbia*) bushes are growing, performs pūja to the plant, and cuts a twig with five sub-branches, which is taken to the temple and worshipped. On the wedding day, the brother of the bride is fantastically dressed, with margosa (*Melia Azadirachta*) leaves tied to his turban, and carries a bow and arrow. This kodangi (buffoon) is conducted in procession to the

* H. Moegling, Coorg Memoirs.

† S. Mateer, Journ. Anth. Inst., XII, 1883.

‡ Mysore Census Report, 1901.

temple by a few married women, and made to walk on cloths spread in front of him by the village washerman. On reaching the temple, he and the women worship a vessel placed in a tray along with betel leaves, plantain fruits, and a mirror. The boy, while thus worshipping, is surrounded by a screen, and at the conclusion of the ceremony, goes three times round the vessel and screen. At the close of each revolution, three plantains and sweet cakes are stuck on to the arrow which he carries.

At the pudamuri (pudaya, a woman's cloth; muri, cutting) form of marriage among the Nāyars of Malabar, in a room decorated and turned into a bed-room for the occasion, are placed a number of lighted lamps, and ashtamangaliam, which consists of eight articles symbolical of mangaliam or marriage. These are rice, paddy, the tender leaves of the cocoanut, an arrow, a looking-glass, a well-washed cloth, burning fire, and a small round wooden box called cheppu, made in a particular fashion.* At the Nāyar tāli-kettu (tāli-tying) ceremony, the girl is brought before the manavālan (bridegroom), covered up like a gōsha woman, and holding an arrow in her hand. Basavi women (dedicated prostitutes) are sometimes married to a dagger, sometimes to an idol. In making a female child over to the service of the temple, she is taken, and dedicated for life to some idol. A khanjar or dagger is placed on the ground, and the girl who is undergoing the ceremony puts a garland thereon. Her mother then puts rice on the girl's forehead. The officiating priest weds the girl to the dagger, just as if

* Report of the Malabar Marriage Commission, 1894.

he was uniting her to a young man, by reciting the marriage stanzas, a curtain being held between the girl and the dagger.*

Among the Kavarais (Telugu traders), who have settled in Tinnevelly, a custom, which is now dying out, was the wearing by the bridegroom of a dagger, called jintadu, at the waist. The Vakkaligas (cultivators) of Mysore use a katar or vanki (dagger) during the marriage ceremony. The best man usually carries it in his hand. The bridegroom's sister carries a pot of rice, into which a four-anna piece has been dropped. When the bridegroom goes to the temple, prior to the tying of the tāli, he is accompanied by these articles. The dagger, which has a red cloth tied round the blade, must be close to the bridegroom when he comes to the marriage booth. On the third day, when he goes to his father-in-law's house, the dagger must go with him, and is then returned to its owner. Just before the tāli is tied, a screen is stretched between the bridal couple, over whom jaggery (molasses) and cummin seeds are thrown. The screen is then removed, and the tāli and silver bracelets are placed in the bridegroom's hands. The bride places her hands beneath his, and the relations pour milk over the tāli. The tāli and bracelets are then placed in the bride's hands, and the bridegroom sets his hands beneath hers. The milk-pouring is repeated. The tāli is placed on a piece of jaggery, and passed round to be blessed. It is then tied on the bride's neck by the bridegroom.

* Balfour, Cyclopædia of India.

At a marriage among the Okkiliyans (cultivators) of Coimbatore, the bridegroom carries a katar (dagger) with a lime stuck on the point, wrapped up in a cloth, which he keeps by him until the kankanam (marriage wrist-thread) is untied. An Odde (navvy) bridegroom, when he proceeds to the bride's house, carries a curved knife partly concealed by a cloth. When the tāli is tied round the bride's neck, she stoops down, and the bridegroom touches the knot of the tāli string thrice with the knife, implying thereby that the knot has been so firmly tied that even a knife cannot cut it. Hence their union will also be strong. At a Toreya (Canarese fisherman) marriage, the Brāhman priest ties on the head of both bride and bridegroom an ornament made of gold leaf or tinsel, called mandai-kattu. The bridegroom puts on the sacred thread, and, holding a katar in his hand, sits in the wedding booth with a cloth screen surrounding him on all sides. The tying of a bashingam, made of pith or flowers, on the forehead (plate III) during the marriage ceremony is a general custom among the Telugu and Canarese classes.

Concerning the marriage ceremony of the Tottiyans or Kambalas (Telugu cultivators) of Madura and Tinnevelly, I gather that it is carried out in two temporary huts, one for the bridegroom, the other for the bride. The tāli is tied round the bride's neck by an elderly male or female belonging to the family. If the marriage is contracted with a woman of a lower class, the bridegroom's hut is not made use of, and he does not personally take part in the ceremony. A dagger

Plate III.

Vakkaliga Bride.

(katar), or sword is sent to represent him, and the tāli is tied in the presence thereof. In a Zamindāri suit some years ago, details of which are published in the Madras Law Reports, Vol. XVII, 1894, the Judge found that the plaintiff's mother was married to the plaintiff's father in the dagger form ; that a dagger is used by the Saptūr Zamindars, (landlords) who are called Kattari Kamaya, in the case of inequality in the caste or social position of the bride ; that, though the customary rites of the Kambla caste were also performed, yet the use of the dagger was an essential addition ; and that, though she was of a different and inferior caste to that of the plaintiff's father, yet that did not invalidate the marriage. The defendant's argument was that the dagger was used to represent the Zamindar bridegroom as he did not attend in person, and that, by his non-attendance, there could have been no joining of hands or other essential for constituting a valid marriage. The plaintiff argued that the nuptial rites were duly performed, the Zamindar being present; that the dagger was there merely as an ornament, and that it was customary for people of the Zamindar's caste to have a dagger paraded on the occasion of marriages. The Judge found that the dagger was there for the purpose of indicating that the two ladies, whom the Zamindar married, were of an inferior caste and rank.

At a wedding in the Gōda section of the Kammas (Telugu cultivators), one or more daggers are placed near a pīpal (*Ficus religiosa*) tree, round which a yellow cotton thread is wound three or five times. The tree is then worshipped. As a substitute for the sacrifice of a sheep or goat, lime fruits are cut.

In an account of the initiation ceremony of the Basavis (dedicated prostitutes) of the Bellary district, Mr. F. Fawcett writes as follows.* "A sword with a lime stuck on its point is placed upright beside the novice, and held in her right hand. It represents the bridegroom, who, in the corresponding ceremony of the Hindu marriage, sits on the bride's right. A tray, on which are a kalasyam (vessel of water) and a lamp, is then produced, and moved thrice in front of the girl from right to left. She rises, and, carrying the sword in her right hand, places it in the god's sanctuary. Among the dancing girls very similar ceremonies are performed. With them the girl's spouse is represented by a drum instead of a sword, and she bows to it. Her insignia consist of a drum and bells." Concerning the ceremony of dedication of a girl as a Basavi, Mr. F. Fawcett writes further :† "A tāli, on which is depicted the nāmam of Vishnu, fastened to a necklace of black beads, is tied round her neck. She is given, by way of insignia, a cane as a wand carried in the right hand, and a gopālam or begging basket, which is slung on the left arm." She is then branded with the emblems of the chank shell (*Turbinella rapa*) and chakra (discus).

In another account of the marriage ceremony among dancing girls, it is stated that the Bhōgams or dancing girls, who are without exception prostitutes, though

* Journ. Anth. Soc., Bomb., 1891. † *Ibid.*

they are not allowed to marry, go through a marriage ceremony, which is rather a costly one. Sometimes a wealthy native bears the expense, makes large presents to the bride, and receives her first favours. Where no such opportunity presents itself, a sword or other weapon represents the bridegroom, and an imaginary nuptial ceremony is performed. Should the Bhōgam woman have no daughter, she invariably adopts one, usually paying a price for her, the Kaikōlan (weaver) caste being the ordinary one from which to take a child.* The custom of sending a sword to represent an unavoidably absent bridegroom at a wedding is not uncommon among the Telugu Rāzus and Velamas.† The Rāzus at their weddings worship a sword, which is a ceremony usually denoting a soldier caste. They say they are Kshatriyas, and at marriages use a wrist string made of cotton and wool, the combination peculiar to Kshatriyas, to tie the wrists of the happy couple.‡

Sūdra girls in Ganjam can, if a marriage has not been arranged in time, be married to the sun; and, if this ceremony is performed, they are eligible for marriage with a man, notwithstanding that they have arrived at womanhood.§

The Maravan Zamindars of Tinnevelly celebrate marriage by means of a stick, which is sent by the bridegroom, and set up in the marriage booth in his place.

* Manual of the North Arcot district.

† H. G. Prendergast, Ind. Ant., XX, 1891.

‡ Madras Census Report, 1901.

§ Manual of the Ganjam district.

The tāli is tied by some one representing the bridegroom, and the marriage then becomes complete.*

On the first day of a marriage among the Palayakkārans (Telugu cultivators), the bridegroom worships a jammi (*Prosopis spicigera*) twig by offering milk, ghī, and incense to it, and ties it to the central post of the marriage booth. On the morning of the second day, the married couple go in procession to a white-ant (*Termites*) hill outside the village, pour milk and ghī over it, and carry home five baskets of earth from it. The bridegroom mixes the earth with water, and places a lump of it at each of the twelve posts of the booth. On the third day he goes, accompanied by some of his relations, to a plot of ground outside the village, taking with him two bullocks, a plough, two yokes, and nine kinds of grain. He yokes the bullocks to the plough, turns up a small space of ground, and sows the grain.† At a wedding among the jungle Irulas, it is necessary that the two front posts of the marriage booth should have twelve twigs of the pāla (milk) tree tied to them. The happy pair have to fetch a basketful of earth from an ant-hill, and place it beneath the pāla twigs. The binding part of the ceremony is said to consist in the woman smoking the bridegroom's cheroot, or eating out of the same dish with him.‡ All castes erect certain posts, called pāla-kambam (milk posts) or pāla maram (milk tree), for the marriage booth. Some sections of Sūdras set up posts made of branches of the pāla tree (*Mimusops hexandra*), but the

* Madras Census Report, 1891. † Manual of the North Arcot district.
‡ Madras Census Report, 1901.

tree commonly used is the pīpal (*Ficus religiosa*). On the occasion of a marriage among the Oddes (navvies) of Coimbatore, three female relations of the bridegroom proceed to a white-ant hill, and, after worshipping it by breaking cocoanuts and burning camphor, fill their baskets with earth from the hill, and carry them to the marriage booth. They then bring from the potter's house three decorated pots and an earthen tray, and place them in the booth. A bit of turmeric with betel leaves is tied to each pot, and they are filled with water. In front of the booth a small platform is made with the ant-earth mixed with water. A wild sugar-cane, twig of *Ficus religiosa*, and of the milk-hedge (*Euphorbia Tirucalli*) are tied together, and planted in the centre of the platform. The bridegroom among the hunting Boyas of the Deccan districts has to collect some earth from an anthill, in which seeds are then sown, and he carries a dagger.* A Lambādi bride and bridegroom pour milk down an ant-hill, where a snake is said to live, and offer it cocoanuts, flowers, etc.†

Of marriage among the Arayans (fishing caste) of Travancore the Rev. A. W. Painter writes as follows.‡ "A curious ceremony prevails, copied, I believe, from the custom of Nairs and Chogans, though differing in several particulars. As soon as the woman attains maturity, relatives and friends are summoned to a feast.

* Madras Census Report, 1901.

† Mysore Census Report, 1901. The Lambādis, Sugālis, or Banjāris are commonly described as gipsies. Some are nomad, while others have settled down as agriculturists.

‡ Journ. Anth. Soc., Bomb., 1890.

The pooshāri (priest) having fixed the propitious hour, the girl is brought in, and made to stand on a plank of jack-wood (*Artocarpus integrifolia*), a tree considered sacred by the Arayans. The father's sister then ties the tāli round her neck. A feast is then partaken of, and the ceremony is considered complete."

A curious mock marriage ceremony is celebrated among Brāhmans when an individual marries a third wife. It is believed that a third marriage is very inauspicious, and that the bride will become a widow. To prevent this mishap, the man is made to marry the arka plant (*Calotropis gigantea*), and the real marriage thus becomes the fourth. If this ceremony is carried on in orthodox fashion, it is generally celebrated on some Sunday or Monday, when the constellation Astham is visible. The bridegroom and a Brāhman priest, accompanied by a third Brāhman, repair to a spot where the arka plant (a very common weed) is growing. The plant is decorated with a cloth and piece of string, and symbolised by the priest into the sun. The bridegroom then invokes it thus: "Oh! master of three lōks, Oh! the seven-horsed, Oh! Rāvi, avert the evils of the third marriage." Next the plant is addressed with the words "You are the oldest of the plants of this world. Brāhma created you to save such of us as have to marry a third time, so please become my wife." The Brāhman who accompanies the bridegroom becomes his father-in-law for the moment, and says to him "I give you in marriage Aditya's great granddaughter, Savi's granddaughter, and my daughter Arkakanya." All the ceremonies, such as making hōmam (sacred fire), tâli-tying, etc., are performed as at a regular marriage, and, after the recitation of a few sentences from the Vēdas, the plant is cut down. "The plant," Mr. A. Srinivasan writes,* "is named arka after the sun. When the car of the sun turns towards the north, every Hindu applies the leaves of this plant to his head before he bathes, in honour of the event. The plant is, besides, believed to be a willing scapegoat to others' ills. Oil and ghī applied to the head of the victim of persistent illness has only to be transferred to this plant, when it withers and saves the man, even as Baber is said to have saved his son. The poet Kalidāsa describes sweet Sakuntala, born of a shaggy dweller of the forest, as a garland of jasmine thrown on an arka plant. 'May the arka grow luxuriant in your house' is the commonest form of curse. 'Be thou belaboured with arka leaves' is familiar in the mouths of reprimanding mothers. Adulterers were, half a century ago, seated on an ass, face towards the tail, and marched through the village. The public disgrace was enhanced by placing a garland of the despised arka leaves on their head. A Telugu proverb asks in triumph 'Does the bee ever seek the arka flower'? The reasons for the ill-repute that this plant suffers from are not at all clear. The fact that it has a partiality for wastes has evidently brought on its devoted head the dismal associations of desolation, but there would seem to be more deep-seated hatred to the plant than has been explained." A Tamil proverb has it that "he earns merit who crushes the bud

* Madras Christian College Magazine, March 1903.

of the arka." Some Telugu and Kanarese Brāhmans, who follow the Yajur Vēda or Rig Vēda, consider the arka plant as sacred, and use the leaves thereof during the nanthi (ancestor invoking) ceremony, which is performed as one of the marriage rites. Two or three arka leaves, with betel leaves and nuts, are tied to the cloth, which is attached to a stick as representing the ancestors (pithrus). With some the arka leaves are replaced by leaves of *Pongamia glabra*. Brāhmans who follow the Sāma Vēda, during the annual upākarmam ceremony,* make use of arka leaves and flowers in worshipping the rishis and pithrus. On the upākarmam day the Sāma Vēdis invoke their sixty-two rishis and the last three ancestors, who are represented by sixty-five clay balls placed on arka leaves. To them are offered arka flowers, fruits of karai-chedi (*Canthium parviflorum*) and nāval (*Eugenia Jambolana*). In addition to this worship, they perform the rishi and pithru tharpanam by offering water, gingelly (*Sesamum indicum*) seeds, and rice. The celebrant, prior to dipping his hand into the water, places in his hands two arka leaves, gingelly and rice. The juice of the arka plant is a favourite agent in the hands of suicides. Among the Tangalān Paraiyans, if a young man dies before he is married, a ceremony called kannikazhiththal (removing bachelorhood) is performed. Before the corpse is laid on the bier, a garland of arka flowers is placed round its neck, and balls of mud from

* Upakarmam (bringing the Vedas near) is a religious rite observed by Hindus on the full-moon day in the month of Sravanam. On this day all Brahmachāris commence the study of the Vedas.

a gutter are laid on the head, knees, and other parts of the body. In some places a variant of the ceremony consists in the erection of a mimic marriage booth, which is covered with leaves of the arka plant, flowers of which are also placed round the neck as a garland.

At a form of marriage called rambha or kathali (plantain tree) marriage, the *Calotropis* plant is replaced by a plantain tree (*Musa*). It is performed by those who happen to be eldest brothers, and who are incapable of getting married, so as to give a chance to younger brothers, who are not allowed to marry unless the elder brother or brothers are already married.

With the Billavas, or toddy-tappers of South Canara, sexual licence within the caste before matrimony is tolerated, but a woman who indulges in it is married with a different ceremony from that performed by virgins. She is first married to a plantain tree, and then the joining hands ceremony takes place, but pouring of water is omitted.* By the Chakkiliyans or Telugu leather-workers, the āvaram or tangēdu (*Cassia auriculata*) tree, the bark of which is widely used as a tanning agent, is held in much veneration, and the tāli is tied to a branch of it as a preliminary to marriage.† It is a curious fact that, in the Madura district, while the Chakkiliyan men belong to the right-hand faction, the women belong to, and are most energetic supporters of the left. It is even said that, during the entire period of a faction riot, the women keep aloof from their husbands, and deny

* Manual of the South Canara district.

† Manual of the North Arcot district.

them their marital rights.* The origin of the division of the Hindu castes of Southern India into right hand (valankai) and left hand (idankai) is lost in obscurity. "The fact of such a distinction," Surgeon-Major W. R. Cornish writes, "has frequently intruded itself unpleasantly upon the attention of Government, and, in many feuds between the rival 'hands,' the peace has only been restored by calling out the troops. Whatever the origin of the dispute, it seems certain that the castes of the right hand fraternity claim certain privileges, which they jealously deny to those of the left hand. The right hand castes, for instance, claim the prerogative of riding on horseback in processions, and of appearing with standards bearing certain devices, and of erecting twelve pillars to sustain their marriage booths, while the left hand castes may not have more than eleven pillars, nor use the standards and ensigns belonging to the right hand fraternity.†

At a wedding among the Cherumans (agricultural serfs) of Malabar, when the wedding party sets out, they form a large gang of people, and at intervals the men set to at stick play, the women singing in chorus to encourage them "Let us see—let us see—the stick play (paditallu) Oh! Cherumar." At their weddings men and women mingle indiscriminately in dancing. On the arrival of the bride at the bridegroom's hut, she is expected to weep loudly and deplore her fate; and, on entering, she must tread on a pestle placed across the

* Manual of the Madura district. † Madras Census Report, 1871.

threshold.* When a Gūdala (Telugu basket-maker) widow is married, the tāli is put on near a mortar.† At the marriage of a Malai Vellāla (hill cultivator) girl of the Coimbatore district, she has to cry during the whole ceremony, which lasts three days. Otherwise she is considered an "ill woman." When she can no longer produce genuine tears, she must proceed to bawl out. If she does not do this, the bridegroom will not marry her. Two curious points in connection with the marriage ceremony of the Lambādis may be noticed. The women are said to weep and cry aloud at their weddings, which may be a relic of marriage by capture, and the bride and bridegroom are stated to pour milk down some snake's hole, and offer to the snake cocoanuts, flowers, and so on. Brāhmans are sometimes engaged to celebrate weddings, and, failing a Brāhman, a youth of the tribe will put on the marriage thread, and perform the ceremony.‡

Of substitutional child-marriage many examples are forthcoming. The custom, which illustrates the Hindu love of offspring, prevails, for example, among the Malaiālis (hill cultivators) of the Salem district. "The sons, when mere children, are married to mature females, and the father-in-law of the bride assumes the performance of the procreative function, thus assuring for himself and his son a descendant to take them out of Put. When the putative father comes of age, and in their turn his wife's male offspring are married, he performs for them the same

* Manual of Malabar.

† Madras Census Report, 1901.

‡ *Ibid.*

office which his father did for him. Thus not only is the religious idea involved in the words Putra and Kumāran (both meaning son)* carried out, but also the premature strain on the generative faculties, which this tradition entails, is avoided. The accommodation is reciprocal, and there is something on physiological grounds to recommend it."† Writing to me recently concerning this custom among the Malaiālis, a native says that "the custom of linking a boy in marriage to a mature female, though still existing, has, with the advance of the times, undergone a slight yet decent change. The father-in-law of the bride has relieved himself of the awkward predicament into which the māmūl (custom) drove him, and now leaves the performance of the procreative function to others accepted by the bride." The Malaiālis claim to be Vellālas who emigrated to the hills from the city of Kānchipuram (Conjeveram); and, like them, a section of Vellālas in the Coimbatore district is said to have had the custom of the father of a family living in incestuous intercourse with his own daughter-in-law during the period that his son, the youthful husband, was in nonage.‡ The Kanarese proverb "stealing cotton is no theft; to go with a mother-in-law is no sin" would seem to indicate the practice of cohabitation with a wife's mother, but any knowledge of such a custom is firmly denied. The Kammas (Telugu cutivators) tie a bunch of

* Putra means one who saves from put, a hell into which those who have not produced a son fall. Kumāran is the second stage the life of an individual, which is divided into infancy, childhood, manhood and old age.

† Manual of the Salem district.

‡ J. Shortt, Tribes of the Neilgherries, 1868.

dhāl (*Cajanus indicus*) leaves to the north-east post of the marriage booth, to commemorate the escape of a party of Kammas who concealed themselves in a field of dhāl. Consummation does not take place till three months after the marriage ceremonies, as it is considered unlucky to have three heads in a household within a year of marriage. By the delay, the birth of a child should take place only in the second year, so that, during the first year, there will be only two heads, husband and wife. In like manner, it is noted by Mr. Francis that among the Gangimakkulu and Mālas, as among the Mādigas, the marriage is not consummated for three months after its celebration.*

Among the Kammas of the Tamil country, the bridegroom is sometimes much younger than the bride, and a case is on record of a wife of twenty-two years of age, who used to carry her boy-husband on her hip, as a mother carries her child. A parallel is to be found in Russia, where, not very long ago grown-up women were to be seen carrying about boys of six, to whom they had been betrothed.† Among the western Kunnuvans of the Madura hills, when an estate is likely to descend to a female in default of male issue, she is forbidden to marry an adult, but goes through the ceremony of marriage with some young male child, or a portion of her father's dwelling house, on the understanding that she shall be at liberty to amuse herself with any man of her caste, to whom she may take a fancy. And her issue, so begotten,

* Manual of the Bellary district.

† Hutchinson, Marriage Customs in Many Lands, 1897.

inherits the property, which is thus retained in the woman's family. Numerous disputes originate in this singular custom, and Madura magistrates have sometimes been puzzled not a little by evidence to show that a child of three or four years was the son or daughter of a child of ten or twelve.* At the marriage of Kongas, (Tamil cultivators) barbers officiate as the priests, and the tāli is tied round the neck of the bride, not by the bridegroom, but by a person known as the arumaikkāran, who is assisted by the barber. Marriage with a maternal uncle's daughter is looked upon as the most desirable union, and this frequently results in a boy of seven or eight being married to a girl twice his age, who lives with her father-in-law until her husband grows up. This custom is said to be dying out.† Among the Tottiyans (Telugu cultivators) the custom of marrying boys to their paternal aunt's or maternal uncle's daughter, however old she may be, obtains, and, in such cases, the bridegroom's father is said to take upon himself the duty of begetting children to his own son.‡ In like manner, among the Kāppiliyans (Canarese-speaking farmers) the right of a man to marry his sister's or aunt's daughter is so strong that it frequently happens that small boys are married to adult women, and, in such cases, morality is naturally lax. Children of such ill-matched unions inherit the property of the nominal father, even though he was quite a child at the time of their birth.§ Among the Reddis (Telugu cultivators) who have settled in

* Manual of the Madura district.

† Madras Census Report, 1891.

‡ Madras Census Report, 1901.

§ *Ibid.*

Tinnevelly, a young woman of sixteen or twenty years of age, is frequently married to a boy of five or six years, or even of a more tender age. After marriage she lives with some other man, a near relative on the maternal side, frequently an uncle, and sometimes with her boy-husband's own father. The progeny so begotten are affiliated on the boy-husband. When he comes of age he finds his wife an old woman, and perhaps past child-bearing. So he, in his turn, contracts a *liaison* with some other boy's wife, and procreates children for him.* Khond boys of ten or twelve years of age are said to be married to girls of fifteen or sixteen. The wife lives with her boy-husband in his father's house, occupying the same couch. When her husband grows up, he gets a house of his own, unless he is the youngest son.† Marriage among the Kallans is said to depend entirely upon consanguinity. The most proper alliance is one between a man and the daughter of his father's sister; and, if an individual has such a cousin, he must marry her, whatever disparity there may be between their respective ages. A boy, for example, of fifteen must marry such a cousin, even if she be thirty or forty years old, if her father insists upon his so doing. Failing a cousin of this sort, he must marry his aunt or his niece, or some near relative. If his father's brother has a daughter, and insists upon his marrying her, he cannot refuse: and this whatever may be the woman's age.‡ Among the Vallambans (Tamil cultivators), the maternal uncle's

* Shortt. *Op. cit.* † Macpherson. *Op. cit.*
‡ Manual of the Madura district.

or paternal aunt's daughter is said * to be claimed as a matter of right by a boy, so that a lad of ten may be wedded to a mature woman of twenty or twenty-five years, if she happens to be unmarried and without issue. Any elderly male member of the boy's family—his elder brother, uncle, or even his father—will have intercourse with her, and beget children, which the boy, when he comes of age, will accept as his own, and legitimatise. One of the customs of the Kōmatis (Telugu traders) is that which renders it the duty of a man to marry his uncle's daughter, however sickly or deformed she may be. This custom is known as mēnarikam, and is followed by a number of Dravidian castes, but it is perhaps more strictly observed by the Kōmatis than by others.† Some Kōmatis have, in recent times, given up this custom, and, as the common folk among them put it, have suffered by the loss of their sons-in-law and other mishaps. Kanyakapurānam, the sacred book of the Kōmatis, is a lasting monument of the rigidity with which mēnarikam was maintained in ancient days. The custom has apparently been copied by the Dēsāsta Brāhmans of Southern India, in whom it would, but for modern enlightenment, have almost been crystallised into law. The Ayyar Brāhmans have adopted it in order to keep the family property intact within it.‡

A Nattamān (Tamil cultivator) man has a right to marry the daughter of his father's sister, and, if she is given to another man, the father's sister has to return

* Manual of the Madura district.

† C. Hayavadana Rao, MS.

‡ *Ibid.*

to her father or brother the dowry, which she received at the time of her marriage, and this is given to the man who had the claim upon the girl.*

Among the Goundans (cultivators) of Coimbatore, a boy of seven or eight is occasionally married to a maternal uncle's or paternal aunt's daughter of sixteen or eighteen. In this case it is said that the boy's father is the *de facto* husband. But this barbarous and objectionable custom is more honoured in the breach than in the observance, and is hardly practised, though it is alleged that it can be enforced by appeal to the community, and that, upon any objection, the boy's mother is entitled (to threaten) to drown herself in a well, or (as is not unfrequently the case), she will incite her friends to tie a tāli on the girl by fraud or force. The maternal uncle's daughter is absolutely the correct relationship for a wife. It is the bride's maternal uncle who carries her to the nāttu-kal (place where grain seedlings are raised) at the village boundary, and this is the equivalent to a publication of the banns.† A Paraiyan bride, at Coimbatore, is carried in the arms of her maternal uncle thrice round the wedding booth. At the same place, after the tāli has been tied round the Odde (navvy) bride's neck, her maternal uncle ties a four-anna piece in her cloth, and carries her in his arms to the marriage booth. The Idaiyan (Tamil shepherd) bridegroom makes a present of four annas and betel to each of the bride's maternal uncles' sons, who have a natural right to marry her. The acceptance of

* Madras Census Report, 1901.

† Manual of the Coimbatore district.

the presents indicates their consent to the marriage. One of the bride's maternal uncles carries her in his arms to the marriage booth, while another uncle carries a lighted torch on a mortar. The light is placed in front of the contracting couple, who are seated side by side. The bride and bridegroom's wrists are tied together by the maternal uncles' sons. When they retire to the bride's house, she is carried in the arms of the elder brother of the bridegroom. They are stopped by the maternal uncles' sons, who may beat the man who is carrying the bride. But, on payment by the bridegroom of four annas to each of his cousins, he and his bride are permitted to enter the house. Among the Yerukalas (a nomad tribe in the Telugu country) polygamy is practised, and the number of wives is only limited by the means of the husband. Marriage of relations within the degree of first cousins is not allowed. The rule is relaxed with respect to a man marrying the daughter of his father's sister, which is not only allowed, but a custom prevails that the two first daughters of a family may be claimed by the maternal uncle as wives for his sons.* "The value of a wife," Dr. Shortt writes,† "is fixed at twenty pagodas. The maternal uncle's right to the first two daughters is valued at eight out of twenty pagodas, and is carried out thus. If he urges his preferential claim, and marries his own sons to his nieces, he pays for each only twelve pagodas; and, similarly, if he, from not having sons or any other cause, foregoes his claim, he receives eight pagodas out of the twenty

* Manual of the Nellore district.

† Trans. Eth. Soc. N.S., VII.

Plate IV₈

Naidu Bride and Bridegroom.

paid to the girl's parents by anybody else who may marry them." In the formal marriage ceremony among the jungle Shōlagas of Coimbatore, the tāli is tied by the bridegroom inside a booth. The maternal uncle, if he can afford it, presents a new cloth to the bride, and a feast is held. Sometimes even this simple rite is dispensed with, and the couple, without any formality, live together as man and wife on the understanding that, at some time, a feast must be given to a few of the community.

At a Sembadavan (Tamil fishermen) wedding small gold and silver plates, called pattam, are tied to the foreheads of the bride and bridegroom. Of these, the most conspicuous are those tied by the maternal uncles, which have for the bridegroom a V-shape like a nāmam, and fort he bride the shape of a pīpal (*Ficus religiosa*) leaf.

On the wedding day among the Mādigas (Telugu Pariahs) the bridegroom's party bring betel nuts, limes, a golden head, a bonthu (unbleached cotton thread), rice, and turmeric paste. The maternal uncle of the bride gives five betel leaves and nuts to the Pedda Mādiga (head-man), and putting the bonthu round the bride's neck, ties the golden bead thereon. At a wedding among the Jōgis (Telugu mendicants) the kankanam (wrist threads), which are made of human hair, are tied by the maternal uncles to the wrists of the bride and bridegroom.

Among many of the classes which inhabit the plains of Ganjam, the younger brother has a claim to marry the widow of an elder brother.

The Pulluvans (astrologers and medicine men) of Malabar, it is said, permit marriage between even brother and sister. Whatever the truth may be, it is probable that something of the kind was once the case, for, when a man is suspected of incest, they say "He is like the Pulluvans." *

A quaint custom among the Lambādis of Mysore is that the officiating Brāhman priest is the only male who is permitted to be present. Immediately after the betrothal, the females surround and pinch him on all sides, and try to strip him stark naked, repeating all the time songs in their mixed Kutni dialect. The vicarious punishment, to which the solitary male Brāhman is thus subjected, is said to be apt retribution for the cruel conduct of a Brāhman parent, who, in an age gone-by, heartlessly abandoned his two daughters in the jungle, as they had attained puberty before marriage. The pinching episode is a painful reality. It is said, however, that the Brāhman willingly undergoes the operation in consideration of the fee paid.† An equally mauvais quart d'heure is passed by a Brāhman at a wedding among the Lingayats (Kannadiyans) of Chingleput. On the tāli-tying day a Brāhman (generally a Saivite) is formally invited to attend, and pretends that he is unable to do so. But he is, with mock gravity, pressed hard to come, and, after repeated guarantees of good faith, he finally consents with great reluctance and misgivings. On his arrival at the marriage booth, the headman of the family in which the marriage is taking

* Madras Census Report, 1891. † Mysore Census Report, 1891.

place seizes him roughly by the head, and ties five cocoanuts as tightly as possible to his kudumi, or bunch of hair at the back of his head, amid the loud, though not real protestations of the victim. Those present, with all seriousness, pacify him, and he is cheered by the sight of five rupees, which are presented to him together with a pair of new cloths, and pān-supāri. Meanwhile the young folk have been making sport of him by throwing at his new and old cloths big empty brinjal (*Solanum Melongena*) fruits filled with turmeric powder and chunām (powdered shell-lime). He goes for the boys, who dodge him, and at last the elders beat off the youngsters with the remark that "after all he is a Brāhman, and ought not to be trifled with in this way." The Brāhman then takes leave, and is heard of no more in connection with the marriage rites. The whole ceremony has a decided ring of mockery about it, and leads one to the conclusion that it is celebrated more in derision than in honour of the Brāhmans. It is notorious that the Lingayats will not even accept water from a Brāhman's hands, and do not, like many other castes, require his services in connection with marriage or funeral rites. The ceremony of tying cocoanuts to the hair of the Brāhman appears to be observed by the bamboo section of the Kannadiyans, and not by the rattan section. These two sections carry their pots of curds in rattan and bamboo baskets respectively. By the rattan section a quaint ceremonial is observed. The village barber is invited to be present, and the infant bride and bridegroom are seated before him in a state of nudity. He is provided with some good ghī in a cocoanut shell, and has to sprinkle this over the heads of the contracting couple by means of a grass or reed. This he is prevented from doing by a cruel contrivance. A large stone is suspended from his neck by a rope, and, by means of another rope, he is kept nodding backwards and forwards by urchins at his back. Eventually he succeeds in his efforts, and, after receiving a small fee, ghī, and pān-supāri, he is dismissed. The bride and bridegroom then take an oil bath, and the marriage ceremony it proceeded with.* The stone round the neck probably represents the linga, and the barber becomes for the moment a Lingayat.

In an account of the marriage ceremony among the Lambādis, Mr. Francis writes † that the right hands of the couple are joined, and they walk seven times round two grain-pounding pestles, while the women chant the following song, one line being sung for each journey round the pestle :—

> To yourself and myself marriage has taken place.
> Together we will walk round the marriage pole.
> Walk the third time. Marriage has taken place.
> You are mine by marriage.
> Walk the fifth time. Marriage has taken place.
> Walk the sixth time. Marriage has taken place.
> Walk the seventh time. Marriage has taken place.
> We have walked seven times. I am yours.
> Walk the seventh time. You are mine.

This Lambādi ceremonial, at which a Brāhman is present, may be compared with the Brāhmanical saptapadi

* C. Hayavadana Rao, MS.

† Manual of the Bellary district.

(seven feet), which has already (p. 1) been described as the essential and binding portion of the marriage ceremony.

At a wedding among the Lingayats, in the case of a four-day marriage, the first day is spent in worshipping ancestors. On the second day, rice and oil are sent to the local mutt (place where the priest stays) and oil alone to the relatives. New pots are brought with much shouting, and deposited in the room in which the household god is kept. A booth is erected, and the bridegroom sits under it side by side with a married female relative, and goes through a performance called surigi. An enclosure is made round them with cotton thread passed ten times round four earthen pitchers placed at the four corners. Five married women come with boiled water, and wash off the oil and turmeric, with which the bride and bridegroom and his companion have been anointed. The matrons then clothe them with the new cloths offered to the ancestors on the first day. After some ceremonial, the thread forming the enclosure is removed, and given to a Jangam (priest). The surigi being now over, the bridegroom and his relative are taken back to the god's room. The bride and one of her relations are now taken to the booth, and another surigi is gone through. When this is over, the bride is taken to her room, and decorated with flowers. At the same time the bridegroom is decorated in the god's room, and, mounting on a bullock, goes to the village temple, where he offers a cocoanut. A chaplet of flowers (bashingam) is tied to his forehead, and he returns to the house. In the god's room a pānchakalāsam, consisting of five metal vessels, with betel and vibhūti (sacred ashes) has been arranged, one vessel being placed at each corner of a square, and one in the middle. By each kalasam is a cocoanut, a date-fruit, a betel leaf and areca nut, and one pice (copper coin) tied in a handkerchief. A cotton thread is passed round the square, and round the centre kalasam another thread, one end of which is held by the family guru (priest), the other by the bridegroom, who sits opposite to him. The guru wears a ring made of kusa grass on the big toe of his right foot. The bride sits on the left of the bridegroom, and the guru ties their right and left hands together with kusa grass. The joined hands are washed, and bilva (*Ægle Marmelos*) leaves and flowers are offered. The officiating priest then consecrates the tāli and the kankanam (consecrated thread); ties the latter on the wrist of the joined hands; and gives the tāli to the bridegroom, who ties it round the bride's neck, repeating some words after the priest. On the fourth day the married couple worship Jangams and the elders, and take off the kankanam from their wrists, and tie it to the doorway.

In a report by Lieutenant Evans in 1820, it is stated that the marriages of the Kotas of the Nīlgiri hills remind one of what is called bundling in Wales. The young man and girl, being together for the night, the girl is questioned next morning by her relatives whether she is pleased with her husband-elect. If she answers in the affirmative, it is a marriage; if not, the young man is immediately dismissed, and the girl does not suffer in reputation if she thus discards half a dozen suitors.

At a wedding among the Muhammadan Māppillas or Moplahs of Malabar, the bridegroom and his suite are conducted to a room in the bride's house specially prepared for their reception. After a few minutes' stay in the room, the party withdraws, leaving the bridegroom alone. The bride is next introduced into the room by her female relations, and the door is closed by them. The bridegroom and the bride are left together for a few minutes. The bride then leaves, and the bridegroom's party enters, and take him back to his house. In some places the bride and bridegroom are permitted to spend the whole night together, and the latter takes leave only the next morning. In some of the southern talūks (divisions) the custom is the reverse of what has just been described. The bride is first conducted into the room, and persuaded or forced to lie on a sofa, and the bridegroom is next introduced into it, tarries there a few moments, and then leaves. This is practicable only in the case of girls of tender age, who are ignorant of the meaning of what they are made to do.*

The marriage customs of the Nayādis of Malabar have recently been described by Mr. Gopal Panikkar, who writes as follows.† "A large hut is constructed of leaves, inside which the girl is ensconced. Then all the young men and women of the village gather round the hut, and form a ring about it. The girl's father, or the nearest male relative, sits at a short

* P. Kunjain, Malabar Quart. Review, II, 1903.

† Malabar and its Folk, 1900. The Nayādis are a very polluting class, who live by begging, etc.

distance from the crowd with a tom-tom in his hands. Then the music commences, and a chant is sung by the father, which has been freely translated as follows :—

> Take the stick, my sweetest daughter;
> Now seize the stick, my dearest love;
> Should you not capture the husband you wish for;
> Remember, 'tis fate decides whom you shall have.

All the young men who are eligible for matrimony arm themselves with a stick each, and begin to dance round the little hut, inside which the girl is seated. This goes on for close on an hour, when each of them thrusts his stick inside the hut through the leaf covering. The girl has then to take hold of one of these sticks from the inside, and the owner of the stick which is seized by her becomes the husband of the concealed bride. This ceremony is followed by feasting, after which the marriage is consummated." Among the jungle Kurumbas of the Nīlgiris there is, as a rule, no marriage rite. A man and woman will mate together, and live as man and wife. And, if it happens that in a family there has been a succession of such wives for one or two generations without the woman deserting her man in favour of another, it becomes an event, and is celebrated as such. The pair sit together, and pour water over each other from pots. They then put on new cloths, and a feast is partaken of. Among the jungle Shōlagas, when a man falls in love with a girl, and she likes him, they go off to the jungle for three days. On the fourth day the whole village turns out with tom-toms and other musical instruments. They go into the jungle and find the young couple, whom they bring in procession to the temple, where the marriage ceremony is performed. According to another account, the couple elope to a distant jungle, and return home only after the bride has become a mother.*

There exists, among the hill Urālis of Coimbatore, a kind of informal union called kuduvali. A man and woman will, by mutual consent, elope into the jungle, and live there together till they are discovered, and brought back by their relations. A council-meeting is held, and they are recognised as man and wife if the bride-money and fine inflicted are paid. Failure to pay up would render them liable to excommunication. To celebrate the event, a feast must be given by the man, and, if he should die without having fed the community, any children born to him are considered as illegitimate. In such a case, the widow or her near relatives are asked to give food to at least a few before the corpse is removed, so as to legitimatise the children.

Shubernagiri, in the Ganjam Māliahs, has two tryst-ing trees, consisting of a jāk and mango growing close together. The custom was for a Khond, unable to pay the marriage fees to the Patro, (head-man) to meet his love here at night and plight his troth, and then for the two to retire into the jungles for three days and nights before returning to the village. Afterwards, they were considered to be man and wife.

In one form of marriage among the jungle Chenchus, a man, wishing to marry, selects his bride, and both retire for one night by mutual consent from the gudēm

* Mysore Census Report, 1891.

(village). On the following morning, when they return, their parents invite their friends and relatives, and, by formally investing them with new cloths, declare them duly married. To complete the ceremony, a meal is given to those assembled.*

Until she is seven or eight years old, a Thanda Pulayan (agrestic serf) girl of Cochin, wears no covering except a strip of the tender bark of the areca palm. When she assumes the garment made of the leaves of the thanda (a sedge), a ceremony called thanda kalyānam (marriage) is celebrated at an auspicious hour on an appointed day. The garment is generally made by a female relative. The investiture is the occasion of a feast of curry and rice, fish and toddy.

With the Tangalān Paraiyans, the betrothal ceremony, or pariyam, is binding as long as the contracting couple are alive. They may live together as man and wife without performing the marriage ceremonial, and children born to them are considered as legitimate. But, when their offspring marry, the parents must first go through the marriage rites, and the children are then married in the same pandal on the same day.

I have previously stated † that "the Yerukalas of the Kistna district are divided into two classes—sheep and goats practically. Of these, the latter are the bastard offspring of the former. They are not allowed to marry among the legitimate members. But, in order to prevent them from becoming a separate caste, the sons and

* Manual of the Kurnool district.

† Madras Mus. Bull., IV, 3.

daughters of a bastard couple are not allowed to marry a bastard. They must marry a legitimate, and so the second generation is clean again." The Collector of the district informs me that legitimate may not marry illegitimate. Illegitimate must marry illegitimate. The offspring thereof is *ipso facto* whitewashed, and becomes legitimate, and must marry a legitimate. According to the Rev. J. Cain, * on the birth of a daughter to a Yerukala, the father of an unmarried little boy often brings a rupee, and ties it in the cloth of the father of the newly born girl. When the girl is grown up, he can claim her for his son. For twenty-five rupees he can claim her much earlier.

Among the Nanga Porojas (cultivating hill tribe) of Vizagapatam, pits are dug in the ground, in which during the cold season the children are put at night to keep them warm. The pit is about nine feet in diameter. In the spring all the marriageable girls of a settlement are put into one pit, and a young man, who has really selected his bride with the consent of his parents, comes and sings to her by name. Whereupon, if she likes him, she comes out, a fire is lighted, and a dance takes place. If the girl sings back that she will not have him, he tries some other girl's name. On one occasion a leopard jumped into the pit, and killed some of the maidens. According to another version, a number of Bhonda youths, who are candidates for matrimony, start off for a village, where they hope to find a corresponding number of young women, and make known their

* Ind. Ant., III 1874.

wishes to the elders, who receive them with all due ceremony. The juice of the salop (sago palm, *Caryota urens*) in a fermented state is in great requisition, as nothing can be done without the exhilarating effects of this, their favourite beverage. The youths excavate an underground chamber (if one is not already prepared) having an aperture at the top, admitting of the entrance of one at a time. Into this the young gentlemen, with a corresponding number of young girls, are introduced, when they grope about and make their selection, after which they ascend out of it, each holding the young lady of his choice by the forefinger of one of her hands. Bracelets are then put on her arms by the elders.*

Dr. Rivers informs me that, when a Toda marriage is arranged, the future husband gives a cloth, and salutes (head to foot) the father, mother and brothers of his future bride. I am told that, in like manner, the prospective bride bows down with her face to the ground, and her husband-elect places first the right, and then the left foot on her head.

Unusual details in the marriage ceremony of the Chettis (traders) are the wearing of a toe-ring by the bridegroom, and a custom, said to be now dying out, of inviting a carpenter to bless the happy pair. Unmarried girls usually wear a necklace of cowry (*Cypræa moneta*) shells and beads. This is noteworthy, for, though married women in many castes are distinguished by the tāli round their necks and the silver rings on their second toes, and in the case of Brāhmans by wearing one end

* J. A. May, Ind. Ant., II, 1875.

of their cloths passed between their legs, it is unusual for unmarried girls to wear any badge of their condition.*

The Ilaiyāttakudi section of the Chettis has seven exogamous sub-divisions, called kovils or temples, which derive their names from seven favourite temples. Ilaiyāttakudi is considered the parent temple, and, when a man of any of the other six kovils is married, he has to obtain two garlands of flowers, one from the temple at that place, and one from the temple after which his sub-division is named.*

The Kondayamkottai Maravans, Mr. F. Fawcett tells us,† are divided into six sub-tribes or trees. Each tree or kothu (branch) is divided into three khilais or branches. Those of the khilais belonging to the same tree or kothu are never allowed to intermarry. "A man or woman must marry with one of a khilai belonging to another tree than his own, his or her own being that of his or her mother, and not of the father. But marriage is not permissible between those of any two trees or kothus. There are some restrictions. For instance, a branch of betel-vine or leaves may marry with a branch of cocoanut, but not with areca nuts or dates. The tāli must be obtained at the cost of the bridegroom's sister. The bride's father, uncle, or other relations, present the bridegroom with money, the amount of which must be an odd number."

Among Telugu Brāhmans, the interposition of a cloth as a screen between the bride and bridegroom, just before

* Madras Census Report, 1901. † Journ. Anthrop. Inst., XXXIII, 1903.

the tying of the mangala suthram (tāli) is fairly common. It is resorted to, so that the bride may not be seen by the bridegroom. Further, the bride is, like the Santhal bride in Bengal, made to sit in a capacious basket, which is either empty or partly filled with paddy. The tāli is tied while she is in the basket. Among all the Telugu-speaking castes, from Brāhmans to Mādigas, small black glass beads form part of the mangala suthram. At a marriage among the Izhavans or Iluvans (toddy-drawers) of Travancore, it is a barber woman that ties the pratisaram or the diksha thread (the equivalent of the kankanam) round the bride's wrist, and formally hands over the tāli to the bridegroom. It is pointed out by Mr. N. Subramani Iyer * that shaving was originally not a mere question of personal toilette, but a sacrament, and the priestly function was combined with that of the barber. On the wedding day among the Iluvans of Malabar, the bridegroom's face is shaved, and, after being rubbed with oil, he is bathed by seven young men. He is carried, or walks on planks from the bathing-place to the marriage booth, and must not touch the ground with his feet. The barber cuts the nails of an Okkiliyan bride and bridegroom. The barber also, after worshipping, shaves the face of an Idaiyan bridegroom, and receives as his fee four annas, some rice, and the cloth which the young man was wearing. An Odde may not shave his face till it has been shaved by the barber on his wedding day.

* Travancore Census Report, 1901.

It is the barber, at a marriage among the Konga Vellālas (cultivators) of the Salem district, who officiates at the marriage rites, and ties the tāli. Brāhmans are invited to the wedding, and treated with due respect, and presented with money, rice, betel leaves and nuts. The barber, when he ties the tāli, mutters something about Brāhman and Vēdas in a respectful manner. The story goes that, during the days of the Chēra, Chola, and Pandyan kings, a Brāhman and an Ambattan (barber) were both invited to a marriage feast. But the Brāhman, on his arrival, died, and the folk, believing his death to be an evil omen, ruled that, the Brāhman being missing, they would have the Ambattan; and it has ever since been the custom for the Ambattan to officiate at weddings. The purōhits (priests) of the Kallan Muppans (stone workers) of Malabar are Tamil barbers, who officiate at their marriages. The barber shaves the bridegroom before the marriage ceremony, and the purōhit has to blow the conch shell all the way from the bridegroom's house to that of the bride.*

At a wedding among the low-class Mālas of the Telugu country, a barber pares the bridegroom's toe-nails, and, as a mere form, touches his chin with a razor. Then, taking two rice-pounders, he dips the ends in milk and ghī, and touches the shoulders of the bride and bridegroom as a signal to retire for bathing, while he salutes them with the words "Good be to you."† In like manner, at a Kamma wedding, the barber pares

* C. Karunakara Menon. † Manual of the Nellore district.

the nails of the bridegroom, and touches those of the bride with a mango leaf dipped in milk. A Kāpu (Telugu agriculturist) bridegroom is invested with a new cloth, and the bride placed beside him. Their cloths are then tied together in a knot. A barber next approaches with a brass cup of water, and a plate containing rice stained with turmeric is placed upon the ground. Each of the visitors takes up a few grains of rice, and sprinkles them on the head of the couple, and waves round their heads some small pieces of money to avert the evil eye. The coins so used are thrown into the barber's cup. The barber then cuts the toe-nails of the bridegroom. This, with the Sūdras, answers to the ceremony of shaving the head among the Brāhmans. Later, a cloth is held up between the bride and bridegroom, and she is presented to him by her father. The couple unite hands, and walk round the dais thrice. Then, the veil being again held up between them, the bridegroom places his right foot upon a black pounding stone, and the bride puts her left foot three times upon his right. Then she treads with her right foot upon the stone, and he places his left foot upon it three times. The temporary screen is then again removed, and the bride puts on the saffron-coloured cloth brought as a present for her by the bridegroom's father. Bride and bridegroom look up at the sky to catch a glimpse of the pole-star, (Arūndati) and then enter the apartment, when the marriage feast commences. At a Brāhman marriage ceremony, the bridegroom shows the bride the pole-star, and recites the following text: "Heaven is stable; the earth is stable; this universe is stable; these mountains are stable. May this woman be stable in her husband's family."

At an Idaiyan (Tamil shepherd) wedding, at Coimbatore, the bridegroom places his right foot, and the bride her left foot on a grindstone, and they look at the pole-star, which represents the wife of the ascetic Vashista, who is the pattern of chastity. The grindstone represents Ahalliya, who was the wife of a saint, Gauthama. She was cursed by her husband for her misconduct with Indra, and turned into a stone. By placing their feet on the grindstone, the young couple express a wish to keep in check unchaste desires. The bride decorates a small grindstone with cloths and ornaments, gives it to the bridegroom, and takes it to all the assembled relations who give her something, and bless her with a hope that she will bring forth many children.

During the marriage ceremony among the Oddes (navvies) of Coimbatore, a woman, belonging to a Pedda (big) Boyan family, puts turmeric water mixed with chunām (burnt lime), betel leaves, and a coral necklet in a vessel, and waves it in front of the bridegroom's face. This is arathi, and is done to avert the evil eye. At the close of the ceremony the bride and bridegroom tie the ends of a single cloth round their bodies, and are bathed in turmeric water, which they pour over each other. They then look at the sky, and, taking water in both hands, throw it down thrice. The kankanams (wrist threads) are then untied.

Many variants of the Kāpu screen-scene occur in the Telugu country, and it has been adopted by the less civilised classes. For example, at a Yānādi (Telugu forest tribe), wedding, the bride and bridegroom sit side by side on two planks upon a raised platform. The mothers of the contracting parties then anoint them with oil, turmeric, and sandal paste. The pair retire to bathe, and return from the bath decorated with jewelry, and wearing new cloths, which have been dipped in turmeric water and dried. They next stand, one at each end of the platform, and a cloth is interposed as a screen between them, after the kankanam, or cotton thread dipped in turmeric water, has been tied to the wrist. To this thread a folded mango (*Mangifera indica*) leaf is sometimes attached. The couple next approach the screen, and the bridegroom, stretching his right leg underneath the screen, places his right foot on the right foot of the bride. He then takes up the bottu, or gold ornament, attached to a cotton thread dyed with turmeric, and ties it round the neck of the bride, his foot still on hers. In some cases a cotton thread (bashingam) with a folded mango leaf attached to it is further tied on the head, in imitation of the custom among the Nayudus, Kāpus, and others.

The marriage ceremonies of the Kavarais (Tamil synonym for Balija) who are settled in Tinnevelly are like those of many other Telugu castes, and the interposition of a screen between the bride and bridegroom, and tying of the second tāli or string of black beads on the nagavali day (sacrifice to the Dēvas) are performed. But those who belong to the Sīmaneli sept go through two additional ceremonies. One of these, called Krishnamma parantalu, is performed on the day previous to the tying of the tāli. It consists in the worship of the soul of Krishnamma, a married woman. A new cloth is purchased, and presented, together with money, betel, etc., to a married woman, who eats before those who are assembled. All the formalities of the srādh, (memorial ceremony) are observed, except the burning of the sacred fire (hōmam) and repeating of mantrams from the Vēdas. This ceremony is very commonly observed by Brāhmans, and castes which employ Brāhman priests for their ceremonials. The main idea is the propitiation of the soul of the deceased married woman. If in a family a married woman dies, every ceremony of an auspicious nature should be preceded by the worship of the Sumangali (married woman), which is known as Sumangali-prarthana. Orthodox women think that, if the soul of Sumangali is not thus worshipped, she may do some injury to those who are performing the ceremony. On the tāli-tying day the Kavarai bride and bridegroom proceed to the temple to worship. A few small pots are placed on the turban of the bridegroom, and on the head of the bride, where they are kept in position by the kongu or free end of her cloth. The sacred thread is worn during the marriage ceremony, but not afterwards.

On the occasion of a wedding among the Kurubas (Canarese shepherds) of western Bellary, a square space is marked out by pots filled with water, which are placed at each corner. Round the pots five turns of cotton thread are wound. Within the square a pestle, painted with red and white stripes, is placed, on which the bridal couple, with two young girls, sit. Rice is thrown over them, they are anointed and washed, and receive presents. Later on, the marriage dais is covered with a blanket (kambli), on which a mill-stone and basket filled with cholum (*Andropogon Sorghum*), are placed. The bridegroom standing with a foot on the stone, and the bride with a foot on the basket, the tāli is tied by the officiating Brāhman priest, while those assembled throw rice over the happy pair. On the night of the sixth day after marriage, a large metal plate or gangalam is filled with rice, ghī, curds, and sugar. Round this some of the relatives of the bride and bridegroom sit, and finish off the food. The number of those who partake thereof must be an odd one, and they must eat the food as quickly as possible. If anything goes wrong with them while eating or afterwards, it is regarded as an omen of impending misfortune. Some even consider it as an indication of the bad character of the bride.

The Patnūlkārans found in the Tamil districts have adopted some of the marriage customs of the Telugus, and a number of small pots are set up in a room, and worshipped daily throughout the marriage ceremony. A figure of a car (plate V) is drawn on the wall with red earth or laterite stone, and on it the gōtra of the bridegroom is written. The Patnūlkārans are a caste of weavers, who speak a dialect of Gujarati, and migrated to the south from Gujarat. They claim to be Saurashtra Brāhmans.

During the wedding ceremony among the Paraiyans of Coimbatore, a pestle is placed in the marriage booth,

Plate V.

Patnūlkāran Wall Design.

and the bridegroom sits on it. The bride's father and brothers rub oil over his head, and he is bathed. The bride then sits on the pestle, and is in like manner anointed with oil and bathed. The pestle is then removed, and a plank placed in its stead. A four-anna piece, and a small chank shell (*Turbinella rapa*) such as is used as a baby's pap-bowl, are thrown into a pot containing turmeric water, from which the bride is expected to pick up the shell, and the bridegroom the coin. This is repeated three times, and the kankanams (wrist threads) are then untied, and put into the pot. When an Odde bride and bridegroom enter the bride's house, a pot of water is brought, and they put their hands into it. A ring is dropped into the pot, and they both try to pick it up. Whoever first does so is considered to be the more clever. This is repeated three times. At a wedding among the Dēvāngas (weavers), a pap-bowl and ring are put into a pot. If the bride picks out the pap-bowl, her first child will be a girl; if the bridegroom picks out the ring, it will be a boy. At an Idaiyan (Tamil shepherd) wedding, a gold and silver ring are placed in a large pot, and in another pot a style, such as is used for writing on palm leaves, and a piece of palm leaf are placed. The bride and bridegroom then struggle to catch hold of these objects. Included among the presents to a Nānchināt Vellāla bridegroom in Travancore are an iron writing style and a knife.*

* Travancore Census Report, 1901.

At a marriage among the Iluvans (toddy-tappers) of Malabar, the bridegroom removes seven threads from the new cloth brought for the bride, and makes a string with them, which is coloured yellow with turmeric. To the string he attaches the tāli, which he places on betel leaves, and hands over to his sister. During the ceremony the bride stands on rice, and covers her face with betel leaves. To bring good luck to the young couple, a married woman with a child meets them as they approach the bridegroom's house.

At a wedding among the Holeyas (agrestic serfs) of South Canara, the bridegroom's party go to the bride's house with rice, betel-leaves and areca-nuts, and wait the whole night outside the bride's hut, the bridegroom being seated on a mat specially made by the bride. Next morning the bride is made to sit opposite the bridegroom with a winnowing fan, filled with betel-leaves, etc., between them. Meanwhile the men and women throw rice over the heads of the contracting couple. The bride then accompanies the bridegroom to his hut, carrying the mat with her. The marriage ceremony lasts four days, during which time none of the party should fail to sit on the mat. On the last day the couple take the mat to a river or tank (pond), where fish are to be found, and catch some fish, which they let go after kissing them.* At a wedding among the leaf-wearing Koragas of South Canara, the bride and bridegroom take a cold bath, and seat themselves side by side on a mat with a handful of rice between them. The blessings

* Manual of the South Canara district.

of the sun are invoked, and then an elderly man of the tribe takes up a few grains of rice, and sprinkles them over the heads of the couple. His example is followed by the others present. The bridegroom has then to present two silver pieces to the bride.* At a wedding among the Kannadiyans (Canarese shepherds), married women are selected, who are required to bathe as each of the more important ceremonies is performed, and are alone allowed to cook for or to touch the happy couple. Weddings last eight days, during which time the bride and bridegroom must not sit on anything but woollen blankets.†

The custom of the bridal couple bathing in water brought from seven different villages obtains among many Oriya castes, including Brāhmans. It is known by the name of pāni-tula. The water is brought by married girls who have not reached puberty on the night preceding the wedding day, and the bride and bridegroom wash in it before dawn. This bath is called koili-pāni-snāno, or cuckoo water bath. The koil is the Indian koel or cuckoo (*Eudynamis honorata*), whose crescendo cry ku-il, ku-il, is trying to the nerves during the hot season.

The essential and binding part of the marriage ceremony among the Bants (cultivators) of South Canara is called dhāre. The right hand of the bride being placed over the right hand of the bridegroom, a silver vessel (dhāre gindi) filled with water, with a cocoanut over the mouth and the flower of the areca palm over the

* Manual of the South Canara district. † Madras Census Report, 1901.

cocoanut, is placed on the joined hands. The parents, the managers of the two families, and the village headmen, all touch the vessel, which, with the hands of the bridal pair, is moved up and down three times. In some families the water is poured from the vessel into the united hands of the couple, and this betokens the gift of the bride. The bride and bridegroom then receive the congratulations of the guests, who express a hope that they may become the parents of twelve sons and twelve daughters. An empty plate, and another containing rice, are next placed before the pair, and their friends sprinkle them with rice from the one, and place a small gift, generally four annas, in the other. The bridegroom then makes a gift to the bride, which is called tirdochi, and varies in amount according to the position of the parties. Among the Ares* the pot contains a mixture of water, milk, ghī, honey, and curds instead of plain water. In the dhāre ceremony as performed by the Gaudas (Canarese farmers), the bridal pair hold in their joined hands five betel leaves, an areca nut, and four annas; and, after the water has been poured, the bride-groom ties a tāli on the neck of the bride.† At marriages among the Mogers (Canarese fishermen) the bride and bridegroom sit under a pandal, and join hands, palms uppermost. Upon their hands the maternal uncle of the bride places first some rice, next five betel leaves, then an unhusked arecanut, and last of all a lighted wick. The bridal couple slowly lower their hands, and deposit

* The Ares are said to be closely allied to the Marathis, and speak Marathi or Konkani.

† Manual of the South Canara district.

all these things on the ground. The bride's maternal uncle then takes her by the hand, and formally makes her over to the maternal uncle of the bridegroom.*

Among various Oriya classes in Ganjam, a bachelor wishing to marry a widow, or a widower wishing to remarry, has first to marry a sahāda or shādi tree, called in Telugu bharinike chettu, which is afterwards cut down. This tree is apparently *Streblus asper*, the twigs of which are struck in and around thatched houses to ward off lightning.

The essential portion of the marriage ceremony among the Badhoyis (Oriya carpenters and blacksmiths) is the tying together of the hands of the bride and bridegroom.† In like manner, at a wedding among the Bolāsis and Samantiyas (Oriya cultivators), the binding portion of the ceremony is hasthōgonthi, or the tying together of the hands of the bridal pair with a cotton thread soaked in turmeric water.† The contracting parties at a wedding among the jungle Kādirs of the western ghāts link together the little fingers of their right hands as a token of their union, and walk in procession round the marriage booth. So, too, the Pāno (hill tribe of Ganjam) bride and bridegroom have to join their little fingers to make the ceremony binding.‡ At a marriage among the Paraiyans of Coimbatore, the little finger of the bridegroom's right hand is linked with the little finger of the bride's left hand, the two hands being covered with a cloth. The ends of the

* Manual of the South Canara district.

† Madras Census Report, 1901. ‡ *Ibid.*

cloth of an Okkiliyan (cultivator) bride and bridegroom, with betel leaves and nuts in them, are tied together, and the little fingers of their right hands are linked. The contracting parties, among the hill Urālis, sit on a plank with their little fingers linked, while the bride-money is paid to the father-in-law and the milk-money to the mother-in-law. In one form of the marriage ceremony among the Kondayamkottai Maravans, the Brāhman priest ties together the little fingers of the right hands of the contracting couple, which are interlocked, with a silken thread.* Among the Kāppiliyans (Canarese cultivators) who have settled in the Madura district, the tāli is entirely dispensed with. The binding portion of the marriage ceremony is the locking of the fingers of the bridal couple under a cloth by their maternal uncles. The wedding-day is called kai kudako dhina (hand-joining day).

A curious ceremony during a marriage among the Goundans (cultivators) of Coimbatore is the visit of the bride to the nāttu-kal (place where seedlings are raised) where a Pillayar (elephant god) is made of cow-dung or mud, worshipped, and broken up. At this spot the nāttu-kal and the sun are also worshipped.†

At a marriage among the Pallans (agricultural labourers) of Coimbatore, cocoanuts are broken, and offered to a Pillayar made of cow-dung. The tāli is taken round in one of the fragments, to be blessed by those assembled. When a marriage is contemplated among

* F. Fawcett, Journ. Anthrop. Inst., XXXIII, 1903.

† Manual of the Coimbatore district.

the Idaiyans (Tamil shepherds) of the same place, the parents of the prospective bride and bridegroom go to the temple, and throw before the idol a red and a white flower, each wrapped in a betel-leaf. A small child is then asked to pick up one of the leaves. If the one selected contains the white flower, it is considered auspicious, and the marriage will be contracted. During the marriage ceremony the officiating Brāhman places a cow-dung Pillayar in the marriage booth. The bride husks some paddy. The relations of the bride and bridegroom fetch from the potter's house seven pots called adukupanai (pots kept one over the other), two large pots called arasanipanai, and seven earthen trays, and place them in front of the mud platform. The pots are filled with water, and a small piece of gold is dropped into each. The pots are worshipped daily during the marriage ceremony.

The match-making among the hill Urālis of Coimbatore is carried out by the boy's parents, who, with his other relations, pay two visits, one with and one without the boy, to the parents of the girl. The party must be received with due respect, which is shown by taking hold of the walking-sticks of the guests on arrival, and receiving them on a mat. A flower is placed on the top of a stone or figure representing the tribal goddess, and, after pūja has been done to it, it is addressed in the words "Oh! swāmi (god), drop the flower to the right if the marriage is going to be propitious, and to the left if otherwise." Should the flower remain on the image without falling either way, it is greeted as a very happy omen. On the occasion of the betrothal ceremony, if the bridegroom's party, on their way to the bride's village, have to cross a stream, running or dry, the bridegroom is not allowed to walk across it, but must be carried over on the back of his maternal uncle. During the marriage ceremony, after the bridal couple have worshipped at a pond, they must, on their return thence, be accompanied by their maternal uncles, who should keep on dancing, while cocoanuts are broken in front of them till the house is reached.

As a preliminary to marriage among the Kurubas, (Canarese shepherds) the bridegroom's father observes certain marks or curls on the head of the proposed bride. Some of these are believed to forbode prosperity, and others misery to the family into which the girl enters. They are, therefore, very cautious in selecting only such girls as possess curls (suli) of good fortune. This curious custom is observed by others only in the case of the purchase of cows, bulls, and horses. One of the good curls is the bāshingam found on the forehead, and the bad ones are the pēyanākallu at the back of the head, and the edirsuli near the right temple. As a nuptial tie, the ends of the garments of the contracting Kuruba parties are, at the wedding, tied together.* The curl on the forehead appears to be considered a good omen by the Kurubas at Hospet, and bad by those at Sandūr. A curl on the chest (theggu) is considered unlucky by both. Like the Kurubas, the Pallis (Tamil agriculturists) also

* Manual of the North Arcot district.

examine the curls in the selection of a bride. A curl on the forehead is considered as an indication that the girl will become a widow; and one on the back of the head portends the death of the eldest brother of her husband. On the subject of curls in the horse Mr. J. Walhouse writes as follows. "When a wealthy Hindu meditates purchasing a horse, he looks to the presence or not of certain circles or curls on particular parts of the body. These are called in Tamil suri or flowers, and by them a judgment is formed of the temper and quality of the horse. Each curl indicates a particular god, and a Hindu will not purchase unless the hair-curls are present, turning in the proper direction, and in their right places." * Of omens from the examination of horses' curls, the following may be cited. (1) The horse which has a ringlet under the eyes, in the chin, cheek, heart, neck, the part between the nostrils, temples, the buttocks, part below the nostrils, knees, testicles, navel, hump on the back, anus, right belly and feet, will bring on evil. (2) The horse which has ringlets in the upper lip, neck, ears, back, loins, eyes, lips, thighs, front legs, belly, sides and forehead, will bring on prosperity.†

I have heard of a Eurasian police officer, who attributed the theft of five hundred rupees, his official transfer to the Cuddapah district, and other strokes of bad luck, to the purchase of a horse with unlucky curls. All went well with him after he had got rid of the animal.

At the marriage ceremony of some Kurubas, a golden image of the tribal hero is taken out of the saffron

* Ind. Ant., XI, 1881. † Brihat Samhita.

powder, in which it has lain in its casket, and placed before the bride and bridegroom, who call aloud the hero's name. The pūjāri (officiating priest) then breaks a few cocoanuts on the heads of the hereditary cocoanut-breakers, and ties a piece of saffron to the right arm of the bride. With the Patha Kurubas the string used must be of cotton and wool mixed; with the Kottha Kurubas of wool alone; and with the Andē Kurubas of wool alone, this being regarded as an important distinction. Next the gaudu (head-man) and pūjāri throw rice upon the bride's head, and, the bridegroom tying a tāli round her neck, the ceremony is completed.* According to another account † "the Kurubas are divided into three endogamous divisions, viz., attikankana, unnekankana, and andē. In Canarese atti means cotton, unne woollen, while kankana is a thread tied round the wrist at the time of marriage, and the first and second subdivisions use respectively cotton and woollen threads at their marriages. Andē is a small vessel used by the Andē Kurubas for milking goats. According to a popular legend, an ancestral Kuruba, by name Undala Padmanna, whose material welfare was provided for by Sīva, contracted alliances with a Brāhman girl whom he rescued from rākshasas (giants), and with a girl of his own caste. At the marriage of his sons, a cotton (atti) kankanam was tied to the wrist of the caste woman's offspring, and a woollen (unni) kankanam to that of the Brāhman girl's sons. Marriage is celebrated in the bridegroom's house, and, if the bride belongs to a different

* Madras Census Report, 1891. † Manual of the North Arcot district.

village, she is escorted to that of the bridegroom, and made to wait in a particular spot outside it. On the first day of the marriage, purna kumbam, a small decorated vessel containing milk or ghī, with a two-anna piece and a cocoanut placed on the betel-leaf spread over the mouth of it, is taken by the bridegroom's relations to meet the bride's party. There the distribution of pān supāri takes place, and both parties return to the village. Meanwhile the marriage booth is erected, and twelve twigs of nāval (*Eugenia Jambolana*) are tied to the twelve pillars, the central or milk post, under which the bridal pair sit, being smeared with saffron, and a yellow thread being tied thereto. At an auspicious hour of the third day, the couple are made to sit in the booth, the bridegroom facing the east and the bride facing west. On a blanket spread near the kumbam 2½ measures of rice, a tāli or bottu, a cocoanut, betel-leaf, and camphor are placed. The gaudu places a ball of vibhūti (sacred ashes) thereon, breaks a cocoanut, and worships the kumbam, while camphor is burnt. The gaudu next takes the tāli, blesses it, and gives it to the bridegroom, who ties it round the bride's neck. The gaudu then, throwing rice on the heads of the pair, recites certain verses. The girl next removes her veil, and the men and women assembled throw rice on the heads of the bridal pair. The ends of their garments are then tied together, and two girls and three boys are made to eat out of the plates placed before the married couple. A feast completes the ceremony.

At a Coorg wedding, the Aruva (family adviser) puts three pebbles in the hands of the bride, who ties them in one of the corners of her garment as a token of sealing her right to her husband's property. The bridegroom throws some coloured rice on the head of his new wife, gives a little milk to her to drink, and presents her with a gift, such as a ring, or anything according to his means. When the bridegroom enters the bride's house on the evening of the marriage day, several thick plantain tree trunks are placed across the entrance, each of which he has to cut in a single stroke, showing his strength of arm, and confirming thereby his fitness to marry the bride.*

"It is generally believed that, when a marriage takes place in the family of a Kōmati (Telugu merchant),† some member of this family is obliged to go through the form of inviting the low-class Mādigas (leather-workers) of the place. If the Mādigas were to hear the invitation, the Kōmati would certainly be assaulted, and treated roughly; for the Mādigas look on the invitation as an insult and unlucky. In order to prevent the Mādigas hearing the invitation, the Kōmati takes care to go to the back of the Mādiga's house at a time when he is not likely to be seen, and whispers into an iron vessel commonly used for measuring out grain an invitation in the following words: 'In the house of the small ones (*i.e.*, Kōmatis) a marriage is going to take place. The members of the big house (*i.e.*, Mādigas) are to come.' The light to kindle the fire during the marriage ceremony must be obtained from a Mādiga's house, but, since the Mādigas object to giving it, some artifice has to be used in getting this

* A. Rea, Ann. Report, Arch. Survey, Madras, 1901–1902.

† The Kōmatis (Telugu traders) claim to be Vaisyas.

fire."* It is a curious fact, though many Kōmatis deny it, that at their marriage ceremonies they have to present betel-nuts and leaves to some Mādiga family.† Concerning this custom Mr. W. Francis writes as follows:‡ "The statement about the presentation of the betel-leaf and nut seems to be accurate, though no doubt the custom is not universal. It rests on the authority of Sir Walter Elliot ('Trans. London Ethn. Soc.,' 1869) and Major Mackenzie ('Ind. Ant.,' Vol. VIII, p. 36); and, in a foot-note on p. 55 of the 'Original Inhabitants of Bharata Varsha or India,' Dr. Oppert states that he has in his possession documents which confirm the story. It is said that now-a-days the presentation is sometimes veiled by the Kōmati concerned sending his shoes to be mended by the Mādiga a few days before the wedding, deferring payment till the wedding day, and then handing the Mādiga the leaf and nut with the amount of his bill." According to another account, the Kōmati of set purpose unbinds the toe-ring of his native shoes (chĕruppu), and summons a Mādiga, whose profession it is to make and repair these articles of attire. The Mādiga quietly accepts the job, and is paid more amply than is perhaps necessary in the shape of pān supāri, flowers and money. "Formerly," the Rev. J. Cain writes,§ "before a marriage took place between two Vaisyalu (Kōmatis), they had to arrange for, and pay all the marriage expenses of two Mādigas, but this custom has been

* J. S. F. Mackenzie, Ind. Ant., VIII, 1879.
† Madras Census Report, 1891.
‡ Madras Census Report, 1901.
§ Ind. Ant., VII, VIII, 1879.

abandoned, and they content themselves by giving an invitation to their wedding." "I cannot," Mackenzie writes,* "discover the connection between two such different castes as the Kōmatis and Mādigas, who belong to different divisions. The Kōmatis belong to the 18 pana division, while the Mādigas are members of the 9 pana. One reason has been suggested. The caste goddess of the Kōmatis is the virgin Kannikā Amma, who destroyed herself rather than marry a prince, because he was of another caste. She is usually represented by a vessel full of water, and, before the marriage ceremonies are commenced, she is brought in state from her temple, and placed in the seat of honour in the house. The Mādigas claim Kannikā as their goddess, worship her under the name of Māhatangi, and object to the Kōmatis taking their goddess." There is said to be another queer custom among the Kōmatis, and one from which some of the families derive their distinguishing names. After a marriage has been completed, the figure of a cow is made of flour, and into its stomach is put a mixture of turmeric, lime, and water, called wokale. After the cow has been worshipped in due form, it is cut up, and to each different family is secretly sent that portion of the cow which, according to custom, they are entitled to receive. For example, the Kōmarlavaru receive the horns, the Guntla the neck, etc.† It is noted by Frazer ‡ as a remarkable feature of some of the Oraon totems, that they are not

* Ind. Ant., VIII, 1879. The pana divisions correspond to the right and left hand sections.

† Mackenzie, *loc. cit.*

‡ Totemism, 1887.

whole animals, but parts of animals, as the head of a tortoise, the stomach of a pig. And, he adds, in such cases (which are not confined to Bengal) it is of course not the whole animal, but only the special part which the clansmen are forbidden to eat.

The Kōmatis, at the present day, during the marriage ceremonial, perform a rite called gōtra pūja. On the fifth day, they offer two large lumps of flour paste to the goddess Kannikamma, out of which they make a number of small balls, the number being usually twice or four times that of the gōtras among the local Kōmatis. On the second or third day after the tying of the tāli, the goddess is worshipped by two Kōmati women, who have to fast during the entire day. When the Kōmati males have partaken of a meal, a member of the community, carrying a cup containing turmeric water coloured red with chunām, makes a mark therewith on the cloth over the right thigh of all the castemen present, beginning with an individual belonging to the Pendlikūla gōtra. Towards evening Kannikamma, represented by a kalasam (brass vessel), is worshipped with an elaborate ritual.

The Mādigas (Telugu Pariahs) are divided into endogamous sections called dhomptis. During the marriage ceremonies, dhomptis, or offerings of food to the gods, are made, with variations according to the dhompti to which the celebrants belong. An illustration may be taken from the Gampa (basket) dhompti. The contracting parties procure a quantity of rice, jaggery, and ghī, which are cooked, and moulded into an elongated mass, and placed in a new bamboo basket. In the middle of the mass, which is determined with a string, a twig with a wick at one end is set up, and two similar twigs are stuck into the ends. Pūja is performed, and the mass is distributed among the daughters of the house and other near relations, but not among members of other dhomptis. The bride and bridegroom take a small portion from the mass, which is called dhonga muddha, or the mass that is stolen.

Among the Urālis (Tamil agricultural labourers), a man detected in an intrigue with an unmarried woman is fined, and has to marry her; and, at the wedding, his waist string is tied round her neck instead of a tāli.* Among the Korāmas (nomad Telugu tribe) the tāli is replaced by a string of black beads. The story goes that once upon a time a bridegroom forgot to bring the tāli, and he was at once told off to procure the necessary piece of gold from a goldsmith. The parties waited and waited, but the young man did not return. Since then the tāli has not been forthcoming, and the little string of beads is used as a substitute.† Instead of the tāli, the Reddis (Telugu cultivators) use a plain twisted cord of cotton thread besmeared with saffron, and devoid of ornament of any kind. They have a legend, which accounts for this. In days of yore a Reddi chief was about to be married, and he accordingly sent for a goldsmith, and, desiring him to make a splendid tāli, gave him the price of it beforehand. The smith was a drunkard, and neglected his work. The day for the celebration of the marriage arrived, but there was no tāli. Whereupon the old chief,

* Madras Census Report, 1901.

† Madras Mail, 1900.

plucking a few threads from his garment, twisted them into a cord, and tied it round the neck of the bride, and this became a custom.* The insigne of marriage among the Gāndlas (oil-pressers) is a bundle of 101 yellow coloured threads without a tāli or bottu, which is put on only after the marriage ceremony.†

Some Kāpus, especially the Motāti Kāpus, do not wear the tāli during marriage, its place being taken by a cotton string. Concerning the origin of this custom, the following story is narrated. During the reign of Bharatha, the brother of Rāma, Pillala Mari Belthi Reddi and his sons deceived him by appropriating all the grain, and giving up only the straw. On the return of Rāma from exile, he, to punish the Kāpus, directed them to bring *Cucurbita* (pumpkin) fruits for the srādh of Dasaratha. They eagerly consented, and cultivated the plant. A few days before the ceremony, Hanumān uprooted all the plants, so that, on the appointed day, they could not comply with Rāma's order. They, however, promised to pay a sum of money equal in weight to a pumpkin fruit. This proposal was accepted, and the Kāpus brought all the money they possessed, and yet the scale containing the fruit did not rise. They, accordingly, took the tālis from their wives' necks, and placed them on the scale containing the money, when the pumpkin immediately rose. A similar legend is current among the Vakkaligas (cultivators) of Mysore, who, instead of giving up the tāli, seem to have abandoned the cultivation of the plant.

* J. F. Kearns, Kalyana Shatanku.

† Manual of the North Arcot district.

The legend is thus narrated by Mr. Narasimmiyengar.* In the days of Rāma, when he was exiled to the wilds of Dandaka, Bharatha was appointed regent. The rayats (agriculturists) waxed rich, and tried every dodge to cozen the king, and defraud him of his revenues. If required to give to Government the upper crop as rent, they cultivated roots, ground-nuts, saffron, etc., and brought only the stalks and straw to the treasury; and when, in the following year, the state officers wanted the lower crop, they sowed rice, rāgi, wheat, etc., and the tax-gatherer was obliged to be content with the straw. The result of this state of things was emptiness of the exchequer. On Rāma's return and restoration, he examined the treasury, and hit upon an expedient for replenishing it. He sent for a grey pumpkin, took out the seeds, and, keeping one for himself, had the remainder boiled in milk. He then sent for all the rayats, gave each of them a seed, and told them that each rayat should pay a pumpkin as rent. At the time of the kist (payment of revenue) the rayats pleaded that their seeds were useless, and, on Râma showing them his own pumpkin, which had grown, offered to pay its weight in gold. But not until the rayat placed his wife's tāli in the scale did the beam kick, and, in this manner, all the gold in the realm found its way to the public treasury. As it was the means of their ruin, the Vakkaligas do not cultivate the grey pumpkin, or taste it even at the present day.

* Ind. Ant., III, 1874.

At a wedding among the Rājpūts of North Arcot, the marriage booth must be made with mango posts, and not with those of *Ficus religiosa*, and the bride and bridegroom must walk round it seven times. These people assert that they are true Kshatriyas, who came south from Rājputāna with the Muhammadan armies.* In the marriage ceremony of the Vanniyans or Pallis (agriculturists), the first of the posts supporting the booth must be cut from the vanni (*Prosopis spicigera*), a tree which they hold in much reverence because they believe that the five Pāndava princes, who were like themselves Kshatriyas, during the last year of their wanderings, deposited their arms in a tree of this species. On the tree the arms turned into snakes, and remained untouched till the owners' return.* The *Prosopis* tree is worshipped in order to obtain pardon from sins, success over enemies, and the realisation of the devotee's wishes. The Jālāris (Telugu fishermen) are divided into two endogamous sections called the people of the twelve poles and the people of the eight poles, according to the number of poles or posts used for the marriage booths. Similar sections are said to exist among the Pallis.†

At a wedding among the Jōgis (Telugu beggars), the marriage booth must contain twelve posts, and both bride and bridegroom must present four sheep and ten pots to the assembled guests. Should either fail, he or she receives three blows on the hand, is fined three rupees, and has cowdung and water poured over the head. Part

* Manual of the North Arcot district.

† Madras Census Report, 1901.

of the fine goes to the head of the caste, and the rest is spent in liquor, with which the party make merry.*

The milk-post, at a wedding among the Okkiliyans (cultivators) of Coimbatore, is made of the milk-hedge (*Euphorbia Tirucalli*), to which mango leaves and a kankanam (wrist thread) are tied. To the marriage post of the weaver Kaikōlans a cloth dipped in turmeric, in which pearls, coral, pieces of gold, and nine kinds of grain are tied up, is fixed. A four-anna piece, wrapped in a cloth, is tied to the milk-post of the Oddes (navvies). At a wedding among the Bēri Chettis (merchants), who belong to the left-hand faction, they are not allowed to tie plantain trees to the posts of the wedding booth with the trees touching the ground. If they do so, the Paraiyans, who belong to the right-hand section, cut them down. This custom is still observed in some out-of-the-way villages.

The mother of a Paraiyan bride, at Coimbatore, places seven rice cakes on the bridegroom's body, viz., on the head, above the shoulders, in the bend of the elbows, and in each hand. She removes all except the one on the head, and replaces them three times, when the cake on the head is removed with the others. A similar ceremony is performed on the bride.

The Toreyan (Canarese fisherman) bridegroom places his hands together, and small rice cakes are placed on his body in the following positions: one on the head, two above the shoulders, two in the bends of the elbows, two

* Madras Census Report, 1901.

in the knees, and four between the fingers. Cakes are, in like manner, placed on the bride's body. At a Toreya wedding cooked rice, white and coloured red, yellow, black, and green, is placed in trays, and waved before the contracting couple. Then nine lighted wicks are placed in a tray, and waved to avert the evil eye. Marriage, among the Toreyans, is always celebrated at the house of the bridegroom, never at that of the bride, as there is a legend that there was once a Rājah belonging to this caste, whose son was taken to the house of his bride-elect, and there murdered.

The marriage ceremony among the nomad Kuravans merely consists in tying a thread soaked in turmeric round the bride's neck, feasting the relations, and paying the bride-price.* The Kuravans seem to be even more previous than fathers who enter their infant sons for a popular house at a public school. For their children are said to be espoused even before they are born. Two men, who wish to have marriages between their children, say to one another: "If your wife should have a girl and mine a boy (or *vice versâ*), they must marry." And, to bind themselves to this, they exchange tobacco, and the bridegroom's father stands a carouse of arrack or toddy to the future bride's relations. But if, after the children are grown up, a Brāhman should pronounce the omens unpropitious, the marriage is not consummated, and the bride's father pays back the cost of the spirits used at the betrothal. When a marriage is arranged, a pot of water is placed before the couple, and a grass called thurvi

* Madras Census Report, 1901.

(*Cynodon Dactylon*) put into the water. This is equal to a binding oath between them.* Of this grass it is said in the Atharwana Vēda: "May this grass, which rose from the water of life, which has a hundred roots and a hundred stems, efface a hundred of my sins, and prolong my existence on earth for a hundred years." Writing concerning the Kuravans, Mr. Francis says: † "Kuravas have usually been treated as being the same as the Yerukalas . . . . But they do not intermarry or eat together. The Kuravas are said to tie a piece of black thread soaked in turmeric water round the bride's neck at weddings, while the Yerukalas use a necklace of black beads . . . . The (Kuravan) wife is apparently regarded as of small account, and, in a recent case in the Madras High Court, a husband stated that he had sold one of his wives for Rs. 21. The marriage ceremony consists merely in tying the thread soaked in turmeric round the woman's neck, feasting the relations, and paying the bride-price. Among the Kongu sub-division this latter can be paid by instalments in the following manner. A Kurava can marry his sister's daughter, and, when he gives his sister in marriage, he expects her to produce a bride for him. His sister's husband accordingly pays Rs. 7½ out of the Rs. 60, of which the bride-price consists at the wedding itself, and Rs. 2½ more each year until the woman bears a daughter." A Yerukala man can claim a girl in marriage for his son, when she attains a marriageable age, by tying, with the consent of the Berumanusan (headman), some money in her

* J. F. Kearns, *loc. cit.*

† Madras Census Report, 1901.

father's cloth, or at least give a treat of toddy to the headman, the girl's father, and others.

At a Cheruman (agriculture serf) wedding, the groom receives from his brother-in-law a kerchief, which the giver ties round his waist, and a bangle which is placed on his arm. The bride receives a pewter vessel from her brother. Next her cousin ties a kerchief round the groom's forehead, and sticks a betel-leaf into it. The bride is then handed over to the bridegroom.* A Boya (Telugu hunter) bride, besides having a golden tāli tied to her neck, has an iron ring fastened to her waist with a black string, and the bridegroom has the same.† An unusual item in the marriage ceremony of the Malasars (forest tribe) of Coimbatore is the tying of an iron ring to the bridegroom's wrist.‡ The tāli is, among the Nāttukottai Chettis (traders) tied, not by the bridegroom, but by some old man who is the father of many children. During the ceremony, the bridegroom should invariably carry on his shoulder a bag containing betel-leaves and nuts. At a wedding among the jungle Kānikars of Travancore, the bridegroom offers a cloth as a present to the bride's mother, besides one to the bride; and a present of 5½ fanams (coins) in the case of a bride who has reached puberty, and 7½ fanams in the case of a bride who has not, to the uncle or father-in-law, four chuckrams (small coins) of which go to the bride's father. A silver tāli is tied by the bridegroom himself

* Madras Mail, 1899.

† Manual of the North Arcot district.

‡ Madras Census Report, 1901.

in the case of a girl of the latter kind, and through his sister to one of the former. On the marriage day the feast is held at the bride's father's house, and on the next at the bridegroom's.*

The chief ceremonies at a marriage among the Bāvuris (basket-makers and earth-diggers) of Ganjam are the tying of betel-leaf and nut in the cloths of the bridal pair, the throwing of rice over the shoulder of the bridegroom by the bride, and the adornment of the bride with bangles.† Unusual items at a wedding among the Konda Doras (hill cultivators) of Vizagapatam are that the bridegroom is bathed in saffron water, and that the tāli is handed to him by an old man.†

In years gone by, members of the Gūna Velama class (Telugu cultivators), who were desirous of getting married, had to arrange and pay the expenses of the marriage of two of the Palli (fisherman) caste, but now it is regarded as sufficient to hang up a net in the house during the time of the marriage ceremony. The custom had its origin in a legend that, generations ago, when all the members of the caste were in danger of being swept off the face of the earth by their enemies, the Pallis came to the rescue with their boats, and carried the Velamas to a place of safety.‡

A custom called araveni or aireni is described as being observed at weddings of Sūdras in the Nellore district. Previous to the marriage day a potter is called

* M. Ratnasami Aiyar, Indian Review, 1902.
† Madras Census Report, 1901.
‡ Rev. J. Cain, Ind. Ant., VIII, 1879.

on to make from nine to twenty-one pots, the largest of which is about twelve feet in circumference, and the smallest a foot. These pots are painted outside with ornamental designs. The bride's relatives take two or three plates full of rice, pulse, and cakes under a canopy, and offer them to the pots. The offering is taken by the potter. The pots are then brought to the dwelling of the bride, and red coloured rice is whirled round each, to avert the evil eye, and then thrown away. The pots are brought into the house, and ranged each upon a settle of paddy. Lights are kept burning near this day and night, and are not allowed to go out. The married couple repair to the pots and worship them, and repeat the ceremony morning and evening for five days. Each morning and evening some matrons take the smaller pots to a well under a canopy, accompanied by music, and, after worshipping the well, they fill the pots with water, and bear them to the house. This water is for the bride and bridegroom to bathe with. Both morning and evening the bridal couple are seated upon a bedstead, and benedictory hymns are sung round them.* The marriage ceremony among the Uppiliyans (salt workers) is unusual. The couple are made to sit inside a wall made of piled-up water pots. The ends of their cloths are tied together, and then the women present pour the contents of some of the pots over them.†

The Panta Reddis (cultivators) of the Telugu country worship, at their marriages, the Ganga idol, which is

* Manual of the Nellore district. † Madras Census Report, 1901.

kept in the custody of a washerman belonging to a particular section of the Tsākalis. On the morning of the wedding day the Tsākali brings the idol, represented by a wooden head, and deposits it in the room where the araveni pots are kept. It is worshipped daily during the marriage ceremony, just before pūja is done to the pots. Towards evening on the fourth day, the idol, together with a goat and a kāvadi (bamboo pole with baskets of rice, cakes, betel leaves and nuts) is carried in procession to a pond or temple. The Tsākali, dressed up like a woman, heads the procession, and keeps on dancing and singing till the destination is reached. The idol is placed inside a rude triangular hut made of three sheaves of straw, and the articles brought in the baskets are spread before it. On the heap of rice small lumps of flour paste are placed, and these are made into lights by scooping out cavities, and feeding the wicks with ghī. One of the ears of the goat is then cut, and it is brought near the food. This done, the lights are extinguished, and the assembly return home without the least noise. The washerman takes charge of the idol, and goes his way. With the Panta Reddis of the southern (Tamil) districts, the details of the ceremony are somewhat different. The idol is taken in procession by the washerman two or three days before the marriage, and he goes to every Reddi house, and receives a present of money. The idol is then set up in the verandah, and worshipped daily till the conclusion of the marriage ceremony. Concerning the origin of the Ganga pūja the following legend is narrated. The Reddis who came southward had to cross the Silanathi, or petrifying river, and, if they

Plate VI.

Pūni Golla Muggu.

passed through the water, they would have become petrified. So one of the Reddis took the party back to a place called Dhonakonda, and, after worshipping Ganga, the head of the idol was cut off, and brought to the river-bank. The waters, like those of the Red Sea in the time of Pharoah, were divided, and the Reddis crossed on dry ground.

To propitiate their ancestors, the Pūni Gollas (Telugu cultivators), on the occasion of a marriage, go through an elaborate ceremonial called Ganga pūja, which was witnessed by Mr. K. Rangachari. Nine devices (muggu) are drawn on the floor of the court-yard by Mādigas or Mālas in five colours, viz., rice-flour (white), turmeric (yellow), turmeric and chunām (red), powdered leaves of *Cassia auriculata* (green), and charred paddy husk (black). These patterns represent a lotus flower, pandal or booth, tridents, snakes, throne of Sakti, a hero and his wife, Rāni's palace, offerings of food, and a female figure of Ganga. Of these the last is the most elaborate (plate VI). People, especially boys, are not allowed to witness the drawing of the devices, as the sight of the muggu in preparation would bring on illness, especially to boys and those of weak mind. Near the head of the figure of Ganga, an old bamboo box containing metal idols, ropes, betel, flowers, and a sword is placed. On its left side are set a brass vessel representing Sīva, three brass vessels (called bonalu or food-vessels), topped with betel, a small empty box tied up in a turmeric-dyed cloth called Brāmayya, and a sword. On the right side are an earthen tray and lamp. Near the legs are placed a brass pot filled with water, a lump of food coloured red, and frankincense. Food is piled up, in large and small conical heaps, and broom-sticks, bearing betel leaves, are placed on them. The pūja commenced with waving of the red food and incense. A fowl was then smoked over the vessel containing the incense, and, after being waved over the Ganga figure, its neck was wrung. Cocoanuts and fruit were then offered. One of the men officiating at the ceremonial, tying to his legs bells like those used by dancing-girls, became possessed by the spirit of an ancestor, and cut himself with a sword, which was wrested from him, and placed on the figure. The bridegroom then arrived, and seated himself by the feet of Ganga. He, too, becoming inspired, threw off his turban and body-cloth, and began to kick about, while declaring that he was Kariyāvala Rāja (an ancestor). Gradually becoming calm, he began to cry. Incense and lights were then carried round the figure, and the bride and bridegroom were blessed by those assembled.

Among the Vellūr-nādu Kallans a curious custom is said to be followed in the seventh month of a woman's pregnancy. Patterns are drawn on her back with rice flour, and milk is poured over them. The husband's sister decorates a grinding stone in the same way, invokes blessings on the woman, and expresses a hope that she may have a male child as strong as a stone.*

Concerning a form of marriage between the living and the dead among the Kōmatis, if a man and woman have

* Madras Census Report, 1901.

been living together and the man dies, Mr. Hutchinson writes as follows : * "The sad intelligence of her man's death is communicated to the neighbours ; a guru or priest is summoned, and the ceremony takes place. According to a writer who once witnessed such a proceeding, the dead body of the man was placed against the outer wall of the verandah of the house in a sitting posture, attired like a bridegroom, and the face and hands besmeared with turmeric. The woman was clothed like a bride, and adorned with the usual tinsel ornament over the face, which, as well as the arms, was daubed over with yellow. She sat opposite the dead body, and spoke to it in light unmeaning words, and then chewed bits of dry cocoanut, and squirted them on the face of the dead man. This continued for hours, and not till near sunset was the ceremony brought to a close. Then the head of the corpse was bathed, and covered with a cloth of silk, the face rubbed over with some red powder, and betel leaves placed in the mouth. Now she might consider herself married, and the funeral procession started." At the funeral of an unmarried Toda girl, which I witnessed, the corpse was made to go through a form of marriage ceremony. A small boy, three years old, was selected from among the relatives of the dead girl, and taken by his father in search of a grass and the twig of a shrub (*Sophora glauca*), which were brought to the spot where the corpse was lying. The mother of the dead child then withdrew one of its hands from the putkūli (cloth) in which it was wrapped, and the boy placed the grass

* *Op. cit.*

and twig in the hand, and limes, plantains, rice, jaggery, honey-comb and butter in the pocket of the putkūli, which was then stitched with needle and thread. The boy's father then took off his son's putkūli, and covered him with it from head to foot. Thus covered, the boy remained outside the hut till the morning of the morrow, watched through the night by near relatives of himself and his dead bride. When an unmarried member of the Vāniyan or Onti-eddu Gāniga (Canarese oil-pressers) communities dies, a mock marriage ceremony is performed, and the corpse is decorated with a wreath of arka (*Calotropis gigantea*) flowers. Among the Maravars, if the parties are too poor to afford all the rites and entertainments, the tying of the tāli is alone performed at first, and the man and woman begin to cohabit forthwith. But the other ceremonies must be performed at some time, or, as the phrase goes, "the defect must be cured." Sometimes the ancillary ceremonies will take place after the wife has borne three or four children. And, should the husband happen to die before he can afford to cure the defect, his friends and relations will at once borrow money, and the marriage will be duly completed in the presence and on behalf of the corpse, which must be placed on one seat with the woman, and be made to represent a bridegroom. The tāli is then taken off, and the widow is free to marry again.* In Malabar an unmarried woman cannot be cremated until the tāli has been tied round the neck of the corpse, while it lies on the funeral

* Manual of the Madura district.

Plate VII.

Gāniga Bride and Bridegroom.

pyre by some relation. The following horrible rite has been described by the Abbé Dubois as existing among the Nambūtiri Brāhmans. "Observant Nambudrii morem quam pravissimum turpissimumque. Apud hos immaturæ adhuc nubunt plerumque puellæ. Si forte mortua fuerit virgo, apud quam exstiterint jam pubertatis indicia, more gentili quasi religio est in cadaver ejus exercendum esse stuprum monstruosum. Necesse est igitur mercede conducant parentes qui tam obscæni conjugii munere fungi velit, quo omisso sibi quasi maculam hærere existimant propinqui." But Mr. T. A. Kalyanakrishna Aiyar, writing recently,* stated that he had had the advantage of an interview with the greatest living authority among the Nambūtiris on their customs and observances, who assured him that not only did the custom not exist at the present day, but there was not the slightest vestige of any tradition that it ever existed among them at any time.

In bygone days there was, in Coorg, a custom of so-called cloth marriages. "In these," F. Kittel writes † "a man gave a cloth to a girl, and she, accepting it, became his wife without any further ceremonies. He might dismiss her at any time without being under the least obligation of providing either for her or the children born during the connection. The custom was abolished by one of the Lingayat Rājas, who, being unable to obtain as many girls for his harem as he wished, from wanton selfishness put a stop to it."

* Malabar Quart. Review, I, 1902. † Ind. Ant., II, 1873.

I pass on to the custom of polyandry. As an example of *quasi*-polyandry, the Tottiyans or Kambalattars (Telugu cultivators) may be cited. When a marriage has been agreed to, two booths are erected outside the village, and decked with leaves of the pongu tree. In each of them is placed a bullock-saddle, and upon these the bride and bridegroom are seated while the relations are marshalled and addressed by the priest. After marriage it is customary for the women to cohabit with their husband's brothers and near relatives, and with their uncles; and, so far from any disgrace attaching to them in consequence, their priests compel them to keep up the custom if by any chance they are unwilling.* Among the Kāppiliyans (Canarese cultivators) who have settled in the Tamil country, it is said to be permissible for a woman to cohabit with her brothers-in-law, without thereby suffering any social degradation. One of the customs of the western Kallans is specially curious. It constantly happens that a woman is the wife of ten, eight, six, or two husbands, who are held to be the fathers jointly and severally of any children that may be born of her body, and, when the children grow up, they will call themselves the children not of ten, but of eight and two fathers. This is probably to avoid mentioning the number ten, which is inauspicious.

Concerning the system of polyandry, as carried out by the Todas of the Nīlgiris, Dr. Rivers writes as follows.† "The Todas have long been noted as a polyandrous people,

* Manual of the Madura district. † Man. No. 97, 1903.

and the institution of polyandry is still in full working order among them. When the girl becomes the wife of a boy, it is usually understood that she becomes also the wife of his brothers. In nearly every case at the present time, and in recent generations, the husbands of a woman are own brothers. In a few cases, though not brothers, they are of the same clan. Very rarely do they belong to different clans. One of the most interesting features of Toda polyandry is the method by which it is arranged who shall be regarded as the father of a child. For all social and legal purposes, the father of a child is the man who performs a certain ceremony about the seventh month of pregnancy, in which an imitation bow and arrow are given to the woman. When the husbands are own brothers, the eldest brother usually gives the bow and arrow, and is the father of the child, though, so long as the brothers live together, the other brothers are also regarded as fathers. It is in the cases in which the husbands are not own brothers that the ceremony becomes of real social importance. In these cases it is arranged that one of the husbands shall give the bow and arrow, and this man is the father, not only of the child born shortly afterwards, but also of all succeeding children, till another husband performs the essential ceremony. Fatherhood is determined so absolutely by this ceremony that a man who has been dead for several years is regarded as the father of any children borne by his widow, if no other man has given the bow and arrow. There is no doubt that, in former times, the polyandry of the Todas was associated with female infanticide, and it is probable that the latter custom still exists to some extent, though strenuously denied. There is reason to believe that women are now more plentiful than formerly, though they are still in a distinct minority. Any increase, however, in the number of women does not appear to have led to any great diminution of polyandrous marriages, but polyandry is often combined with polygyny. Two or more brothers may have two or more wives in common. In such marriages, however, it seems to be a growing custom that one brother should give the bow and arrow to one wife, and another brother to another wife. It seems possible that the Todas are moving from polyandry to polygyny through an intermediate stage of combined polyandry and polygyny."

In the ceremony referred to by Dr. Rivers, according to the account given to me by several independent witnesses, the Toda woman proceeds, accompanied by members of the tribe, on a new moon day in the fifth or seventh month of her pregnancy, to a shola (grove), where she sits with the man who is to become the father of her child near a kiaz tree (*Eugenia Arnottiana*). The man asks the father of the woman if he may bring the bow, and, on obtaining his consent, goes in search of a shrub (*Sophora glauca*), from a twig of which he makes a mimic bow. The arrow is represented by a blade of grass called nark. Meanwhile a triangular niche has been cut in the kiaz tree, in which a lighted lamp is placed. The woman seats herself in front of the lamp, and, on the return of the man, asks thrice " Whose bow is it " ? or " What is it?" meaning to whom, or to which mand does the child belong? The answer varies according to the group of mands which is concerned. Those, for example, who belong to the school mand group say Pulkoroff, and those who belong to the Tarnād mand say Purzesthi. The bow and arrow are handed to the woman, who raises them to her head, touches her forehead with them, and places them near the tree. From this moment the lawful husband of the child is the man from whom she has received the bow and arrow. He places on the ground at the foot of the tree some rice, various kinds of grain, chillies, jaggery, and salt tied in a cloth. All those present then leave, except the man and woman, who remain near the tree till about six o'clock in the evening, when they return to the mand. The time is determined, in the vicinity of Ootacamund, by the opening of the flowers of *Œnothera tetraptera*, a garden escape called by the Todas āru mani puff (six o'clock flower), which opens towards evening.

A few years ago (1902) the Todas, in a petition to Government, prayed for special legislation to legalise their marriages on the lines of the Malabar Marriage Act. The Government was of opinion that legislation is at present unnecessary, and that it is open to such of the Todas as are willing to sign the declaration prescribed by section 10 of the Marriage Act, III of 1872, to contract legal marriages under the provision of that Act. The Treasury Deputy Collector of the Nīlgiris was appointed Registrar of Toda Marriages. No marriage has been registered up to the present time, because, I am informed, the Act requires a declaration of being unmarried, which cannot be made by a Toda who has gone through a form of marriage according to Toda rites, and whose marriage has not been formally dissolved.

The custom of fraternal polyandry is said to still survive among the Tiyans (toddy tappers) in a few talúks of Malabar, but to be dying out. After he has married his elder brother's wife, a man can marry again, and have a wife for himself. Property, however, devolves through the eldest brother's wife. A girl will not be given to an only son, for, they say "Where is the good? He may die, and she will have nothing. The more brothers, the better the match."* I am told that the Tiyan woman sleeps in a room, and her husbands outside. When one of them is engaged with her, a knife is placed on the door-frame as a signal that entrance into the room is forbidden to the other husbands.

In Ceylon the children of polyandrous marriages acknowledged all the husbands of their mother as their fathers, calling them, like the Nambūtiri Brāhman, Tiyan, and Nāyar, great father, little father, etc. It is recorded of a certain highland chieftain in Ceylon that, in speaking of the insolent behaviour of a certain lad towards him, he remarked: "He behaves thus to me who am one of his fathers."† And a native of Ceylon, speaking contemptuously of the inhabitants of a village in which Professor Haeckel was staying, spoke as follows. "Their reprobate nature is not to be wondered at. For these low country people have always had a number

* F. Fawcett, Madras Mus. Bull., MS.

† Papers on the custom of Polyandry as practised in Ceylon.

of fathers, and, as they inherit all the bad qualities of so many fathers, it is only natural that they should grow worse and worse."*

Among the jungle Kurumbas of the Nīlgiris it is said to be the custom for several brothers to take one wife in common, and they do not object to their women being open to others also.† In the Madras Census Report, 1891, Mr. H. A. Stuart states that he is "informed that polyandry of the fraternal type exists among the Panta sub-division of the Reddis, but the statement requires verification." I have been unable to establish the existence of the custom, belief in which seems to have been based on the fact that, among the Reddi sub-division of the Yānādis, who are employed by Panta Reddis as domestic servants, if a woman's husband dies, abandons or divorces her, she may marry his brother. The Kanisans (astrologers) of Malabar admit that polyandry of the fraternal type was formerly common among them, but this has now died out.‡ It is generally believed that fraternal polyandry once prevailed among the Krishnavakkakars of Travancore, and even to-day a widow may be taken as a wife by a brother of the deceased husband, even though he is younger than herself. Issue, thus procreated, is the legitimate issue of the deceased, and acquires full right of inheritance to his property.§

Of the fraternal form of polyandry in Malabar, Bartolomeo writes ‖ that "on the coast of Malabar, a

* Haeckel. A visit to Ceylon, 1883. † A. Rajah Bahadur Mudaliar, MS.

‡ Madras Census Report, 1891. § N. Subramani Iyer, MS.

‖ Voyage to the East Indies, 1776-89.

custom prevails, in the caste to which the braziers belong, that the eldest, brother alone marries ; but the rest, when he is absent, supply his place with their sister-in-law."

Of polyandry as practised by the Kammālans (artisans) of Malabar, I learn that, when a marriage is thought of, the village astrologer is summoned, and the horoscopes of the contracting parties are consulted. It is sufficient if the horoscope of one of the sons agrees with that of the girl. On the wedding day the bride and bridegrooms sit in a row, and the girl's parents give them fruits and sugar. A feast is then held, and a priest of the Kammālans takes some milk in a vessel, and pours it into the mouths of the bride and bridegrooms, who are seated in a row, the eldest on the right, the others in order of seniority, and lastly the bride. During the nuptials the parents of the bride have to present a water-vessel, lamp, eating-dish, cooking vessel, spittoon, and a vessel for drawing water from the well. The eldest brother cohabits with the bride on the wedding day, and special days are set apart for each brother. There seems to be a belief among the Kammālan women that, the more husbands they have, the greater will be their happiness. If one of the brothers, on the ground of incompatibility of temper, brings a new wife, she is privileged to cohabit with the other brothers. In some cases a girl will have brothers, ranging in age from twenty-five to five, whom she has to regard as her husbands, so that, by the time the youngest brother reaches puberty, she may be over thirty, and the young man has to perform the duties of a husband with a wife who is twice his age. Polyandry is said to be most prevalent among the blacksmiths, who lead the most precarious existence, and have to observe the strictest economy.* The Kanisans, or astrologers of the west coast, Mr. Logan writes, "† like the Pāndava brothers, as they proudly point out, used formerly to have one wife in common among several brothers, and this custom is still observed by some of them." The custom among the Kāraikkāt Vellālas (Tamil cultivators) according to which wives are accustomed to grant the last favour to their husband's relations, is, it has been suggested, a survival of fraternal polyandry.‡

In illustration of the custom of polyandry among the Nāyars of Malabar in bygone days, the following extracts may be quoted:—

"On the continent of India," it is recorded in Ellis' edition of the Kural, "polyandry is still said to be practised in Orissa, and among particular tribes in other parts. In Malayālam, as is well known, the vision of Plato in his ideal republic is more completely realised, the women among the Nāyars not being restricted to family or number, but, after she has been consecrated by the usual rites before the nuptial fire, in which ceremony any indifferent person may officiate as the representative of her husband, being in her intercourse with the other sex only restrained by her inclinations; provided that the male with whom she associates be of an equal or superior tribe. But it must be stated, for the glory of the female character,

* S. Appadorai Iyer, MS. † Malabar Manual.
‡ Manual of the Madura district.

that, notwithstanding the latitude thus given to the Nāyattis, and that they are thus left to the guidance of their own free will and the play of their own fancy (which in other countries has not always been found the most efficient check on the conduct of either sex), it rarely happens that they cohabit with more than one person at the same time. Whenever the existing connexion is broken, whether from incompatibility of temper, disgust, caprice, or any of the thousand vexations by which, from the frailty of nature, domestic happiness is liable to be disturbed, the woman seeks another lover, the man another mistress. But it mostly happens that the bond of joint paternity is here, as elsewhere, too strong to be shaken off; and that the uninfluenced and uninterested union of love, when formed in youth, continues even in the decline of age."

Writing in the latter half of the eighteenth century, Grose * says that "it is among the Nairs that principally prevails the strange custom of one wife being common to a number; in which point the great power of custom is seen from its rarely or never producing any jealousies or quarrels among the co-tenants of the same woman. Their number is not so much limited by any specific law as by a kind of tacit convention, it scarce ever happening that it exceeds six or seven. The woman, however, is under no obligation to admit above a single attachment, though not less respected for using her privilege to its utmost extent. If one of the husbands happens to come

* Travels to the East Indies.

to the house, when she is employed with another, he knows that circumstance by certain signals left at the door that his turn is not come, and departs very resignedly." Writing about the same time, Sonnerat * says that "these Brāhmans do not marry, but have the privilege of enjoying all the Nairesses. This privilege the Portuguese, who were esteemed as a great caste, obtained and preserved, till their drunkenness and debauchery betrayed them into a commerce with all sorts of women. The following right is established by the customs of the country. A woman without shame may abandon herself to all men who are not of an inferior caste to her own, because the children (notwithstanding what Mr. De Voltaire says) do not belong to the father, but to the mother's brother; they become his legitimate heirs at his birth, even of the crown if he is king." In his 'Voyages and Travels' Kerr writes as follows: † "By the laws of their country these Nayres cannot marry, so that no one has any certain or acknowledged son or father; all their children being born of mistresses, with each of whom three or four Nayres cohabit by agreement among themselves. Each one of this cofraternity dwells a day in his turn with the joint mistress, counting from noon of one day to the same time of the next, after which he departs, and another comes for the like time. Thus they spend their time without the care or trouble of wives and

* Voyage to the East Indies, 1774 and 1781.

† R. Kerr, General History and Collection of Voyages and Travels, 1811, chapter VI, History of the Discovery and Conquest of India by the Portuguese between the years 1497 and 1525: from the original Portuguese of Herman Lopes de Castaneda.

children, yet maintain their mistresses well according to their rank. Any one may forsake his mistress at his pleasure; and, in like manner, the mistress may refuse admittance to any one of her lovers when she pleases. These mistresses are all gentlewomen of the Nayre caste, and the Nayres, besides being prohibited from marrying, must not attach themselves to any woman of a different rank. Considering that there are always several men attached to one woman, the Nayres never look upon any of the children born of their mistresses as belonging to them, however strong a resemblance may subsist, and all inheritances among the Nayres go to their brothers, or the sons of their sisters, born of the same mothers, all relationship being counted only by female consanguinity and descent. This strange law prohibiting marriage was established that they might have neither wives nor children on whom to fix their love and attachment: and that, being free from all family cares, they might be more willingly devote themselves entirely to warlike service." The term son of ten fathers is used as a term of abuse among Nāyars to this day.* Tīpū Sultān is said to have issued the following proclamation to the Nāyars, on the occasion of his visit to Calicut in 1788. "And, since it is a practice with you for one woman to associate with ten men, and you leave your mothers and sisters unconstrained in their obscene practices, and are thence all born in adultery, and are more shameless in your connections than the beasts of the field; I hereby require you to forsake these sinful practices, and live like the rest of

* Wigram, Malabar Law and Custom, Ed. 1900.

mankind."* As to the existence or non-existence of what has been called an expansive form of polyandry, which assumes as a postulate that the wisest child cannot be expected to know its own father, and that a man's heir-at-law is his sister's son, I must call recent writers into the witness box The Rev. S. Mateer, Mr F. Fawcett writes,† "informed me ten years ago—he was speaking of polyandry among the Nāyars of Travancore—that he had 'known an instance of six brothers keeping two women, four husbands to one, and two to the other. In a case where two brothers cohabited with one woman, and one was converted to Christianity, the other brother was indignant at the Christian's refusal to live any longer in this condition.' I have not known an admitted instance of polyandry amongst the Nāyars of Malabar at the present day, but there is no doubt that, if it does not exist now (and I think it does here and there), it certainly did not long ago." Mr. Gopal Panikkar says ‡ that "to enforce this social edict upon the Nairs, the Brāhmans made use of the powerful weapon of their aristocratic ascendancy in the country, and the Nairs readily submitted to the Brāhman supremacy. Thus it came about that the custom of concubinage so freely indulged in by the Brāhmans with Nair women obtained such firm hold upon the country that it has only been strengthened by the lapse of time. At the present day there are families, especially in the interior of the district, who look upon

* T. A. Kalyanakrishna Aiyar, Malabar Quart. Review, II, 1908.
† Madras Museum Bull., III, 1901.
‡ Malabar and its Folk, 1900.

it as an honour to be thus united with Brāhmans. But a reaction has begun to take place against this feeling; and Brāhman alliances are invariably looked down upon in respectable Nair tarwads.* This reactionary feeling took shape in the Malabar Marriage Act." And Mr. Justice K. Narayana Marar says: † "there is nothing strange or to be ashamed of in the fact that the Nāyars were originally of a stock that practised polyandry, nor if the practice continued till recently. Hamilton in his 'Account of the East Indies' and Buchanan in his 'Journey' say that, among the Nāyars of Malabar, a woman has several husbands, but these are not brothers. These travellers came to Malabar in the eighteenth and the beginning of nineteenth centuries. There is no reason whatever to suppose that they were not just recording what they saw. For I am not quite sure whether, even now, the practice is not lurking in some remote nooks and corners of the country." Lastly, Mr. Wigram writes as follows: ‡ "Polyandry may now be said to be dead, and, although the issue of a Nāyar marriage are still children of their mother rather than of their father, marriage may be defined as a contract based on mutual consent, and dissoluble at will. It has been well said (by Mr. Logan) that nowhere is the marriage tie, albeit informal, more rigidly observed or respected than it is in Malabar: nowhere is it more jealously guarded, or its neglect more savagely avenged."

* Tarwad: a Marumakkatāyam family consisting of all the descendants in the female line of one common female ancestor.

† Malabar Quart. Review, No. 1, 1902.

‡ Malabar Law and Custom, 1882.

Reference may be here appropriately made to the curious ceremony called Tāli-kettu-kalyānam (tāli-tying marriage), or mock marriage ceremony which every girl in a Nāyar tarwad goes through while still a child. For an account of this ceremony I must resort to Mr. K. R. Krishna Menon's evidence before the Malabar Marriage Commission.* "The Tāli-kattu-kalyānam is somewhat analogous to what a dēva-dāsi (dancing girl attached to temples) of other countries (districts) undergoes before she begins her profession. Among royal families, and those of certain Edaprabhus, a Kshatriya, and among the Charna sect a Nedungādi is invited to the girl's house at an auspicious hour appointed for the purpose, and, in the presence of friends and castemen, ties a tāli round her neck, and goes away after receiving a certain fee for his trouble. Among the other sects, the horoscope of the girl is examined along with those of her enangan (a recognised member of one's own class) families, and the boy whose horoscope is found to agree with hers is marked out as a fit person to tie the tāli, and a day is fixed for the tāli-tying ceremony by the astrologer, and information given to the karanavan (senior male in a tarwad) of the boy's family. On the appointed day the boy is invited to a house near that of the girl, where he is fed, with his friends, by the head of the girl's family. The feast is called ayaniūnu, and the boy is thenceforth called manavālan or pillai (bridegroom). From the house in which the manavālan is entertained a procession is formed, preceded by men with swords and shields shouting a kind of war-cry. In

* Report of the Malabar Marriage Commission, 1894.

the meantime a procession starts from the girl's house, with similar men and cries, and headed by a member of her tarwad, to meet the other procession, and, after meeting the manavālan, he escorts him to the girl's house. After entering the booth erected for the purpose, he is conducted to a seat of honour, and his feet are washed by the brother of the girl, who receives a pair of cloths. The manavālan is then taken to the centre of the booth, where bamboo mats, carpets, and white cloths are spread, and seated there. The brother of the girl then carries her from inside the house, and, after going round the booth three times, places her at the left side of the manavālan. The father of the girl then presents new cloths tied in a kambli (blanket) to the pair, and with this new cloth (called manthravadi), they change their dress. The wife of the karnavan of the girl's tarwad, if she be of the same caste, then decorates the girl by putting on anklets, etc. The purōhit (officiating priest) called Elayath (a low class of Brāhmans) then gives the tāli to the manavālan, and the family astrologer shouts muhurtham (auspicious hour), and the manavālan, putting his sword on the lap, ties the tāli round the neck of the girl, who is then required to hold an arrow and a looking glass in her hand. In rich families a Brāhmani sings certain songs intended to bless the couple. In ordinary families, who cannot procure her presence, a Nāyar, versed in songs, performs the office. The boy and girl are then carried by enangans to a decorated apartment in the inner part of the house, where they are required to remain under a sort of pollution for three days. On the fourth day they bathe in some neighbouring tank or river, holding each other's hands. After changing their cloths, they come home, preceded by a procession. Tom-toms (native drums) and elephants usually form part of the procession, and saffron water is sprinkled. When they come home, all the doors of the house are shut, and the manavālan is required to force them open. He then enters the house, and takes his seat in the northern wing thereof. The aunt and female friends of the girl then approach, and give sweetmeats to the couple. The girl then serves food to the boy, and, after taking their meal together from the same leaf, they proceed to the booth, where a cloth is severed into two parts, and each part given to the manavālan and girl separately in the presence of enangans and friends. The severing of the cloth is supposed to constitute a divorce." Several variations of the rite as practised prevail in different localities, and it is said that, when the family is poor, a bridegroom is sometimes dispensed with altogether. The girl's mother makes an idol of clay, adorns it with flowers, and invests her daughter with the tāli in the presence of the idol. This would seem to be an almost exact counterpart of the consecration of the east coast dēva-dāsi to her profession as a temple prostitute. The opinion was expressed by Mr. (now Sir Henry) Winterbotham, one of the Malabar Marriage Commissioners, that the Brāhman tāli-tier was a relic of the time when the Nambūtiris were entitled to the first fruits, and it was considered the high privilege of every Nāyar maid to be introduced by them to womanhood.

Without giving any opinion as to the correctness or otherwise of this view, Mr. Justice Moore * draws attention to the following passage from Captain Hamilton's new account of the East Indies (1744). "When the Zamorin marries, he must not cohabit with his bride till the Nambūdri, or chief priest, has enjoyed her, and he, if he pleases, may have three nights of her company, because the first fruits of her nuptials must be an holy oblation to the god she worships. And some of the nobles are so complaisant as to allow the clergy the same tribute, but the common people cannot have that compliment paid to them, but are forced to supply the priests' places themselves."

Concerning the Kammālans (artisans) of Malabar Mr. S. Appadorai Iyer writes that as with the Nāyars, the tāli-kettu-kalyānam has to be celebrated. For this the parents of the child have to find a suitable manavālan or bridegroom by the consultation of horoscopes. An auspicious day is fixed, and new cloths are given to the manavālan. The girl bathes, and puts on new clothes. The bride and bridegroom are brought to the marriage booth, where the tāli-tying ceremony takes place. This concluded, the bridegroom takes a thread from the new cloth, and breaks it in two, saying that his union with the girl has ceased. He then walks away without looking back.

With the Iluvans (toddy tappers) of Malabar the vītil kettu corresponds to the tāli-kettu ceremony of other castes. The girl is bathed by seven maidens, and made

* Malabar Law and Custom, 3rd Edition, 1905. The chapter therein devoted to quasi-marriage customs, is well worthy of careful study.

to stand on a plank. The boy's sister then ties the tāli round her neck. The maidens husk a measure of paddy, and they and the girl eat it. On the fourth day the girl is taken to a tank, and bathed. Flowers and three lighted wicks are placed on a raft made of a plantain stem, and floated on the water while she bathes. On her return from the tank, she is given a little jaggery and cocoanut to eat. The girl's father asks the boy's people that the marriage tie should be severed. Her mother, or one of her female relations, takes a thread from her cloth, and, saying that the girl and boy are separated, puts it in a vessel containing cooked rice. This vessel, and two other vessels containing curry and other food-stuffs, are sent to the boy's house. The girl is no longer his wife, and may be married to any one else. If a girl is to be married before the vītil-kettu has been performed, the sister of the bridegroom-elect carries a new cloth as a present from him to the bride's house. Instead of the tāli, a gold ring is tied on the girl's neck. The remaining ceremonies are as at any ordinary wedding. This form of marriage is called kannannī.

It is stated in a recent article * that among the Konars (cow-herds) of Pūndurai near Erode, in the Tamil country, who, according to tradition, originally belonged to the same tribe as the Gopas living in the southern part of Kerala, and now forming a section of Nāyars, the former matrimonial customs were exactly the same as those of the Nāyars. They, too, celebrated kettu-kalyānam, and, like the Nāyars, did not make it

* K. Kannan Nāyar, Malabar Quart. Review, 1903.

binding on the bride and bridegroom of the ceremony to live as husband and wife. They have now, however, abandoned the custom, and have made the tying of the tāli the actual marriage ceremony.

Of those who gave evidence before the Malabar Commission, some thought the tāli-kettu was a marriage, some not. Others called it a mock marriage, a formal marriage, a sham marriage, a fictitious marriage, a marriage sacrament, the preliminary part of marriage, a meaningless ceremony, an empty form, a ridiculous farce, an incongruous custom, a waste of money, and a device for becoming involved in debt. "While," the report states, "a small minority of strict conservatives still maintain that the tāli-kettu is a real marriage intended to confer on the bridegroom a right to cohabit with the bride, an immense majority describe it as a fictitious marriage, the origin of which they are at a loss to explain. And another large section tender the explanation accepted by our President (Sir T. Muttusami Aiyar) that in some way or other it is an essential caste observance preliminary to the formation of sexual relations."

In a recent note on marriage customs in Malabar,* Mr. T. A. Kalyanakrishna Aiyar states that "in some parts of Travancore and Cochin, and in the tarwads of Tirumalpāds and others belonging to the Kshatriya caste, the tāli-kettu ceremony is said to be performed after puberty. In a few Sūdra families also, here and there, such as at Manapuram and other places, now-a-days the ceremony is performed after the girl attains puberty."

* Malabar Quart. Review, 1902.

The tāli-kettu ceremony is, it may be noted, referred to by Kerr,* who, in his translation of Castaneda, states that "these sisters of the Zamorin, and other kings of Malabar, have handsome allowances to live upon; and, when any of them reaches the age of ten, their kindred send for a young man of the Nayre caste, out of the kingdom, and give him great presents to induce him to initiate the young virgin; after which he hangs a jewel round her neck, which she wears all the rest of her life, as a token that she is now at liberty to dispose of herself to any one she pleases as long as she lives."

In summing up the evidence collected by him, Mr. Justice Moore states that it seems to prove beyond all reasonable doubt that "from the sixteenth century at all events, and up to the early portion of the nineteenth century, the relations between the sexes in families governed by marumakkathayam were of as loose a description as it is possible to imagine. The tāli-kettu-kalyānam, introduced by the Brāhmans, brought about no improvement, and indeed in all probability made matters much worse by giving a quasi-religious sanction to a fictitious marriage, which bears an unpleasant resemblance to the sham marriage ceremonies performed among certain inferior castes elsewhere as a cloak for prostitution. As years passed, some time about the opening of the nineteenth century, the Kērala Mahatmyam and Kēralotpathi were concocted, probably by Nambūdris, and false and pernicious doctrines as to the obligations laid on the Nāyars by divine law to administer to the

* *Op. cit.*

lust of the Nambūdris were disseminated abroad. The better classes among the Nāyars revolted against the degrading system thus established, and a custom sprang up, especially in north Malabar, of making sambandham a more or less formal contract, approved and sanctioned by the karnavan (senior male) of the tarwad to which the lady belonged, and celebrated with elaborate ceremonies under the pudamuri form. That there was nothing analogous to the pudamuri prevalent in Malabar from A.D. 1550 to 1800 may, I think, be fairly presumed from the absence of all allusion to it in the works of the various European writers." According to Act IV, Madras, 1896, sambandham means an alliance between a man and a woman, by reason of which they, in accordance with the custom of the community to which they belong, or either of them belongs, cohabit or intend to cohabit as husband and wife.

Since the passing of the Malabar Marriage Act in 1896, only the following applications to register sambandhams were received until 1904:—

—	Nāyars.	Tiyans.	Others.	Total.
1897	28	6	2	36
1898	8	2	4	14
1899	8	2	4	14
1900	8	...	9	17
1901	3	...	1	4
1902	.	...	...	...
1903	2	...	...	2
Total ...	57	10	20	87

In his report for 1898–99, the Registrar-General of Marriages states that "the power conferred by the marriage law to make provision for one's wives and children has hitherto acted as some inducement to persons to register their sambandhams; but as the new testamentary law (Act V of 1898) enables the followers of marumakkatayam law to attain this object without registering their sambandhams, and thus 'unnecessarily curtailing their liberty of action, and risking the chance of divorce proceedings,' the Registrar of Calicut thinks it unlikely that registrations under the marriage law would increase in future." In the report for 1900–01, he writes further that "the mass of the population of the west coast is so strongly opposed to the provisions of the Act that even the educated classes find it difficult, if not impossible, to act upon their convictions, and run counter to popular opinion. This is especially the case in North Malabar, where not a single notice to register sambandhams has been received during the past two years, and only twelve sambandhams (confined chiefly to officials and vakils *) have been registered since the Marriage Act came into force. Since the passing of the Malabar Testamentary Act in 1898, the necessity for registering sambandhams, with the main object of making provision for their offspring, has practically disappeared, and there has been a large increase in the number of testamentary dispositions of property and deeds of gift registered in several of the registration offices."

* Law pleaders.

In the Madras Census Report, 1901, Mr. Francis refers to the form of hypergamy between different castes which exists on the west coast, where "women of castes equal to or higher than the Nāyars are prohibited from forming unions with men of castes below them in rank, though the men of these castes are not similarly restricted." Nāyars, for example, may marry Erumān (buffalo-drivers and keepers) women, but their men may not marry Nāyar girls. In this and other respects the Erumāns resemble the Erumān sub-division of the Kōlayān (cow-herd) caste, whose women may marry Nāyars, though the offspring of such unions cannot claim the same privileges in the temples as pure-bred Kōlayāns.* Of the children of marriages between Maravans and Agamudaiyan women, the females marry Maravans, the males Agamudaiyan.† Oriya Zamindar get wives from the Khondāita sub-caste of Odiyas or Oriyas, but the men of this sub-caste cannot marry into the Zamindar's families.*

A friend was, on one occasion, out after big game in the Jeypore hill-tracts, and shot a tiger. He asked his shikāri (tracker) what reward he should give him for putting him on to the beast. The shikāri replied that he would be quite satisfied with twenty-five rupees, as he wanted to get his younger brother out of pledge. Asked what he meant, he replied that, two years previously, he had purchased as his wife a Bhumia woman, who belonged to a caste higher than his own, for a

* Madras Census Report, 1901. † Rev. A. C. Clayton, MS.

hundred rupees. He obtained the money by pledging his younger brother to a sowcar (money-lender), and had paid it all back except twenty-five rupees. Meanwhile his brother was the bondsman of the sowcar, and cultivating his land in return for simple food.

DEATH CEREMONIES.

At the present day, many Hindus disregard certain ceremonies, in the celebration of which their forefathers were most scrupulous. Even the daily ceremonial ablutions, which are all-important to a Brāhman from a shastraic point of view, are now neglected by a large majority, and the prayers (mantrams), which should be chanted during their performance, are forgotten. But no Brāhman, orthodox or unorthodox, dares to abandon the death ceremonial, and annual srādh (memorial rites). A Brāhman beggar, when soliciting alms, invariably pleads that he has to perform his father or mother's srādh, or upanayanam (thread ceremony) of his children, and he rarely goes away empty-handed. "The constant periodical performance," Monier Williams writes,* "of commemorative obsequies is regarded in the light of a positive and peremptory obligation. It is the simple discharge of a solemn debt to one's forefathers, a debt consisting not only in reverential homage, but in the performance of acts necessary to their support, happiness, and progress onward in the spiritual world. A man's deceased relatives, for at least three generations, are among his cherished divinities, and must be honoured by daily offerings and adoration, or a nemesis of some kind is certain to overtake his living family. The

* Religious Thought and Life in India.

object of a Hindu funeral is nothing less than the investiture of the departed spirit with an intermediate gross body—a peculiar frame interposed, as it were parenthetically, between the terrestrial gross body, which has just been destroyed by fire, and the new terrestrial body, which it is compelled to ultimately assume. The creation of such an intervenient frame, composed of gross elements, though less gross than those of earth, becomes necessary, because the individualised spirit of man, after the cremation of the terrestrial body, has nothing left to withhold it from re-absorption into the universal soul, except its incombustible subtle body, which, as composed of the subtle elements, is not only proof against the fire of the funeral pile, but is incapable of any sensations in the temporary heaven, or temporary hell, through one or other of which every separate human spirit is forced to pass before returning to earth, and becoming re-invested with a terrestrial gross body."

When a Brāhman is on the point of death, he is removed from his bed, and laid on the floor. If there is any fear of the day being a danishtapanchami (inauspicious), the dying man is taken out of the house, and placed in the court-yard or pial (raised verandah). Some prayers are uttered, and a cow is presented (gōdhanam). These are intended to render the passage of life through the various parts of the body as easy as possible. The spirit is supposed to escape through one of the nine orifices of the body, according to the character of the individual concerned. That of a good man leaves the body through the brāhmarandhra (top of the skull), and that of a bad man through the anus. Immediately after death, the body is washed, religious marks are made on the forehead, and parched paddy (unhusked rice) and betel are scattered over and around it by the son. As a Brāhman is supposed always to have his fire with him, the sacred fire is lighted. At this stage, certain purificatory ceremonies are performed, if death has taken place on a day or hour of evil omen, or at midnight. Next, a little rice is cooked in a new earthen pot, and a new cloth is thrown over the corpse, which is roused by the recitation of mantrams. Four bearers, to each of whom dharba grass is given in token of his office, are selected to carry the corpse to the burning-ground. The space, which intervenes between the dead man's house and the burning-ground, is divided into four parts. When the end of the first of these is reached, the corpse is placed on the ground, and the sons and nephews go round it, repeating mantrams. They untie their kudumis (hair knot), leaving part thereof loose, tie up the rest into a small bunch, and keep on slapping their thighs. [When children at play have their kudumi partially tied, and slap their thighs, they are invariably scolded, owing to the association with funerals.] A little cooked rice is offered to the path as a pathi bali (wayside offering), to propitiate evil spirits, or bûthas. The same ceremonial should, strictly speaking, be performed at two other spots, but now-a-days it is the custom to place the corpse on the ground near the funeral pyre, moving its position three times, while the circumambulation and pathi bali are gone through only once. As soon as the corpse has reached the spot where the pyre is, the celebrant of the rites sprinkles water thereon, and throws a quarter of an anna on it as the equivalent of purchase of the ground for cremation. The sacred fire is lighted, and the right palm of the corpse is touched with a gold coin. The nine orifices of the body are then smeared with ghī (clarified butter), and rice is thrown over the corpse, and placed in its mouth. The son takes a burning brand from the sacred fire, lights the pyre, and looks at the sun. Then he, and all the relations of the deceased, squat on the ground, facing east, take up some dharba grass, and, cutting it into small fragments with their nails, scatter them in the air, while repeating some Vēdic verses, which are chanted very loudly and slowly, especially at the funeral of a respected elder. The celebrant then pours a little water on a stone, and sprinkles himself with it. This is also done by the other relations, and they pass beneath a bundle of dharba grass and twigs of *Ficus glomerata* held by the purōhit (officiating priest), and gaze for a moment at the sun. Once more they sprinkle themselves with water, and proceed to a tank (pond), where they bathe. When they return home, two rites, called nagna (naked) srādh, and pashana sthapanam (stone-fixing), are celebrated. The disembodied spirit is supposed to be naked after the body has been cremated. To clothe it, offerings of water, with balls of cooked rice, are made, and a cloth, lamp, and money are given to a Brāhman. Then two stones are set up, one in the house and the other on the bank of a tank, to represent the spirit of the deceased. For ten days, libations of water mixed with gingelly (*Sesamum indicum*) seeds, called thīlothakam, and a ball of cooked rice, must be offered to the stones. The ball of rice is left for crows to eat. The number of libations must be seventy-five, commencing with three on the first day, and increasing the number daily by one. In addition, three further libations are made daily by dipping a piece of cloth from the winding-sheet in water, and rinsing it over the stone (vasothakam).

A Brāhman widow removes her tāli (marriage badge) on the tenth day after the death of her husband, and should have the head shaved, and wear white cloths. Every month, for a year after a death in a family, srādh is performed, and corresponds in detail with the annual srādh, which is regularly performed, unless a visit is paid to Gaya, which renders further performance of the rite not obligatory. For the performance of this ceremony by the nearest agnate of the deceased (eldest son or other), three Brāhmans should be called in, to represent respectively Vishnu, the Dēvatas, and the deceased ancestors. Sometimes two Brāhmans are made to suffice, and Vishnu is represented by a sālagrāma stone. In extreme cases, only one Brāhman assists at the ceremony, the two others being represented by dharba grass. The sacred fire is lighted, and ghī, a small quantity of raw and cooked rice, and vegetables are offered up in the fire. The Brāhmans then wash their feet, and are fed. Before they enter the space set apart for the meal, water, gingelly, and rice are sprinkled about it, to keep off evil spirits. As soon as the meal is finished, a ball of rice, called vayasa pindam (crow's food) is offered to the pithru dēvatas (ancestors of three generations), and thrown to the crows. If they do not eat the rice, the omens are considered to be unfavourable. The Brāhmans receive betel and money in payment for their services.

Burial in a sitting posture, which is still practised by many castes in Southern India, is said to be a survival from neolithic times. "There can," Lord Avebury writes,* "be no doubt that, in the neolithic stone age, it was usual to bury the corpse in a sitting or contracted posture."

Among the Dēvānga and Karnabattu weavers, the dead are usually buried in a sitting attitude. The Dēvāngas are said to erect, in some places, a hut of milk-hedge (*Euphorbia Tirucalli*) branches over the grave.† Before the grave of a Dēvānga is filled in, a rope is tied to the kudumi (hair of the head) and brought towards the surface. Over the end of the rope, when the grave has been filled in, a lingam (phallic emblem) is placed, so as to be above the head of the corpse, and worshipped daily throughout the death rites. By the Paththars or Acharapākam Chettis, who likewise bury their dead in a seated attitude, a bamboo stick is tied to the kudumi instead of a rope. Many of the Kammālans bury their dead in a seated posture.‡ Certain of the Vellālas have

* Prehistoric Times.

† Madras Census Report, 1901; South Canara and North Arcot Manuals.

‡ Madras Census Report, 1891.

a custom called padmāsanam, in reference to the treatment of the dead, who are not laid out, but trussed up in a squatting posture, a string being passed round the neck, and made fast behind, to keep the body upright.* Among the Paraiyans (Pariahs) and Okkiliyans of Coimbatore, if the deceased was a married man, he is buried in a sitting posture.

Before a Lingayat man dies, the ceremony called vibhūti-velai is performed. He is given a bath, and made to drink holy water, in which the Jangam's (priest) feet have been washed. He is made to give the Jangam a handkerchief with vibhūti (sacred ashes), rudraksha (*Elæocarpus*) beads, coins, and betel leaf. This is followed by a meal, of which all the Jangams present, and the friends and relations of the sick man partake. It appears to be immaterial whether he is still alive or not. It is stated that, if the invalid survives this ceremony, he must take to the jungles and disappear, but in practice this is not observed. The death party resembles, in some respects, an Irish wake, though the latter does not commence until the deceased is well on his way to the next world. The dead are buried in a sitting posture (a fact which was noted by the traveller Pietro della Valle in 1623), facing towards the north, but an exception is made in the case of unmarried people, who are buried in a reclining posture. After death, the corpse is placed in a sitting attitude, and the Jangam who has received the offering before death places his left foot on the right thigh of the body. The people present worship the

* Manual of the Salem district.

corpse, and the usual distribution of coins and betel to Jangams follows. The body is carried in a vimānam or bamboo chair decorated with plantain stems, coloured cloths, and flags, to the burial-ground. The grave should be a cube of nine feet dimensions, with a niche on one side, in which the corpse is to sit. The lingam which the man wears, in a silver-casket or tied up in a silk cloth, is untied, and placed in the left hand. Bilva (*Ægle Marmelos*) leaves and vibhūti are placed at the side; the body is wrapped in an orange-coloured cloth, and the grave is filled in. A Jangam stands on the grave, and, after receiving the usual *douceur*, shouts out the name of the deceased, and announces that he has gone to kailāsa or heaven. Memorial ceremonies are contrary to Lingayat tenets, but in this, as in other matters, Brāhman influence appears, and among some sections an annual ceremony is performed.*

The death ceremonies of a Pishārati (temple servant) in Travancore are peculiar, and resemble those of a Sanyāsi (ascetic). The body is placed in a sitting posture, and buried in a pit with salt, ashes and sand. As in the case of a Sanyāsi who is liberated from the bondage of the flesh, though alive in body, few death rites are performed. But, on the eleventh day, a ceremony corresponding to the ekōddishta srādh of the Brāhman is performed. A knotted piece of kusa (*Eragrostis*) grass, representing the departed soul, is taken to a neighbouring temple, where a lighted lamp, symbolical of Māha Vishnu,

* Madras Mus. Bull. MS.

is worshipped, and prayers are offered. Since the Sanyāsi is considered to be above all sin, and to have acquired sufficient merit for salvation, no srādh is performed by the children born to him before he became an anchorite.*

The jungle Yeruvas of Coorg bury their women in a sitting posture, in a hole scooped out of the side of an ordinary grave, so that the earth does not touch her body.† In like manner, the dead among the Kudubis of South Canara are buried, and no ceremonies are performed for the deceased, except the distribution of rice to a few Brāhmans. Writing about the Irulas of the Nilgiris in 1832, Harkness states‡ that the sepulchres are "pits about thirty or forty feet square, and of considerable depth, over which are placed large planks. Above is erected a shed, covering in the whole, and protecting it from the weather. In the centre of the planks is an opening about a cubit square, over which are placed other pieces of wood, and on these is raised a small mound of earth in the form of an altar, the surface being decorated with pebbles placed there as memorials of the departed, and as objects of future worship. When a casualty occurs, and another burial becomes necessary, the mound of earth is removed, and the body thrown in. Some ten or twelve days after, a mound of fresh earth is raised in room of the one which had been removed. The pebbles, which in the first instance had been put carefully

* Travancore Census Report, 1901.

† Richter. Eth. Compendium of the Castes and Tribes of Coorg.

‡ Aboriginal Race inhabiting the Neilgherry hills, 1832.

aside, are again replaced, and another pebble added to them in memory of the deceased. All this is done with much ceremony, the pebbles being anointed with oil, perfumed with frankincense, and decorated with flowers. Food is also distributed to the assembly, according to the ability of the relatives of the deceased. Should one of this tribe die in an Irula village to which he does not belong, these villagers will not bury him with their dead, but, digging a fresh grave, place the body in it. And, when his relations hear of his death, they come and disinter the body, or whatever may remain of it, in order to deposit it in their own place of sepulture, when they go through the same observances as though the deceased had died among themselves."

When a Nīlgiri Irula dies, two jungle Kurumbas come to the village, and one shaves the head of the other. The shorn man is fed, and presented with a new cloth, which he wraps round his head. This quaint ceremonial is believed, in some way, to bring good luck to the departed. Outside the house of the deceased, in which the corpse is kept till the time of the funeral, men and women dance to the music of the Irula band. The dead are buried in a sitting posture, with the legs crossed tailorwise. Each settlement has its own burial-ground. A pit is dug, at the lower end of which a chamber is excavated, in which the corpse, clad in its own clothes, jewelry, and a new cloth, is placed, and the mouth of the chamber closed with planks or sticks. The pit is then filled in, and the position of the grave marked by a mound. Sometimes an old grave is reopened, and a further corpse placed in it, either in the original chamber, or in a newly excavated chamber. The following account of an Irula annual memorial service was given to me. A lamp and oil are purchased, and rice is cooked in the village. They are then taken to the shrine at the burial-ground, offered up on stones on which some of the oil is poured and pūja done. At the shrine a pūjāri, with three white marks on the forehead when on duty, officiates. Like the Badaga Dēvadāri, the Nīlgiri Irula priest at times becomes inspired by the god. The Irulas of the North Arcot district are, likewise, said to bury their dead in a sitting posture, with a lamp beside the corpse, and mark the grave with a small upright stone.* The Irulas or Villiyans (bowmen) of the Chingleput district bury their dead lying flat on the face, with the head to the north, and the face turned towards the east. When the grave has been half filled in, they throw into it a prickly-pear (*Opuntia Dillenii*) shrub, and make a mound over it. Around it they place a row or two of prickly-pear stems, to keep off jackals. No monumental stone is placed over the grave. Among other castes, which bury their dead in a sitting posture, are the Yōgi-Gurukkal, who are professional beggars, temple priests, and village schoolmasters in Malabar; the Pandārams, or Saivite beggars in the Tinnevelly district; the Kurnis, who are Kanarese weavers in Bellary; and the Killēkyatas, who speak Marathi, and amuse people with their marionette shows in the little state of Sandūr in the Bellary district, and other places.

* Madras Census Report, 1891.

The Head Magistrate of Coimbatore informs me that the Shōlagas of Gandai near Sirumugai dispose of their dead in a curious way. They have, in the depths of the jungle, a huge bottomless pit, which has been there from time immemorial. When a Shōlaga dies, the body is wrapped in a new cloth, garlanded, and carried to the pit, into which it is thrown. The pit mouth is sealed with a large rock. As soon as this is done, the party return to the village, and no one may look back on the way, as to do so would bring bad luck.

The Kādirs of the Anaimalai hills are buried in a grave, or, if death occurs in the depths of the jungle, with a paucity of hands for digging, the corpse is placed in a crevice between the rocks, and covered over with stones. The grave is dug from four to five feet deep, at some place not far from the scene of death. A band, composed of drum and fife, plays weird dirges outside the hut of the deceased. The body is carried on a bamboo stretcher, lying on a mat, and covered over with a cloth and mat. As it leaves the hut, rice is thrown over it. The corpse is laid in the grave on a mat in a recumbent posture, with head towards the east, and covered over with a mat and leaves. The grave is then filled in. No stone or sepulchral monument is erected to indicate the spot. A memorial service, called karrumantram, with feasting and dancing, is held two years after death.

When a death occurs among the Paniyans of Malabar, a trench, four or five feet deep, is dug due north and south near the village. At the bottom of this excavation the earth is scooped out from the western side on a level with the floor, so as to form a receptacle for the corpse, which, placed on a mat, is laid therein upon its left side with the head to the north and feet to the south. After a little cooked rice has been put into the grave, the mat, which has been made broad enough for the purpose, is folded up, and tucked in under the roof of the cavity, and the trench filled up. It has probably been found by experience that the corpse, when thus protected, is safe against the ravages of scavenger jackals and pariah dogs. For seven days after death a little rice gruel is placed at a distance of fifty to a hundred yards from the grave by the Jenmi (landlord), who claps his hands as a signal to the evil spirits in the vicinity, who, in the shape of a pair of crows, are supposed to partake of the food, which is hence called kāka kanji or crow's rice. At a memorial service, held once in every three or four years in honour of those who are specially respected, the Jenmi (landlord), holding on his crossed arms two winnowing sieves, each containing rice, walks round three times, and finally deposits the sieves in a pandal. One of the relatives, or a professional, becomes possessed, and performs the functions of an oracle, working himself up into a frenzied state of divination, while the mourners cry out, and ask why the dead have been taken from them. Meanwhile, food has been prepared for all present, except the mourners, and, when it has been partaken of, dancing is kept up round the central group till daybreak.

On the seventh day after the cremation or burial of a Male (hill) Kudiya, a booth is erected over the grave or place of cremation, and a bleached cloth is spread on it by the washerman. A wick, floating in a half cocoanut shell full of oil, is then lighted, and placed at each corner of the booth. The relations of the deceased then gather round the place, and throw a handful of rice over the spot.* It has been noted as one of the first indications of a jungle tribe being adopted into the Hindu fold, that they replace burial by cremation. Many of the lower classes now-a-days bury or burn their dead, according to the worldly circumstances of the relations of the deceased, burying being cheaper than burning, which necessitates the purchase of wood for the pyre.

At the green funeral of a Toda, which took place when I was on the Nīlgiris in 1900, the corpse was placed in front of the entrance to a circle of loose stones about a yard and a half in diameter, which had been specially constructed for the occasion. Just before the buffalo sacrifice took place, a Toda of the Paiki clan, standing near the head of the corpse, dug a hole in the ground with a cane, and asked a man of the Kenna clan, who was standing opposite, "Shall I throw the mud three times"? To which the Kenna replied "Throw the mud thrice." The Paiki then threw some earth three times over the corpse, and three times into the kraal. According to Breeks,† "it appears that

* Manual of the South Canara district.

† Primitive Tribes and Monuments of the Nīlgiris, 1873.

sometimes a circle of old date is used, and sometimes a new one is formed. The ashes of the deceased are scraped together, and buried under a large stone at the entrance of the āzāram. At the dry funeral of a Toda Mr. Walhouse noticed that within the circle several fires were lighted, and bamboo vessels ornamented with cowries and filled with grain, rattans bent to represent buffalo horns, a mimic bow and arrows, ornamented umbrellas, knives, coins, etc., placed in the fire. When the various articles had been consumed, and the fire sunk into embers, the ashes were scraped together, and put into a hole within the circle near the entrance, over which a stone was rolled.

The temples of the Kurubas of North Arcot are said * to be "rude, low structures, resembling an enclosed mantapam (shrine) supported upon rough stone pillars. A wall of stones encloses a considerable space round the temple, and this is covered with small structures formed of four flat stones. The stone facing the open side often has a figure sculptured upon it, representing the deceased gaudu or pūjāri (headman or priest), to whom it has been dedicated. For each deceased person of this rank one of these monuments is erected, and here periodically, and always during the annual feasts, pūja is made, not only to the spirits of the deceased chiefs, but also to those of all who have died in the clan. It seems impossible not to connect this with those strange structures called by the natives Pāndava's temples. They are numerous where the Kurubas are now found,

* Manual of the North Arcot district.

and are known to have been raised over the graves of the dead." Writing concerning the Kurumbas and Irulas,* Mr. Walhouse states that "after every death among them, they bring a long water-worn stone (dēva kotta kallu), and put it into one of the old cromlechs, which are sprinkled over the Nīlgiri plateau. Some of the larger of these have been found piled up to the capstone with such pebbles, which must have been the work of generations. Occasionally, too, the tribes mentioned make small cromlechs for burial purposes, and place the water-worn pebbles in them." According to Mr. Grigg,† some of the Kurumbas of the Nīlgiris "deposit a bone from the pyre in a sāvumauē or death-house—a small cromlech surrounded by upright stones, and bearing some resemblance to the more ancient cromlechs found on the hills. These sāvumanēs, they say, were made by their forefathers." The suggestion is hazarded by Fergusson ‡ that the Kurumbas of the southern hills are the remnant of a great and widely spread race, who may have erected dolmens. Writing concerning the Kurumbas, or shepherd caste of Kaladgi, a correspondent of the Indian Antiquary states § that he came across the tomb of one only four years old. "It was a complete miniature dolmen about eighteen inches every way, composed of four stones, one at each side, one at the rear, and a capstone. The interior was occupied by two round stones about the size of a man's fist, painted red, the deceased man resting in his mother earth below."

* Ind. Ant., IV, 1877.

† Manual of the Nilgiri district.

‡ Rude Stone Monuments.

§ Ind. Ant., VI, 1877.

The Pāndava temples, pāndu kūlis or kistvaens, referred to above are, Mr. Walhouse writes,* "in many places believed to have been built by a dwarf race a cubit high, who could nevertheless lift the huge stones with ease. I have heard, too, of a large mound near Chingleput, not far from Madras, surrounded by kistvaens, and inhabited by a bearded race of Pāndayar three feet high, ruled by a king who lives in the top of the mound. One of the native notions respecting pāndu kūlis is that men of old constructed them for the purpose of hiding treasure. Hence it is that antiquaries find so many have been ransacked. It is also believed that spells were placed over them as a guard, the strongest being to bury a man alive in the cairn, and bid his ghost protect the deposit against any but the proprietor. The ghost would conceal the treasure from all strangers, or only be compelled to disclose it by a human sacrifice being offered."

In the mountains inhabited by the Mala Arayans of Travancore are many tumuli, and vaults called pāndikuri. The latter stand north and south, with the circular opening to the south. "A round stone," the Rev. S. Mateer writes,† "is fitted to this aperture, with another acting as a long lever, to prevent its falling out. The sides, as also the stones of the top and bottom, are single slabs. To this day the Arayans make similar little cells of pieces of stone, the whole forming a box a few inches square; and, on the death of a member of any family, the spirit is supposed to pass, as the body

* Ind. Ant., V, 1876.

† Native Life in Travancore.

is being buried, into a brass or silver image, which is shut into this vault. If the parties are very poor, an oblong smooth stone suffices. A few offerings of milk, rice, toddy and ghī are made, a torch is lighted and extinguished, the figure placed inside the cell, and the covering stone hastily placed on. Then all leave. On the anniversary, similar offerings being made, the stone is lifted off, and again hastily closed. The spirit is thus supposed to be enclosed. No one ventures to touch the cell at any other time."

In an account of his excavations at the extensive "prehistoric" burial site at Aditanallur in the Tinnevelly district, Mr. A. Rea writes as follows * concerning a series of gold ornaments, which were found in most cases lying at the bottom of large urns, crusted and crumpled, apparently intentionally, at the time of deposit. "It seems certain that they are diadems. Diadems of the same shape were found at Mycenæ, and are described † as long, thin, oval gold plates, bound round the head by a small gold wire, the holes for which are at each extremity. This description applies equally to the present examples, except as to the gold wire, of which none was seen. The tying material was probably thread, of which I found traces in some bronze necklaces. Nowadays no custom is known in the neighbourhood of tying diadems on the dead, but what may be a relic of it is described as pattayam kattaradu, meaning literally in Tamil 'the tying of a plate' to the forehead of a corpse,

* Arch. Survey of India, Ann. Report, 1902-03.

† Journ. Soc. Arts. No. 2595, Vol. I, 777.

but which now consists in the sprinkling of some grains of gold and silver on the breast of the dead. I also learn that, among some castes in the east of the Madura district, there still exists a custom of tying a plain rectangular strip of gold, an inch or two in length, on the forehead of the dead. In this case, the custom is known by the same name, and its forms have been preserved in their entirety. In Aditanallur the custom could not have been a general one, for, out of many urns excavated, only a few gold ornaments were found. It must have been limited to persons of rank or importance."

The Jains cremate their dead, placing the corpse on a stone, in order to avoid taking the life of any stray insect during the process.

The Nayādis of Malabar burn their dead close to the dwelling hut. The bones are collected on the seventh day, and preserved in a pot, which is kept close to the hut of the deceased. Pollution is observed for ten days. On the tenth day all the sons of the deceased go with their relations to the nearest stream, and bury the bones on the bank. The sons bathe, and perform beli (offering). A heap of sand, representing the deceased, is constructed, and on it are placed a piece of plantain (*Musa*) leaf, some unboiled rice, and karuka grass (*Cynodon*). Over these water is poured twelve times, and the sons reverently prostrate themselves before the heap. The Nayādi is an ancestor worshipper, and keeps representations of the departed near the hut, to which rice, toddy, and arrack are offered at certain fixed times,

Plate VIII.

Nayādi Ancestral Circle.

e.g., at the Onam and Vishu festivals. "I visited," Mr. S. Appadorai Iyer writes,* "one of the spots, where the Nayādis keep these memorial monuments to deceased ancestors. Beneath a mango tree in a paramba (garden) I counted forty-four stones set up in a circle round the tree (plate VIII). One of these stones was a beli-kal (beli stone), such as is placed round the inner shrines of temples. The remainder resembled survey stones, but were smaller in size. I asked a Nayādi what the stones indicated. He stated that they represented forty-four grown-up Nayādis who had left the world. The stone is set up immediately after the cremation of the body. On the ceremonial occasions mentioned above, solemn prayers are offered that the souls of the departed may protect them from the ravages of wild beasts and snakes. I enquired of a Nayādi how he can expect assistance when a tiger comes in his way. The reply was that he would invoke the aid of his ancestors, and that immediately the mouth of the beast would be sealed, and the animal rendered harmless. The purport and object of their prayers are that all the superior castes, who give them alms, may have long life and prosperity; that they themselves, and their families, may have as great peace and as much food in the future as they had yesterday; and that tigers, snakes, and other beasts may not hurt them. When asked why the Nayādis are not thieves, they replied that they are not so much afraid of tigers as of man, and that they would rather die of hunger than steal. Some time ago an old Nayādi, who had the reputation of being a good shot, died, and was buried. His bones were subsequently collected, and his son, who had obtained a handful of gunpowder from a gun license-holder, set fire to it near the grave with a view to satisfying the soul of the deceased, whose bones, after suspension in a pot beneath a mango tree, were carried to the river."

Of the three endogamous sections of the Tottiyans of the Madura district, two—the Yerrakollas and Vekkiliyans—observe the worship of ancestors, who are represented by a number of stones set up somewhere within the village boundaries. Such places are called mālē. The stones are arranged in an irregular circle. The circles of the Yerrakollas are exceedingly simple, and recall to mind those of the Nayādis, but without the tree. The stones are set up in an open space close to the burning-ground. When a death occurs, a stone is erected among the ashes of the deceased, on the last day of the funeral ceremonies (karmandhiram), and worshipped. It is immediately transferred to the ancestral circle. The mālē of the Vekkiliyans consists of a massive central wooden pillar, carved with male and female human figures (plate IX), set up in a cavity in a round boulder, and covered over by a conical canopy supported on pillars (plate X). When this canopy is set in motion, the central pillar appears to be shaking. This illusion, it is claimed, is due to the power of the ancestral gods. All round the central pillar, which is about ten feet high, a number of stones of different sizes are set up. The central pillar represents Jakkamma and other remote ancestors. The surrounding stones are the representatives of those who

Plate IX.

Tottiyan Mālē.

have died in recent times. Like the Yerrakollas, the Vekkiliyans erect a stone on the karmandhiram day at the spot where the body was cremated, but, instead of transferring it at once to the ancestral circle, they wait till the day of periodical mālē worship, which, being an expensive ceremonial, may take place only once in twelve years. If the interval is long, the number of stones representing those who have died meanwhile may be very large. News of the approaching mālē worship is sent to the neighbouring villages, and, on the appointed day, people of all castes pour in, bringing with them several hundred bulls. The hosts supply their guests with fodder, pots, and a liberal supply of sugar-cane. Refusal to bestow sugar-cane freely would involve failure of the object of the ceremonial. After the completion of the worship, the bulls are let loose, and the animal which reaches the mālē first is decorated, and held in reverence. Its owner is presented with cloths, money, etc.

"For ancestor worship," Mr. A. Rea writes,* "each Coorg house has a kaimatta under a tree in his fields, or in the yard close to his house. This is a raised mud platform, where carved stones, representing the images of their ancestors, are placed. Sacrifices of fowls and pigs are made to them. Sometimes Coorgs become possessed of the spirits of the dead, and express all their desires, when they are sumptuously fed and given drink. The spirits of ancestors are believed to hang over their locality, and become angry now and then." On the final

* Arch. Survey, Madras. Report, 1901-02.

day of the death ceremonies among the Kaikōlans, a small hut is erected, and inside it stones representing the ancestors, brought by a barber, are set up. Some days after the death of a Pallan at Coimbatore, cooked rice, betel leaves, and other articles, are placed near a bābul (*Acacia arabica*) or other thorny tree, and seven small stones, smeared with turmeric, are set up. A cocoanut is broken, and pūja performed. The thorny tree represents the dead person, and the stones are emblematic of the seven Hindu sages, who are worshipped in order to secure salvation to the soul of the deceased.

Near the burial ground of the Irulas of the Nīlgiris is a shed, inside which stones of various sizes are piled up. The larger stones represent adult, and the smaller stones youthful members of the tribe who have died.

An uncommon kind of ancestor worship is recorded * by Mr. Francis from the eastern tāluks of the Anantapur district. " In that quarter, carefully and strongly built tombs may often be seen, each of them provided with a niche, in which a lamp may be placed. At these the Vishnavites of several castes do regular worship to their ancestors on the date of the annual ceremony of the deceased, and on the Mahālaya Amāvāsya day. The tombs are previously whitewashed, and, on the day in question after dark, goats are sacrificed, cocoanuts broken, camphor burnt, and a lamp is lighted in the niche on the tomb."

The Savaras of Ganjam burn their dead, and bury the ashes. A grand feast is given on the day after death, a

* Gazetteer of the Anantapur district.

Plate X.

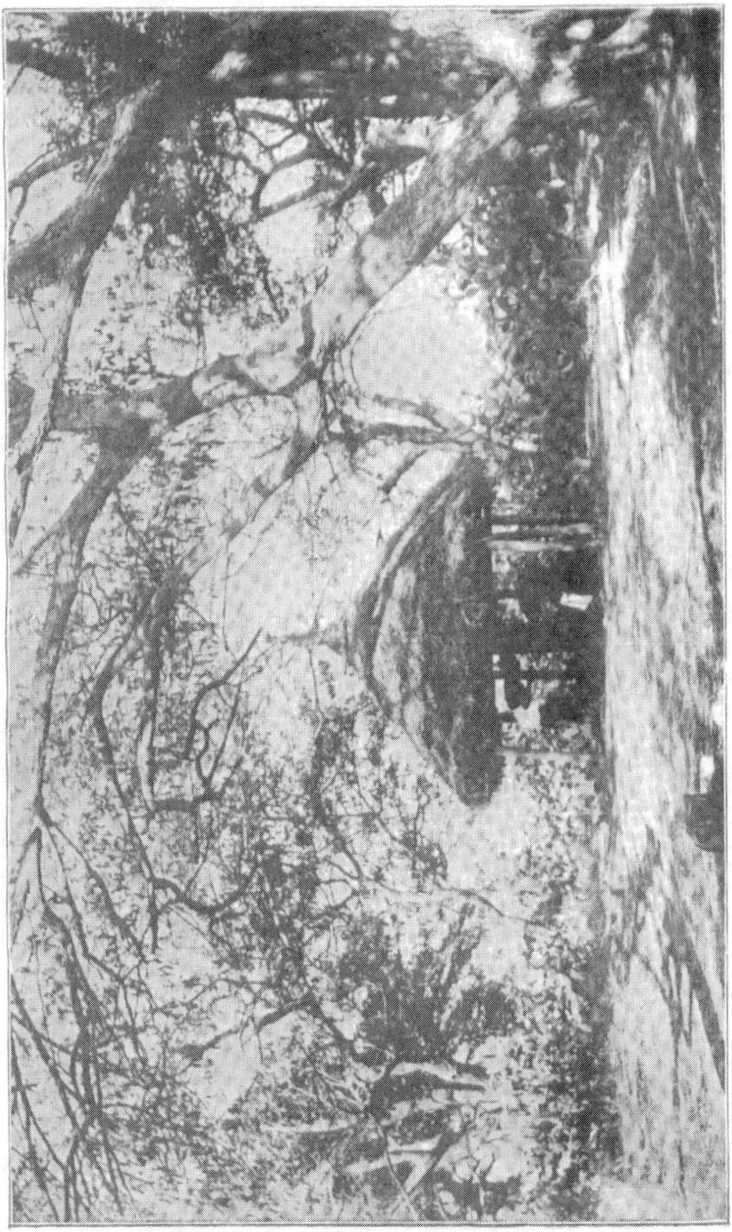

Tottiyan Mālē.

month after that event, and on the anniversary. On the last occasion they dance round the spot where the body was burnt, and set up a stone on end under a tree near the village in memory of the deceased.*

In an account of the death ceremonies of the Kois or Koyis of the Godāvari district, the Rev. J. Cain states,† that "the bodies of children, and young men and women, are buried. If a child dies within a month of its birth, it is usually buried close to the house, so that the rain, dropping from the eaves, may fall upon the grave, and thereby cause the parents to be blessed with another child in due course. With the exception of the above-mentioned, corpses are usually burnt. A cow or bullock is slain, and the tail cut off and put in the dead person's hand, after the cot on which the corpse is carried has been placed upon the funeral pile. If a pūjāri or Koi priest is present, he not unfrequently claims a cloth or two belonging to the dead person. The cot is then removed, and the body burnt. Mr. Vanstavern reports that he has seen part of the liver of the slain animal placed in the mouth of the corpse. The friends of the deceased then retire, and proceed to feast upon the animal slain for the occasion. Three days afterwards they generally return, bringing contributions of cholum (millet: *Sorghum*), and, having slain one or more animals, have another feast. The general idea of the Kois is that the spirits of the dead wander about the forest in the form of pishāchis." I.ˉ G. F. Paddison informs me that in the Mulkanagari tāluk of Vizagapatam he came across a Koya graveyard

* Manual of the Ganjam district. † Ind. Ant. V, 1876.

with upright stones, each of which had a bullock's tail tied to it. He was told that it is the custom to tie a bullock by the tail to the stone, kill it, and then, leaving the tail on the stone, take away the carcase to be eaten. The tail, representing the animal, is left to appease the ghost of the deceased, who thinks that he has got the whole animal. Much in the same way, a lizard, when pursued by a scorpion, sheds its tail, which the scorpion proceeds to sting, while the lizard hurries away to make a new one.

Among the Koragas of South Canara, a handful of earth is removed from the grave on the sixteenth day after burial, and buried in a pit. A stone is erected over it, on which some rice and toddy are placed as a last offering to the departed soul, which is then asked to join its ancestors.* When a death occurs among the Shōlagas of the Coimbatore hills, the corpse is buried. On their return from the funeral, those who have been present salute a lighted lamp. On the spot where the dead person breathed his last, a little rāgi (*Eleusine*) paste and water are placed, and here, on the fourth day, a goat is sacrificed, and offered up to the soul of the departed. After this, the son proceeds to the burial-ground, carrying a stone, and followed by five men selected from each of the exogamous septs. Arrived near the grave, they sit down while the son places the stone on the ground, and they then lift it in succession. The last man to do so is said to fall into a trance. On his recovery, five leaves (plantain, teak, etc.) are

* Manual of the South Canara district.

arranged round the stone, and, on each leaf, five different kinds of food are placed. The five men partake of the food, each from the leaf allotted to his sept. The meal concluded, the son holds the stone in his hands, while his companions pour rāgi and water over it, and then carries it away to the gopamanē (burial-ground) of his sept, and sets it up there.

When a Toreya of the Coimbatore district dies, the corpse is placed inside a pandal made of cocoanut leaves and stems of the milk-hedge (*Euphorbia*). Sect marks are placed on the foreheads of the corpse and the widow. The son dons the sacred thread. At the funeral a mound is piled up over the grave. A Paraiyan places a small twig of the arka plant (*Calotropis gigantea*) in three corners of the grave, leaving out the north-east corner, and the son puts a small coin on each twig. As he goes round the grave with a water-pot and fire-brand, his maternal uncle, who stands at the head of the grave, makes holes in the pot. On the third, fifth, seventh, and ninth days, the widow, dressed in new cloths and decorated with ornaments and flowers, is taken to the burial-ground with offerings of milk, ghī, tender cocoanut, sandal, camphor, etc. Five small stones, smeared with turmeric and lime, are set up at the head of the grave, and worshipped. The widow goes thrice round the grave, and seats herself near the head thereof. Her brother holds up her arms, and one of her husband's male relations breaks her bangles. She breaks her tāli, and throws it on the grave, with the flowers which adorn her. Her ornaments are removed, and she is covered with a cloth, and taken to the river, where she is rubbed with cow-dung, and bathed. The son and other relatives go to the temple with butter and other articles required for pūja. The Brāhman performs a service, and shuts the door of the temple. The son, with his back to the temple, throws a little butter on the doors, which are then opened. This is repeated thrice. On the eleventh day pollution is removed by sprinkling holy water, and the caste people are fed. The widow remains gōsha (not appearing in public) for three months.

On the death of an Odde at Coimbatore, the corpse is, like that of the Toreya, placed under a milk-hedge pandal. When it is borne to the burial-ground, the son carries a new earthen pot filled with water, and the barber the various articles required for pūja, and a pot containing cooked rice. A Paraiyan marches in front, carrying the mat and pillows used by the deceased, and throws them in a place called the idukādu, which has to be passed before the burial-ground is reached. This spot is made to represent the shrine of Arichandra, a king who became a slave of the Paraiyans, and is in charge of the burial-ground. At the idukādu the bier is set on the ground, and the barber makes a mark at the four corners, on each of which the son places a quarter-anna. The barber and the son then go round the bier three times, and the latter, after putting some of the cooked rice on the corpse, breaks the pot containing the rice near its head. The two bearers, who up to this time were at the head of the corpse, now change places with those who were at the feet. From the idukādu to the burial-ground only a single drum may be beaten. Arrived at the burial-ground, the son and other relations place a little raw rice in the mouth of the corpse. The son is shaved, and a piece of cloth, torn from the winding sheet, is given to the Paraiyan. The corpse is laid in the grave with its face to the north, and the grave is filled in. The Paraiyan places a small stone and twig of a thorny tree on it, and again makes a mark in the four corners, in each of which the son once more places a quarter-anna. The coins are the perquisite of the Paraiyan. Placing the pot of water on his right shoulder, the son, with a fire-brand in his left hand, goes, accompanied by the barber, thrice round the grave. Each time the head of the grave is reached, the barber makes a hole in the pot. The son then throws the pot away, and sticks the fire-brand into the grave. All then take their departure without looking back. On the evening of the third day, on which crows are fed with rice at the grave, the figure of a human being is made in rice flour, and placed on a leaf. At the ends of the four extremities, the navel, and on the head, depressions are made, into which a little oil and lighted wicks are placed. The son carries it to the backyard of the house, and places it in a pit filled with water. He then returns to the house without being seen by any one, and enters a room, in which rice has been kept ready for him. He shuts the doors, and eats the food. A calf is placed outside the door, so that, when he opens it, he must see it. He then gazes at the stars. On the day of the anniversary ceremony, the cloths and other belongings of the deceased are worshipped by the near relations.

Somewhat similar are the death ceremonies of the Paraiyans of Coimbatore. The corpse is placed in a pandal made of twigs of the nīm tree (*Melia Azadirachta*) and milk-hedge, and supported behind by a mortar. The widow puts on all her ornaments, and decorates her hair with flowers. She seats herself on the left of the corpse, into the hand of which some paddy and salt are placed. Taking hold of the hands, some one pours the contents into the hands of the widow, who throws them back into those of the corpse. This is done thrice, after which she ties the rice in her cloth. On the way to the burial-ground, the son carries a new pot of water, the barber a pot of cooked rice and brinjal (*Solanum Melongena*) fruits, and other things required for doing pūja. The Paraiyan in charge of the burial-ground carries a fire-brand. The mats, and other articles used by the deceased, and the materials of which the pandal were made, are carried in front by the washerman, who throws them into the idukādu. Here, as before, the son breaks the pot of rice, and the barber makes marks. The son places a quarter-anna on three of the marks, and a little cow-dung on the one at the north-east corner. The widow seats herself at the feet of the corpse, and another widowed woman breaks her tāli-string, and throws it on the corpse. Arrived at the grave the gurukkal (priest) descends into it, does pūja, and applies sacred ashes to its sides. The body is lowered into it, and half a yard of cloth from the winding-sheet is given to the Paraiyan, and a quarter of a yard to an Āndi (religious mendicant). The grave is filled in up to the neck, and bael leaves

(*Ægle Marmelos*), salt, and sacred ashes placed on the head by the gurukkal. The grave is then completely filled in, and a stone and thorny branch placed at the head end. As the son goes round the grave thrice, the barber makes a hole in the water-pot, which is thrown on the stone. The son retires with his head covered with a cloth. The son and other relations bathe, and return to the house, where a vessel containing milk is placed on a mortar, and another containing water placed at the door. They dip twigs of the pīpal (*Ficus religiosa*) into the milk, and throw them on the roof. They also worship a lighted lamp. On the third day, cooked rice, and other food for which the deceased had a special liking, are taken to the grave, and placed on plantain leaves. Pūja is done, and the crows are attracted to the spot. If they do not turn up, the gurukkal prays, and sprinkles water three times. On the seventeenth day the son and others, accompanied by the gurukkal, carry a new brick, and articles required for pūja, to the river. The brick is placed in the water, and the son bathes. The various articles are spread on a plantain leaf, before which the son places the brick. Pūja is done to it, and a piece of new cloth tied to it. It is then again carried to the river, and immersed therein. The ceremony concludes with the lighting of the sacred fire (hōmam). The 'Dead March in Saul' has been known to be played at a Paraiyan funeral in Madras. At royal death ceremonies in Travancore, the same march is played by the band of the Nayar Brigade.

When a Mukkuvan (fishing caste of Malabar) dies, the body is placed on a bier brought by the barber, dressed in new clothes, and decked with ornaments. Four persons are deputed to carry the bier. They bathe in the sea, and carry the corpse to the grave. Four old women engage in loud lamentations. A few pieces of the clothes on the dead body are torn off, and preserved by the son, and others who perform the burial rites. The bearers and near relations of the deceased then bathe in the sea, and the body is placed in the grave. A small piece of gold, and a little water and flowers, are placed in the nose, and all present drop water into the mouth of the corpse. The grave is then filled in. Some use coffins. The son, or other person who conducts the ceremonies, goes round the grave three times with a pot of water on his head, and breaks the pot at the head of the grave. After the interment, all return to the house, and worship a lamp, which is lighted by a barber woman. The next-of-kin is then taken by the barber to the sea-shore, where oblations of water and cooked rice are offered to the deceased. Until the fourteenth day, the barber woman sprinkles water on those who observe pollution. On the fourteenth day the barber makes an image of the deceased in rice, and the relations worship it. The barber then gives them salt and tamarinds, which they eat. He and the headman are then paid their fees. Rice and cocoanuts are distributed to all the houses of the dēsam (sub-division), and the son performs the final ceremony at the grave. That night all go in procession to the shore, and the funeral cakes and a piece of the hair of the son are thrown into the sea. There is a feast on that, and the following day. On the fifteenth day, after the feast, the barber distributes sandal and jaggery to the assembled people, and they leave the house without touching the eaves. If the deceased has a wife of the first class (*i.e.*, married to him with all the marriage rites), her tāli is broken by the barber woman, and put into the grave. A cloth is thrown on her head, and a pot of water poured over it. She is then confined to the house for a year. On the death of such a wife, if her husband is alive, three pots of water are poured over his head, and he remains in the house for three days.

At the funeral of a Thanda Pulayan of Cochin, a pot of water is broken at the head of grave. At the four corners thereof a few grains of rice are placed, and a pebble is laid on it, with mantrams (charms), to keep jackals away, and to prevent the spirit of the departed from molesting people. The Cherumans (agrestic serfs) of Malabar, like other classes, observe death pollution. But, as they cannot, at certain seasons, afford to be idle for fourteen consecutive days, they resort to an artifice to attain this end. They mix cow-dung and paddy, and make it into a ball, and place the ball in an earthen pot, the mouth of which they carefully close with clay. The pot is laid in a corner of the hut, and as long as it remains unopened, they remain free from pollution, and can mix among their fellows. On a convenient day they open the pot, and are instantly seized with pollution, which continues for forty days. Otherwise fourteen days' consecutive pollution is all that is required. On the forty-first or fifteenth day, as the case may be, rice is thrown to the ancestors, and a feast follows.*

The Koramas of Mysore are said to experience considerable difficulty in finding men to undertake the work of carrying the corpse to the grave. Should the dead Korama be a man who has left a young widow, it is customary for some one to propose to marry her the same day, and, by so doing, to engage to carry out the principal part of the work connected with the burial. A shallow grave, barely two feet deep, is dug, and the corpse laid therein. When the soil has been loosely piled in, a pot of fire, carried by the chief mourner in a split bamboo, is broken, and a pot of water placed on the raised mound. Should the spot be visited during the night by a pack of jackals, and the water drunk by them, to slake their thirst after feasting on the dead Korama, the omen is accepted as proof that the liberated spirit has fled away to the realms of the dead, and will never trouble man, woman, child, or cattle. On the sixth day the chief mourner must kill a fowl, and mix its blood with rice. This he places, with some betel leaves and nuts, near the grave. If it is carried off by crows, every thing is considered to have been settled satisfactorily. When a Hasalara or Hasala (forest tribe) of Mysore dies, somebody's evil spirit is credited with the mishap, and an astrologer is consulted, to ascertain its identity. He throws cowry (*Cypræa moneta*) shells or rice for divination, and mentions the name of some neighbour as the

* Malabar Manual.

owner of the devil. Thereupon the spirit of the dead is redeemed by the heir or relative by means of a pig, fowl, or other guerdon. The spirit is then considered to be released, and is thenceforward domiciled in a pot, which is periodically supplied with water and nourishment. This, it is suggested, may be the elementary germ of the posthumous care taking, or srādh, in the more civilised members of the Hindu community.*

On the day following the funeral of a Khond, a little rice is cooked, placed on a dish, and laid on the spot where the corpse was burnt. An incantation is then pronounced, requesting the spirit of the deceased person to eat the rice, and enjoy itself, and not to change itself into a devil or tiger, and come bothering the survivors in the village. Three days after death, the madda, or ceremony, is performed. An effigy of the deceased is prepared out of straw, and stuck up in front of, or on the roof of the house. The relations and friends assemble, mourn, and eat at the expense of the people of the deceased's house. Each person brings a present of some kind or other, and, on his departure next day, receives something of slightly higher value. The death of a person in a village requires a purification, which is made by the sacrifice of a buffalo. If a man has been killed by a tiger, the purification is made by the sacrifice of a pig, the head of which is cut off with a tangi (axe) by a Pāno (hill weaver), and passed between the legs of the men in the village, who stand in a line astraddle. It is a bad omen to him, if the head

* Mysore Census Report, 1891.

touches any man's legs. If the Patro (head of a group of villages) attends a funeral, he gets a fee of a goat for firing his gun, to drive away the dead man's ghost.*

At the final death ceremonies of the Gānigas, food is offered to crows and the soul of the dead person, who is represented by a wooden post decorated with his clothes. The bangles of a widow are broken near the post, which is finally thrown into a tank or stream.

At a funeral of a Nambūtiri Brāhman in Travanore, when the corpse is almost reduced to ashes, the principal performer of the ceremonies and his brothers bathe, and, taking some earth from the adjoining stream or a tank make it into a representation of the deceased.†

When a Yānādi (Telugu forest tribe) is buried, at a fixed spot near the grave, on which all corpses are placed, a cross is drawn on the ground, the four lines of which represent the four cardinal points of the compass. Close to the corpse are placed betel leaves and nuts, and a copper coin. All present then proceed to the spot where the grave is to be dug, while the corpse is left in charge of a Yānādi called the Bathyasthadu, who, as a rule, belongs to a different sept from that of the deceased. The corpse is laid on a cloth, face downwards, in the grave. The eldest son, followed by the other relatives, then throws three handfuls of earth into the grave, which is filled in. On their return home the mourners undergo purification by bathing before entering their huts. In front of the dead man's hut, two broken chatties (pots) are placed, whereof one contains ash-water, the other

* Manual of the Ganjam district. † Travancore Census Report, 1901.

turmeric-water. Into each chatty a leafy twig is thrown. Those who have been present at the funeral stop at the chatties, and, with the twig, sprinkle themselves first with the ash-water, and then with the turmeric-water. Inside the hut a lighted lamp, fed with gingelly-oil, is set up, before which those who enter make obeisance before eating. The chinnadinamu (little day) ceremony, whereof notice is given by the Bathyasthadu, is usually held on the third day after death. Every group (gudem) or village has its own Bathyasthadu, specially appointed, whose duty it is to convey the news of death, puberty of girls, and other events, to all the relatives. On the morning of the chinnadinamu, the eldest son of the deceased cooks rice in a new pot, and makes curries and cakes according to his means. These are made up into six balls, which are placed in a new basket, and taken to the burial ground. On reaching the spot where the cross-lines were drawn, a ball of rice is placed thereon, together with betel leaves and nuts and a copper coin. The Bathyasthadu remains in charge thereof, while those assembled proceed to the grave, whereon a pot of water is poured, and a stone planted at the spot beneath which the head lies. The stone is anointed with shi-kai (fruit of *Acacia concinna*) and red powder, and milk poured over it, first by the widow or widower, and then by the relations This ceremony concluded, the son places a ball of rice at each corner of the grave, together with betel and money. Milk is poured over the remaining ball, which is wrapped in a leaf, and buried over the spot where the abdomen of the deceased is situated.

Close to the grave, at the southern or head end, three stones are set up in the form of a triangle, whereon a new pot full of water is placed. A hole is made in the bottom of the pot, and water trickles out towards the head of the corpse. This concludes the ceremony, and, as on the day of the funeral, purification by bathing, ash-water and turmeric-water is carried out. The peddadinamu (big day) ceremony is performed on the sixteenth, or some later day after death. As at the chinnadinamu, the son cooks rice in a new pot. Opposite the entrance to the hut a handful of clay is squeezed into a conical mass, representing the soul of the deceased, and stuck up on a platform. The eldest son, taking a portion of the cooked rice, spreads it on a leaf in front of the clay image before which incense is burnt, and a lamp placed. The image, and the remainder of the food made up into four balls, are then carried by the son to a tank. As soon as the relatives have assembled there, a recumbent effigy of a man is made, close to the edge of the tank, with the feet towards the north. The conical image is set up close to the head of this effigy, which is anointed by the relatives as at the chinnadinamu, except that no milk is poured over it. The four balls of rice are placed close to the hands and feet of the effigy, together with betel and money, and the son salutes it. The agnates then seat themselves in a row between the effigy and the water, with their hands behind their backs, so as to reach the effigy, which is moved slowly towards the water, into which it finally falls, and becomes disintegrated. The proceedings

Plate XI.

Gammala Muggu.

conclude with the distribution of cloths and tobacco and purification as before. The more prosperous Yānādis now engage a Brāhman to remove the pollution by sprinkling water over them. During the peddadinamu incessant music and drum-beating has been going on, and is continued till far into the night, and sometimes the ceremonial is made to last over two days, in order that the Yānādis may indulge in a bout of music and dancing.

Like the Yānādis, the Mādigas, at the peddadinamu ceremony, make an effigy of the deceased, but only if a female, to which food, winnowing sieves, and glass bangles are offered.

On the last day (peddadinamu) of the funeral ceremonies of the Gamallas (Telugu toddy-drawers), it is customary to engage Pambalas and Bainēdis (musicians and story-tellers) to recite the story of Ankamma, or some other god or goddess. After food has been offered to the dead person, the musician and reciter turn up in the evening, and draw on the floor of the house figures (muggu, plate XI) of a male and female ancestor in powders of five colours, red, yellow, white, green, and black. To these figures a fowl and cocoanuts are offered, and the story-telling is continued until dawn. It is customary among the Padmā Sālē weavers, in some places, to offer up a fowl to the corpse before its removal from the house. If a death occurs on a Saturday or Sunday, a fowl is tied to the bier, and burnt with the corpse. This is done, as there is a belief that otherwise another death will very shortly occur. The Tamulians, in like manner, have a proverb "A Saturday corpse will not go alone."

On the final day of the death ceremonies among the Paraiyans of the Chingleput district, all concerned proceed to a tank with cooked rice, cakes, etc. A Pillayar (figure of Ganēsa) is made with earth, and five kalasams (vessels) are placed near it. The various articles which have been brought are set out in front of it. Two bricks, on which figures of a man and woman are drawn, are given to the son, who washes them, and does pūja to them, after an effigy has been made at the waterside by a washerman. He then says "I gave you calves and money. Enter kailāsam (the abode of Sīva). Find your way to paralokam (the other world). I gave you milk and fruit. Go to the world of the dead. I gave gingelly and milk. Enter yamalokam (the abode of the god of death). Eleven descendants on the mother's side, and ten on the father's, twenty-one in all, may they enter heaven." He then puts the bricks in the water.

At the funeral of an Okkiliyan of Coimbatore, as the procession proceeds towards the burial ground, the relations and friends of the deceased throw small coins, fruits, cakes, fried rice, etc., on the road, to be picked up by poor people. If the funeral is in high life, they may throw flowers made in silver or gold, but not images, as is done by some of the higher classes. A small quantity of salt is placed on the abdomen of the corpse before the grave is filled in. Leaves of the arka plant or tangēdu (*Cassia auriculata*) are placed at three corners of the grave, and a stone is set up over the head. On the third day, dried twigs of several species of *Ficus* and the jāk tree (*Artocarpus integrifolia*), milk, a new cloth, plantains, tender cocoanuts, cheroots, raw rice, betel, etc., are taken to the grave. The twigs are burnt, and reduced to ashes, with which, mixed with water, the figure of a human being is made. It is covered with the new cloth, and flowers are thrown on it. Pūja is done to the plantains, cocoanuts, etc., and milk is poured on the figure by the relations and friends of the deceased. The widow breaks her tāli string, and throws it on the figure. The son, and the four bearers who carried the corpse to the grave, are shaved. Each of the bearers stands up, holding a pestle. The barber touches their shoulders with sacred grass dipped in gingelly oil. Raw rice, and other eatables, are sent to the houses of the bearers by the dead person's son. And, at night, his cloths, turban, and other personal belongings, are worshipped.

The Myāsa Bēdas (hunters) of Mysore, on the day after cremation, scatter the ashes on five tangēdu trees.* On the last day of the funeral rites of a Pattanāvan (Tamil fishing caste) married man, the tāli of his widow is cut off, and thrown into a new pot containing water. Those who come to condole with her on her loss must first set eyes on the tāli on a tray, and afterwards on the widow. A common form of abuse among Pattanāvan women is "Let your tāli be thrown into water."

At the funeral of the Jōgis various articles of food, and tobacco, are placed in a hole scooped out in the floor of the grave. On the last day of the funeral rites,

* Mysore Census Report, 1891.

a widower cuts through his waist-thread, and a widow removes her tāli.

Turning now to the tribes which inhabit the Nīlgiri plateau. Full details of the funeral ceremonies of the Todas will, I know, be published ere long by Dr. Rivers. And it must suffice for the moment to describe those funerals, at which I have been present as an eye-witness.

It was my good fortune to have an opportunity of witnessing the dry funeral ceremony (kēdu) of a woman who had died from small-pox two months previously. On arrival at a mand (Toda settlement) on the open downs about five miles from Ootacamund, we were conducted by a Toda friend to the margin of a dense shola (grove), where we found two groups seated apart, consisting of (*a*) women, girls, and brown-haired female babies, chatting round a camp fire; (*b*) men, boys, and male babies carried, with marked signs of paternal affection, by their fathers. The warm copper hue of the little girls and young adults stood out in noticeable contrast to the dull, muddy complexion of the elder women. In a few minutes a murmuring sound commenced in the centre of the female group. Working themselves up to the necessary pitch, some of the women (near relatives of the dead woman) commenced to cry freely, and the wailing and lachrymation gradually spread round the circle, until all, except little girls and babies who were too young to be affected, were weeping and moaning, some for fashion, others from genuine grief. The men meanwhile showed no signs of sorrow, but sat talking together, and expressed regret that we had not brought the hand dynamometer, to amuse them with trials of strength. In carrying out the orthodox form of mourning, the women first had a good cry to themselves, and then, as their emotions became more intense, went round the circle, selecting partners with whom to share companionship in grief. Gradually the group resolved itself into couplets of mourners, each pair with their heads in close contact, and giving expression to their emotions in unison. Before separating, to select a new partner, each couple saluted by bowing the head and raising the feet of the other, covered by the putkūli (cloth), thereto. From time to time the company of mourners was reinforced by late arrivals from distant mands, and, as each detachment, now of men, now of women, came in view across the open downs, one could not fail to be reminded of the gathering of the clans on some Highland moor. The resemblance was heightened by the distant sound as of pipers, produced by the Kota band (with two police constables in attendance), composed of four Kotas, who made a hideous noise with drums and flutes as they drew near the scene of action. The band, on arrival, took up a position close to the mourning women. As each detachment arrived, the women, recognising their relatives, came forward and saluted them in the manner customary among Todas by falling at their feet, and placing first the right then the left foot on their head (ababuddiken). Shortly after the arrival of the band, signals were exchanged, by waving of putkūlis (cloths) between the assembled throng and a small detachment of men some distance off. A general move was made, and an *impromptu* procession formed with men in front, band in the middle, and women bringing up the rear. A halt was made opposite a narrow gap leading into the shola; men and women sat apart as before, and the band walked round, discoursing unsweet music. A party of girls went off to bring fire from the spot just vacated for use in the coming ceremonial, but recourse was finally had to a box of tändstikers lent by one of our party. At this stage of the proceedings we noticed a woman go up to the eldest son of the deceased, who was seated apart from the other men crying bitterly, and would not be comforted in spite of her efforts to console him. On receipt of a summons from within the shola, the assembled Toda men and ourselves swarmed into it by a narrow track leading to a small clear space around a big tree, from a hole cut at the base of which an elderly Toda produced a piece of the skull of the dead woman, wrapped round with long tresses of her hair. It now became the men's turn to exhibit active signs of grief, and all with one accord commenced to weep and mourn. Amid the scene of lamentation, the hair was slowly unwrapt from off the skull, and burned in an iron ladle, from which a smell as of incense arose. A bamboo pot of ghī was produced, with which the skull was reverently anointed, and placed in a cloth spread on the ground. To this relic of the deceased the throng of men, amid a scene of wild excitement, made obeisance by kneeling down before it, and touching it with their foreheads. The females were not permitted to witness this stage of the proceedings, with the exception of one or two near relatives of the departed one, who supported themselves sobbing against the tree. The ceremonial concluded, the fragment of skull, wrapt in the cloth, was carried into the open, where, as men and boys had previously done, women and girls made obeisance to it. A procession was then again formed, and marched on until a place was reached, where were two stone-walled kraals, large and small. Around the former the men, and within the latter the women, took up their position, the men engaging in chit-chat, and the women in mourning, which after a time ceased, and they too engaged in conversation, one of their number (a Toda beauty) entertaining the rest by exhibiting a photograph of herself, with which I had presented her. A party of men, carrying the skull, still in the cloth, set out for a neighbouring shola, where a kēdu of several other dead Todas was being celebrated; and a long pause ensued, broken eventually by the arrival of the other funeral party, the men advancing in several lines, with arms linked, keeping step and crying out U, hah, hah, U, hah, hah, in regular time. This party brought with it pieces of the skulls of a woman and two men, which were placed, wrapt in cloths, on the ground, saluted, and mourned over by the assembled multitude. At this stage a small party of Kotas arrived, and took up their position on a neighbouring hill, waiting, vulture-like, for the carcase of the buffalo which was shortly to be slain. Several young men now went off across the hill in search of buffaloes, and speedily re-appeared, driving five buffaloes before them with sticks. As soon as the beasts approached a swampy marsh at the foot of the hill, on which the expectant crowd of men was gathered together, two young men of athletic build, throwing off their putkūlis, made a rush down the hill, and tried to seize one of the buffaloes by the horns, with the result that one of them was promptly thrown. The buffalo escaping, one of the remaining four was quickly caught by the horns, and, with arms interlocked, the men brought it down on its knees, amid a general scuffle. In spite of marked objection and strenuous resistance on the part of the animal —a barren cow—it was, by means of sticks freely applied, slowly dragged up the hill, preceded by the Kota band, and with a Toda youth pulling at its tail. Arrived at the open space between the two kraals, the buffalo, by this time thoroughly exasperated, and with blood pouring from its nostrils, had a cloth put on its back, and was despatched by a blow on the poll with an axe deftly wielded by a young and muscular man. On this occasion no one was badly hurt by the sacrificial cow, though one man was seen washing his legs in the swamp after the preliminary struggle with the beast. But Colonel Ross-King narrates * how he saw a man receive a dangerous wound in the neck from a thrust of the horn, which ripped open a wide gash from the collar bone to the ear. With the death of the buffalo, the last scene which terminated the strange rites commenced; men, women, and children pressing forward and jostling one another in their eagerness to salute the dead beast by placing their heads between its horns, and weeping

* Aboriginal Tribes of the Nilgiri Hills, 1870.

and mourning in pairs; the facial expression of grief being mimicked when tears refused to flow spontaneously.

It has been suggested * that the numerous figures of large-horned buffaloes, some with bells round their necks, made of clay, which are found in the Nīlgiri cairns, are monuments of the antiquity of the Toda custom of sacrificing buffaloes decorated with bells at funerals.

A few days after the dry funeral ceremony, I was invited to be present at the green funeral of a young girl who had died of small-pox five days previously. I proceeded accordingly to the scene of the recent ceremony, and there, in company with a small gathering of Todas from the neighbouring mands (among them the only white-haired old woman whom I have seen), awaited the arrival of the funeral cortége, the approach of which was announced by the advancing strains of Kota music. Slowly the procession came over the brow of the hill; the corpse, covered by a cloth, on a rude ladder-like bier, borne on the shoulders of four men, followed by two Kota musicians; the mother carried hidden within a sack; relatives and men carrying bags of rice and jaggery, and bundles of wood of the kiaz tree (*Eugenia Arnottiana*) for the funeral pyre. Arrived opposite a small hut, which had been specially built for the ceremonial, the corpse was removed from the bier, laid on the ground, face upwards, outside the hut, and saluted by men, women, and children, with the same manifestations of grief as at the dry funeral. Soon the men moved

* H. Congreve, Madras Journ. Lit. Science, XIV, 1847. The figures referred to are now in the Madras Museum.

away to a short distance, and engaged in quiet conversation, leaving the females to continue mourning round the corpse, interrupted from time to time by the arrival of detachments from distant mands, whose first duty was to salute the dead body. Meanwhile a near female relative of the dead child was busily engaged inside the hut, collecting together in a basket small measures of rice, jaggery, sago, honey-comb, and the girl's simple toys, which were subsequently to be burned with the corpse. The mourning ceasing after a time, the corpse was placed inside the hut, and followed by the near relatives, who there continued to weep over it. A detachment of men and boys, who had set out in search of the buffaloes which were to be sacrificed, now returned driving before them three cows, which escaped from their pursuers to re-join the main herd. A long pause ensued, and, after a very prolonged drive, three more cows were guided into a swampy marsh, where one of them was caught by the horns as at the dry funeral, and dragged reluctantly, but with little show of fight, to the weird strains of Kota drum and flute, in front of the hut, where it was promptly despatched by a blow on the poll. The corpse was now brought from within the hut, and placed, face upwards, with its feet resting on the forehead of the buffalo, whose neck was decorated with a silver chain, such as is worn by Todas round the loins to suspend the languti, as no bell was available, and the horns were smeared with butter. Then followed the same frantic manifestations of grief as at the dry funeral, amid which the unhappy mother fainted from sheer exhaustion. Mourning over, the corpse was made to go through a form of ceremony, resembling that which is performed at the fifth month of pregnancy with the first child. A small boy, three years old, was selected from among the relatives of the dead girl, and taken by his father in search of a certain grass (*Andropogon Schœnanthus*), and a twig of a shrub (*Sophora glauca*), which were brought to the spot where the corpse was lying. The mother of the dead child then withdrew one of its hands from the putkūli, and the boy placed the grass and twig in the hand, and limes, plantains, rice, jaggery, honey-comb, and butter in the pocket of the putkūli, which was then stitched with needle and thread in a circular pattern. The boy's father then took off his son's putkūli, and covered him with it from head to foot. Thus covered, the boy remained outside the hut till the morning of the morrow, watched through the night by near relatives of himself and his dead bride. [On the occasion of the funeral of an unmarried lad, a girl is, in like manner selected, covered with her putkūli from head to foot, and a metal vessel, filled with jaggery, rice, etc. (to be subsequently burnt on the funeral pyre), placed for a short time within the folds of the putkūli. Thus covered, the girl remains till next morning, watched through the dreary hours of the night by relatives. The same ceremony is performed over the corpse of a married woman, who has not borne children, the husband acting as such for the last time, in the vain hope that the woman may produce issue in heaven.] The quaint ceremonial concluded, the corpse was borne away to the burning-ground within the shola, and, after removal of some of the hair by the mother of the newly wedded boy, burned, with face turned upwards,* amid the music of the Kota band, the groans of the assembled crowd squatting on the ground, and the genuine grief of the nearest relatives. The burning concluded, a portion of the skull was removed from the ashes, and handed over to the recently made mother-in-law of the dead girl, and wrapped up with the hair in the bark of the tūd tree (*Meliosma pungens*). A second buffalo, which, properly speaking, should have been slain before the corpse was burnt, was then sacrificed, and rice and jaggery were distributed among the crowd, which dispersed, leaving behind the youthful widower and his custodians, who, after daybreak, partook of a meal of rice, and returned to their mands; the boy's mother taking with her the skull and hair to her mand, where it would remain until the celebration of the dry funeral. No attention is paid to the ashes after cremation, but they are left to be scattered by the winds.

A further opportunity offered itself to be present at the green funeral of an elderly woman on the open downs not far from our head-quarters, in connection with which certain details, not recorded in my original account of the funeral ceremonies, possess some interest. The corpse was, at the time of our arrival, laid out on a rude bier within an improvised arbour covered with leaves and open at each end, and tended by some of the female relatives. At some little distance, a conclave of Toda

* Marshall states that he was "careful to ascertain that the placing the body with its *face downwards* had not been an accidental circumstance."

men, who rose of one accord to greet us, was squatting in a circle, among whom were many venerable white-turbaned elders of the tribe, protected from the scorching sun by palm-leaf umbrellas. Amid much joking, and speech-making by the veterans, it was decided that, as the eldest son of the deceased woman was dead, leaving a widow, this daughter-in-law should be united to the second son, and that they should live together as man and wife. On the announcement of the decision, the bridegroom-elect saluted the principal Todas present by placing his head on their feet, which were sometimes concealed within the ample folds of the body-cloth. At the funeral of a married woman, three ceremonies must, I was informed, be performed, if possible, by a daughter or daughter-in-law, viz. :—

(1) Tying a leafy branch of the tiviri shrub (*Atylosia Candolleana*) in the putkūli of the corpse ;

(2) Tying balls of thread and cowry shells on the arm of the corpse, just above the elbow ;

(3) Setting fire to the funeral pyre, which was, on the present occasion, done by lighting a rag with a match. In an account of a Toda green funeral Mr. Walhouse notes * that, "when the pile was completed, fire was obtained by rubbing two dry sticks together. This was done mysteriously and apart, for such a mode of obtaining fire is looked upon as something secret and sacred." The buffalo capture took place amid the usual excitement and freedom from accident ; and, later in the day, the stalwart buffalo catchers turned up at the travellers'

* Ind. Ant., III, 1874.

bungalow for a *pour boire* in return, as they said, for treating us to a good fight. The beasts selected for sacrifice were a full grown cow and a young calf. As they were dragged near to the corpse, now removed from the arbour, butter was smeared over the horns, and a bell tied round the neck. The bell was subsequently removed by Kotas, in whose custody it was to remain till the next dry funeral. The death blow, or rather series of blows, having been delivered with the butt-end of an axe, the feet of the corpse were placed in the mouth of the buffalo. In the case of a male corpse, the hands are made to clasp the horns. The customary mourning in couples concluded, the corpse, clad in four cloths, was carried on the stretcher to a hollow in the neighbouring shola, and placed by the side of the funeral pyre, which had been rapidly piled up. The innermost cloth was black in colour, and similar to that worn by the holy pālāl (priest) of the tiriēri (sacred mand). Next to it came a putkūli decorated with blue and red embroidery, outside which again was a plain white putkūli covered over by a red cotton cloth of European manufacture. Seated by the side of the pyre, near to which I was courteously invited to take a seat on the stump of a rhododendron, was an elderly relative of the dead woman, who, while watching the ceremonial, was placidly engaged in the manufacture of a holly walking-stick with the aid of a glass scraper. The proceedings were watched on behalf of Government by a forest guard, and a police constable who, with marked affectation, held his handkerchief to his nose throughout the ceremonial. The corpse was decorated with brass rings, and within the putkūli were stowed jaggery, a scroll of paper adorned with cowry shells, snuff and tobacco, cocoanuts, biscuits, various kinds of grain, ghī, honey, and a tin-framed looking-glass. A long purse, containing a silver yen and an Arcot rupee of the East India Company, was tied up in the putkūli close to the feet. These preliminaries concluded, the corpse was hoisted up, and swung three times over the now burning pyre, above which a mimic bier, made of slender twigs, was held. This ceremonial, wherein presumably the spirit was supposed to depart heavenwards (to Amnor), concluded, the body was stripped of its jewelry, and a lock of hair cut off by the daughter-in-law for preservation, together with a fragment of the skull, until the dry funeral. As soon as the pyre was fairly ablaze, the mourners, with the exception of some of the female relatives, left the shola, and the men, congregating on the summit of a neighbouring hill, invoked their god. Four men, seized, apparently in imitation of the Kota dēvādi, with divine frenzy, began to shiver and gesticulate wildly, while running blindly to and fro with closed eyes and shaking heads. They then began to talk in Malayālam, and offer an explanation of an extraordinary phenomenon, which had appeared in the form of a gigantic figure, which disappeared as suddenly as it appeared. At the annual ceremony of walking through fire (hot ashes) in that year, two factions arose owing to some dissension, and two sets of ashes were used. This seems to have annoyed the gods, and those concerned were threatened with speedy ruin. But the whole story was very vague. The possession by some Todas of a smattering of Malayālam is explained by the fact that, when grazing their buffaloes on the northern and western slopes of the Nīlgiris, they come in contact with the Malayālam-speaking people from the neighbouring Malabar district.

The death of a man in a Khond village requires a purificatory ceremony on the seventh day, in the course of which a buffalo is sacrificed. When staying at Kota-giri on the Nīlgiris a few years ago, the weird strains of the Kota band announced to me that death reigned in the Kota village. Soon after daybreak, a detachment of villagers hastened to convey the tidings of the death to the Kotas of the neighbouring villages, who arrived on the scene later in the day in Indian file, men in front and women in the rear. As they drew near to the place of mourning, they all, of one accord, commenced the orthodox manifestations of grief, and were met by a deputation of villagers accompanied by the band. Meanwhile a red flag, tied to the top of a bamboo pole, was hoisted as a signal of death in the village, and a party had gone off to a glade, some two miles distant, to obtain wood for the construction of the funeral car (tēru). The car, when completed, was an elaborate structure, about eighteen feet in height, made of wood and bamboo, in four tiers, each with a canopy of turkey red and yellow cloth, and an upper canopy of white cloth trimmed with red, surmounted by a black umbrella of European manufacture, decorated with red ribands. The car was profusely adorned throughout with red flags and long white streamers, and with young plantain trees at the base. Tied to the car were a calabash and a bell. During the construction of the car the corpse remained within the house of the deceased man, outside which the relatives and villagers continued mourning to the dirge-like music of the band, which plays so prominent a part at the death ceremonies of both Todas and Kotas. On the completion of the car, late in the afternoon, it was deposited in front of the house. The corpse dressed up in a coloured turban and gaudy coat as for a nautch party, with a garland of flowers round the neck, and two rupees, a half rupee, and sovereign gummed on to the forehead, was brought from within the house, lying face upwards on a cot, and placed beneath the lowest canopy of the car. Near the head were placed iron implements and a bag of rice, at the feet a bag of tobacco, and beneath the cot baskets of grain, rice, cakes, etc. The corpse was covered by cloths offered to it as presents, and before it those Kotas who were younger than the dead man prostrated themselves, while those who were older touched the head of the corpse, and bowed to it. Around the car the male members of the community executed a wild step-dance, keeping time with the music in the execution of various fantastic movements of the arms and legs. During the long hours of the night mourning was kept up to the almost incessant music of the band, and the early morn discovered many of the villagers in an advanced stage of intoxication. Throughout the morning dancing round the car was continued by men, sober and inebriated, with brief intervals of rest, and a young buffalo was slaughtered as a matter of routine form, with no special ceremonial, in a pen outside the village, by blows on the back and neck administered with the keen edge of an adze. Towards midday presents of rice from the relatives of the dead man arrived on the back of a pony, which was paraded round the funeral car. From a vessel containing rice and rice water, rice was crammed into the mouths of the near relatives, some of the water poured over their heads, and the remainder offered to the corpse. At intervals a musket, charged with gunpowder, which proved later on a dangerous weapon in the hands of an intoxicated Kota, was let off, and the bell on the car rung. About 2 P.M., the time announced for the funeral, the cot bearing the corpse, from the forehead of which the coins had been removed, was carried outside the village, followed by the widow and a throng of Kotas of both sexes, young and old, and the car was carried to the foot of the hill, there to await the arrival of the corpse after the performance of various ceremonies. Seated together at some distance from the corpse, the women continued to mourn until the funeral procession was out of sight, those who could not cry spontaneously, or compel the tears to flow, mimicking the expression of woe by contortion of the grief muscles. The most poignant grief was displayed by man, in a state of extreme intoxication, who sat apart by himself, howling and sobbing, and wound up by creating considerable disturbance at the burning ground. Three young bulls were brought from the village, and led round the corpse. Of these, two were permitted to escape for the time being, while a vain attempt, which would have excited the derision of the expert Toda buffalo catchers, was made by three men hanging on to the head and tail to steer the third bull up to the head of the corpse. The animal, however, proving refractory, it was deemed discreet to put an end to its existence by a blow on the poll with the butt-end of an adze, at some distance from the corpse, which was carried up to it, and made to salute the dead beast's head with the right hand in feeble imitation of the impressive Toda ceremonial. The carcase of the bull was saluted by a few of the Kota men, and subsequently carried off by Paraiyans. Supported by females, the exhausted widow of the dead man, who had fainted earlier in the day, was dragged up to the corpse, and, lying back beside it, had to submit to the ordeal of removal of all her jewelry, the heavy brass bangle being hammered off the wrist, supported on a wooden roller, by oft-repeated smart blows with mallet and chisel, delivered by a village blacksmith assisted by a besotten individual noted as a consumer of twelve grains of opium daily. The ornaments, as removed, were collected in a basket, to be worn again by the widow after several months. This revolting ceremony concluded, and a last salutation given by the widow to her dead husband, arches of bamboo were attached to the cot, which was covered over with a coloured table-cloth hiding the corpse from sight. A procession was then formed, composed of the corpse on the cot, preceded by the car and musicians, and followed by male Kotas and Badagas, Kota women carrying the baskets of grain and cakes, a vessel containing fire, burning camphor, and, bringing up the rear, a high dignitary of the church, an amateur photographer, and myself. Quickly the procession marched to the burning ground beyond the bazār, situated in a valley by the side of a stream running through a glade in a dense undergrowth of bracken fern and trailing passion-flower. On arrival at the selected spot, a number of agile Kotas swarmed up the sides of the car, and stripped it of its adornments, including the umbrella, and a free fight for the possession of the cloths and flags ensued. The denuded car was then placed over the corpse, which, deprived of all valuable ornaments, and still lying on the cot face upwards, had been meanwhile placed, amid a noisy scene of brawling, on the rapidly constructed funeral pyre. Around the car faggots of fire-wood, supplied, in lieu of wreaths, by different families in the dead man's village, as a tribute of respect to the deceased, were piled up, and the pyre was lighted with torches kindled at a fire which was burning on the ground close by. As soon as the pyre was in a blaze, tobacco, cheroots, cloths, and grain were distributed among those present, and the funeral party dispersed, discussing the events of the day as they returned to their homes, leaving a few men behind in charge of the burning corpse. And peace reigned once more in the Kota village. A few days later the funeral of an elderly Kota woman took place with a very similar ceremonial. But, suspended from the handle of the umbrella on the top of the car was a rag doll, which, in appearance, resembled an 'Aunt Sally.'

Of the death rites as carried out by the Badaga subdivision of the Badagas of the Nīlgiris the following note was recorded during a recent visit to Kotagiri. When death is drawing near, a gold coin, called Vīraraya hana or fanam, dipped in butter or ghī, is given to the dying man to swallow. If he is too far gone to be capable of swallowing, the coin is, according to Mr. S. M. Natesa Sastri,* tied round the arm. But our informants told us that this is not done at the present day. "If," Mr. Gover writes,† "the tiny coin slip down, well. He will need both gold and ghee, the one to sustain his strength in the dark journey to the river of death, the other to fee the guardian of the fairy-like bridge that spans the dreaded tide. If sense remain to the wretched man, he knows that now his death is nigh. Despair and the gold make recovery impossible, and there are none who have swallowed the Birianhana, and yet have lived. If insensibility or deathly weakness make it impossible for the coin to pass the thorax, it is carefully bound in cloth, and tied to the right arm, so that there may be nought to hinder the passage of a worthy soul into the regions of the blessed." The giving of the coin to the dying man is apparently an important item, and in the Badaga folktales a man on the point of death is made to ask for a Vīraraya fanam. When life is extinct, the corpse is kept within the house until the erection of the funeral car (gudikattu) is completed. Though Mr. Gover states that the burning must not be delayed more than twenty-four hours, at the present day the Badagas postpone the

* Madras Christ. Coll. Magazine, 1892.

† Folk Songs of Southern India, 1871.

funeral till all the near relations have assembled, even if this necessitates the keeping of the dead body for two or three days. Cremation may take place on any day, except Tuesday. News of a death is conveyed to distant hamlets (hattis) by a Toreya,* who is paid a rupee for his services. On approaching a hamlet, he removes his turban, to signify the nature of his errand, and, standing on the side of a hill, yells out "Dho! Dho! Who is in the hamlet"? Having imparted his news, he proceeds on his journey to the next hamlet. On the morning of the day fixed for the funeral, the corpse is taken on a charpoy or native cot to an open space, and a buffalo led thrice round it. The right hand of the corpse is then lifted up, and passed over the horns of the buffalo. A little milk is drawn, and poured into the mouth of the corpse. Prior to this ceremony, two or three buffaloes may be let loose, and one of them captured, after the manner of the Todas, brought near the corpse, and conducted round the cot. The funeral car (frontispiece) is built up in five to eleven tiers, decorated with cloths and streamers, and one tier must be covered with black chintz. By the poorer members of the community the car is replaced by a cot covered with cloth, and surmounted by five umbrellas. Immediately after the buffalo ceremony, the corpse is carried to the car, and placed in the lowest storey thereof, washed, and dressed in coat and turban. A new dhupati (coarse cloth) is wrapped round it. Two silver coins—Japanese yens or rupees—are stuck on the forehead. Beneath the cot are placed a crowbar, and baskets containing

* The Toreyas are the lowest endogamous sub-division of the Badagas.

cakes, parched paddy, tobacco, chick pea (*Cicer arietinum*), jaggery, and sāmai (*Panicum miliare*) flour. A number of women, relations and friends of the dead man, then make a rush to the cot, and, sitting on it round the corpse, keep on wailing, while a woman near its head rings a bell. When one batch is tired, it is replaced by another. Badaga men then pour in in large numbers, and salute the corpse by touching the head, Toreyas and female relations touching the feet. Of those who salute, a few place inside the dhupati a piece of white cloth with red and yellow stripes, which has been specially prepared for the purpose. All then proceed to dance round the car to the music of the Kota band, near male relations removing their turban or woollen nightcap, as a mark of respect, during the first three revolutions. Most of the male dancers are dressed up in gaudy petticoats and smart turbans. "No woman," Mr. Natesa Sastri writes, "mingles in the funeral dance if the dead person is a man, but, if the deceased is a woman, one old woman, the nearest relative of the dead, takes part in it." But, at the funerals of two men which we witnessed, a few women danced together with the men. Usually the tribesmen continue to arrive until 2 or 3 P.M. Relations collect outside the village, and advance in a body towards the car, some, especially the sons-in-law of the dead man, riding on ponies, some of which carry sāmai grain. As they approach the car, they shout "Ja! hoch; Ja! hoch." The Muttu Kotas * bring a double iron sickle

* Each Badaga family has its Muttu Kota, who has to make iron implements, ploughs, etc., in return for an annual present of grain.

with imitation buffalo horns on the tip, which is placed, with a hatchet, buguri (flute), and walking-stick, on the cot or on the ground beside it. When all are assembled, the cot is carried to an open space between the house and the burning ground, followed by the car and a party of women carrying the baskets containing grain, etc. The car is then stripped of its trappings, and hacked to pieces. The widow is brought close to the cot, and removes her nose-screw (elemukkuththi), and other jewels. The nose-screw may be only worn by a woman married to a man of the Madavē exogamous sept on two occasions, at the funeral of her husband, and at the mandēdanda festival, when the first born child is taken to the temple. At both the funerals which we witnessed the widow had a narrow strip of coloured chintz over her shoulders. Standing near the corpse, she removed a bit of wire from her ear-rings, a lock of hair, and a palm-leaf roll from the lobe of the ear, and tied them up in the cloth of her dead husband. After her, the sisters of the dead man cut off a lock of hair, and, in like manner, tied it in the cloth. Women attached to a man by illegitimate ties sometimes also cut off a lock of hair, and, tying it to a twig of *Dodonæa viscosa*, place it inside the cloth. Very impressive is the recitation, or after-death confession of a dead man's sins by an elder of the tribe standing at the head of the corpse, and rapidly chanting the following lines, or a variation thereof, while he waves his right hand during each line towards the feet. The reproduction of the recitation in my phonograph never failed to impress the daily audience of Badagas, Kotas and Todas.

This is the death of Andi.
In his memory the calf of the cow Bellē has been set free.
From this world to the other
He goes in a car.
Everything the man did in this world.
All the sins committed by the ancestors.
All the sins committed by his forefathers.
All the sins committed by his parents.
All the sins committed by himself.
The estranging of brothers.
Shifting the boundary line.
Encroaching on a neighbour's land by removing the hedge.
Driving away brothers and sisters.
Cutting the kalli tree stealthily.
Cutting the mulli tree outside his boundary.
Dragging the thorny branches of the kotte tree.
Sweeping with a broom.
Splitting green branches.
Telling lies.
Uprooting seedlings.
Plucking growing plants, and throwing them in the sun.
Giving young birds to cats.
Troubling the poor and cripples.
Throwing refuse water in front of the sun.
Going to sleep after seeing an eclipse of the moon.
Looking enviously at a buffalo yielding an abundance of milk.
Being jealous of the good crops of others.
Removing boundary stones.
Using a calf set free at the funeral.
Polluting water with dirt.
Urinating on burning embers.
Ingratitude to the priest.
Carrying tales to the higher authorities.
Poisoning food.

Not feeding a hungry person.
Not giving fire to one half frozen.
Killing snakes and cows.
Killing lizards and blood-suckers.
Showing a wrong path.
Getting on the cot, and allowing his father-in-law to sleep on the ground.
Sitting on a raised verandah, and driving thence his mother-in-law.
Going against natural instincts.
Troubling daughters-in-law.
Breaking open lakes.
Breaking open reservoirs of water.
Being envious of the prosperity of other villages.
Getting angry with people.
Misleading travellers in the forest.
Though there be three hundred such sins,
Let them all go with the calf set free to-day.
May the sins be completely removed!
May the sins be forgiven!
May the door of heaven be open!
May the door of hell be closed!
May the hand of charity be extended!
May the wicked hand be shrivelled!
May the door open suddenly!
May beauty or splendour prevail everywhere!
May the hot pillar become cooled!
May the thread bridge * become tight!
May the pit of perdition be closed!
May the thorny path become smooth!
May the mouth of the worm-hole be closed!
May he reach the golden pillar!
May he rub against the silver pillar!

* The bridge spanning the river of death, which the blessed cross in safety.

Holding the feet of the six thousand Athis,
Holding the feet of the twelve thousand Pathis,
Holding the feet of Brāhma,
Holding the feet of the calf set free to-day,
May he reach the abode of Sīva!

So mote it be.

The recitation is repeated thrice, and a few Badagas repeat the last words of each line after the elder. As the ceremony witnessed by us differs materially from the account thereof given by Gover thirty-four years ago, I may appropriately quote his description. "By a conventional mode of expression, the sum total of sins a man may do is said to be thirteen hundred. Admitting that the deceased has performed them all, the performer cries aloud 'Stay not their flight to God's pure feet.' As he closes, the whole assembly chants aloud 'Stay not their flight.' Again the performer enters into details, and cries 'He killed the crawling snake. It is a sin.' In a moment the last word is caught up, and all the people cry 'It is a sin.' As they shout, the performer lays his hand upon the calf. The sin is transferred to the calf. Thus the whole catalogue is gone through in this impressive way. But this is not enough. As the last shout 'Let all be well' dies away, the performer gives place to another, and again confession is made, and all the people shout 'It is a sin.' A third time it is done. Then, still in solemn silence, the calf is let loose. Like the Jewish scape-goat, it may never be used for secular work." At the funerals of which we were spectators, no calf was brought near the corpse, and the celebrants of the rites were satisfied with the mere mention by name of a calf, which is male or female according to the sex of the deceased. If a dead man leaves a widow in a state of pregnancy, who has not performed the kanni-kattu, or marriage thread ceremony, this must be gone through before the corpse is taken to the pyre, in order to render the child legitimate. A man cannot, during life, claim the paternity of a child unless he has thrown the kanni round his wife's neck during the seventh month of her first pregnancy. The pregnant woman is, at the time of the funeral, brought close to the cot, and a near relation of the deceased, taking up a cotton thread twisted in the form of a necklace without any knots, throws it round her neck. Sometimes the hand of the corpse is lifted up with the thread, and made to place it round the neck. Soon after the recitation of the sins, all the agnates go to the house of the dead man, at the entrance to which a gunny-bag is spread, whereon a small quantity of paddy is poured, and a few culms of *Cynodon Dactylon* and a little cow-dung are placed on it. The eldest of the agnates, sickle in hand, takes some of the paddy, and moves on, raising both hands to his forehead. The other agnates then do the same, and proceed, in Indian file, males in front and females in the rear, to the corpse. Round it they walk, men from left to right, and women in the reverse direction, and at the end of each circuit put some of the paddy on its face. The cot is then carried to the burning-ground, a woman heading the procession, and shaking the end of her cloth all the way. The corpse is laid on the pyre with its feet to the south, and the pyre lighted by the eldest son standing at the head. The sticks of which the car was constructed are added to the fuel, of which the pyre is built up. In some places the son, when lighting the pyre, repeats the words "Being begotten by my father and mother, I, in the presence of all and the dēva, set fire at the head after the manner of my ancestors and forefathers." On the day following the funeral, the bereaved family distribute rice to all the Badagas of the hamlet, and all the near relations of the deceased go to the burning ground, taking with them two new pots. The fire is extinguished, and the fragments of the bones are collected. A tray is made of the fronds of the bracken fern (*Pteris aquilina*) covered with a cloth, on which the bones are placed together with culms of *Cynodon* grass and ghī. The Badagas of the hamlet who are younger than the deceased salute the bones by touching them, and a few men, including the chief mourner, hold the tray, and convey it to the bone pit, which every hamlet possesses. Into it the bones are thrown, while an elder repeats the words "Become united with the line of your relations, with your clan, and with the big people," or "May the young and old who have died, may all those who have died from time immemorial up to the present time, mingle in one." When the pit has been closed up, all return to the spot where the body was burnt, and, clearing a space, make a puddle, round which they stand, and throw into it a handful of korali (*Setaria italica*), uttering the words "May deaths cease; may evils cease; may good prevail in the village; in virtue of the good deeds of the ancestors and forefathers, may this one mingle with them." This ceremony concluded, they repair to a stream, where a member of the bereaved family shaves a Toreya partially or completely. Some take a razor, and, after removing a patch of hair, pass the Toreya on to a barber. All the agnates are then shaved by a Badaga or a barber. The chief mourner then prostrates himself on the ground, and is blessed by all. He and the Toreya then proceed to the house of the deceased. Taking a three-pronged twig of *Rhodomyrtus tomentosus*, and placing a minige (*Argyreia*, sp.) leaf on the prongs, he thrusts it into a rubbish heap near the house. He then places a small quantity of sāmai grain (which is called street food) on the leaf, and, after sprinkling it thrice with water, goes away. The final death ceremonies are carried out on a Sunday following the day of death.

The funeral rites of the Udaya (Lingayat) sub-division of the Badagas differ in some important details from those of the Badaga sub-division. The buffalo catching, and leading the animal round the corpse are omitted. But a steer and heifer are selected, and branded on the thigh, by means of a hot iron, with the lingam and other emblems. Bedecked with cloths and jewels, they are led to the side of the corpse, and made to stand on a blanket spread on the ground. They are treated as if they were lingams, and pūja is done to them by offering cocoanuts and betel leaves, and throwing flowers over them. Round their necks kankanams (marriage threads) are tied. They are made to turn so as to face away from the corpse, and their tails are placed in the hands thereof. An elder then proceeds with the recitation of the dead person's sins. The Udayas bury their dead in a sitting posture in a cell dug out of the side of the grave, and, like the Irulas, prefer to use a grave in which a previous burial has taken place. At the four corners of the grave they place in the ground a plant of *Leucas aspera*, and pass a cotton thread laterally and diagonally across the grave, leaving out the side opposite the cell. Two men descend into the grave, and deposit the corpse in its resting place with two lighted lamps.

Quite recently (1905) an elaborate Badaga memorial ceremony for ancestors, called manavalai, which takes place at long intervals, was held on the Nīlgiris. I gather from the notes of a native official that an enormous car, called elu kudi tēru (seven-storeyed car) was built of wood and bamboo, and decorated with silk and woollen fabrics, flags, and umbrellas. Inside the ground floor were a cot with a mattress and pillow, and the stem of a plantain tree. The souls of the ancestors are supposed to be reclining on the cot, resting their heads on the pillow, and chewing the plantain, while the umbrellas protect them from the sun and rain. The ear ornaments of all those who have died since the previous ceremony should be placed on the cot. "A Badaga fell and hurt himself during the erection of the car. Whereupon, another Badaga became possessed, and announced that the god was angry because a Kurumba had something to do with the building of the structure. A council meeting was held, and the Kurumba fined twenty-five rupees, which were credited to the god. Sixty-nine petty bazārs and three beer taverns had been opened for the convenience of all classes of people that had assembled. One very old Badaga woman said that she was twelve years old when the first European was carried in a chair by the Todas, and brought up the ghāt to the Nīlgiris from Coimbatore. On Wednesday at 10 A.M. people from the adjoining villages were announced, and the Kota band, with the village people, went forward, greeted them, and brought them to the tower (car). As each man approached it, he removed his turban, stooped over the pillow and laid his head on it, and then went to form a ring for the dance. The dancers wore skirts made of white long-cloth, white and cream silks and satins with border of red and blue trimming, frock dresses, and dressing-gowns, while the coats, blouses, and jackets were of the most gaudy colours of silk, velvet, velveteen, tweed, and home-spun. As each group of people arrived, they went first to the temple door, saluted the god, and went to the basement of the tower to venerate the deceased, and then proceeded to join the ring for the dance, where they danced for an hour, received their supplies of rice, etc., and cleared off. Thursday and Friday were the grandest days. Nearly three thousand females and six thousand males assembled on Thursday. To crown all the confusion, there appeared nearly a thousand Badagas armed with new mamoties (spades). They came on dancing from some distance, rushed into the crowd, and danced round the tower. These Badagas belonged to the gang of public works, local fund, and municipal maistries. On the last day a sheep was slaughtered in honour of the deity. The musicians throughout the festivities were Kotas and Kurumbas. The dancing of men of three score showed that they danced to music, and the stepping was admirable, while the dancing of young men did not show that they had any idea of dancing, or either taste or knowledge of music. They were merely skipping and jumping. This shows that the old art of the Badaga dance is fast decaying." The cot is eventually burnt at the burning-ground, as if it contained a corpse.

The Urālis of the Coimbatore hills are familiar with the Badagas, who have a settlement not many miles distant, and their death ceremonies are, to some extent, copied from those of the Badagas. As soon as a member of the tribe dies, the corpse is anointed, washed, and dressed in new clothes and a turban. On the face three silver coins are stuck, viz.:—a rupee on the forehead, and a quarter rupee outside each eye. When all have assembled for the funeral, the corpse is brought out and placed within a car (tēru) of six storeys, made of bamboo and sticks, covered with coloured cloths and flags, and having at the top a kalasa (brass vessel) and umbrella. To the accompaniment of a band a dance takes place around the car, and the procession then moves on to the burial ground, where a cow-buffalo is brought near the car, and a little milk drawn, and poured three times into the mouth of the corpse. A cow and one or two calves are then taken round the car, and the calves presented to the sister of the deceased. The car is broken up, after the decorations have been stripped off. The corpse

26

is buried either on the spot, or taken away to distant Nīrgundi, and buried there. On the eighth day after the funeral or return from Nīrgundi, the eldest son of the deceased has his head shaved, and, together with his brother's wife, fasts. If the funeral has been at Nīrgundi, the son, accompanied by his relations, proceeds thither after tying some cooked rice in a cloth. On arrival he offers this to all the memorial stones in the burial ground (goppamanē), and erects a stone, which he has brought with him, in memory of the deceased. He then anoints all the stones with ghī, which is contained in a green bamboo measure. He next collects the rice, which has been offered, and one of the party, becoming inspired, gives vent to oracular declarations as to the season's prospects, the future of the bereaved family, etc. The collected rice is regarded as sacred, and is partaken of by all. Each sept has its own goppamanē, which is a rectangular space with mud walls on three sides. In cases in which the corpse has been buried close to the village, the grave is marked by a pile of stones. Two or three years afterwards the body is exhumed, and the bones are collected, and placed in front of the house of the deceased. All the relations weep, and the son conveys the bones to Nīrgundi, where he buries them. On the eighth day he revisits the spot, and erects a stone with due ceremony.

On the twelfth day after the death of a Bant in South Canara, a barber, washerman, and carpenter, erect a lofty structure made of bamboo and areca palm, on the spot where the corpse was burnt. The structure must be supported on an odd number of posts, and possess an odd number of tiers. It is dressed with red, white, and black cloths, fruits, tender cocoanuts, sugar-cane, mango leaves, etc., and a fence is set up round it. The sons and nephews of the dead person bring three balls of rice (pinda) coloured with turmeric, raw rice, green plantain fruit, pumpkin and cocoanut on trays, and go thrice round the structure, carrying the trays on their heads. They then deposit the various articles within the structure, and a little of the raw rice is thrown into it. One of the castemen present then sprinkles water contained in a mango leaf over their hands, and they bathe, and return home, where a further ceremonial is carried out.

On the eleventh or thirteenth day after a death among the Baidyas (Billavas) of South Canara, a ceremony called bojja is performed. Its celebration is essential, as the dead are believed to fast until it has been carried out. For this ceremony the near relations of the deceased come in a body in procession, accompanied by music, and bringing loads of provisions. Sometimes devil-dancers don their professional costume, and accompany the procession. Early in the morning a few handfuls of earth from the burial place are burnt with various kinds of grain, as a symbol of cremation, and the ashes are deposited in the garden of the house of the deceased. Over them a barber erects a lofty bamboo structure, called doope, composed of five, seven, or nine conical tiers, and topped with a wooden dome covered with gilt paper. The doope is decorated with coloured cloths. Within the house, where the females have to sit, a similar structure, but on a smaller scale, is set up. When the guests have arrived, uncooked rice mixed with saffron paste, and rice cakes are handed to them by the female mourners, and are carried on a palanquin brought by the barber in procession, with music, to the doope, in the lowest tier whereof they are deposited. The ghost of the dead person is believed to be propitiated thereby, and to be admitted to the ghost fraternity by the ancestors.* By the Baidyas a further quaint ceremony called kale deppuni (driving the ghost) is carried out. The ghost of a dead person is believed to haunt the house until the fifth day. Before retiring to bed on the evening of this day, the inmates sprinkle the portico with ashes from the spot where the deceased breathed his last, and take great care to abstain from walking thereon, or approaching the sprinkled spot, lest the ghost should strike them. Early next morning they examine the ashes, to see if the marks of the cloven feet of the ghost are left thereon. If the marks are clear, it is a sign that the ghost has departed; otherwise a magician is called in to drive it out. My informant naively remarks that, when he has examined the marks which are left on the ashes, they were those of the family cat.

The origin of the funeral cars, which play a conspicuous part in the death ceremonies of the Badagas, Kotas, Urālis, Okkiliyans, Bants, Baidyas, and others, must, I imagine, be sought for in the vimānam or bamboo chair decorated with plantain stems, coloured cloths, and flags, which has already (p. 139) been referred to in the account of the Lingayat death ceremonies.

* M. Venkatappa, M.S.

"The Eastern Kullans sometimes, after a corpse has been buried, bring a bier to the grave. The brother of the widow of the deceased digs up the body, removes the skull, which he washes, and smears with sandalwood powder and spices. This man, whose relation to the deceased is an indication of the matriarchate, is seated on the bier, and, holding the skull in his hands, is carried to a shed erected in front of the dead man's house. The skull is set down, and all the relations mourn over it till the next day at noon. The following twenty-four hours are given over to drunken revelry. Then the brother-in-law is again seated on the bier, skull in hand, and is carried back to the grave. The son, or heir of the deceased, then burns the skull, and breaks an earthen pot, apparently with the object of releasing the ghost."*

"The Coorgs," Mr. A.Rea writes, † "bury the corpses of women and boys under sixteen years of age, while those of men are burnt. One male and one female of every house in the village must attend the funeral. A light is lit in the half of a broken cocoanut, the oil being clarified butter. This is set on a quantity of rice in a dish, which is placed close by the corpse. There is also a dish with cocoa-milk, saffron, rice and water, into which each of the villagers who attend the rites puts some money, after they have poured some water into the mouth of the corpse. This collection goes towards the funeral expenses. The dead is honoured by the firing of guns. At the burial ground, all the villagers moisten the lips of the corpse

* W. Crooke. *Fide* Folk-lore, V, 86.

† Arch. Survey, Madras. Ann. Report, 1901–02.

with a drop or two of water, and put a coin in a dish placed for the purpose. On the twenty-eighth day after death all the villagers are invited to a feast." As soon as a Malaiāli of the Javādi hills dies, guns are fired off at short intervals, till the burial is over. A few bundles of tobacco are buried with the dead body.* As soon as a Savara dies, a gun is fired off at the door, to frighten away the kulba (spirit). The dead body is washed and carried away to the family cremation ground, where it is burned. Every thing a man has—his bows and arrows, tangi (axe), dagger, necklaces, cloths, rice, etc.—are burnt with his body.† Among the jungle Chenchus, if an old man dies, leaving no children or other near relations, his bows and arrows, axe, clothing, etc., are buried with him.

Of the death ceremonies among the Nāyars of Malabar, the following detailed account is given by Mr. F. Fawcett.‡ "When the dying person is about to embark for that bourne from which no traveller returns, and the breath is about to leave his body, the members of the household, and all friends who may be present, one by one, pour a little water, a few drops from a tiny cup made of a leaf or two of the tulsi (*Ocimum*) plant, into his mouth, holding in the hand a piece of gold or a gold ring; the idea being that the water should touch gold ere it enters the mouth of the person who is dying. If the taravād (or tarwad) is rich enough to afford it, a small gold coin (a Rāsi fanam, if one can be procured) is

* Manual of the North Arcot district.

† Madras Census Report, 1891.

‡ Madras Mus. Bull., III, 3, 1901.

placed in the mouth, and the lips are closed. As soon as death has taken place, the corpse is removed from the cot or bed, and carried to the vatakkini (a room in the northern end of the house), where it is placed on long plantain leaves spread out on the floor; and while it is in the room, whether by day or by night, a lamp is kept burning, and one member of the taravād holds the head in his lap, and another the feet in the same way; and here the neighbours come to take a farewell look at the dead. As the Malayālis believe that disposal of a corpse by cremation or burial as soon as possible after death is conducive to the happiness of the spirit of the departed, no time is lost in setting about the funeral. The bodies of senior members of a taravād, male or female, are burned; those of children under two are buried; so too are the bodies of all persons who have died of cholera or small-pox.* When preparations for the funeral have been made, the corpse is removed to the natumuttam or central yard of the house if there is one (there always is in the larger houses), and, if there is not, is taken to the front yard, where it is again laid on plantain leaves. It is washed and anointed, the usual marks are made with sandalwood paste and ashes as in life, and it is neatly clothed. There is then done what is called the pota-vekkuka ceremony, or placing new cotton cloths (kōti mundu) over the corpse by the senior member of the deceased's taravād followed by all the other members, also sons-in-law and daughters-in-law, and all relatives.

* It is the same among the Khonds of Ganjam.

These cloths are used for tying up the corpse, when being taken to the place of burial or cremation. In some parts of Malabar the corpse is carried on a bier made of fresh bamboos, tied up in these cloths, while in others it is carried, well covered in the cloths, by hand. In either case it is carried by the relatives. Before the corpse is removed, there is done another ceremony called pāra virakkuka (filling up pāras—a pāra is a measure nearly as big as a gallon). All adult male members of the taravād take part in it under the direction of a man of the Atikkurissi clan, who occupies the position of director of the ceremonies during the next fifteen days, receiving as his perquisite all the rice and other offerings made to the deceased's spirit. It consists in filling up three pāra measures with paddy, and one edangāli ($\frac{1}{10}$ of a pāra) with raw rice. These offerings of paddy and rice are placed very near the corpse, together with a burning lamp of the kind commonly used in Malabar, called nela villāku.* If the taravād is rich enough to afford one, a silk cloth is placed over the corpse before removal for cremation. As much fuel as is necessary having been got ready at the place of cremation, a small pit about the size of the corpse is dug, and across this are placed three long stumps of a plantain tree, one at each end, one in the middle, on which as a foundation the pyre is laid. The whole, or at least a part of the wood used should be that of the mango tree. As the corpse is being removed to the pyre, the senior

* In this connection it is interesting to note that, amongst many Tamil castes, it is the custom to place a measure filled with paddy, and a lamp, at the head of the corpse, and to take them round it.

Anandravan * who is next in age (junior) to the deceased, tears from one of the new cloths laid on the corpse a piece sufficient to go round his waist, ties it round his waist, and holds in his hand, or tucks into his cloth at the waist a piece of iron, generally a long key. This individual is throughout chief among the offerers of pindam (balls of rice) to the deceased. The corpse is laid on the bier, with the head to the south, with the fuel laid over it, and a little camphor, sandalwood and ghī, if these things are within the means of the taravād. Here must be stated the invariable rule that no member of the taravād, male or female, who is older than the deceased shall take any part whatever in the ceremony, or in any subsequent ceremony following on the cremation or burial. All adult males junior to the deceased should be present when the pyre is lighted. The deceased's younger brother, or, if there is none surviving, his nephew (his sister's eldest son), sets fire to the pyre at the head of the corpse. If the deceased left a son, this son sets fire at the same time to the pyre at the feet of the corpse. In the case of the deceased being a woman, her son sets fire to the pyre; failing a son, the next junior in age to her has the right to do it. It is a matter of great importance that the whole pyre burns at once. The greatest care is taken that it burns as a whole, consuming every part of the corpse. While the corpse is being consumed, all the members of the deceased's taravād who carried it to the

* The eldest male member of the Malabar taravād is called the Kāranavan. All male members, brothers, nephews and so on, who are junior to him, are called Anandravans of the taravād.

pyre go and bathe in a tank (there is always one in the compound or garden around every Nāyar's house). The eldest, he who bears the piece of torn cloth and the piece of iron (the key), carries an earthen pot of water, and all return together to the place of cremation. It should be said that, on the news of a death, the neighbours assemble, assisting in digging the grave, preparing the pyre, and so on, and, while the members of the taravād go and bathe, they remain near the corpse. By the time the relatives return it is almost consumed by the fire, and the senior Anandravan carries the pot of water thrice round the pyre, letting the water leak out by making holes in the pot as he walks round. On completing the third round, he dashes the pot on the ground close by where the head of the dead had been placed. A small image of the deceased is then made out of raw rice representing the deceased, and to this image a few grains of rice and gingelly seeds are offered. When this has been done, the relatives go home and the neighbours depart, bathing before entering their houses. When the cremation has been done by night, the duty of sēshakriya (making offerings to the deceased's spirit) must be begun the next day between 10 and 11 A.M., and is done on seven consecutive days. In any case the time for this ceremony is after 10 and before 11, and it continues for seven days. It is performed as follows. All male members of the taravād younger than the deceased go together to a tank and bathe, *i.e.*, they souse themselves in the water, and return to the house. The eldest of them, the man who tore off the strip of cloth from the corpse, has with him the same strip of cloth and the piece of iron, and all assemble in the central court-yard of the house, where there has been placed ready by an enangan, some rice which has been half boiled, a few grains of gingelly, a few leaves of the cherūla (*Ærua lanata*) some curds, a smaller measure of paddy, and a smaller measure of raw rice. These are placed in the north-east corner with a lamp of the ordinary Malabar pattern. A piece of palmyra leaf, about a foot or so in length and the width of a finger, is taken, and one end of it knotted. The knotted end is placed in the ground, and the long end is left sticking up. This represents the deceased. The rice and other things are offered to this. The belief concerning this piece of palmyra leaf is explained thus. There are in the human body ten humours:--Vāyūs; Prānan; Apānan; Samānan; Udānan; Vyānan; Nāgan; Kūrman; Krikalan; Dēvadattan; Dhananjayan. These are called Dasavāyu, *i.e.*, ten airs. When cremation was done for the first time, all these, excepting the last, were destroyed by the fire. The last one flew up, and settled on a palmyra leaf. Its existence was discovered by some Brāhman sages, who, by means of mantrams, forced it down to a piece of palmyra leaf on the earth. So it is thought that by making offerings to this dhananjayan leaf for seven days, the spirit of the deceased will be mollified, should he have any anger to vent on the living members of the taravād. The place where the piece of leaf is to be fixed has been carefully cleaned, and the leaf is fixed in the centre of this prepared surface. The offerings made to it go direct to the spirit of the deceased, and the peace of the taravād is ensured. The men who have bathed and returned have brought with them, plucked on their way back to the house, some grass (karuka pulla). They kneel in front of the piece of palmyra. with the right knee on the ground. Some of the grass is spread on the ground near the piece of leaf, and rings made with it are placed on the ring finger of the right hand by each one present. The first offerings consist of water, sandalwood paste, and leaves of the cherūla, the eldest of the Anandravans leading the way. Boys need not go through the actual performance of offerings; it suffices for them to touch the eldest as he is making his offerings. The half-boiled rice is made into balls (pindams), and each one present takes one of these in his right hand, and places it on the grass near the piece of palmyra leaf. Some gingelly seeds are put into the curd, which is poured so as to make three rings round the pindams. It is poured out of a small cup made with the leaf on which the half-boiled rice had been placed. It should not be poured from any other kind of vessel. The whole is then covered with this same plantain leaf, a lighted wick is waved, and some milk is put under the leaf. It is undisturbed for some moments, and the leaf is tapped gently with the back of the fingers of the right hand. The leaf is then removed, and torn in two at its midrib, one piece being placed on either side of the pindams. The ceremony is then over for the day. The performers rise, and remove the wet clothing they have been wearing. The eldest of the Anandravans should, it was omitted to mention, be kept somewhat separated from the other Anandravans while in the courtyard, and before the corpse is removed for cremation; a son-in-law or a daughter-in-law, or some such kind of relation remaining, as it were, between him and them. He has had the piece of cloth torn from the covering of the corpse tied round his waist, and he has had the piece of iron in the folds of his cloth, or stuck in his waist during the ceremony which has just been described. Now, when it has been completed, he ties the piece of cloth to the pillar of the house nearest to the piece of palmyra leaf which has been stuck in the ground, and puts the piece of iron in a safe place. The piece of palmyra leaf is covered with a basket. It is uncovered every day for seven days at the same hour, while the same ceremony is repeated. The balls of rice are removed by women and girls of the taravād who are junior to the deceased. They place them in the bell-metal vessel, in which the rice was boiled. The senior places the vessel on her head, and leads the way to a tank, on the banks of which the rice is thrown. It is hoped that crows will come and eat it; for, if they do, the impression is received that the deceased's spirit is pleased with the offering; but, if somehow it is thought that the crows will not come and eat it, the rice is thrown into the tank. Dogs are not to be allowed to eat it. The women bathe after the rice has been thrown away. When the ceremony which has been described has been performed for the seventh time, *i.e.*, on the seventh day after death, the piece of palmyra leaf is removed from the ground, and thrown on the ashes of the deceased at the place of cremation. During these seven days, no member of the taravād goes to any other house. The house of the dead, and all its inmates are under pollution. No outsider enters it but under ban of pollution, which is, however, removable by bathing. A visitor entering the house of the dead during these seven days must bathe before he can enter his own house. During these seven days, the Kāranavan of the family receives visits of condolence from relatives and friends to whom he is "at home" on Monday, Wednesday or Saturday. They sit and chat, chew betel and go home, bathing ere they enter their houses. It is said that, in some parts of Malabar, the visitors bring with them small presents in money or kind, to help the Kāranavan through the expenditure to which the funeral rites necessarily put him. To hark back a little, it must not be omitted that on the third day after the death, all those who are related by marriage to the taravād of the deceased combine, and give a good feast to the inmates of the house and to the neighbours, who are invited, one man or one woman from each house. The person so invited is expected to come. This feast is called patni karigi. On the seventh day a return feast will be given by the taravād of the deceased to all relatives and neighbours. Between the seventh and fourteenth day after death no ceremony is observed; but the members of the taravād remain under death pollution, and then on the fourteenth day comes the sanchayanam. It is the disposal of the calcined remains; the ashes of the deceased. The male members of the taravād go to the place of cremation, and, picking up the pieces of unburnt bones which they find there, place these in an earthen pot which has been sun-dried (not burnt by fire in the usual way), cover up the mouth of this pot with a piece of new cloth, and, all following the eldest who carries it, proceed to the nearest river (it must be running water), which receives the remains of the dead. The men then bathe, and return home. In some parts of Malabar the bones are collected on the seventh day, but it is not orthodox to do so. Better by far than taking the remains to the nearest river is it to take them to some specially sacred place, Benares, Gāya, Ramēsvaram, or even to some place of sanctity much nearer home, as to Tirunelli in Wynād, and there dispose of them in the same manner. The bones or ashes of any one having been taken to Gāya and there deposited in the river, the survivors of the taravād have no need to continue the annual ceremony for that person. This is called ashta-gāya srādh. It puts an end to the need for all earthly ceremonial. It is believed that the collection and careful disposal of the ashes of the dead gives peace to his spirit, and, what is more important, the pacified spirit will not thereafter injure the living members of the taravād, cause miscarriage to the women, possess the men (as with an evil spirit), and so on. On the fifteenth day after death is the purificatory ceremony. Until this has been done, any one touched by any member of the taravād should bathe before he enters his house, or partakes of any food. A man of the Athikkurisī clan officiates. He sprinkles milk oil, in which some gingelly seeds have been put, over the persons of those under pollution. This sprinkling, and the bath which follows it, remove the death pollution. The purifier receives a fixed remuneration for his offices on this occasion, as well as when there is a birth in the taravād. In the case of death of a senior member of a taravād, well-to-do and reckoned as of some importance, there is the feast called pinda atiyantaram on the sixteenth day after death, given to the neighbours and friends. The word neighbours, as used here, does not mean those who live close by, but, owing to the custom of Malabar under which each house is in its own paramba (garden or enclosure) which may be a large one, those of the caste living within a considerable area round about. I am not sure whether in connection with these ceremonies there is mutual assistance in preparation for the funeral; or whether there is any recognized obligation between members of the same amsham, dēsam, or tara; or whether this kind of mutual obligation obtains generally between any taravād and those of the caste round about, irrespective of boundaries. With the observance of the pinda atiyantaram or feast of pindams, there is involved the dīkṣha, or leaving the entire body unshaved for forty-one days, or for a year. There is no variable limit between forty-one days or a year. Forty-one days is permissible as the period for the dīkṣha, but a year is correct. The forty-one day period is the rule in North Malabar.

"I have seen many who were under the dīkṣha for a year. He who lets his hair grow may be a son or nephew of the deceased. One member only of the taravād bears the mark of mourning by his growth of hair, remarkable enough in Malabar where every one as a rule, excepting the Māppila Muhammadans (and they shave their heads), shaves his face, head (except the patch on the crown) chest and arms, or at any rate his wrists. He who is under the dīkṣha offers half-boiled rice and gingelly seeds to the spirit of the deceased every morning after his bath; and he is under restriction from women, from alcoholic drinks, and from chewing betel, also tobacco. When the dīkṣha is observed, the ashes of the dead are not deposited as described already (in the sun-dried vessel) until its last day—the forty-first or a year after death. When it is carried on for a year there is observed every month a ceremony called bali. It is noteworthy that, in this monthly ceremony and for the conclusion of the dīkṣha, it is not the thirtieth or three hundred and sixty-fifth day which marks the date for the ceremonies, but it is the day (of the month) of the star which was presiding when the deceased met his death: the returning day on which the star presides.* For the bali, a man of the Elāyatu caste officiates. The Elāyatus are priests for the Nāyars. They wear the Brāhman's thread, but they are not Brāhmans. They are not permitted to study the Vēdas, but to the Nāyars they stand in the place of the ordinary purōhit. The officiating Elāyatu prepares the rice for the bali, when the deceased, represented by karuka grass, is offered boiled rice, curds, gingelly seeds and some other things. The Elāyatu

* All caste Hindus who perform the srādh ceremony calculate the day of death, not by the day of the month, but by the thithis (day after the full or new moon).

should be paid a rupee for his services, which are considered necessary even when the man under dīkṣha himself is familiar with the required ceremonial. The last day of the dīkṣha is one of festivity. After the bali the man under dīkṣha is shaved. All this over, the only thing to be done for the deceased is the annual srādh or yearly funeral commemorative rite. Rice balls are made, and given to crows. Clapping of hands announces to these birds that the rice is being thrown for them, and, should they come at once and eat it, it is obvious that the spirit of the deceased is pleased with the offering, and is not likely to be troublesome. But, on the other hand, should they not come and eat, it is evident that the spirit is displeased, and the taravād had better look out. The spirits of those who have committed suicide, or met death by any violent means, are always particularly vicious and troublesome to the taravād, their spirit possessing and rendering miserable some unfortunate member of it. Unless pacified, they will ruin the taravād, so Brāhman priests are called in, and appease them by means of tilahōmam, a rite in which sacrificial fire is raised, and ghī, gingelly, and other things are offered through it."

Among the Tiyans of Malabar, on the morning of the third day the kurup, or caste barber, adopts measures to entice the spirit of the deceased out of the room in which the deceased breathed his last. This is done by the nearest relative bringing into the room a steaming pot of savoury funeral rice. It is immediately removed, and the spirit, after three days' fasting, is understood to greedily follow the odour of the tempting food. The **kurup** at once closes the door, and shuts out the spirit.*

After the cremation of an Ambattan of Travancore, a rope is held by two of the relations between the cremated body and the **karta** (chief mourner), and is cut in two, as if to indicate that all connection between the **karta** and the deceased has ceased. This is called bandham aruppu (severing of connection).†

The Ambalakārans employ Brāhman purōhits and wear the sacred thread at funerals, and perform srādh. Yet they eat mutton, pork and fowls, and drink alcohol, and allow the marriage of widows and divorced women. A curious custom among the Nānchināt and other Vellālas is that, for their funeral ceremonies, the head of the chief mourner is shaved clean, while, in the case of other castes, his hair is kept sacred from the barber's hand for a variable period. He wears the Brāhmanical thread during the period of pollution.‡ The Bhatrāzus, who were formerly bards and panegyrists in the Telugu country, employ Brāhman priests for their marriages, but Jangams and Sātānis for funerals, and follow the lower Purānic, instead of the higher Vēdic ritual.§

A curious mode of carrying the dead among the Namadari or Vaishnavite Nagarthas of Mysore is that the corpse is rolled up in a blanket, and carried by its four corners to the burial-ground. In like manner, the corpse of an unmarried Yerukala man is carried to the burial-ground, not on a bier, but wrapped up in a mat or cloth.

* Malabar Manual.

† Travancore Census Report, 1901.

‡ Travancore Census Report, 1901.

§ Madras Census Reprt, 1901.

On the last day of the death rites, a new cloth is purchased, and on it a human figure, representing the deceased, is drawn. Pumpkins, onions, brinjals, pork, and fowls are spread on castor-oil leaves, and offered to the deceased. By some Oddes a corpse is carried to the burial-place by four men on a dhupati (cloth). The corpse may not be washed in the house, but is bathed and decorated *en route* to the graveyard. A widower cuts through his waist-string on the peddhadinam ceremony for his deceased wife.

The nomad Kuravans, on the third day after the funeral, offer toddy and pork to the spirit of the deceased.*

A ceremonial rite, called mayanakollai, or robbery in the smasānam or mayanam (burning-ground), forms part of the festival celebrated by the Sembadavan fishermen on a new-moon day in honour of the goddess Ankalamma. Its origin is based on the following legend. One Vallāla Māharāja, by severe penance and austerity, secured a boon, whereby to beget a child capable of destroying everything in the universe. Learning this, the Dēvas hurried to the three Murtis, Brāhma, Vishnu, and Sīva. Sīva placed a curse on the Rāja, so that his wife should not conceive. After some years, however, the Rāni became pregnant, but still no child was born. Finally, Ankalamma, a Sembadavan woman married to the god Sīva, came to the Rāja's territory disguised as a midwife. Hearing of her arrival, Vallāla Rāja sent for her, and asked her to assist the Rāni. This the mock midwife promised to do, on condition that no male should

* Madras Census Report, 1901.

Plate XII.

Şembadavan Māyana Kollai.

be allowed to enter the precincts of the building, in which the Rāni was to be delivered. Securing this condition, Ankalamma went to the Rāni, and assumed her real form. The Rāni thereon fainted, and Ankalamma tore open her abdomen and destroyed the child. Simultaneously, her son Vīrabhadra entered the palace, and killed Vallāla Rāja. The whole town was then sacked, and it was converted into a burning-ground. In commemoration of this event, the festival is celebrated. On the last day, or in the afternoon if it lasts only for a single day, the god and goddess are carried in procession to the burning-ground. Two people dress up to represent Vīrabhadra and Ankalamma, and a boy, disguised as Katteri (a devil) accompanies them. Vīrabhadra carries in one hand a long sword with a lime-fruit stuck on the point, and in the other the head of Vallāla Rāja. Ankalamma, in like manner, carries a scimitar with a lime on the point, and a new winnow containing the well-washed and cleaned viscera of a sheep. A portion of the intestines is kept in the mouth of the mock goddess (plate XII) till the return of the god and goddess, at the end of ten or twelve hours, to the village temple. When the burning-ground is reached, a plantain leaf is placed on the recent ashes of a corpse, or on the bare ground, where a body has once been cremated. On the leaf are set a small quantity of mutton, cooked rice, dried fish, cakes, pulses, a piece of a human bone, and a bottle of arrack (liquor). The men disguised as Vīrabhadra and Ankalamma, accompanied by the Katteri, go thrice round the plantain leaf, which is then lifted, and thrown high into the air. The crowd then scramble for a share of the food-stuffs, and for some minutes there is a regular melée.

My Assistant, Mr. Govindan, was present at the festival called Smasānakollai, held at Walajapet in honour of Ankamma, the goddess of Malayanūr, on the day following Sīvarātri. A huge figure, representing the goddess, was made at the burning-ground out of the ashes of burnt bodies mixed with water, the eyes being made of two hens' eggs painted black in the centre to represent the pupils. It was covered with a yellow cloth, and a sweet-smelling powder (kadambam) was sprinkled over it. The following articles, which are required by a married woman, were placed on it—a comb, a pot containing colour-powder, glass bangles, rolls of palm-leaf for dilating the ear-lobes, and a string of black beads. Devotees presented as offerings limes, plantains, toddy, arrack, sugar-cane, and various kinds of cooked grains and other eatables. About midday the goddess was taken in procession from her shrine to the burning-ground, and placed in front of the figure. The pūjāri (a fisherman), who wore a special dress for the occasion, walked in front of the idol, carrying in one hand a brass cup representing the skull which Sīva carried in his hand, and in the other a piece of human skull-bone, which he bit and chewed as the procession moved onwards. When the burning-ground was reached, he performed pūja by breaking a cocoanut, and going round the figure with burning camphor in his hand. Goats and fowls were sacrificed. A woman, possessed by a devil, seated herself at the feet of the figure, and became wild and agitated. The pūja completed, the assembled multitude fell on the figure, and carried off whatever they could grab of the articles placed on it, which are believed to possess healing and other virtues. They also smeared their bodies with the ashes. The pūjāri, and some of the devotees, then became possessed, and ran about the burning-ground, seizing and eating partly burnt bones. Tradition runs to the effect that, in olden times, they used to eat even the dead bodies, if they came across any, and the people are so afraid of their doing this that, if a death should occur, the corpse is not taken to the burning-ground till the festival is over. "In some cases," Herbert Spencer writes,* "parts of the dead are swallowed by the living, who seek thus to inspire themselves with the good qualities of the dead; and we saw that the dead are supposed to be honoured by this act."

The celebration of the smasāna or mayanakollai at Malayanūr is thus described by Mr. K. Rangachari. The village of Malayanūr is famous for its Ankalamma temple, and during the festival, which takes place immediately after the Sīvarātri, some thousands of people congregate at the temple, which is near the burning-ground. In front of the stone idol is a large ant-hill, on which two copper idols are placed, and a brass vessel, called korakkūdai, is placed at the base of the hill, to receive the various votive offerings. Early in the day

* Principles of Sociology.

the pūjāri (a Sembadavan fisherman) goes to a tank, and brings a decorated pot, called pūngkaragam, to the temple. Offerings are made to a new pot; and, after a sheep has been sacrificed, the pot is filled with water, and carried on the head of a pūjāri, who shows signs of possession by the deity, through the streets of the village to the temple, dancing wildly, and never touching the pot with his hands. It is believed that the pot remains on the head, without falling, through the influence of the goddess. When the temple is reached, another pūjāri takes up a framework, to which are tied a head made of rice flour, with three faces coloured white, black, and red, representing the head of Brāhma which was cut off by Sīva, and a pot with three faces on it. The eyes of the flour figure are represented by hen's eggs. The pot is placed beneath the head. Carrying the framework, and accompanied by music, the pūjāri goes in procession to the burning-ground, and, after offerings of a sheep, arrack, betel and fruits have been made to the head of Brāhma, it is thrown away. Close to the spot where corpses are burnt, the pūjāris place on the ground five conical heaps representing Ganēsa, made of the ashes of a corpse. To these are offered the various articles brought by those who have made vows, which include cooked pulses, bangles, betel, parts of the human body modelled in rice flour, etc. The offerings are piled up in a heap, which is said to reach ten or twelve feet in height. Soon afterwards, the people assembled fall on the heap, and carry off whatever they can secure. Hundreds of persons are said to become possessed, eat the ashes of the corpses, and bite any human bones, which they may come across. The ashes and earth are much prized, as they are supposed to drive away evil spirits, and secure offspring to barren women. Some persons make a vow that they will disguise themselves as Sīva, for which purpose they smear their faces with ashes, put on a cap decorated with feathers of the crow, egret, and peacock, and carry in one hand a brass vessel called Brāhma kapalam. Round their waist they tie a number of strings, to which are attached rags and feathers. Instead of the cap, Paraiyans and Valluvans wear a crown. The brass vessel, cap, and strings are said to be kept by the pūjāris, and hired out for a rupee or two per head. The festival is reputed to be based on the following legend. Sīva and Brāhma had the same number of faces. During the swayamvaram, Parvati, the wife of Sīva, found it difficult to recognise her husband, so Sīva cut off Brāhma's head. The head stuck on to Sīva's hand, and he could not get rid of it. To get rid of the skull, and throw off the crime of the murder, Sīva wandered far and wide, and came to the burning-ground at Malayanūr, where various Bhūthas were busy eating the remains of corpses. Parvati also arrived there, and failed to recognise Sīva. Thereon the skull laughed, and fell to the ground. The Bhūthas were so delighted that they put various kinds of herbs into a big vessel, and made out of them a sweet liquor, by drinking which Sīva was absolved from his crime. For this reason, arrack is offered to him at the festival.

An unpleasant reflection is that the Vannāns, or washermen, add to their income by hiring out the cloths of their customers for funeral parties, who lay them on the ground before the pall-bearers, so that they may not step upon the ground.* On one occasion a party of Europeans, when out shooting near the village of a hill-tribe, met a funeral procession on its way to the burial-ground. The bier was draped in many folds of clean cloth, which one of the party recognised by the initials as one of his bed-sheets. Another identified as his sheet the cloth on which the corpse was lying. He cut off the corner with the initial, and a few days later the sheet was returned by the dhobi (washerman) who pretended ignorance of the mutilation, and gave as an explanation that it must have been done, in his absence, by one of his assistants.

The Boras, or Muhammadan converts from Bombay, who in Madras have their own high-priest and mosque, are said to have a custom that, when one of their community dies, the high-priest writes a note to the Archangels Michael, Israel, and Gabriel, asking them to take care of him in Paradise, and the note is placed in the coffin.†

The bones of a dead person are consigned by Panta Reddis of the Tamil districts by parcel-post to a paid agent at Benares, and thrown into the Ganges.

Among various Hindu castes it is the custom, if a death occurs on an inauspicious day, to remove the

* Manual of the North Arcot district.

† Madras Census Report, 1901.

corpse from the house not through the door, but through a temporary hole made in the wall.

To bring down rain, Brāhmans, and these non-Brāhmans who copy their ceremonial rites, have their Varūna japam, or prayers to Varūna. Some of the lower classes, instead of addressing their prayers to the rain-god Varūna, try to induce a spirit or dēvata named Kodumpāvi (wicked one) to send her paramour Sukra to the affected area. The belief seems to be that Sukra goes away to his concubine for about six months, and, if he does not then return, drought ensues. The ceremony consists in making a huge figure of Kodumpāvi in clay, which is placed on a cart, and dragged through the streets for seven to ten days. On the last day, the final death ceremonies of the figure are celebrated. It is disfigured, especially in those parts which are usually concealed. Vettiyans (Paraiyan grave-diggers), who have been shaved, accompany the figure, and perform the funeral ceremonies. This procedure is believed to put Kodumpāvi to shame, and to get her to induce Sukra to return, and stay the drought.

In conclusion I may make a brief reference to death songs, for the following note on which I am indebted to Mr. Hayavadana Rao. These songs are sung over the bodies of dead relations by most castes in Southern India, including Brāhmans. They are taught, together with festival and other songs, to little girls, and are sung by females, not only immediately after the death of a relation, but also once a fortnight or more frequently until the first annual ceremony is performed. A woman should know at least one song about her grandparents, parents, brothers and sisters, husband, children, and father and mother-in-law. On the occurrence of a death in a family, all the members of the household collect at the death-bed, weeping aloud, and embracing each other. Female relations, friends, and neighbours, as they arrive, sit down, and, putting their arms round each others' necks, raise up a cry of lamentation. Their long tresses of hair fall dishevelled to the ground, and they strike their uncovered bosoms with the hands, as they sing the appropriate song. Each song is divided into the following four parts :—

1. Pulambal, or the cry.
2. Mār adippu or breast-beating.
3. Mayir azhivu, or hair separation. The songster runs her fingers through, and disentangles her dishevelled locks.
4. Marupadiyum ninrudukkam, or standing bemoaning. The mourners collect in a circle, and go round and round with their arms on each others' shoulders.

Writing nearly a century ago concerning similar songs among Hindus in Ceylon, Colebrook remarks * that "whether the feelings which these lamentations express have existence in all cases in the hearts of the mourners or otherwise, is not at present the consideration. The observance implies that such feelings are held in high estimation, and the striking resemblance which these lamentations bear to those in the scripture, and in

* Journ. Roy. As. Soc. II.

particular to that over Saul, appealing to the common sympathies which the occasion naturally calls forth, and uttered in short emphatic and unconnected sentences, renders them not the less worthy of observation." The authorship of the songs is attributed to the great Tamil poet Pughalēnthi Pulavar. Born in a village in what is now the Chingleput district, he is said to have become the court poet of the Pāndyan king Varaguna, and to have been part of the dowry of the king's daughter who married a Chola prince. When at the Chola court, he was, at the instigation of a local bard, imprisoned, and, during his confinement, amused himself by composing the death songs, and teaching them to women who passed by on their way to the tank for water.

The following fragmentary examples of the songs are selected from a very large repertoire :—

A.—Song sung by the Wife in Honour of her dead Husband.

1. *The cry.*

My protector, my lord. Oh ! God.
The apple of mine eye. We cannot find
My husband, my lord. Oh ! God.
My wealth we cannot see.
Me, in my fifth year, my lord,
Me, when I was an infant.
In my tenth year, my lord,
In my milk-sucking age.
Thou, beautiful-visaged, garlanded me, * my lord.

* The reference is to the custom of exchanging garlands on the occasion of marriage.

And kept me splendidly.
Thou, graceful-visaged, garlanding me, my lord,
Kept me with great affection.
My sight thou hast plundered, my lord.
Thou hast reached the Lord Protector's feet.
Thou hast destroyed my pleasure, my lord.
Thou hast gone and laid thyself on earth.
With what rare love you took me, my lord.
With what splendour we came in procession.
Making me now the world's laughing-stock, my lord.
Thou hast travelled away to Kylās.*
The majesty of thy bedroom, my lord.
The service under the Pāndya (king).
The golden palace, my lord.
Thy forbearing words.
Thy office and audience hall, my lord.
While crores of persons are come,
While elephants are beautified, my lord,
While thousands of persons are waiting for thee,
Thou, discarding all these, my lord,
Hast travelled away to heaven.

2. *Breast beating.*

Oh! protector; Oh! my lord. Hast
Thou reached Kylās? Oh! the superior, my lord.
Hast thou reached the lord of heaven? Leaving me alone.
Is it just for thee
To run away, making me solitary?
Is it right to jump away? Not separating
Even for a day, thou hast separated thyself from thy wife.
For many days not separating, why hast thou separated thyself.

* Kylas, the abode of Síva, whither the blessed go after death.

From the servant? Leaving me solitary. [law.*
Thou hast gone away somewhere. Oh! my golden brother-in-
Even after thou hast gone, would I survive thee in this
world.
Oh! thou beautiful-visaged, separated from thee could I
With these eyes, Oh! my king, separated from thee, [live?
Could I wander on this earth? Oh! my protector.

3. *Hair separation.*

I have untied the false hair † Oh! my golden brother-in-law.
I have cast down the flower (from my head) on this earth.
I have loosened the string of the hair-knot, Oh! my golden
brother-in-law.
In thy side-room I have pulled off the flower,
The hair-knot that I had combed and worn, Oh! my golden
brother-in-law.
Thou hast wrecked my usual toilet.
In thy ruby-like side-room, Oh! my golden brother-in-law,
It is time that I should dishevel my hair.
On my chāndu ‡ adorned forehead, Oh! my golden brother-
in-law,
Thou hast settled ashes. §
On my chāndu-adorned forehead, Oh! my lord,
Thou hast settled mud.
To me saffron has become rare, Oh! my golden brother-
in-law.
To me marudāni‖ has become bitter.
To me flowers have become rare, Oh! my golden brother-
in-law.

---

* Term by which, in the Tamil country, a wife calls her husband.

† False hair worn by married women.

‡ Chāndu, a round moon-shaped dot made with black paste on the forehead. Widows may not adorn themselves with it.

§ Widows mark their foreheads with the sacred ashes (vibhuthi).

‖ Henna (*Lawsonia alba*) leaves, with which women stain their nails red. Widows are not allowed to do this.

To me my husband's face has become bitter.
Taking out the saffron-stringed tāli,* Oh! my golden brother-in-law.
I stood in thy mansion and mourned.
Rubbing out the kunkunam† dot, Oh! my lord,
I stood in thy fort and mourned.
Born in a family of sisters, Oh! my golden brother-in-law,
I stood in thy ornamented house and mourned.
Bred up in a mansion, Oh! my lord,
I stood in thy house and mourned.
Having lost thy golden head, Oh! my golden brother-in-law.
I have cast off the tāli thread.‡
Having lost thy golden head, Oh! my lord,
I have forgotten the flower.
Is it not by losing my neck jewel, Oh! my golden brother-in-law,
That I have become half-necked? §
Is it not by losing my grass-like tāli, || Oh! my lord,
That I have become dwarf-necked?

4. *Standing bemoaning.*

Oh! my golden brother-in-law; Oh! my lord,
Hast thou reached the golden abode?
Me, thy most precious servant while here, Oh! my golden brother-in-law,
Why hast thou gone to Kylās?
Me, thy most beloved servant while here, Oh! my lord,
Why hast thou gone to the golden abode?
Me, as a husbandless woman, Oh! my golden brother-in-law,
People will backbite me.

---

* The tāli is generally daubed with saffron before it is tied round the neck.

† Anilin powder, with which married women mark their foreheads.

‡ A woman, on the death of her husband, removes her tāli.

§ A term of abuse for a widow.

|| Tāli which has proved as unsubstantial as grass.

Even though I behave with humility, Oh ! my lord,
They will call me the rulerless sinner.
Even though I conduct myself trembling, Oh ! my golden brother-in-law,
They will call me the lordless woman.
For thy palanquin's service, * Oh ! my lord,
If I accompanied thee, it would be no mistake.
Riding upon an elephant, Oh ! my god,
Oh ! my lord, if thou camest to the river bank,
Hearing the elephant bell ringing,
I would light the cooking fire.
Riding a horse, Oh ! my god, Oh ! my lord,
If thou camest to the tank bund,
Hearing the horse-bell ringing,
I would get thy hot bath ready.
We, like milk and water, Oh ! my lord,
Were affectionately bound to each other.
We like milk and water, to be separated, Oh ! my golden brother-in-law,
Is it the decree of lord Siva ?
We, like the small bird for a while, Oh ! my lord,
Building its nest.
We, as husband and wife, Oh ! god.
While we were united together.
For that bull-like Yama † to come, Oh ! lord,
And separate us, is there any right ?
For that Yama, who comes to call thee, Oh ! my golden brother-in-law.
I say that I will give a goat as a sacrifice.
For that Yama, who comes to kill thee, Oh ! my lord,
I say that I will give a cock as a sacrifice.
He, refusing even that, Oh ! my golden brother-in-law,
Wants to plunder thy beautiful head,
Whilst we were enjoying our better days, Oh ! my lord,

* The bier is often constructed in the form of a palanquin.

† Yama, the god of death.

Thou hast reached the feet of Sīva. [brother-in-law.
When we were entering on a life of plenty Oh! my golden
Thou hast reached the feet of Hara.
The children crying, Oh! my lord,
Me, the housewife mourning,
The voice of thy children crying, Oh! god,
Dost thou not hear even a little? [law.
Seeing the faces of thy children, Oh! my golden brother-in-
Wouldst thou not leave that place, and come?

B.—Song of a Mother on the Death of the Child.

Oh! the apple of my eye; Oh! my darling; my blissful paradise.
Oh! the apple of my eye, where hast thou hidden thyself?
Oh! my golden bead; Oh! my eyes;
Oh! my flower, where hast thou hidden thyself?
Oh! gem-like apple of my eye; Oh! my blissful paradise,
I do not know how thou hast gone away.
Even as a capering deer leaps, Oh! the apple of my eye.
Hast thou leaped into the well.
Even as the capering deer, Oh! my blissful paradise,
Hast thou jumped into the tank.

* * * *

From the moment thou wast born in my bosom, Oh! the apple of my eye,
Thou hast lit a ceaseless fire therein.
From the time thou wast born in my belly, Oh! my darling,
Thou hast put inextinguishable fire therein.
Is this anyone's curse on me? Oh! the apple of my eye.
Is this the worst sin of my sons?
Is this anyone's curse on me? Oh! my darling.
Is this God's wickedness?
As the yak leaps, Oh! the apple of my eye,
Why has Yama carried you off?

The ornaments which you wore not sufficing, Oh ! my darling,
We are searching for more.
The jewelry with which we decorated thee,
Not sufficing, Oh ! the apple of my eye,
We are searching for more. [my eye,
We are taking ships, and traversing ports, Oh ! the apple of
And searching for valuable jewels for thee.
Traversing islands, Oh ! my darling,
We are searching for many jewels.
All of them not caring, Oh ! my gold,
Why hast thou gone to Indra's feet? [of my eye
Was it for the white-ant eaten burial ground, Oh ! the apple
We reared thee up fondly? [garland.
Was it for the beetle-trodden burial ground, Oh ! my
We combed, and brought thee up? [diamond.
Thou hast thought of borrowed fire * for me, Oh ! my
Thou hast thought of a borrowed pot † for me.

C.—Lament of a Daughter for her Mother.

Oh ! my mother ; Oh ! my mother.
Oh ! my mother, who gave birth to me.
Losing a mother's love, Oh ! my mother,
Could we stay in this world?
Losing our progenitor, Oh ! my mother,
Could we live in this world?
Separated from our mother, Oh ! my mother,
Could we live on this earth?
Feeling our stomachs, Oh ! my mother,
Didst thou give us plenty of rice?
Feeling our sides, Oh ! my mother,
Didst thou nourish us with milk?

* It is the sacred duty of a son who outlives his parents to light the funeral pyre.

† The son should go round the pyre, carrying a pot of water on his shoulder.

While thy children are here, Oh! my mother,
Thou hast reached the golden world.
While thy begotten are here, Oh! my mother.
Thou hast graced Yama's feet.
While thy kith and kin are here, Oh! my mother,
Thou hast graced Siva's feet.
While thy beloved ones are here, Oh! my mother,
Thou hast reached Indra's feet.

D.—Song of a Daughter-in-law on the Death of her Mother-in-law.

Oh! my eye-like mother-in-law,
Thou hast travelled away to mount Kylās.
Mounting the flower-car, Oh! mother,
Thou hast gone to the golden abode.
Mounting the golden car, Oh! my mother,
Thou hast gone slowly away.
I have not known my own mother, Oh! mother.
I have heard of her being talked of by others.
I have not known her who reared me, Oh! mother.
I have heard of her being talked of.
On curds didst thou bring me up, Oh! mother,
And made me forget my mother.
On milk diet didst thou bring me up, Oh! mother,
And made me forget my ties (to my mother).
I have forgotten my mother, Oh! mother,
I have forgotten every one.
Thou hast cast away all my ties, Oh! mother.
Thou hast made us beggars.

* * * *

Bird-like, thou hast flown away.
Is there no time when thou wilt come back? Oh! mother.

Shall I not expect thee ?
The expectant eye, Oh ! mother,
Thou has blindfolded.
While we, servants and others, are here, Oh ! mother.
Why hast thou gone to Yama's feet ?
Whilst thine own men are here, Oh ! mother.
Why hast thou gone away to Svarga * ?
Thou, remaining some time longer here, Oh ! mother,
Shouldst thou not help us awhile ?
Thou remaining some time longer here, Oh ! mother,
Shouldst thou not help us on a little ?

* The Vaishnava abode of bliss.

OMENS, EVIL EYE, CHARMS, ANIMAL SUPERSTITIONS, SORCERY, ETC., VOTIVE OFFERINGS.

IN seeking for omens, natives consult the so-called science of omens or science of the five birds, and are guided by them. Selected omens are always included in native calendars or panchāngams. To the quivering and throbbing of various parts of the body as omens, repeated reference is made in the Hindu classics. Thus, in Kalidāsa's Sakuntala, king Dushyanta says:—"This hermitage is tranquil, and yet my arm throbs. Whence can there be any result from this in such a place? But yet the gates of destiny are everywhere." Again, Sakuntala says:—"Alas! why does my right eye throb?", to which Gautami replies:—"Child, the evil be averted. May the tutelary deities of your husband's family confer happy prospects!" In the Raghuvamsa the statement occurs that "the son of Paulastya, being greatly incensed, drove an arrow deep into his right arm, which was throbbing, and which, therefore, prognosticated his union with Sīta." A quivering sensation in the right arm is supposed to indicate marriage with a beautiful woman; in the right eye some good luck. A tickling sensation in the right sole foretells that the person has to go on a journey.

Night, but not day dreams are considered as omens for good or evil. Among those which are auspicious may be mentioned riding on a cow, bull, or elephant; entering a temple or palace; a golden horse; climbing a mountain or tree; drinking liquor; eating flesh, curds and rice; wearing white cloths, or jewels set with precious stones; being dressed in white cloths, and embracing a woman, whose body is smeared with sandal paste. A person will be cured of sickness if he dreams of Brāhmans, kings, flowers, jewels, women, or a looking-glass. Wealth is ensured by a dream that one is bitten in the shade by a snake, or stung by a scorpion. If a person has an auspicious dream, he should get up, and not go to sleep again. But, if the dream is of evil omen, he should pray that he may be spared from its effects, and may go to sleep again.

Of omens, both good and bad, in Malabar, the following comprehensive list is given in the Malabar Manual:—

"Good.—Crows, pigeons, etc., and beasts as deer, etc., moving from left to right, and dogs and jackals moving inversely, and other beasts found similarly and singly; wild crow, cock, ruddy goose, mongoose, goat and peacock seen singly or in couples either at the right or left. A rainbow seen on the right or left, or behind, prognosticates good, but the reverse if seen in front. Buttermilk, raw rice, puttalpira (*Trichosanthes anguina*, snake-gourd); priyangu flower; honey; ghī; red cotton juice; antimony sulphurate; metal mug; bell ringing; lamp; lotus; karuka grass; raw fish; flesh; flour; ripe fruits; sweetmeats; gems; sandal-wood; elephants; pots filled with water; a virgin; a couple of Brāhmans; Rājas;

respectable men; white flower; white yak tail;* white cloth; and white horse. Chank shell; flagstaff; turban; triumphal arch; fruitful soil; burning fire; elegant eatables or drinkables; carts with men in; cows with their young; mares; bulls or cows with ropes tied to their necks; palanquin; swans; peacock and Indian crane warbling sweetly. Bracelets, looking-glass; mustard; bezoar; any substance of white colour; the bellowing of oxen; auspicious words; harmonious human voice; such sounds made by birds or beasts; the uplifting of umbrellas; hailing acclamations; sound of harp, flute, timbrel, tabor, and other instruments of music; sounds of hymns of consecration and Vēdic recitations; gentle breeze all round at the time of a journey.

"Bad.—Men deprived of any of their limbs; lame or blind; a corpse or wearer of a cloth put on a corpse; coir (cocoanut fibre); broken vessels; hearing of words expressive of breaking, burning, destroying, etc.; the alarming cry of alas! alas!; loud screams; cursing; tumbling; sneezing; the sight of a man in sorrow; one with a stick; a barber; a widow; pepper and other pungent substances. A snake; cat; iguana (*Varanus*); blood-sucker (lizard); or monkey passing across the road; vociferous beasts such as jackals, dogs, and kites; loud crying from the east; buffalo, donkey, or temple bull; black grains; salt; liquor; hide; grass; dirt; faggots; iron; flowers used for funeral ceremonies; a eunuch; ruffian; outcaste; vomit; excrement; stench; any horrible figure; bamboo; cotton; lead; cot; stool

* Used as a fly-flapper (chamara).

or other vehicle carried with legs upward; dishes, cups, etc., with mouth downward; vessels filled with live coals, which are broken and not burning; broomstick; ashes; winnow; hatchet, etc."

Hindus are very particular about catching sight of some auspicious object on the morning of new year's day, as the effects of omens seen on that occasion are believed to last throughout the year. In Malabar, on new year's eve, a room is decorated with garlands of flowers, and small stools or benches covered with silk or white cloth are placed therein. Various kinds of sweets, fruits, flowers, and other auspicious things are arranged, together with jewels and gold coins. The room is well lighted, incense burnt, and the door closed. Early on the following morning the inmates of the house get up, and, with eyes shut, proceed to the door, which is then opened, so that they are greeted with all the articles of good omen within the room.

It is a good omen for the day if when he gets up in the morning, a man sees any of the following:—his wife's face, the lines on the palm of his right hand, his face in a mirror, the face of a rich man, the tail of a black cow, the face of a black monkey, or his rice fields. There is a legend that Sīta used to rise early and present herself, bathed and well dressed, before her lord Rāma, so that he might gaze on her face, and be lucky during the day. This custom is carried out by all good house-wives in Hindu families. A fair-skinned Paraiyan or a dark-skinned Brāhman should not, in accordance with a proverb, be seen the first thing in the morning.

The omens are favourable if a person comes across any of the following, when starting on a journey or special errand :—

- Married woman.
- Virgin.
- Prostitute.
- Two Brāhmans.
- Playing of music.
- One carrying musical instruments.
- Money.
- Fruit or flowers.
- A light, or clear blazing fire.
- Umbrella
- Cooked food.
- Milk or curds.
- Cow.
- Deer.
- Corpse.
- Two fishes.
- Recital of Vēdas.
- Sound of a drum or horn.
- Spirituous liquor.
- Bullock.
- Mutton.
- Precious stones.
- One bearing a silver armlet.
- Sandal wood.
- Rice.
- Elephant.
- Horse.
- Pot full of water.
- Married woman carrying a water pot from a tank.
- Pot of toddy.
- Black monkey.
- Dog.
- Royal eagle.
- Honey.
- Parrot.
- Hearing kind words.
- A Gāzula Balija with his pile of bangles on his back.

If, on similar occasions, a person comes across any of the following, the omens are unfavourable :—

- Widow.
- Lightning.
- Fuel.
- Smoky fire.
- Pot of oil.
- Leather.
- Dog barking on a house top.

Hare.	Bundle of sticks.
Crow flying from right to left.	Butter-milk.
Snake.	Empty vessel.
New pot.	A quarrel.
Blind man.	Man with dishevelled hair.
Lame man.	Oil-man.
Sick man.	Leper.
Salt.	Mendicant.
Tiger.	

In a recent judicial case a witness gave evidence to the effect that he was starting on a journey, and, when he had proceeded a short way, a snake crossed the road. This being an evil omen, he went back, and put off his journey till the following day. On his way he passed through a village, in which some men had been arrested for murder, and found that one of two men, whom he had promised to accompany, and had gone on without him, had been murdered.

Inauspicious days for starting on a journey are vāra-sūlai, or days on which Sīva's trident (sula) is kept on the ground. The direction in which it lies varies according to the day of the week. For example, Sunday before noon is a bad time to start towards the west, as the trident is turned that way. To one proceeding on a journey, a dog crossing from right to left is auspicious. But, if it gets on his person or his feet, shaking its ears, the journey will be unlucky. If the dog scratches its body, the traveller will fall ill, and, if it lies down and wags its tail, some disaster will follow. If a dog scratches the wall of a house, it will be broken into by thieves; and, if it makes a hole in the ground within a cattle-shed, the cattle will be stolen. A dog approaching a person with a bit of shoe-leather augurs success; with flesh gain; with a meaty bone good luck; with a dry bone death. If a dog enters a house with wire or thread in its mouth, the master of the house must expect to be put in prison. A dog barking on the roof of a house during the dry weather portends an epidemic, and in the wet season a heavy fall of rain. House dogs should, if they are to bring good luck, possess more than eighteen visible claws. The sight of a jackal is very lucky to one proceeding on an errand. Its cry to the east and north of a village foretells some thing good for the village, whereas the cry at midday means an impending calamity. If a jackal crys towards the south in reply to the call of another jackal, some one will be hung; and, if it cries towards the west, some one will be drowned. A bachelor, who sees a jackal running, may expect to be married shortly. The sight of a cat, on getting out of bed, is extremely unlucky, and he who sees it will fail in all his undertakings during the day. "I faced the cat this morning," or "Did you see a cat this morning"? are common sayings when one fails in anything. The Paraiyans are said to be very particular about omens, and if, when a Paraiyan sets out to arrange a marriage with a certain girl, a cat or a Valiyan crosses his path, he will give up the girl. I have heard of a superstitious European police officer, who would not start in search of a criminal, because he came across a cat. Even the braying of a donkey is considered a good or bad omen, according to the direction from which it proceeds.

I have already (pp. 84–85) referred briefly to the examination of horses' curls as omens. "Throughout India," Mr. J. D. E. Holmes writes, * "but more especially in the Southern Presidency, among the native population, the value of a horse or ox principally depends on the existence and situation of certain hair marks on the body of the animal. These hair marks are formed by the changes in the direction in which the hair grows at certain places, and, according to their shape, are called a crown, ridge, or feather mark. The relative position of these marks is supposed to indicate that the animal will bring good luck to the owner and his relatives. There is a saying that 'a man may face a rifle and escape, but he cannot avoid the luck, good or evil, foretold by hair marks.' So much are the people influenced by these omens that they seldom keep an animal with unlucky marks, and would not allow their mares to be covered by a stallion having unpropitious marks." The following are some of the marks recorded by Mr. Holmes :—

(*a*) *Horses.*

1. Deobund (having control over evil spirits), also termed dēvuman or dēvumani. Said by Muhammadans to represent the Prophet's finger, and by Hindus to represent a temple bell. This mark is a ridge, one to three inches long, situated between the throat and counter along the line of the trachea. It is the most

* Madras Agricultural Bulletin II. 42. 1900.

lucky mark a horse can possess. It is compared to the sun, and therefore, when it is present, none of the evil stars can shine, and all unlucky omens are overruled.

2. Khorta-gad (peg-driver) or khila-gad is a ridge of hair directed downwards on one or both hind legs. It is said that no horse in the stable will be sold, so long as the horse with these marks is kept.

3. Badi (fetter), a ridge of hair directed upwards on one or both forearms on the outer side, and said to indicate that the owner of the animal will be sent to jail.

4. Thanni (teat). Teat-like projections on the sheath of the male are considered unlucky.

(b) Cattle.

5. Bhashicam suli is a crown on the forehead above the line of the eyes. Bhashican is the name of the wreath worn by bride and bridegroom during the marriage ceremony. If the purchaser be a bachelor or widower, this mark indicates that he will marry soon. If the purchaser be a married man, he will either have the misfortune to lose his wife and marry again, or the good fortune to obtain two wives.

6. Mukkanti suli. Three crowns on the forehead, arranged in the form of a triangle, said to represent the three eyes of Sīva, of which the one in the forehead will, if opened, burn up all things within the range of vision.

7. Pādai suli. Two ridges of hair on the back on either side of the middle line, indicating that the purchaser will soon need a coffin.

8. Tattu suli. A crown situated on the back between the points of the hips, indicating that any business undertaken by the purchaser will fail.

9. A bullock with numerous spots over the body, like a deer, is considered very lucky.

It is said that, if a cow voids urine at the time of purchase, it is considered a very good omen, but, if she passes dung, a bad omen. The reverse is the case with a bullock.

The sight of a Brāhmani kite on a Sunday morning is very auspicious, so on this day people may be seen throwing pieces of mutton or lumps of butter to these birds. If the bird is seen flying, the omen is good, but, if seen perching, bad. I am told that the Khonds show no reverence for the Brāhmani kite, but will kill it if it carries off their chickens.

Sometimes people leave their house, and sleep elsewhere on the night preceding an inauspicious day, on which a journey must be made. When a student starts for the examination hall, he will, if he sees a widow or a Brāhman, retrace his steps, and start again after the lapse of a few minutes. Meeting two Brāhmans would indicate good luck, and he would press forward.

If, when a person is leaving the house, the head or feet strike accidentally against the threshold, he should not go out, as it forebodes some impending mischief. If one dines with a friend or relation on Monday, Wednesday, Friday, or Saturday, it is well; if on a Tuesday, ill-feeling will ensue; if on a Thursday, endless enmity; if on a Sunday, hatred. If one places the head towards the east when sleeping, he will obtain wealth and health; if towards the south, a lengthening of life; if towards the west, fame; if towards the north, sickness. The last position should, therefore be avoided.* It is unlucky to go westward on Friday or Sunday, eastward on Monday or Saturday, north on Tuesday or Wednesday, south on Thursday. A journey begun on Tuesday is liable to result in loss by thieves or fire at home. Loss, too, is likely to follow a journey begun on Saturday, and sickness a start on Sunday. Wednesday and Friday are both propitious days, and a journey begun on either with a view to business will be lucrative. The worst days for travelling are Tuesday, Saturday, and Sunday.†

Sneezing once is a good sign, twice a bad sign. More than twice is not regarded. When a child sneezes, those near it usually say "dīrgayus" (long life), or sathāyus (a hundred years). Adults who sneeze pronounce the name of some god, the common expression being "Srīmadrangam." When a Badaga baby is born, it is a good omen if the father sneezes before the umbilical cord has been cut, and an evil one if he sneezes after its severance. Gaping is an indication that evil spirits have effected an entrance into the body. Hence many Brāhmans, when they gape, snap their fingers as a preventive.‡ It was noted by Alberuni that Hindus "spit out and blow their noses without any respect for the elder ones present, and crack their lice before them. They consider the *crepitus ventris* as a good omen, sneezing as a bad omen." When a great man yawns, his sleep is promoted by all the company with

* K. Srikantaliyar. Ind. Ant., XXI., 1892.

† M. J. Walhouse. Ind. Ant., X, 1881. ‡ *Ibid.*, V, 1876.

him snapping their fingers with great vehemence, and making a singular noise. In the Telugu country, when a child is roused from sleep by a thunder-clap, the mother, pressing it to her breast, murmurs "Arjuna Sahādēva." The invocation implies the idea that thunder is caused by the Mahābhārata heroes Arjuna and Sahādēva.*

If a child is born with the umbilical cord round its neck like a garland, it is believed to be inauspicious for its uncle, who is not allowed to see it for ten days, or even longer. and then a propitiatory ceremony has to be performed. If the cord is entwined across the breast, and passes under the armpit, it is believed to be an unlucky omen for the father and paternal uncle. In such cases, some special ceremony, as looking into vessels of oil, is performed. When the tāli of a Brāhman woman is lost, it is an omen that her husband will fall ill, or be lost soon.

Arrack (liquor) vendors consider it unlucky to set their measures upside down. Sometime ago, the Excise Commissioner informs me, the Madras Excise Department had some aluminium measures made for measuring arrack in liquor shops. It was found that the arrack corroded the aluminium, and the measures soon leaked. The shop-keepers were told to turn their measures upside down, in order that they might drain. This they refused to do, as it would bring bad luck to their shop. New measures with round bottoms were evolved, which would not stand up. But the shop-keepers began to use rings of

* M. N. Venkataswami, Ind. Ant., XXXIV, 1905.

India-rubber from soda water bottles, to make them stand. An endeavour has since been made to induce them to keep their measures inverted by hanging them on pegs, so that they will drain without being turned upside down. The case illustrates well how important a knowledge of the superstitions of the people is in the administration of their affairs. So trifling an innovation as the introduction of a new arrangement for maintaining tension in the warp during the process of weaving gave rise quite recently to a strike among the hand-loom weavers at the Madras School of Arts.

A bazār shopkeeper who deals in colours will not sell white paint after the lamps have been lighted. And, in like manner, a cloth dealer refuses to sell black cloth, and the dealer in hardware to sell nails, needles, etc., lest poverty should ensue. Digging operations with a spade must be stopped before the lamps are lighted. A betel-vine cultivator objects to entering his garden or plucking a leaf after the lighting of the lamps, but, if some leaves are urgently required, he will, before plucking them, pour water from a pot at the foot of the tree on which the vine is growing.

In teaching the Grāndha alphabet to children, they are made to repeat the letter ça twice quickly without pausing, as the word ça means "die." To mention the number seven in Telugu is unlucky, because the word is the same as that for weeping (yeḍu). Even a Treasury officer, who is an enlightened University graduate, in counting money, will say six and one. In Tamil the word ten is, in like manner, inauspicious, because, on the tenth day after the death of her husband, a widow removes all the emblems of married life. Probably for this reason the offspring of Kallan polyandrous marriages style themselves the children of eight and two, not ten fathers. Lābha is a Sanskrit word meaning profit or gain, and has its equivalent in all the vernacular languages. Hindus, when counting, commence with this word instead of the word signifying one. And, in like manner, Muhammadans use the words Bismillah or Burketh, apparently as an invocation like the medicinal ℞ (Oh! Jupiter aid us). When the number a hundred has been counted, they again begin with the substitute for one, and this serves as a one for the person who is keeping tally. Oriya merchants say lābo instead of eko (one), when counting out the seers of rice for the elephants' rations.

The birth of a male child on the day in which the constellation Rohini is visible portends evil to the maternal uncle; and a female born under the constellation Moolam is supposed to carry misery with her to the house which she enters by marriage. While eating, one should face east, south, west, or north, according as one wishes for long life, fame, to become vain-glorious, or for justice or truth. Chewing a single betel nut along with betel leaves secures vigour; two nuts are inauspicious; three are excellent; and more bring indifferent luck. The basal portion of the betel leaf must be rejected, as it produces disease; the apical part as it induces sin; and the midrib and veins as they destroy the intellect. A leaf on which chunām (lime) has been kept should be avoided, as it may shorten life.

It is considered by a Hindu unlucky to get shaved for ceremonial purposes in the months of Ādi, Purattāsi, Margali, and Māsi, and in the remaining months Sunday, Tuesday, and Saturday should be avoided. Further, the star under which a man was born has to be taken into consideration, and it may happen that an auspicious day for being shaved does not occur for some weeks. It is on this account that orthodox Hindus are sometimes compelled to go about with unkempt chins.

Even for anointing the body, auspicious and inauspicious days are prescribed, *e.g.*, anointing on Sunday causes loss of beauty, on Monday brings increase of riches, on Thursday loss of intellect. If a person is obliged to anoint himself on Sunday, he puts a bit of the root of *Nerium* (oleander) in the oil, and heats it before applying it. This is supposed to avert the evil influence. Similarly, on Tuesday dry earth, on Thursday roots of *Cynodon Dactylon*, and on Friday ashes must be used. The Kalinga Kōmatis of Vizagapatam will not reside at any place from which the Padmanābham hill near Bimlipatam can be seen, owing to a tradition that residence near these formerly proved inauspicious to their class.*

It is considered auspicious if a girl attains puberty on a Monday, Wednesday, Thursday, or Friday, and the omens vary according to the month in which the first menstrual period occurs. Thus the month of Vaiyāsi ensures prosperity; Āni male issue; Māsi happiness; Margali well-behaved children; Punguni long life and many children.

* Manual of the Vizagapatam district.

Plate XIII.

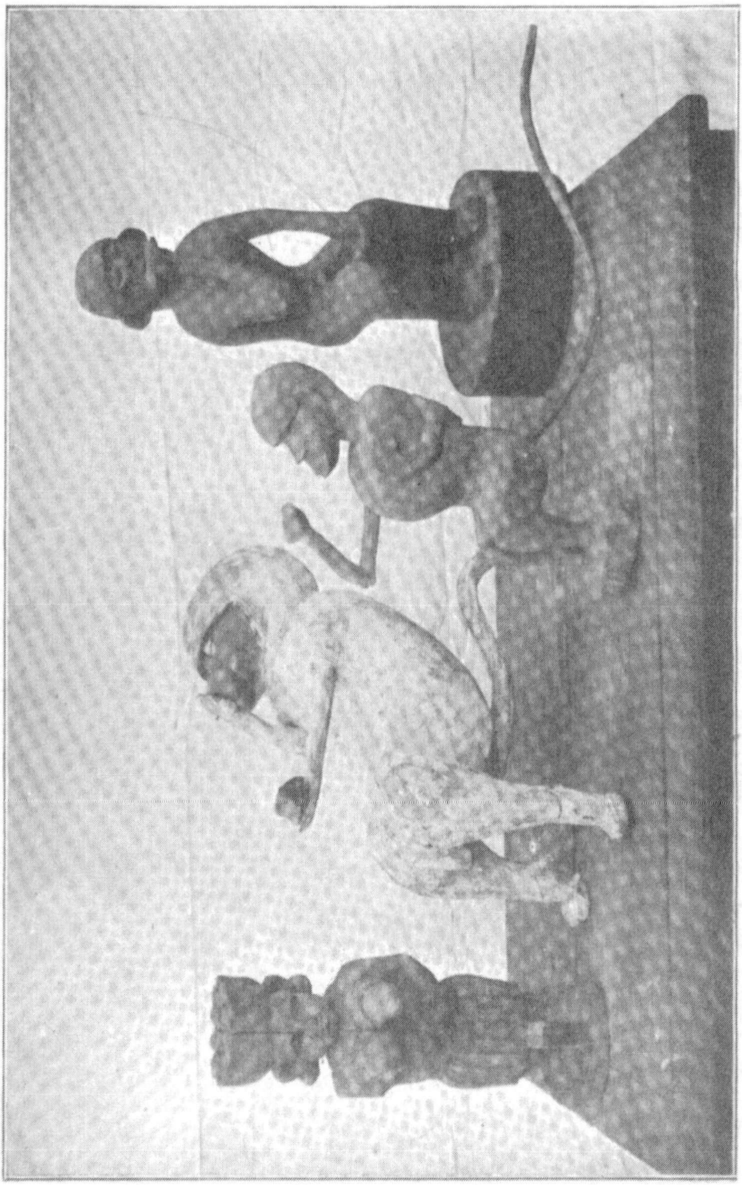

Evil Eye Figures.

It is believed that the sight or breath of Muhammadans, just after they have said their prayers at a mosque, will do good to children suffering from various disorders. For this purpose women carry or take their children, and post themselves at the entrance to a mosque at the time when the worshippers leave it. Most of them are Hindus, but sometimes poor Eurasians may be seen there.

Evil eye.—The indecent carvings on temple cars are introduced thereon to avert the evil eye. During temple or marriage processions, two huge human figures, male and female, made of bamboo wicker-work, are carried in front for the same purpose. In Malabar, fear of the evil eye is very general. At the corner of the upper storey of almost every Nāyar house near a road or path is suspended some object, often a doll-like hideous creature, on which the eye of the passer-by may rest (plate XIII).* "A crop is being raised in a garden visible from the road. The vegetables will never reach maturity unless a bogey of some sort is set up in their midst. A cow will stop giving milk, unless a conch shell is tied conspicuously about her horns. When a house or shop is being built, there surely is to be found exposed in some conspicuous position an image, sometimes of extreme indecency, a pot covered with cabalistic signs, a prickly branch of cactus, or what not, to catch the evil eye of passers by, and divert their attention from the important work in hand."† Many of the carved wooden images recall

* F. Fawcett., Madras Mus. Bull., III. 3, 1901.

† Logan. Malabar Manual.

forcibly to mind the Horatian ode "Olim truncus eram. . . Obscenoque ruber porrectus ab inguine palus." Monstrous Priapi made in straw, with painted clay pots for beads, pots smeared with chunām and studded with black dots, or palmyra palm fruits coated with chunām, (plate XIV) may often be seen set up in fields, to guard the ripening crop. For the following note on the evil eye in Malabar I am indebted to Mr. S. Appadorai Iyer. "It is not the eye alone that commits the mischief, but also the mind and tongue. Man is said to do good or evil through the mind, word and deed, *i.e.* manasa, vācha, and karmana. When a new house is being constructed, or a vegetable garden or rice field are in a flourishing condition, the following precautions are taken to ward off the evil eye:—

a. In buildings—

1. A pot with black and white marks on it is suspended mouth downwards.

2. A wooden figure of a monkey, with pendulous testes, is suspended.

3. The figure of a Malayāli woman, with protuberant breasts, is suspended.

b. In fields and gardens.

1. A straw figure covered with a black cloth daubed with black and white dots, is placed on a long pole. If the figure represents a male, it has pendent testes, and, if a woman, well developed breasts. Sometimes male and female figures are placed together in an embracing posture.

2. Pots, as described above, are placed on bamboo poles.

Plate XIV.

Evil-eye Scare-crows.

3. A portion of the skull of a bull, with horns attached, is set up on a long pole.

The figures, pots and skulls are primarily intended to scare away crows, stray cattle, and other marauders, and secondly to ward off the evil eye. Instances are quoted, in which handsome buildings have fallen down, and ripe fruits and grain crops have withered through the influence of the eye, which has also been held responsible for the bursting of a woman's breasts."

In Madras, human figures are made of broken bricks and mortar, and kept permanently in the front of the upstairs verandah. In this city, too, cows may be seen, with a chank shell (*Turbinella rapa*) tied with a black string round the neck, to ward off the evil eye. Māppilla cart-drivers in Malabar tie black ropes round the neck or across the face of their bullocks, for the same purpose. In villages, strangers are not allowed to be present when the cows are milked. Sudden failure of milk, or blood-stained milk, are attributed to the evil eye, to remove the influence of which the owner of the affected cow resorts to the magician. Matrons among all castes make the faces of children ugly by painting two or three black dots on the chin and cheeks, and painting the eyelids black with lamp-black paste. On occasions of auspicious ceremonies, coloured water (arathi), or balls of rice, are waved in front of or around the parties concerned. In like manner, at weddings among some castes, when the bridegroom's party reach the bride's house, her sister waves a vessel containing turmeric water, etc., in front of his face, to ward off the evil eye. Later on in the ceremonial, rice-cakes are placed on various parts of the bodies of the bride and bridegroom, and seven vessels containing turmeric water, charcoal, rice, salt, betel, fruits, and flowers are waved in front of their faces. Sometimes a figure is made of rice-flour paste, and five kinds of flowers are placed near it. Copper coins are stuck on the head, hands, and abdomen of the figure, which is waved in front of a sick person, and taken to a place where three roads or paths meet, and left there. For curing sprains, it is a common practice to have in front of the patient a sickle, an iron measure, or any article made of iron which is at hand. Sometimes a hole is made in a gourd (*Benincasa cerifera* or *Lagenaria vulgaris*), which is filled with turmeric and chunām, and waved round a sick person. It is then taken to a place where three roads meet, and broken. The sudden illness of children is often attributed to the evil eye. In such cases, the following remedies are considered efficacious :—

(1) A few sticks from a new unused broom are set fire to, waved several times round the child, and placed in a corner. With some of the ashes the mother makes a mark on the child's forehead. If the broom burns to ashes without making a noise, the women cry "Look at it. It burns without the slightest noise. The creature's eyes are really very bad." Abuse is then heaped on the person, whose eyes are supposed to be wicked.

(2) Some chillies, salt, human hair, nail-cuttings, and finely powdered earth from the pit of the door-post are mixed together, waved three times in front of the

baby, and thrown on to the fire. Woe betide the possessor of the evil eye, if no pungent, suffocating smell arises while it is burning.

(3) A piece of burning camphor is waved in front of the baby.

(4) Cooked rice-balls, painted red, black and yellow, and white (with curds) are waved in front of the child.

Loss of appetite in children is attributed by mothers to the visit of a supposed evil person to the house. On that person appearing again, the mother will take a little sand or dust from under the visitor's foot, whirl it round the head of the child, and throw it on the hearth. If the suspected person is not likely to turn up again, a handful of cotton seeds, red chillies, and dust from the middle of the street, are whirled round the child's head, and thrown on the hearth. If the chillies produce a strong smell, the evil eye has been averted. If they do not do so, the suspect is roundly abused by the mother, and never again admitted to the house. It is a good thing to frighten any one who expresses admiration of one's belongings. For example, if a friend praises your son's eyes, say to him "Look out. There is a snake at your feet." If he is frightened, the evil eye has been averted.

During a marriage among the Mādigas, a sheep or goat is sacrificed to the marriage (aravēni) pots. The sacrificer dips his hands in the blood of the animal, and impresses the blood on his palms on the wall near the door leading to the room in which the pots are kept. This is said to ward off the evil eye. The nomad

Tottiyans kill a fowl near the pots, and with its blood make a mark on the foreheads of the bride and bridegroom on their entry into the marriage booths erected outside the village. The Vekkiliya Tottiyans sacrifice a goat or sheep instead of a fowl, and the more advanced among them substitute the breaking of a cocoanut for the animal sacrifice.

The objection which a high-caste Brāhman has to being seen by a low-caste man when he is eating his food is based on a belief allied to that of the evil eye. The Brāhmanical theory of vision, as propounded in the sacred writings, and understood by orthodox pandits corresponds with the old corpuscular theory. The low-caste man being inferior in every respect to the Brāhman, the matter or subtle substance proceeding from his eye, and mixing with the objects seen by him, must of necessity be inferior and bad. So food, which is seen by a low-caste man, in virtue of the *radii perniciosi* which it has received, will contaminate the Brāhman.

If a man of another caste enters the house of a Mysore Holeya, the owner takes care to tear the intruder's cloth, and turn him out. This will avert any evil, which might have befallen him.* It is said that Brāhmans consider great luck will wait upon them, if they can manage to pass through a Holeya village unmolested. Should a Brāhman attempt to enter their quarters, the Holeyas turn him out, and slipper him, in former times it is said to death.†

* J. S. F. Mackenzie. Ind. Ant., II, 1873. † *Ibid.*

Charms.—Mantrams, or consecrated formulæ, are supposed to be very powerful, and by their aid even gods can be brought under control. Such charms are *inter alia* believed to be efficacious in curing disease, in protecting children against devils, and women against miscarriage, in promoting development of the breasts, in bringing offspring to barren women, and warding off misfortune consequent on marriage with a girl who has a bad mark on her, in keeping wild pigs from the fields, and warding off cattle disease. For the last purpose the magical formula is carved on a stone pillar, which is set up in the village. They are divided into four classes, viz., mantrasara, or the real essence of magic; yantrasara, or the science of cabalistic figures; prayogasara, or the method of using the above for the attainment of any object; tanthrasara, or the science of symbolical acts with or without words.

Mantrasara includes all mantrams, with their efficacy for good and evil, and the methods of learning or reciting them with the aid of the guru (spiritual instructor). Mantrams are combinations of the five initial letters of the five sacred elements, which produce sounds, but not words. These are believed to vibrate on the ether, and act on latent forces which are there.

Yantrasara includes all cabalistic figures, and the method of drawing and using them, and objects to be attained by them. They are drawn on thin plates of gold, silver, copper or lead. The efficacy of the figures, when drawn on gold, will, it is said, last for a century, while those drawn on the less precious metals will only be effective for six months or a year. Leaden plates are made use of when the mantrams have to be buried underground. These figures should possess the symbols of life, eyes, tongue, the eight cardinal points of the compass, and the five elements.

Prayogasara includes attraction or summoning by enchantment, driving out evil spirits, stupefaction, tempting or bringing a deity or evil spirits under control, and enticement for love, destruction, and separation of friends. The mantras are effective only when the individual who resorts to them is pure in mind and body. This can be attained by the recital of ajapagayithry (216,000 exhalations and inhalations in twenty-four hours). These have to be divided among the deities Ganēsa, Brāhma, Vishnu, Rudra, Jīvathma, Paramathma, and the guru in the proportion of 600, 6000, 6000, 6000, 1000, 1000, 1000. A man can only become learned in mantrams (mantravādi) by the regular performance of the recognised ceremonial, by learning them from a guru, by proper recitals of them, burning the sacred fire (hōmam), and taking food. As examples of yantrams, the following, selected from a very large repertoire, may be cited.

Ganapathi yantram should be drawn on metal, and worship performed. It is then enclosed in a metal cylinder, and tied by a thread round the neck of females, or the waist or arm of men. It will cure disease, conquer an enemy, or entice any one. If the sacred fire is kept up while the formula is repeated, and dry cocoanut, plantain fruits, money, ghī, beaten rice and sweet bread put into it, its owner will be blessed with wealth and prosperity.

Bhadrakāli yantram.—The figure is drawn on the floor with flour of rice, turmeric, charcoal powder, and leaves of the castor-oil plant; and, if pūja is done at night to the deity, it will lead to the acquisition of knowledge, strength, freedom from disease and impending calamities, wealth and prosperity. If the pūja is celebrated by a mantravādi for twelve days with his face turned towards the south, it will produce the death of an enemy.

The utterance of a certain mantram, and recital of purusha sooktham (a Vēdic hymn) before 11 A.M., and the distribution of milk among children, will produce increase of children, wealth, cows, and prosperity. If butter is taken by barren women, with the recital of this mantram, they will be blessed with children.

Sudarsana yantram, when drawn on a metal sheet, and enclosed in a cylinder worn round the neck or on the arm, will relieve those who are ill or possessed of devils. For driving out devils, an oblation to Agni must be offered, while the mantram Om nama sahasrarahun pul is uttered. If the yantram Sudarsana is drawn on butter spread on a plantain leaf, pūja performed, and the butter given to a barren woman, there will be no danger to herself or future issue.

Suthakadhosham yantram.—Children under one year of age are supposed to be affected, if they are seen by a woman on the fourth day of menstruation with wet clothes and empty stomach after bathing. She may not even see her own baby or husband till she has changed her clothes, and taken food. To avert the evil, a waistband, made of the bark of the arka plant (*Calotropis gigantea*), is worn.

Sarabha yantram will cure persons suffering from epilepsy or intermittent fever.

Subramaniya yantram, if drawn and regularly worshipped, will expel devils from both those attacked by them, and from houses.

Hanumān yantram, when worn, will protect those who are out on dark nights, and produce bodily strength and wisdom. If drawn on a gold sheet, enclosed in a casket, and pūja performed to it every Saturday, it will bring prosperity, and help pregnant women during their confinement.

Pakshi yantram, if drawn on a sheet of lead, and kept in several places round a house, will keep snakes away.

Moolathrigona yantram, if drawn on the floor, and a knife placed on it, will drive out devils from those attacked thereby.

Vatugabhairava yantram cures disease in those who are under eighteen years old, and drives out all kinds of evil spirits. If ashes are smeared on the face, and the mantram uttered sixteen times, it will be very effective.

Varati yantram is very useful to any one who wishes to kill an enemy. He should sit in a retired spot at night, with his face turned towards the south, and repeat the mantram a thousand times for twenty days.

Prathingiri yantram is drawn on a sheet of lead, and buried at a spot over which a person, whose death is desired, will pass. It is then placed on the floor, on which the sacred fire is kindled. The mantram should be repeated eight hundred times for seven nights.

Chāmundi and Raktha Chāmundi are used for causing the death of enemies. The mantram should be written on a sheet of lead, and pūja, with the sacrifice of toddy and mutton, performed.

To produce an ulcer, which will cause the death of an enemy in ninety days, a mantram is written on a piece of cadjan (palm-leaf), enclosed in an egg with a small quantity of earth on which he has urinated, and buried in an ant-hill. A fowl is killed, and its blood and some toddy are poured over the egg. To cure fever, the formula is written with the finger in water contained in a basin, and the appropriate words repeated while the water is being drunk.

A charm, called the Asvārūda yantram enables a person wearing it to cover long distances on horseback; and he can make the most refractory horse amenable by tying it round its neck.* An inhabitant of Malabar presented Mr. Fawcett with a yantram against the evil eye, which, if whispered over a piece of string, and tied round any part of the body affected, would work an instantaneous cure. In a note regarding moon-shaped amulets against the evil eye described by Professor Tylor,† Mr. Walhouse mentions that crescents, made of thin plates of metal, sometimes gold, are worn by children on the west coast, suspended upon the breast with the

* F. Fawcett, Madras Mus. Bull., III, 3, 1901.

† Journ. Anthrop. Inst., XIX, 1890.

points upwards. Neck ornaments in the form of crescents are commonly worn by Muhammadan children.

The story of a stone slab in the main street of Rāyalcheruvu, known as the yantram rāyi or magic stone, is narrated by Mr. Francis.* "The charm consists of 81 squares, nine each way, within a border of tridents. Each square contains one or more Telugu letters, but these will not combine into any intelligible words. At the bottom of the stone are cut a lingam and two pairs of foot-prints. Some twelve years ago, it is said, the village suffered severely from cholera for three years in succession, and a Telugu mason, a foreigner who was in the village at the time, cut this charm on the stone to stop the disease. It was set up with much ceremony. The mason went round the village at night without a stitch of clothing on him, and with the entrails of a sheep hanging round his neck Many cocoanuts were offered on the stone, and many sheep slain before it. The mason tossed a lamb into the air, caught it as it fell, tore its throat open with his teeth, and then bounded forward, and spat out the blood. More sheep and more cocoanuts were offered, and then the slab was set up The mason naturally demanded a substantial return for the benefit he had conferred upon the inhabitants. When cholera now breaks out, the villagers subscribe together, and do pūja to the stone in accordance with directions left them by him. A washerman acts as pūjāri, and 101 pots of water are poured over the slab; thread is wound round it 101 times; 101 dots are made

* Gazetteer of the Anantapur district.

on it with kunkumam; and 101 limes, cocoanuts, and quarter anna bits are offered to it."

The tooth or claw of a tiger, worn on the neck or near the loins, wearing an iron ring set with pearls, a lime placed in the turban, or a figure of Hanumān (the monkey god) graven on an ornament, are considered effective against evil demons. A tiger's whiskers are held to be a most potent poison when chopped up; so, when a tiger is killed, the whiskers are immediately singed off.* They are represented in stuffed heads by the delicate bristles of the porcupine.

The hair or chēdu of the bear is enclosed in amulets and tied to the girdle round the loins of male children, and in strings round the neck of female children, as a remedy against fever, and to prevent involuntary discharge of urine during sleep †. The Rev. S. Nicholson informs me that, if a Māla child grinds its teeth in its sleep, a piece of a broken pot is brought from a graveyard, and, after being smoked with incense, tied round the neck of the child with a piece of string rubbed with turmeric, or with a piece of gut. Further, among the Mālas, the dried up umbilical cord is highly prized as a remedy for sterility. The upper lip and chin of a girl are rubbed with the cord so that they may not develop moustache and beard.

A Lambādi has been seen repeating mantrams over his patients, and touching their heads at the same time with a book, which was a small edition of the Telugu

* M. J. Walhouse, Ind. Ant., V, 1876.

† Manual of the Kurnool district.

translation of St. John's gospel. Neither the physician nor the patient could read, and had no idea of the contents of the book.*

Mercury cups, said to be made of an amalgam of mercury and tin, are stated to possess the property of allowing mercury, when poured in, to ooze through them, and pass out. Milk kept overnight in such a cup, or an amulet made from the cup materials, and worn round the waist, are believed to exercise a most potent influence over the male fertilising element. Such an amulet, applied to the neck of a chorister, is said to have increased his vocal powers three or four times. Piles and other bodily ailments are believed to be cured by wearing rings, in the composition of which mercury is one of the ingredients.

In the Diary of Ananda Ranga Pillai † the following method of catching slaves is recorded. "The slave-dealer sent out his men to collect these; they purchased some, and inveigled others into their clutches. They either mixed some deleterious material in the lime which their victims used with their betel and nut, or placed them under a spell by means of the magic paint which they carried in a box in their hands, and then, overpowering them. reduced them to slavery."

The following are interesting as cases in which a European, who was well versed in the theory and practice of native magic, was called in to administer to natives, who were under the spell of devils. In the first case, a

* Rev. J. Cain, Ind Ant., VIII, 1879.

† Edited by Sir J. F. Price, Vol. I, 1904.

Telugu girl, about seventeen years old, had been for some time possessed by her sister's husband, under whose influence she used to eat abnormal quantities of food, tear off her clothes, and use indecent language in a voice other than her own. When the European arrived in her room, the devil, speaking through the girl, threatened to kill her, or the European, or the individual who put it into her. Under the spell of a suitable mantram, the devil departed, and its return was prevented by the wearing of a yantram. The girl is said to have entirely recovered, and to have married and settled down. The other case was that of a boy, who was possessed by a devil. He was found, on the occasion of the visit of the European, lying down in the court-yard of his house, clad in an ample loin-cloth, and with a high temperature. Suddenly through some invisible agency, a corner of the loin-cloth caught fire, which was stamped out. It then caught fire in another place, and eventually was riddled with burnt holes. This was the way in which the devil manifested its influence, and sometimes the boy got burnt. A mantram was recited, with the result that the burning ceased, and the fever abated. An impromptu yantram was made out of vibhūti (sacred ashes), and tied round the boy's neck. A religious mendicant came along a short time afterwards, and treated the boy for some ordinary sickness unconnected with the devil, but the medicine did him no good. Finding the yantram round his neck, the mendicant asserted that it was the cause of his failure, and ordered its removal. This the boy's relations refused to permit. But the holy man ripped it off. Whereon the boy instantly fell down comatose. In recording these two cases, I have reproduced my notes made on the occasion of an interview with the European.

A notorious Māppilla dacoit, who was shot by the police a few years ago, and whom his co-religionists tried to make a saint, was at the time of his death wearing five copper and silver mantram cylinders round his waist. In a case which was tried before a Magistrate in Travancore, the accused, in order to win his case, had concealed in his under-cloth some yantrams, which had been prepared for him by a sorcerer. The plaintiff, having got scent of this, gave information, and the charms were handed over to the Magistrate. In Vizagapatam a most efficacious charm, supposed to render a man invulnerable to every ill, consists of a small piece of block wool, given to every one who takes a black sheep for the priest of a temple on the top of the Bopelli ghāt. A European official in the same district informed me that his autograph and seal were put to a strange use. A Magistrate told him that he wanted to tear up some old abkāri (liquor) licenses, but a man implored him not to do so, as they had brought him life for a year, and were therefore worshipped. So the medicine was water, in which an old license had been dipped. In Vizagapatam a mixture of gingelly oil, the red dye which women use, and other ingredients, put into a small piece of hollow bamboo, and worn on the arm, is said to protect a man against being shot with a bow or musket.

Lean children, especially of the Māla, Mādiga and Chakkiliyan classes, are made to wear a leather strap specially made for them by a Chakkiliyan, which is believed to help their growth.

Animal superstitions.—One of the occupations of the Kuruvikārans (bird-men), a class of Marathi-speaking bird-catchers, pig-breeders, and beggars, is the manufacture and sale of spurious jackal horns, known as narikombu. To catch the jackals, they make an enclosure of a net, inside which a man seats himself, armed with a big stick. He then proceeds to execute a perfect imitation of the jackal's cry, on hearing which the jackals come running to see what is the matter, and are beaten down. Sometimes the entire jackal's head is sold, skin and all. The process of manufacture of the horn is as follows. After the brain has been removed, the skin is stripped off a limited area of the skull, and the bone at the place of junction of the sagittal and lambdoid sutures above the occipital foramen is filed away, so that only a point, like a bony outgrowth, is left. The skin is then brought back, and pressed over the little horn, which pierces it. The horn is also said to be made out of the molar tooth of a dog or jackal introduced through a small hole in a piece of jackal's skin, round which a little blood or turmeric paste is smeared, to make it look more natural. In most cases, only the horn, with a small piece of skull and skin, is sold. Sometimes, instead of the skin from the part where the horn is made, a piece of skin is taken from the snout, where the long black hairs are. The horn then appears surrounded by long black bushy hairs. The Kuruvikarans explain that, when they see a jackal with such long hairs on the top of his head, they know that he possesses a horn. A horn vendor, whom I interviewed, assured me that the possessor of a horn is a small jackal, which comes out of its hiding-place on full-moon nights to drink the dew. According to another version, the horn is only possessed by the leader of a pack of jackals. The Sinhalese and Tamils alike regard the horn "as a talisman, and believe that its fortunate possessor can command the realization of every wish. Those who have jewels to conceal rest in perfect security if, along with them, they can deposit a narri-comboo." * The ayah of a friend of mine, who possesses such a talisman, remarked "Master going into any Law Court, sure to win case." Two of these spurious horns, which I acquired from a wandering Kuruvikāran, were promptly abstracted from my study table, to bring luck to some Tamil member of my staff.

The Gadabas of Vizagapatam will not touch a horse, as they are palanquin-bearers, and have the same objection to the rival animal that a cab-driver has to a motor-car. In South Canara none but the lowest Paraiyan will rub down a horse.

Native physicians, in the Tamil districts, are said to prepare an unguent, into the composition of which the eyes of the slender Loris (*Loris gracilis*), the brain of the dead offspring of a primipara, and the catamenial blood of young virgins enter, as an effective preparation in necromancy. The eye of the Loris is also sought after for making a preparation, which is believed to enable the possessor to kidnap and seduce women. A young

* Tennent, Ceylon.

married student at a college attributed his illness to the administration by his wife of a love philtre containing the brains of a baby, which had been exhumed after burial. Among the Paraiyans, and some other castes, a first born child, if it is a male, is buried near or even within the house, so that its corpse may not be carried away by a witch or sorcerer, to be used in magic rites.* A love philtre, said to be composed of the charred remains of a mouse and a spider was recently sent to the Chemical Examiner to Government for analysis in a suspected poisoning case.

There is a belief that the urine of a wild monkey (kondamuchcha), which it discharges in a thick stream, possesses the power of curing rheumatic pains, if applied to the affected parts with a mixture of garlic. Some of the poorer classes in the villages of Kurnool obtain a sale even for stones on which this monkey has urinated, and hill-people suffering from chronic fever sometimes drink its blood.† The flesh of the black monkey (Nīlgiri langūr) is sold in the Nīlgiri bazaars as a cure for whooping-cough.

It is on record that the Tanjore Nayakar, having betrayed Madura and suffered for it, was told by his Brāhman advisers that he had better be born again. So a colossal cow was cast in bronze, and the Nayakar shut up inside. The wife of his Brāhman guru acted as nurse, received him in her arms, rocked him on her knees,

* A. C. Clayton, Madras Mus. Bull., V, 2, 1906.

† Manual of the Kurnool district.

and caressed him on her breast, and he tried to cry like a baby.*

When a person rises in the morning, he should not face or see a cow's head, but should see its hinder parts. This is because of a legend that a cow killed a Brāhman by goring him with its horns. In some temples a cow is made to stand in front of the temple, with its back towards it, so that any one entering may see its face. A story is told at Cochin that the beautiful blue and white tiles, which adorn the floor of the synagogue, were originally intended for a former Rāja of Cochin. But a wily Jew declared that bullock's blood must have been used in the preparation of the glaze, and offered to take them off the hands of the Rāja, who was only too glad to get rid of them.

At a sale of cattle, the vendor takes a small quantity of straw in his hand, and, putting some cow-dung on it, presents it to the purchaser.† This transaction, which is called erukaziththu koduththal (giving cow-dung) seals the contract. The five products of the cow (pānchagavyam)—milk, curds, butter, urine, and fæces—are taken by Hindus to remove pollution from confinement, and a voyage across the seas to Europe, other causes. Owners of cattle take their sick animals round the hill at Tirukazhukunram on a Tuesday in performance of a vow, with the belief that their health will be thus restored. Sāris (female cloths) with the figures of cows printed on them are made by the cotton-printers of

* J. S. Chandler, Calcutta Review, 1903.

† H. J. Stokes, Ind. Ant., III, 1874.

Masulipatam and other places. Brāhman widows believe that wearing such cloths will bring a blessing on them.

The Sembaliguda Gadabas believe that a piece of wild buffalo horn, buried in the ground of the village, will avert or cure cattle disease.* And the Billavas of South Canara, who are employed as toddy-tappers, believe that, if they beat the spathe of the cocoanut palm with the bone of a buffalo which has been killed by a tiger, the yield of toddy will, if the bone has not touched the ground, be greater than if an ordinary bone is used.

The common striped squirrel was employed in the construction of the bridge which Rāma was constructing to connect Rāmēswaram island with Ceylon. Seeing the squirrel fatigued with its labours, Rāma sympathetically stroked its back with the three middle fingers of his right hand, the marks of which were left behind. In Vizagapatam one of the most valued charms is called chemru mousa, described as being a small musk rat only an inch and-a-half long, very scarce, and only found on rocky hills. It is worn in a gold or silver box on the arm, and is supposed to render a man invulnerable against sword cuts and musket shots.

"At Kolar in Mysore," Mr. S. K. Sundara Charlu writes,† "there is believed to be a regular goddess of scorpions, under whose seat there lives and thrives a brood of scorpions, over whom she presides. Another belief is that scorpions have the power of reviving, even after being completely crushed into pulp. We are,

* H. D. Taylor, Madras Census report, 1891.

† Indian Review, 1905.

therefore, gravely warned not to rest secure till the enemy has been actually cremated. It is commonly said in South India that the scorpion has great reverence for the name of Ganēsa, because it is supposed that when, on seeing a scorpion, one cries out, 'Pulliyar annai' (in the name of Ganēsa), the scorpion will suddenly stop; the truth of the matter being that any loud noise is heard by the scorpion, and arrests its motion."

The peon (attendant) in the zoological laboratory of one of the Madras colleges would put his hand with impunity into a jar of live scorpions, of which he believed that only a pregnant female would sting him with hurt. He was doubtless unaware that, in Senegambia, men of the scorpion class affirm that scorpions of a very deadly kind will run over their bodies without poisoning them.* A sweeper man, who had a mole on his back in shape somewhat resembling a scorpion, believed himself to be immune against scorpion sting, and would confidently insert the poison-spine of a live scorpion into his skin. In a letter to a medical officer a native wrote that "when a pregnant woman is stung by a scorpion, the child which is in the womb at the time of such stinging, when delivered, does not suffer from the sting of a scorpion, if ever it were to be stung in its lifetime." Among quaint remedies for scorpion sting may be noted sitting with an iron crowbar in the mouth, and the application of chopped lizard over the puncture. The excrement of lizards fed on scorpions is believed to be an effective remedy.

* Fraser, Totemism, 1887.

If the offspring of a primipara dies, it is buried in a place where jackals can get at it. It is believed that, if a jackal does not make a sumptuous meal off the corpse, the woman will not be blessed with more children. The hyæna is believed to beat to death, or strangle with its tail people whom it seizes. The head of a hyæna is sometimes buried in cattle-sheds to prevent cattle disease. Its incisor teeth are tied round the loins of a woman in labour, to lessen her pains.* There is a belief that, when a bear seizes a man, it tickles him to death without biting or violence.† Bears are supposed, owing to the multi-lobulated external appearance of the kidneys, to gain an additional pair of these organs every year of their life The bite of a rat, cat, or monkey is commonly believed to give rise to asthma. It is believed that the flesh or blood of some animals, which have certain organs largely developed, will cure disease of corresponding organs in the human subject. For example, the flesh of jackals, which are credited with the possession of very powerful lungs is believed to cure asthma. And the fat of the peacock, which moves gracefully and easily, is supposed to cure stiff joints. For a similar reason women rub the blood of the small garden bat into the dilated lobes of their ears, so as to strengthen them.

In connection with tigers, the following extract from the diary of a native forest officer may be quoted. "Up a tree, where I adhere with much pain and discomposure, while the tiger roaring in a very awful

* Manual of the Kurnool district.

† M. J. Walhouse, Ind. Ant., V, 1876.

manner on the fire-line. This is very inconsiderate tiger, and causes me great griefs, as I have before reported to your honour. This two times he spiled my work, coming and shouting like thunder, and putting me up a tree, and making me behave like an insect. I am not able to climb with agility owing to stomach being a little big from bad water of this jungle. Chenchumans can fly up tree quickly. This is a very awful fate for me." Some years ago, a drinking fountain was erected at the Madras museum, in which the water issued from the mouth of a lion. It entirely failed in its object as the native visitors would not use it, because the animal was represented in the act of vomiting. Some Hindus in Madras believe that it would be unlucky for a newly married couple to visit the museum, as their offspring would be deformed as the result of the mother having gazed on the skeletons and stuffed animals.

Should a crow come near the house, and caw in its usual rapid raucous tones, it means that calamity is impending. But, should the bird indulge in its peculiar prolonged guttural note, happiness will ensue. If a crow keeps on cawing incessantly in a house, it is believed to foretell the coming of a guest. The belief is so strong that some women prepare more food than is required for the household. There is also an insect called virunthoo poochee, or guest insect. The crow is believed to possess only one eye, which moves from socket to socket as occasion demands. The belief is founded on the legend that an Asura, disguised as a crow, while Rāma was sleeping with his head in Sīta's lap in the jungles of Dandaka, pecked at her breasts, so that blood issued therefrom. On waking, Rāma, observing the blood, and learning the cause of it, clipped a bit of straw, and, after infusing it with the Brāhma astra (miraculous weapon, let it go against the crow Asura, who appealed to Rāma for mercy. Taking pity on it, Rāma asked the Asura to offer one of its eyes to the weapon, and saved it from death. Since this time crows are supposed to have only one eye. In Malabar there is a belief that ill-luck will result if, on certain days, a crow soils one's person or clothes. The evil can only be removed by bathing with the clothes on, and propitiating Brāhmans. On other days the omen is a lucky one. On srādh (memorial) days, pindams (balls of cooked rice) are offered to the crows. If they do not touch them, the ceremony is believed not to have been properly performed, and the wishes of the dead man are not satisfied. If the crows, after repeated trials, fail to eat the rice, the celebrant makes up his mind to satisfy these wishes, and the crows are then supposed to relish the balls. On one occasion my assistant was in camp on the Palni hills, the higher altitudes of which are still uninhabited by crows, and he had perforce to march down to the plains, in order to perform the annual ceremony for his deceased father. When an Urāli man has been excommunicated from his caste, he must kill a sheep or goat before the elders, and mark his forehead with its blood. He then gives a feast to the assembly and puts part of the food on the roof of his house. If the crows eat it, he is received back into the caste.* A native

* Madras Census report, 1901.

clerk sometime ago took leave in anticipation of sanction on receipt of news of a death in his family at a distant town. His excuse was that his elder brother had, on learning that his son had seen two crows *in coitu*, sent him a post-card stating that the son was dead. The boy turned out to be alive, but the card, it was explained, was sent owing to a superstitious belief that, if a person sees two crows engaged in sexual congress, he will die unless one of his relation sheds tears. To avert this catastrophe, false news as to the death are sent by the post or telegraph, and subsequently corrected by a letter or telegram announcing that the individual is alive. There is a legend current in the Kavarathi island of the Laccadives, that a Māppilla tāngal (priest) once cursed the crows for dropping their excrement on his person, and now there is not a crow on the island. The Kois of the Godāvari district believe that hell is the abode of an iron crow, which feeds on all who go there. Some years ago a rumour spread in the Koi villages that an iron cock was abroad very early in the morning, and upon the first village in which it heard one or more cocks crow it would send a grievous pestilence, and decimate the village. In one instance at least this led to the immediate extermination of all the unfortunate cocks in that village. I am informed by Mr. Jayaram Mudaliar that the Khonds will not kill crows, as this would be a sin amounting to the killing of a friend. According to their legend, soon after the creation of the world there was a family consisting of an aged man and woman, and four children, who died one after the other in quick succession. Their parents were too aged to take the necessary steps for their cremation, so they threw the bodies away on the ground, at some distance from their home. God appeared to them in their dreams one night, and promised that he would create the crow, so that it might devour the dead bodies.

A grāndha (palm-leaf book), describing how an enemy may be struck down, gives the following details. The head of a fowl with dark-coloured flesh is cut off. The head is then split, and a piece of cadjan, on which are written the name of the person to be injured, and the name of the star under which he was born, is stuck in the split head, which is then sewn up, and the tongue stitched to the beak. The head is then inserted into a certain fruit, which is tied up with a withe of a creeper, and deposited under the enemy's gateway. By the Tiyans a number of evil spirits are supposed to devote their attention to pregnant women, and to suck the blood of the child *in utero*, and of the mother. In the process of expelling these, the woman lies on the ground, and kicks. A cock is thrust into her hand, and she bites it, and drinks its hot blood.* At a marriage among the Malai Vellālas, a live fowl is swung round the heads of the bride and bridegroom. Its neck is then wrung, and the dead bird thrown to the attendant clarionet players. Among some classes in Mysore there is a belief that, if a death occurs in a house on a Tuesday or Friday, another death will quickly follow unless a fowl is tied

* F. Fawcett, Madras Museum Bull., III, 3, 1901.

to one corner of the bier. The fowl is buried with the deceased. Those castes which do not eat fowls replace it by the bolt of the door.* A west coast housewife, when she buys a fowl, goes through a mystic ritual to prevent it from getting lost. She takes it thrice round the fire-place, saying to it "Roam over the country and the forest, and come home safe again." Among the Tamils, if a burial takes place on a Saturday, a fowl must also be buried, or dire calamity will overtake the house.

By some it is considered unlucky to keep pigeons about a dwelling-house, as they are believed, on account of their habit of standing on one leg, to lead to poverty. House sparrows are credited with bringing good luck to a house in which they build their nests. For this purpose, when a house is under construction, holes are left in the walls or ceiling, or earthen pots are hung on the walls by means of nails or pegs, as an attractive site for nesting. One method of attracting sparrows to a house is to make a noise with rupees as in the act of counting out coins. Some native physicians prescribe the flesh and bones of cock sparrows for those who have lost their virility. The birds are cleaned, and put in a mortar together with other medicinal ingredients. They are pounded together for several hours, so that the artificial heat produced by the operation converts the mixture into a pulpy mass, which is taken by the patient in small doses. The flesh of quails and patridges is also believed to possess remedial properties.

* J. S. F. Mackenzie, Ind. Ant., II., 1873.

Ill-luck will follow, should an owl sit on the house top, or perch on the bough of a tree near the house. One screech forebodes death; two screeches success in any approaching undertaking; three the addition by marriage of a girl to the family; four a disturbance; five that the hearer will travel. Six screeches foretell the coming of guests; seven mental distress; eight sudden death; and nine signify favourable results. A species of owl, called pullu, is a highly dreaded and ominous bird. It is supposed to cause all kinds of illness to children, resulting in emaciation. At the sound of its screeching, children are taken into a room, to avoid its furtive and injurious gaze. Various propitiatory ceremonies are performed by specialists to secure its good-will. Amulets are worn by children as a preventive against its evil influences. To warn off the unwelcome intruder, broken pots, painted with black and white dots, are set up on house tops. And sometimes a house, which has been visited by an owl, is locked up and vacated for six months, and then once more occupied after the performance of certain rites. It is stated by Mr. W. Francis * that, in the Bellary district, the flat roofs of many houses may be seen decked with rags fluttering from sticks, piles of broken pots, and so forth. These are to scare away owls, which, it is said, sometimes vomit up blood, and sometimes milk. If they sit on a house and bring up blood, it is bad for the inmates; if milk, good. But the risk of the vomit turning out to be blood is apparently more

* Manual of the Bellary district.

feared than the off chance of its proving to be milk is hoped for, and it is thought best to be on the safe side, and keep the owl at a distance.

There is a curious superstition connected with the Brāhmani kite. When a person is ill in a house, his people vow to offer a few pounds of mutton to the kite on the patient's recovery. It is believed that, should the offering be acceptable, the sick person will speedily get better, and the kite will come to demand its meat, making its presence known by sitting on a tree near the house, and crying plaintively. The shadow of a Brāhmani kite falling on a cobra is said to stupify the snake. A person who has a Garuda machchai or Garuda rēka (Garuda mole or mark) on his body is believed to have such an influence over cobras, that, however fierce they may be, they become quiet on his approach.

The following story is current concerning the sacred vultures of Tirukazhukunram. The Ashtavasus, or eight gods who guard the eight points of the compass, did penance, and Sīva appeared in person before them. But, becoming angry with them, he cursed them, and turned them into vultures. When they asked for forgiveness, Sīva directed that they should remain at the temple of Vedagiri Iswarar. Three pairs of the birds died during the last three yugams, and one pair still survives (plate XV). These birds come to the temple daily at noon for food, and the temple priests say that they will never come together if sinners are present in the crowd which assembles at the temple.

Plate XV.

Sacred Vultures, Tirukazhukunram.

It is believed that, if a young crow-pheasant is tied by an iron chain to a tree, the mother, as soon as she discovers the captive, will go and fetch a certain root, and by its aid easily break the iron chain, which, when it snaps, will be converted into gold. The temple or blue-rock pigeon is greatly venerated by natives, who consider themselves highly favoured if the birds build in their houses. Should a death occur in a house where there is a tame pigeon loft, all the birds will, at the time of the funeral, circle thrice round the loft, and leave the locality for ever. House sparrows are supposed to possess a similar characteristic, but, before quitting the house of mourning, they will pull every straw out of their nests.

Among certain wood-cutter classes, it is believed that, if a crane crosses from left to right, when a man is bringing home wood, he will get a third as much again for his fuel.*

Surgeon-Major Cornish, states † that there is a place near Vaisarpadi, close to Madras, in which the worship of the living snake draws crowds of votaries, who make holiday excursions to the temple, generally on Sundays, in the hope of seeing the snakes, which are preserved in the temple grounds, and, he adds, probably so long as the desire of offspring is a leading characteristic of the Indian people, so long will be worship of the serpent, or of snake-stones, be a popular cult. He describes further how, at Rajahmundry, he came across an old ant-hill by

* Many of the bird superstitions here recorded were published in an article in the Madras Mail, 1895.

† Madras Census Report, 1871.

the side of a public road, on which was placed a modern stone representative of a cobra, and the ground all round was stuck over with pieces of wood curved very rudely in the shape of a snake. These were the offerings left by devotees at the abode taken up by an old snake, who would occasionally come out of his hole, and feast on the eggs and ghī left for him by his adorers. Around this place he saw many women who had come to make their prayers at the shrine. If they chanced to see the cobra, the omén was interpreted favourably, and their prayers for progeny would be granted.

The safety with which snake-charmers handle cobras is said to be due to the removal of a stone, which supplied their teeth with venom, from under the tongue or behind the hood. This stone is highly prized as a snake-poison antidote. It is said to be not unlike a tamarind stone in size, shape, and appearance, and is known to be genuine if, when it is immersed in water, bubbles continue to arise from it, or if, when put into the mouth, it gives a leap, and fixes itself to the palate. When it is applied to the punctures made by the snake's poison-fangs, it is said to stick fast and extract the poison, falling off of itself as soon as it is saturated. After the stone drops off, the poison which it has absorbed is removed by placing it in a vessel of milk, which becomes darkened in colour. A specimen was submitted to Faraday, who expressed his belief that it was a piece of charred bone, which has been filled with blood, and then charred again.*

* *Vide* Yule and Burnell, 'Hobson Jobson.'

In Malabar, Mr. V. Govindan informs me, there are mantravādis, who are believed to possess an hereditary power of removing the effects of snake poison by repeating mantrams, and performing certain rites. If a house is visited by snakes, they can expel them by reciting certain mantrams on three small pebbles, and throwing these on to the roof. In cases of snake-bite they recite mantrams, and wave a cock over the patient's body from the head towards the feet. Sometimes a number of cocks have to be sacrificed before the charm works. The patient is then taken to a tank or well, and a number of pots of water are emptied over his head, while the mantravādi utters mantrams. There are said to be certain revengeful snakes, which, after they have bitten a person, coil themselves round the branches of a tree, and render the efforts of the mantravādi ineffective. In such a case he, through the aid of mantrams, sends ants and other insects to harass the snake, which comes down from the tree, and sucks the poison from the punctures which it has made.

Of serpent worship on the west coast it is written, in the Cochin Census report, 1901, that "no orthodox Hindu will ever kill serpents, even if bitten, for it is believed that any injury done to them would bring on leprosy, sterility, or ophthalmia. They are propitiated by offerings of milk, plantains, etc., on certain days of the year. The Pāmbumēkāt Nambūtiri, in whose house they are fed and nursed, is believed to be proof against their bite and poison. He is the special priest at certain sacrifices offered to the serpents. He alone can remove a serpent grove from one spot to another, or cut and make use of the trees in it. No Hindu, except a Brāhman, will ever make use of even the twig of a plant growing there. The Pulluvans sing in serpent groves, and perform certain ceremonies."

It is recorded by Visscher * that "in the mountains and remote jungles of this country (Malabar) there is a species of snake of the shape and thickness of the stem of a tree, which can swallow men and beasts entire. I have been told an amusing story about one of these snakes. It is said that at Barcelore a chego (Chogan) had climbed up a cocoanut tree to draw toddy or palm wine, and, as he was coming down, both his legs were seized by a snake which had stretched itself up alongside the tree with its mouth wide open, and was sucking him in gradually as he descended. Now, the Indian, according to the custom of his country, had stuck his teifermes (an instrument not unlike a pruning knife) into his girdle with the curve turned outwards; and, when he was more than half swallowed, the knife began to rip up the body of the snake so as to make an opening, by which the lucky man most unexpectedly was able to escape. Though the snakes in this country are so noxious to the natives, yet the ancient veneration for them is still maintained. No one dares to injure them or to drive them away by violence, and so audacious do they become that they will sometimes creep between people's legs when they are eating, and attack their bowls of rice, in which case

* Letters from Malabar.

retreat is necessary until the monsters have satiated themselves and taken their departure."

"A good snake shrine," Mr. J. D. Rees writes,* "in as much an attraction in the case of a house on the Malabar coast as a garden is in the case of a villa at Hampstead or Harrow." Concerning serpent worship in Malabar, Mr. C. Karunakara Menon writes as follows.† "The existence of snake groves is said to owe its origin to Srī Parasurāma, who advised that a part of every house should be set apart for snakes as household gods. These groves have the appearance of miniature reserved forests as they are considered sacred, and there is a strong prejudice against cutting down trees therein. The groves contain a snake king and queen made of granite, and a tower-like structure, made of laterite, for the sacred snakes. An important snake shrine is the one at a Nambūdri house called Pathirikunnath. The whole place looks like a snake asylum. In the front verandah are a series of snake holes, which communicate with ant-hills inside the house. The Nambūdri's source of income is derived from the shrine, to which visitors from all parts of the district bring rich presents for the snakes. Snakes were, in olden days, considered a part of the property. It is on record that a certain family sold their ancestral home to an individual, who cut down the snake grove, and planted it up. Some members of the vendor's family began to suffer from cutaneous disorders. The local astrologer was called in, and attributed the ailment to the wrath of the aggrieved snakes. When a snake is

* Nineteenth Century, 1904.

† Calcutta Review, 1901.

seen inside, or in the neighbourhood of a house, great care is taken to catch it without giving it the least pain. Usually a stick is placed gently on its head, and the mouth of an earthenware pot is shown to it. When it is in, the pot is loosely covered with a cocoanut shell, to allow of free breathing. It is then taken to a secluded spot, the pot destroyed, and the snake set at liberty. It is considered to be polluted by being caught in this way, and holy water is sometimes poured over it. Killing a snake is considered a grievous sin, and even to see a snake with its head bruised is believed to be a precursor of calamities. Pious Malayālis, when they see a snake killed in this way, have it burnt with the full solemnities attendant on the cremation of high-caste Hindus. The carcase is covered with a piece of silk, and burnt in sandalwood. A Brāhman is hired to observe pollution for some days, and elaborate funeral oblations are offered to the dead snake. Snakes are said to fall in love with, and wed mortal girls, whom they constantly pursue when they are at the bath, at meals, etc. Gradually both suffer and die. The snake never uses its fangs against the chosen woman."

Mischievous children and others, when they see two persons quarelling, rub the nails of the fingers of one hand against those of the other, and repeat the words "Mungoose and snake, bite, bite," in the hope that thereby the quarrel will become intensified and grow more exciting from the spectators' point of view.

The fragrant male inflorescence of *Pandanus fascicularis* is believed to harbour a tiny snake, which is more deadly than the cobra. Incautious smelling of the flowers may, it is said, lead to death.

A snake skin is, in some places, kept with valuable clothes, to prevent damage to them.

In Malabar a class of snake-charmers (Kuravan) go about the country exhibiting snakes. It is considered to be a great act of piety to purchase these animals, and set them at liberty.

"It is believed," Mr. Gopal Panikkar writes,* that, "when an eclipse takes place, Rāhu, the huge serpent, is devouring the sun or moon, as the case may be. An eclipse, being thus the decease of one of these heavenly bodies, people must, of necessity, observe pollution for the period during which the eclipse lasts. When the monster spits out the body, the eclipse is over. Food and drink taken during an eclipse possess poisonous properties. At the end of the eclipse they bathe, to get rid of the pollution. People believe in the existence inside the earth of a precious stone called manikkakkallu. These stones are supposed to have been made out of the gold, which has existed in many parts of the earth from time immemorial. Certain serpents of divine nature have been blowing for ages on these treasures of gold, some of which dwindle into a small stone of resplendent beauty and brightness called manikkam. The moment their work is finished, the serpents are transformed into winged serpents, and fly up into the air with the stones in their

* Madras Christ Coll. Magazine, 1896.

mouths." The Rev. S. Nicholson informs me that, during an eclipse, a Māla woman will remain in the house, and burn the hoofs or horns of some animal, in the hope that the smell will keep away the evil spirits.

Among the Telugus, eclipses are said to be caused by the moon intervening between a money-lender and his clients. When the client, exasperated by demands for money, is about to strike the money-lender, the moon intervenes, and is partly obscured by the striker's body. They are also believed to be caused by the moon intervening between a sweeper and his son, when the father is about to strike the son.*

Natives, when seeking for treasure, arm themselves with a staff made from one of the snake-wood trees (pao da cobro), in the belief that the snakes which guard the treasure will retire before it.

When a family, in Malabar, is troubled by the presence of snakes on the premises, or when members thereof are suffering from cutaneous or other disorders, the aid of the astrologer is solicited, and, if the anger of a snake is believed to be the cause of the infliction, a ceremony called pāmbantullel (snake-jumping) or nāgapattu is performed. A Pulluvan, whose caste is said to be descended from the snake deity, acts as the pūjāri or officiating minister. On the day appointed, he draws a geometrical design of a snake on the floor. (plate XVI). The animal is represented in rice flour, and the spaces between the coils are filled in with burnt rice husk,

* M. N. Venkataswami. Ind. Ant., XXXIV, 1905.

Plate XVI.

Casting out Devils.

turmeric powder, powdered green leaves, etc. Five colours are essential, to correspond with the colours which are visible on the necks of serpents. A female member of the afflicted family, who has fasted during the day, bathes, and sits on the floor at the head of the snake. Her hair is untied, and she holds in her hands a bunch of cocoanut flowers. The Pulluvan plays on his earthen pot-drum (Pulluva kudam plate XVII) while a Pulluva woman keeps time with the music by striking a metal vessel. Both man and woman at the same time sing songs in honour of the serpent deity. Gradually the seated woman becomes possessed, and begins to quiver, while waving her dishevelled locks. Moving backwards and forwards, she rubs away the figure of the snake with the cocoanut flowers, and, rising up, bathes once more. It may be necessary to rub away the snake as many as a hundred times, in which case the ceremony is prolonged over several weeks. Each time that the snake design is destroyed, one or two men, with torches in their hands, perform a dance, keeping step to the Pulluvan's music. The family may eventually erect a small platform or shrine in a corner of their grounds, and worship at it annually. The snake deity will, it is believed, not manifest himself if any of the persons or articles required for the ceremony are impure, *e.g.*, if the pot-drum has been polluted by the touch of a menstruating woman. The Pulluvan, from whom a drum was purchased for the museum, was very reluctant to part with it, lest it should be touched by an impure woman.

When a friend was engaged in experiments on snake venom, some Dommaras (jugglers) asked for permission to unbury the corpses of the snakes and mongooses for the purpose of food.

The harmless tree-snake, *Dendrophis pictus*, is more dreaded than the cobra in the Tamil and Telugu countries. It is believed that, after biting a human being, it ascends the nearest palmyra palm, where it waits until it sees the smoke ascending from the funeral pyre of its victim. The only chance of saving the life of a person who has been bitten is to have a mock funeral, whereat a straw effigy is burnt. Seeing the smoke, the deluded snake comes down from the tree, and the bitten person recovers.

An earth-snake, which lives at Kodaikānal on the Palni mountains, is credited with giving leprosy to anybody whose skin it licks.

In the treatment of leprosy, a Russell's viper is stuffed with rice, and put in an earthen pot, the mouth of which is sealed with clay. The pot is buried for forty days, and then exhumed. Chicken are fed with the rice, and the patient is subsequently fed on the chickens.

The fat of the rat-snake is used as an external application in the treatment of leprosy.

A treatment for cobra bite is to take a chicken, and make a deep incision into its beak at the basal end. The cut surface is applied to the punctures made by the snake's fangs, which are opened up with a knife. After

Plate XVII

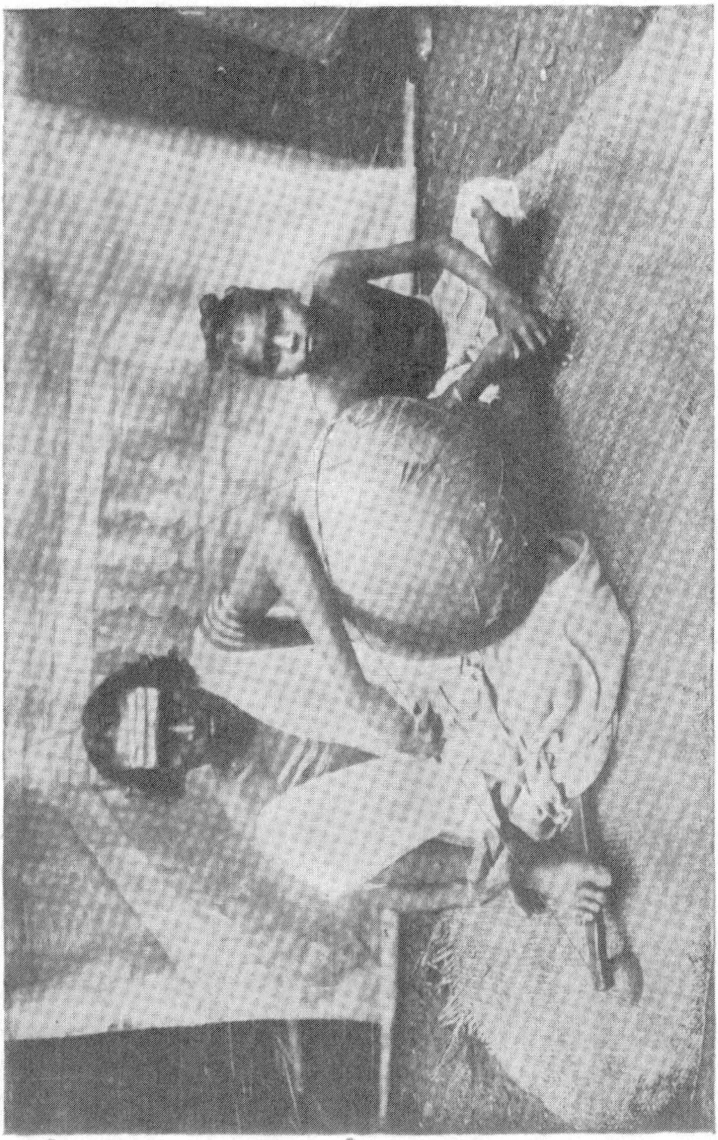

Pulluvan with Pot-drum.

a time the chicken dies, and, if the patient has not come round, more chicken must be applied until he is out of danger. The theory is that the poison is attracted by, and enters the blood of the chicken. A person should postpone an errand on which he is starting, if he sees a cobra or rat snake. One who dreams that he has been bitten by a snake is considered to be proof against snake-bite, and, if he dreams of a cobra, his wife or some near relative is believed to have conceived. The sight of two snakes coiled round each other in sexual congress is considered to portend some great evil. An old woman, during an outbreak of cholera at Bezwāda, used to inject the patients hypodermically with an aqueous solution of cobra venom.

By the Thanda Pulayans of the west coast, the phosphorescence on the surface of the water is supposed to indicate the presence of the spirits of their ancestors, which fish in the backwaters.

The monitor (*Varanus*) and crocodile are believed to proceed from the eggs laid by one animal. They are laid, and hatched near water, and, of the animals which come out of them, some find their way into the water, while others remain on land. The former become crocodiles, and the latter monitors.* The tail of a chamæleon, secured on a Sunday, is an excellent love philtre. There are experts who are able to interpret the significance of the chirping of lizards, which, *inter alia*, foretells the approach of a case of snake-bite, and whether the patient

* T. K. Gopal Panikkar, *op cit.*

will die or not. The fall of a lizard on different parts of the body is often taken as an omen for good or evil, according as it alights on the right or left side, hand or foot, head or shoulder. A native of Cochin foretold from the chirping of a lizard that a robbery would take place in a certain temple. In accordance with the prophecy, the temple jewels were looted, and the prophet was sent to prison under suspicion of being an accomplice of the thieves, but subsequently released as being innocent. There is a widespread belief among children in Malabar that a lizard (*Calotes versicolor*) sucks the blood of those whom it looks at. As soon, therefore, as they catch sight of this creature, they apply saliva to the navel, from which it is believed that the blood is extracted.

The following case was recently brought to my notice by the Chemical Examiner to Government. In Malabar, a young man, apparently in good health, walked home with two other men after a feast, chewing betel. Arriving at his home, he went to sleep, and was found dead next morning. Blood was described as "oozing out of his eyes." It was given out that the cause of death was an insect, which infests betel leaves, and is very poisonous. The belief in death from chewing or swallowing the veththilai or vettila poochi (betel insect) is a very general one, and is so strong that, when a person suffers from giddiness after chewing betel, he is afraid that he has partaken of the poisonous insect. Native gentlemen take particular care to examine every betel leaf, wipe it with a cloth, and smear chunam over it, before chewing.

My assistant has made enquiries concerning the poochi, but no one can tell him what it is like. The poochi is called by Gundert* vettila pāmpu or moorkhan (snake) or vettila thēl (scorpion).

When the umbilical cord of a Khond baby sloughs off, a spider is burnt in the fire, and its ashes are placed in a cocoanut shell, mixed with castor oil, and applied by means of a fowl's feather to the navel. Offerings of milk, fruit and flowers are made, on certain ceremonial occasions, to 'white-ant' (termite) hills, which are also resorted to when people are afflicted with ear-ache, pain in the eye, skin disease, etc. They pour milk and other offerings over the hill, and carry away some of the earth, which they apply to the affected part. The cure is expedited by calling in a Brāhman to repeat mantrams.† A devil, in the disguise of a dung-beetle of large size, is believed to haunt the house wherein a baby has been newly born, and the impact of the insect against the infant will bring about its instant death. Quite recently, a scare has arisen in connection with an insect, which is said to have taken up its abode in imported German glass bangles, which compete with the indigenous industry of the Gāzulas. The insect is believed to lie low in a hole in the bangle till it is purchased, when it comes out and nips the wearer, after warning her to get her affairs in order before succumbing. A specimen of a broken bangle, from which the insect is stated to have burst forth, and stung a girl in the wrist, was recently sent to me. But the insect was not forthcoming.

* Malayalam Dictionary.

† Rev. J. Cain, Ind. Ant., V, 1876.

Witchcraft; Sorcery; etc.—In some places in the Tamil districts, if a temple car does not move from its position when an attempt is made to drag it, a lot of people, who are allowed to get intoxicated, are given toddy mixed with castor-oil. Some of this they spit out upon the wheels of the car, which cannot stand defilement, and proceeds to move. A copper-grant, recently acquired at Tirupati, records that a car was made for the goddess Kālikadēvi of Conjeeveram by certain Pānchālans (members of the artisan classes). While it was being taken to the temple, a magician stopped it by incantations. The help of another magician was sought, and he cut off the head of his pregnant daughter, suspended it on the car, and performed certain other rites. The car then moved, and the woman, whose head had been cut off, was brought back to life. In favour of the magician, who performed these wonders, certain endowments were made by the Pānchālans. The grant is, however, believed to be a forgery. A woman, pregnant for the first time, should not see a car adorned with figures of a lion. If she does, the tradition is that she will give birth to a monster. Some time ago, a man was operated on for a dermoid cyst, and a rumour quickly spread that he had been delivered of twins, on the chance of seeing which a large crowd collected outside the hospital.

Of a remarkable example of demon worship in Tinnevelly, Dr. Caldwell wrote * that "an European was till recently worshipped as a demon. From the rude verses,

* The Tinnevelly Shānars, 1849.

which were sung in connection with his worship, it would appear that he was an English officer, who was mortally wounded at the taking of the Travancore lines in 1809, and was buried about twenty-five miles from the scene of the battle in a sandy waste, where, a few years after, his worship was established by the Shānāns of the neighbourhood. His worship consisted in the offering to his manes of spirituous liquors and cheroots."

At Girigehalli, in the Anantapur district, is a temple concerning which the story goes that the stomach of the village goddess was once opened by an avaricious individual, who expected to find treasure within it. The deity appeared to him in a dream, and said that he should suffer like pain to that which he had inflicted upon her, and he shortly afterwards died of some internal complaint.* A few years ago, in the Bellary district, the god is said to have appeared to a man, and promised him wealth if he would sacrifice his son to him. At that time the man had only one child. But the god said "A son will be born. Do not fear. I shall revive the son, and give you wealth." Within a year a second child was born. Him the father took to the shrine, and cut his throat with a sword, after offerings of a buffalo and goat had proved of no avail in securing the promised riches. The man, whose story I heard from himself in the lock-up, had apparently implicit belief that the god would bring the child to life again.

* Gazetteer of the Anantapur district.

Some years ago, a native of the west coast, believing that treasure was hidden on his property, took council with an astrologer, who recommended the performance of a human sacrifice, which happily was averted. There is a widespread belief that treasure will be found beneath any tree or plant, which exhibits abnormal growth.

In a recent case in Mysore, two men were charged with the kidnapping and murder of a female infant, and one was sentenced to transportation for life. The theory of the prosecution was that the child was killed, to be offered as a sacrifice with the object of securing hidden treasure, believed to be lying underground near the scene of the murder. A witness gave evidence to the effect that the second accused was the pūjāri of the Gāngamma temple. He used to tell people that there was hidden treasure, and that, if a human sacrifice was offered, the treasure might be got. He used to make pūja, and tie yantrams. He also made special pūjas, and exorcised devils. Another witness testified that her mother had buried some treasure during her lifetime, and she asked the pūjāri to discover it. He came to her house, made an earthen image, and did pūja to it. He dug the ground in three places, but no treasure was found. In dealing with this evidence in the Court of Appeal, the Judges expressed their opinion that "the testimony of these witnesses is absolutely irrelevant, as the facts they speak of, even if believed unreservedly, have no logical connection with the guilt of either of the accused men. It is well known that ignorant persons have various superstitions about the discovery of hidden treasure, and the facts that the second accused either shared such superstitious beliefs, or traded on the credulity of his neighbours by his pretensions of special occult power, and that a Sanyāsi had some four years ago given out that treasure might be discovered by means of a human sacrifice, cannot justify any inference that the second accused would have acted on the last suggestion, especially when the witnesses cannot even say that the second accused heard the Sanyāsi's suggestion." The temple was searched, and the following articles were found:—"three roots of the banyan tree having suralay (coil); a suralay of the banyan tree, round which two roots were entwined; a piece of banyan root; and a wheel (alada chakra) made of banyan root. Besides, there were a copper armlet; copper thyati (charm cylinder); nine copper plates on which letters were engraved; a copper mokka mattoo (copper plate bearing figures of deities); a piece of thread coloured red, white and black, for tying yantrams; a tin case containing kappu (black substance), a ball of human hair, and a pen-knife. There was also a deal wood box containing books and papers relating to Bhūta Vidya (black art). Chakrams (wheels) were inscribed on the books and papers."

Theoretically, human sacrifice is efficacious in warding off devils during the construction of a new railway or big bridge. And to the influence of such evil spirits the death of several workmen by accident in a cutting on the railway, which was under construction at Cannanore, was attributed. When a mantapam or shrine was consecrated, a human sacrifice was formerly considered necessary, but a cocoanut is now some times used as a substitute. During the building of a tower at the Madras museum, just before the big granite blocks were placed in position, the coolies contented themselves with the sacrifice of a goat. On the completion of a new building, some castes on the west coast perform certain pūjas, and sacrifice a fowl or sheep, to drive away the devils, which are supposed to haunt it.

In 1840, a religious mendicant, on his way back from Rāmēsvaram, located himself in a village near Ramnād, and gave himself out to be a great swāmi, gifted with the power of working miracles. One evening, the chucklers (leather-workers) of the village, observing crows and vultures hovering near a group of trees, and suspecting that there was carrion for them to feast upon, were tempted to visit the spot, where they found a corpse, mangled most fearfully, and with the left hand and right leg cut off. Many nails were driven into the head, a garland was placed round the neck, and the forehead smeared with sandal paste. It was rumoured that a certain person was ailing, and that the holy man decreed that nothing short of a human sacrifice could save him, and that the victim should bear his name. The holy man disappeared, but was captured shortly afterwards.*

In Coimbatore, some years ago, a Goundan murdered his son, aged nine or ten years, to place a murder at the door of an enemy.

* Chevers. Manual of Medical Jurisprudence in India, 1870.

Plate XVIII.

Pongal Offerings.

In 1900 a hill-man in Vizagapatam gave out that he was an incarnation of one of the Pāndava brothers, and, in the course of a few months, he obtained a following of five thousand people, who firmly believed in his claims to divinity. All his disciples had to go and cut sticks of female bamboos, on the new (or full?) moon of the month Vaisakha. These the holy man blessed, and promised that from them would issue shot and shell, whereas the guns of the sirkar (Government) would discharge only sand and water. The movement eventually assumed a political as well as a religious complexion, but the aims of the leaders were never very definite, and the reason alleged for the murder of two policemen was their refusal to pay homage to the reputed swāmi or god. A force of armed police was sent to arrest the ringleaders, but they and their adherents offered resistance, and a number of the misguided people were killed. The holy man himself was arrested, and charged with abetment of the murder, but he died in jail before the trial.

When a person is taken suddenly ill, a wise woman is consulted, who professes to be able to discover the real cause of the illness. Consultation with this woman is called getha aduguta in Telugu, and kani kelothu in Kanarese. If she says that the illness is due to some evil spirit, *e.g.*, Muniswera, a pongal (boiled rice) and sacrifice of a fowl or goat (plate XVIII) is made to the deity beneath a nīm (*Melia Azadirachta*), in which tree Muni is supposed to live. Or coloured water is waved three times in front of the sick person. On the dish containing the water two cross-lines are made with cow-dung, and at the junction of the lines a pit is made, in which a little oil or ghī is placed, to feed a wick, which is lighted. After the waving, a brass vessel is heated over the wick, and pushed into the cow-dung. On the following morning, the vessel is examined, and, if it is found sticking firmly to the tray, the devil has left the patient. If, on the contrary, it comes easily off the cow-dung, the devil is still there, or the illness is due to some other influence.

At cross-roads in the Bellary district odd geometric patterns may sometimes be noticed. These are put there at night by people suffering from disease, in the belief that the affliction will pass to the person who first treads on the charm.*

From Malabar a correspondent writes as follows: "I came across a funny thing on an embankment in a rice field. The tender part of a young cocoanut branch had been cut into three strips, and the strips fastened one into the other in the form of a triangle. At the apex a reed was stuck, and along the sides and base small flowers, so that the thing looked like a ship in full sail. My Inspector informed me, with many blushes, that it contained a devil, which the sorcerer of a neighbouring village had cut out of a young girl. Mrs. Bishop, in her book on Korea, mentions that the Koreans do exactly the same thing, but, in Korea, the devil's prison is laid by the wayside, and is carefully stepped over by every passer-by, whereas the one I saw was

* Manual of the Bellary district.

laid on a paddy bund, and carefully avoided by my peons (orderlies) and others."

Mr. G. F. Paddison informs me that, in case of sickness among the Savaras of Vizagapatam, a buffalo is tied up near the door of the house. Herbs and rice in small platters, and a little brass vessel containing toddy, balls of rice, flowers and medicine, are brought with a bow and arrow. The arrow is thicker at the basal end than towards the tip. The narrow part goes, when shot, through a hole in front of the bow, which is too small to allow of the passage of the rest of the arrow. The Bēju (wise woman) pours some toddy over the herbs and rice, and daubs the patient over the forehead, breasts, stomach, and back. She croons out a long incantation to the goddess, stopping at intervals to call out "daru", to attract the goddess's attention. She then takes the bow and arrow, and shoots twice into the air, and, standing behind the kneeling patient, shoots balls of medicine, stuck on the tip of the arrow, at her. The construction of the arrow is such that the balls are dislodged from its tip. The patient is thus shot at all over the body which is bruised by the impact of the medicine balls Afterwards the Bēju shoots one or two balls at the buffalo, which is taken to a path forming the village boundary, and killed with a tangi (axe). The patient is then daubed with the blood of the buffalo, rice and toddy, and a feast concludes the ceremonial. Mr. Paddison gave some medicine to the Porojas of Vizagapatam during an epidemic of cholera in a village. They all took it eagerly, but, as he was going away, asked whether it would not be a quicker cure to put the witch in the next village, who had brought on the cholera, into jail. In the same district a man was discovered sitting outside his house, while groans proceeded from within. He explained that he was ill, and his wife was swinging on nails with their points upwards, to cure him.

The annual festival at the temple at Karamadai in the Coimbatore district, is visited by about forty or fifty thousand pilgrims, belonging for the most part to the lower classes. In case of sickness or other calamity they take a vow to perform one of the following :—

(1) To pour water at the feet of the idol inside the temple. Each devotee is provided with a goat-skin bag, or more rarely a new earthen pot. He goes to the tank, and, after bathing, fills the bag with water, carries it to the temple, and empties it before the idol. This is repeated a number of times according to the nature of the vow. If the vow be a life-long one, it has to be performed every year until death.

(2) To give kavalam to Dāsaris (religious mendicants). Kavalam consists of plantain fruits, cut up into small slices, and mixed with sugar, jaggery, fried grain, or beaten rice. The Dāsaris are attached to the temple, and wear short drawers, with strings of small brass bells tied to their wrists and ankles. They appear to be possessed, and move wildly about to the beating of drums. As they go about, the devotee puts some of the kavalam into their mouths. The Dāsaris eat a little, and spit out the remainder into the hands of the devotees, who eat it.

This is believed to cure all diseases, and to give children to those who eat it. In addition to kavalam, some put betel leaves into the mouths of the Dāsaris, who, after chewing them, spit them into the mouths of the devotees, At night the Dāsaris carry large torches made of rags, on which the devotees pour ghī. Some people say that, many years ago, barren women used to take a vow to visit the temple at the festival time, and, after offering kavalam, have sexual intercourse with the Dāsaris. The temple authorities, however, profess ignorance of this practice.

At Bangalore a monthly festival is held in honour of Gurumurthi Swāmi, at which women, disturbed by the spirits of drowned persons, become possessed. She is dragged by the hair of the head to a tree, to which a lock of the hair is nailed. She flings herself about in a frenzy, and throws herself on the ground, leaving the lock of hair, torn out by the roots, fastened to the tree by the nail. Eventually the spirits go up the tree, and the woman recovers herself.*

In some places in Southern India, before a woman is confined, the room in which her confinement is to take place is smeared with cow-dung, and, in the room at the outer gate, to the height of four or five feet from the floor, small wet cow-dung cakes are fixed. They are stuck to the wall, and covered with margosa (*Melia Azadirachta*) leaves and cotton seeds. The cakes, with the leaves and seeds, are supposed to have a great power in averting evil spirits from entering the room, and doing

* F. Fawcett, Journ. Anth. Soc., Bombay, I, 1888.

mischief to the newly-born baby, or the lying-in woman.* In the Telugu country, it is the custom among some castes, *e.g.*, the Kāpus and Gamallas, to place twigs of *Balanites Roxburghii* or *Calotropis gigantea* on the floor or in the roof of the lying-in chamber. Sometimes a garland of old shoes is hung on the door-post of the chamber. A fire is kindled, into which pieces of old leather, hair, nails, horns, hoofs, and bones of animals are thrown, in the belief that the smoke arising therefrom will protect the mother and child against evil spirits. Among some classes, when a woman is pregnant, her female friends assemble, pile up before her door a quantity of rice-husk, and set fire to it. To one door post they tie an old shoe, and to the other a bunch of tulasi (*Ocimum sanctum*), in order to prevent the entry of any demon. A bitch is brought in, painted, and marked in the way that the women daily mark their own foreheads. Incense is burnt, and an oblation placed before it. The woman then makes obeisance to it, and makes a meal off curry and rice, on which cakes are placed. If there is present any woman who has not been blessed with children, she seizes some of the cakes, in the hope that, by so doing, she may ere long have a child.†

A legend is current in the Laccadives that a Māppilla tāngal (priest) of the Kavarathi island, hearing the cries of a woman in labour, prayed to God that the women of the island might suffer from no such pains in future.

* S. M. Natesa Sastri, Ind. Ant., XVIII, 1889.

† Rev. J. Cain, Ind. Ant., IV, 1875.

So strong is the belief in the immunity from the pangs of child-birth, which was thus obtained, that the women of the neighbouring islands go over to Kavarathi for delivery, in order to have an easy confinement.*

In some places, when a woman is in labour, her relations keep on measuring out rice or paddy into a measure close to the lying-in room, in the belief that delivery will be accelerated thereby, and I have heard of a gun being fired off in an adjacent room with the same object. A pregnant woman may not look at a temple car when it is being drawn along with the image of the god seated in it. Nor may such a woman witness an eclipse of the sun or moon, as the off-spring would have hare-lip or other deformity. It is recorded in 'the Travels of the Jesuits' (1762) that the superstitious Indians fancy that a dragon swallows the sun and moon during eclipses, and thereby takes them from our sight. "To make the pretended monster disgorge the mighty morsels, they make a dreadful hurly-burly; and such of their wives as are with child shut themselves up very assiduously, and dare not stir out, for fear lest this terrible dragon, after having swallowed the moon, should do the like to their children." In Malabar the tusks of a wild boar are, in cases of protracted labour, pressed over the abdomen of the woman from above downwards.

Virgins, pregnant women, and children are usually warned not to approach the following, as evil spirits seek them for their abode :—

* Madras Census report, 1891.

The pīpal tree (*Ficus religiosa*), and nīm or margosa tree.

Tamarind tree.*

Some natives believe that sleeping under a tamarind tree causes impotence.

Hysteria, epilepsy, and other disorders are, in Malabar, ascribed to possession by devils, who can also cause cattle disease, accidents, and misfortunes of any kind. Throwing stones on houses, and setting fire to the thatch, are supposed to be their ordinary recreations, and the mere mention of a certain Nambūtiri family name is enough to drive them away.† In Malabar, when epidemics break out, the human representative of the goddess, in whose body she manifests herself in the shape of hysterical leapings, yells, and shouts, goes to any house infected, and, with sword in hand, casts out the evil spirit from the patient, who recovers.‡

An old Brāhman woman, in the Bellary district, complained to the police that a Sūdra woman living in her neighbourhood, and formerly engaged by her as sweeper, had been throwing stones into her house for some nights. The Sūdra woman admitted that she had done so, because she was advised by a Lingayat priest that the remedy for intermittent fever, from which she was suffering, was to throw stones at an old woman, and extract some blood from her body on a new or full moon day. This superstition seems to be fully believed in by the lower classes.

* K. Srikantaliyar, Ind. Ant., XXI, 1892.

† B. Govinda Nambiar, Ind. Review, 1900.

‡ T. K. Gopal Panikkar, Madras Christ. Coll. Mag., 1896.

A few years ago there was very scanty rain in and around Hadagalli in the Bellary district. In these parts it is the belief of superstitious people that, if lepers are buried when they die, rain will not visit that part of the country where their corpses have been deposited. So they disinter the bodies, and throw the remains thereof into the Tungabadra river, or burn them. A man, who was supposed to be a leper, died, and was buried. Some one disinterred his skeleton, put it in a basket, and hung it to a tree with a garland of flowers round its neck. The Superintendent of Police, coming across it, ordered it to be disposed of.

Many years ago, in the Madras Presidency, a woman was supposed to be possessed with a devil, and an exorcist was consulted, who declared that a human sacrifice was necessary. A victim was selected, and made very drunk. His head was cut off, and the blood, mixed with rice, was offered to the idol. The body was then hacked so as to deceive the police, and thrown into a pond.*

Five persons were charged a few years ago at the Coimbatore Sessions with the murder of a young woman. The theory put forward by the prosecution was that two of the accused practised sorcery, and were under the delusion that, if they could obtain the fœtus from the uterus of a woman who was carrying her first child, they would be able to work some wonderful spells with it. With this object they entered into a conspiracy with the

* Lt.-Genl. F. F. Burton, An Indian Olio.

other three accused to murder a young married woman, aged about seventeen, who was seven months advanced in pregnancy, and brutally murdered her, cutting open the uterus, removing the fœtus contained therein, and stealing her jewels. The five accused persons (three men and two women) were all of different castes. Two of the men had been jointly practising sorcery and 'devil driving' for some years. And it was proved that, about two years before, they had performed an incantation near a river with some raw beef, doing pūja near the water's edge in a state of nature. They had also been overheard talking about going to a certain man's house to drive out devils. Evidence was produced to prove that two of the accused decamped after the murder with a suspicious bundle, a few days before an eclipse of the moon, to Tiruchengōdu, where there is a celebrated temple. This bundle, it was suggested, contained the uterus, and was taken to Tiruchengōdu for the purpose of performing some charms. When the quarters in which two of the accused lived were searched, three palm-leaf books were found, containing mantrams regarding the pili suniyam, a process of incantation by means of which sorcerers are supposed to be able to kill people. "There can be little doubt *primâ facie*" the record states, "that the first and fourth accused were taken into the conspiracy in order to decoy the deceased. The inducement offered to them was most probably immense wealth by the working of charms by the second and third accused with the aid of the fœtus." The medical evidence showed that the dead woman was pregnant, and that, after her throat had been cut, the uterus was taken out.

The Rev. J. Castets informs me that he once saw a man being initiated into the mysteries of the magician's art. The apparatus included the top of the skull of a first-born male child inscribed with Tamil characters.

The following forms of sorcery in Malabar are described by Mr. Walhouse.* Let a sorcerer obtain the corpse of a maiden, and on a Sunday night place it at the foot of a bhūta-haunted tree on an altar, and repeat a hundred times Om! Hrim! Hrom! O goddess of Malayāla, who possessest us in a moment! Come! Come! The corpse will then be inspired by a demon, and rise up; and, if the demon be appeased with flesh and arrack, it will answer all questions put to it. A human bone from a burial-ground, over which powerful mantrams have been recited, if thrown into an enemy's house, will cause his ruin.

Concerning sorcery on the west coast the Travancore Census Commissioner, 1901, writes as follows. "The forms of sorcery familiar to the people of Malabar are of three kinds—(1) kaivisham, or poisoning food by incantations; (2) the employment of Kuttichchāttan, a mysteriously-working mischievous imp; (3) setting up spirits to haunt men and their houses, and cause illness of all kinds. The most mischievous imp of Malabar demonology is an annoying quip-loving little spirit, as black as night, and about the size of a well-nourished twelve-year old boy. Some people say that they have seen

* Ind. Ant., V, 1876.

him *vis-à-vis*, having a forelock. There are Nampūtiris in Malabar, to whom these are so many missiles, which they may throw at anybody they choose. They are, like Shakespeare's Ariel, little active bodies, and most willing slaves of the master under whom they happen to be placed. Their victims suffer from unbearable agony. His clothes take fire; his food turns into ordure; his beverages become urine; stones fall in showers on all sides of him, but curiously not one on him; and his bed becomes a literal bed of thorns. He feels, in fact, a lost man. With all this annoying mischief, Kuttichchāttan or Boy-Satan does no serious harm. He oppresses and harasses, but never injures. A celebrated Brāhmin of Changanacheri is said to own more than a hundred of these Chāttans. Household articles and jewelry of value may be left in the premises of the homes guarded by Chāttan, and no thief dares to lay his hand on them. The invisible sentry keeps diligent watch over his master's property, and has unchecked powers of movement in any medium. As remuneration for all these services, the Chāttan demands nothing but food, but that in a large measure. If starved, the Chāttans would not hesitate to remind the master of their power, but, if ordinarily cared for, they would be his most willing drudges. As a safeguard against the infinite power secured for the master by Kuttichchāttan, it is laid down that malign acts committed through his instrumentality recoil on the prompter, who dies either childless or after frightful physical and mental agony. Another method of oppressing humanity, believed to be in the power of sorcerers, is to make men and women possessed with spirits. Here, too, women are more subject to their evil influence than men. Delayed puberty, permanent sterility, and still-births are not uncommon ills of a devil-possessed woman. Sometimes the spirits sought to be exorcised refuse to leave the body of the victim, unless the sorcerer promises them a habitation in his own compound (grounds), and arranges for daily offerings being given. This is agreed to as a matter of unavoidable necessity, and money and lands are conferred upon the mantravādi Nampūtiri to enable him to fulfil his promise." If an evil spirit is not a powerful one, the sorcerer makes it take a vow that it will not trouble any-one in the future, and, in return, offers to it the blood of fowls, a goat, etc. He then orders the spirit to climb a tree, and drives three large iron nails into the trunk thereof. As iron is disliked by spirits, the result is to confine the evil spirit in the tree, for it cannot descend beyond the nails.

Some Bhūtas have human mistresses and concubines. And it is narrated that a Chetti in the Madura district purchased a Malabar demon from a magician for ninety rupees. But hardly a day had passed before the undutiful spirit fell in love with its new owner's wife, and succeeded in its nefarious purpose.*

"There are," Mr. Govinda Nambiar writes,† "certain specialists among Mantravādis (dealers in magical spells), who are known as Odiyans. Conviction is deep-rooted

* M. J. Walhouse, Ind. Ant., V, 1876. † Indian Review, 1900.

that they have the power of destroying whenever they please, and that, by means of a powerful bewitching matter called pilla-thilum (oil extracted from the body of an infant), they are enabled to transform themselves into any shape or form, or even to vanish into air, as their fancy may suggest. When an Odiyan is hired to cause the death of a man, he waits during the night time at the gate of his intended victim's house, usually in the form of a bullock. If, however, the person is inside the house, the Odiyan assumes the shape of a cat, enters the house, and induces him to come out. He is subsequently knocked down, and strangled. The Odiyan is also credited with the power, by means of certain medicines, of inducing sleeping persons to open the doors, and come out of their houses as somnambulists do. Pregnant women are sometimes induced to come out of their houses in this way, and they are murdered, and the fœtus extracted from them. Murder of both sexes by Odiyans was a crime of frequent occurrence before the British occupation of the country."

Concerning odi cult Mr. Anantha Krishna Iyer writes as follows.* "The disciple is taught how to procure pilla thilam (fœtus oil) from the six or seven months fœtus of a young woman in her first pregnancy. He (the Paraiyan magician) sets out at midnight from his hut to the house of the woman he has selected, round which he walks several times, shaking a cocoanut containing gurusi (a compound of water, lime and turmeric), and

* Monograph, Eth. Survey, Cochin.

muttering some mantram to invoke the aid of his deity. He also draws a yantram on the earth, taking special care to observe the omens as he starts. Should they be unfavourable, he puts it off for another favourable opportunity. By the potency of his cult, the woman is made to come out. Even if the door of the room in which she might sleep be under lock and key, she would knock her head against it, until she found her way out. She thus comes out, and yields herself to the influence of the Paraiyan magician, who leads her to a retired spot either in the compound (grounds), or elsewhere in the neighbourhood, strips her naked, and asks her to lie flat. She does so, and the chora kindi (gourd : *Lagenaria*) is placed close to the uterus. The womb expands, and the fœtus comes out in a moment. A few leaves of some plant are applied, and the womb contracts. Sometimes the womb is filled with rubbish, and the woman instantly dies. Care is taken that the fœtus does not touch the ground, lest the purpose be defeated, and the efficacy of the medicine completely lost. It is cut to pieces, dried, and afterwards exposed to the smoke above a fire-place. It is then placed in a vessel provided with a hole or two, below which there is another vessel. The two together are placed in a larger vessel filled with water, and heated by a bright fire. The heat must be so intense as to affect the fœtus, from which a kind of liquid drops down, and collects in the second vessel in an hour and-a-half. He (the magician) then takes a human skull, and reduces it to a fine powder. This is mixed with a portion of the liquid. A mark is made on the forehead with this mixture, and the oil is rubbed on certain parts of the body, and he drinks a measure of cow-dung water. He then thinks that he can assume the figure of any animal he likes, and successfully achieves his object in view, which is generally to murder or maim a person.

"A magic oil, called angola thilum, is extracted from the angola tree (*Alangium Lamarckii*), which bears a very large number of fruits. One of these is believed to be capable of descending and returning to its position on dark nights. Its possession can be attained by demons, or by an expert watching at the foot of the tree. When it has been secured, the extraction of the oil involves the same operations as those for extracting the pilla thilum, and they must be carried out within seven hours. The (odi) cult was practised by the Parayas some twenty years ago to a very large extent in the rural parts of the northern division of the (Cochin) State, and in the taluks of Palghāt and Valuvanād, and even now it has not quite died out. Cases of extracting the fœtus, and of putting persons to death by odi are not now heard of owing to the fear of Government officials, landlords, and others. The records of criminal courts attest the power and prevalence of this persuasion among the more intelligent and higher classes."

In a case which was tried at the Malabar Sessions a few years ago, several witnesses for the prosecution deposed that a certain individual was killed by the process known as odi. One man gave the following account of the process. Shoot the victim in the nape of the neck with a blunt arrow, and bring him down. Proceed to beat him systematically all over the body with two sticks (resembling a policeman's truncheon, and called odivaddi), laying him on his back, and applying the sticks to his chest and up and down the sides, breaking all the ribs and bones. Then raise the person, and kick his sides. After this, force him to take an oath, that he will never divulge the names of his torturers. All the witnesses agreed about the blunt arrow, and some bore testimony to the sticks.

In 1829 several natives of Malabar were charged with having proceeded, in company with a Paraiyan, to the house of a pregnant woman, who was beaten and otherwise ill-treated, and with having taken the fœtus out of her uterus, and introduced in lieu thereof the skin of a calf and an earthen pot. The prisoners confessed before the police, but were acquitted mainly on the ground that the earthen pot was of a size which rendered it impossible to credit its introduction during life.

In 1834 the inhabitants of several villages in Malabar attacked a village of Paraiyas on the alleged ground that deaths of people and cattle, and the protracted labour of a woman in child-bed, had been caused by the practice of sorcery by the Paraiyas. They were beaten inhumanely, with their hands tied behind their backs, so that several died. The villagers were driven, bound, into a river, immersed under water so as nearly to produce suffocation, and their own children were forced to rub sand into their wounds. Their settlement was then razed to the ground, and they were driven into banishment. Some Paniyans of Malabar are believed to be gifted with the power of changing themselves into animals; and there is a belief that, if they wish to secure a woman whom they lust after, one of the men, gifted with the special power, goes to the house at night with a hollow bamboo, and encircles the house three times. The woman then comes out, and the man, changing himself into a bull or dog, works his wicked will. The woman, it is believed, dies in the course of two or three days. Years ago it was not unusual for people to come long distances for the purpose of engaging Paniyans to help them in carrying out some more than usually desperate robbery or murder. The mode of procedure, in engagements of this sort, is evidenced by two cases, which had in them a strong element of savagery. On both these occasions the thatched homesteads were surrounded at dead of night by a gang of Paniyans carrying large bundles of rice-straw. After carefully piling up the straw on all sides of the building marked for destruction, torches were applied, and those of the unfortunate inmates who attempted to escape were knocked on the head with clubs, and thrust into the fiery furnace. In 1904 some Paniyans were employed by a Māppilla to murder his mistress, who was pregnant, and threatened that she would noise abroad his responsibility for her condition. He brooded over the matter, and one day, meeting a Paniyan, promised him ten rupees if he would kill the woman. The Paniyan agreed to commit the crime, and went with his brothers to a place on a hill, where the Māppilla and the woman were in the habit of gratifying their passions. Thither the man and woman followed the Paniyans, of whom one ran out, and struck his victim on the head with a chopper. She was then gagged with a cloth by one of the Paniyans, carried some distance, and killed. Two Paniyans and the Māppilla were sentenced to be hanged.

As bearing on the subject of enchantment and spells, Mr. Logan records * that "the family of famous Kādir trackers, whose services were retained for His Royal Highness the Prince of Wales' (now King Edward) projected shooting tour in the Ānamalai mountains, dropped off most mysteriously, one by one, stricken down by an unseen hand, and all of them expressing their conviction beforehand that they were under a certain individual's spell, and were doomed to certain death at an early date. They were probably poisoned, but how it was managed remains a mystery, although the family was under the protection of a European gentleman, who would have at once brought to light any ostensible foul play."

The jungle Kurumbas of the Nīlgiris are believed to be necromancers, and in league with the devil. The Kurumba is resorted to by the Badagas when they till the land, and sow the seed. Otherwise the harvest will not be prosperous. The Kurumba, therefore, turns the first sod, sows the first handful of seed, and reaps the first sheaf of grain, after invoking the god or evil spirit. The Toda or Badaga requires the services of the Kurumba when he fancies that any member of his household is possessed of the devil, and when he wants to remove the evil eye, to which he fancies that his children

* Manual of Malabar.

have been subjected. The Kurumba does his best to remove the malady by repeating various mantrams. If he fails, and if any suspicion is aroused in the mind of the Toda or Badaga that he is allowing the devil to play his pranks instead of loosing his hold on the supposed victim, woe betide him. The wrath of the entire village, or even the whole tribe, is raised against the unhappy Kurumba. His hut is surrounded at night, and the entire household massacred in cold blood, and their huts set on fire. This is very cleverly carried out, and the isolated position of the Kurumba settlements allows of very little clue for identification. In 1835 no less than fifty-eight Kurumbas were thus murdered, and a smaller number in 1875 and 1882. In 1891 the five inmates of a single hut were murdered, and their hut burnt to ashes, because, it was said, one of them who had been treating a sick Badaga child failed to cure it. The crime was traced to some Kotas in conjunction with Badagas, but the District Judge disbelieved the evidence, and all who were charged were acquitted. Some years ago a Toda was found dead, in a sitting posture, on the top of a hill near a Badaga village, to which a party of Todas had gone to collect tribute. The body was burnt, and a report then made to the police that the man had been murdered. On enquiry it was ascertained that the dead man was supposed to have bewitched a little Badaga girl, who died in consequence and the presumption was that he had been murdered by the Badagas out of spite.

In Mysore, if there is a dispute as to the village boundaries, the Holeya Kuluvādi is believed to be the only person competent to take the oath as to how the boundary ought to run. The old custom for settling such disputes is thus described by Mr. J. S. F. Mackenzie.* "The Kuluvādi, carrying on his head a ball made of the village earth, in the centre of which is placed some water, passes along the boundary. If he has kept the proper line, every thing goes well; but, should he, by accident even, go beyond his own proper boundary, then the ball of earth, of its own accord, goes to pieces. The Kuluvādi is said to die within fifteen days, and his house becomes a ruin. Such is the popular belief."

A few years ago, Mr. H. D. Taylor was called on to settle a boundary dispute between two villages in Jeypore under the following circumstances. As the result of a panchayat (council), the men of one village had agreed to accept the boundary claimed by the other party if the head of their village walked round the boundary and eat earth at intervals, provided that no harm came to him within six months. The man accordingly perambulated the boundary eating earth, and a conditional order of possession was given. Shortly afterwards the man's cattle died, one of his children died of small-pox, and finally he himself died within three months. The other party then claimed the land on the ground that the earth goddess had proved him to have perjured himself. It was urged, in defence, that the man had been made to eat earth at such frequent intervals that he contracted dysentery, and died from the effects of earth eating.

* Ind. Ant., II, 1873.

The name Chedipe (a prostitute) is applied to sorceresses among various classes in the Godāvari district. The Chedipe is believed to ride on a tiger at night over the boundaries of seven villages, and return home at early morn. When she does not like a man, she goes to him bare-bodied at dead of night, the closed doors of the house in which he is sleeping opening before her. She sucks his blood by putting his toe in her mouth. He will then lie motionless and insensible like a corpse. Next morning he feels uneasy and intoxicated, as if he had taken ganja (*Cannabis sativa*), and remains in that condition all day. If he does not take medicine from one skilled in treating such cases, he will die. If he is properly treated, he will be as well as ever in about ten days. If he makes no effort to get cured, the Chedipe will molest him again and again, and, becoming gradually emaciated, he will die. When a Chedipe enters a house, all those who are awake will become insensible, those who are seated falling down as if they had taken a soporific drug. Sometimes she drags out the tongue of the intended victim, who will die at once. At other times slight abrasions will be found on the skin of the intended victim, and, when the Chedipe puts pieces of stick thereon, they burn as if burnt by fire. Sometimes she will hide behind a bush, and, undressing there, fall on any passer-by in the jungle, assuming the form of a tiger with one of the four legs in human form. When thus disguised, she is called Marulupuli (enchanting tiger). If the man is a brave fellow, and endeavours to kill the Chedipe with any instruments he may have with him, she will run away, and, if a man belonging to her village detects her mischief, she will assume her real form, and answer mildly that she is only digging roots. The above story was obtained by a native revenue official, when he visited a Koya village, where he was told that a man had been sentenced to several years' imprisonment for being one of a gang who had murdered a Chedipe for being a sorceress.

In the Vizagapatam district, where a village was supposed to contain a witch, the Dāsari was called upon to examine his books, and name the person. He fixed on some wretched woman, whose front teeth were immediately knocked out, and her mouth filled with filth. She was then beaten with sticks. If she cried out, she was no witch. The only stick that would make a witch cry out was the jorra or castor-oil plant switch. The people believe that a witch, when she wishes to revenge herself on any one, climbs at night to the top of his house, and, making a hole through the roof, drops a thread down till the end of it touches the body of the sleeping man. Then she sucks at the other end, and draws up all the blood out of his body. Witches are said to be able to remove all the bones out of a man's body, or to deposit a fish, ball of hair, or rags in his stomach. The town of Jeypore was said to be haunted by a ghost. It was described as a woman, who paraded the town at midnight in a state of nudity, and from her mouth proceeded flames of fire. She sucked the blood of any loose cattle she found about, and, in the same way, revenged herself on any man who had insulted her.*

* Vizagapatam Manual.

In 1904, a case illustrating the prevailing belief in witchcraft occurred in the Vizagapatam hill tracts. The youngest of three brothers died of fever, and, when the body was cremated, the fire failed to consume the upper portion. The brothers concluded that death must have been caused by the witchcraft of a certain Khond They accordingly attacked the latter, and killed him. After death the brothers cut the body in half, and dragged the upper half of it to their own village, where they attempted to nail it up on the spot where their deceased brother's body failed to burn. The accused were arrested on the spot, with the fragment of the Khond's corpse. They were sentenced to death, and the sentence was confirmed by the High Court.*

Of sorcery among the Oriyas, Mr. S. P. Rice tells us † that a girl was suffering from mental disease, and believed to be possessed of a devil. She declared that she was bewitched by a certain man, who had to be cured of his power over her. Accordingly, the friends and relatives of the girl went to this man's house, dragged him out into the road, laid him on his back, and sat on his chest. They then proceeded to extract his two front teeth with a hammer and pincers. "It does not appear how the cure was to work—whether the operators thought that the words of cursing or magic, coming through the orifice of the teeth, would be mumbled, and thus lose some of their incisive force,

* Police Report, 1904.

† Occasional Essays on Native South Indian Life, 1901.

and therefore of their power for evil, or whether it was thought that the devil wanted room to fly out." In the Kistna district a Māla weaver was suspected of practising sorcery by destroying men with devils, and bringing cholera and other diseases. He was met by certain villagers, and asked for tobacco. While he stopped to get the tobacco out, he was suddenly seized and thrown on the ground. His hands were tied behind his back, and his legs bound fast with his waist-cloth. One man sat on his legs, another on his waist, and a third held his head down by the top-knot. His mouth was forced open with a pair of large pincers, and a piece of stick was thrust between the teeth to prevent the mouth closing. One of the assistants got a stone as big as a man's fist, and with it struck the sorcerer's upper and lower teeth several times until they were loosened. Then nine teeth were pulled out with the pincers. A quantity of milk-hedge (*Euphorbia*) juice was poured on the bleeding gums, and the unfortunate man was left lying on his back, to free himself from his bonds as best he could.* In North Arcot, a few years ago, a man was believed to have great power over animals, of which he openly boasted, threatening to destroy all the cattle of one of his neighbours. This man and his friends believed that they could deprive the sorcerer of his power for evil by drawing all his teeth, which they proceeded to do with fatal results.

At a village near Berhampūr in Ganjam, Mr. Rice tells us,† a number of villagers went out together.

* H. J. Stokes, Ind. Ant., V, 1876. † *Op. cit.*

By-and-bye, according to a preconcerted plan, one of the party suggested a drink. The intended victim was drugged, and taken along to the statue of the goddess, or shrine containing what did duty for the statue. He was then thrown down with his face on the ground in an attitude suggesting supplication, and, while he was still in a state of stupor, his head was chopped off with an axe.

In the Koraput taluk, Vizagapatam, a wizard had a reputation for possessing the power to transplant trees, and it was believed that, if a man displeased him, his trees were moved in the night, and planted in someone else's grounds.

In the Godāvari district a sorcerer known as the ejjugadu (male physician) is believed, out of spite or for payment, to kill another by invoking the gods. He goes to a green tree, and there spreads muggu or chunām (lime) powder, and places an effigy of the intended victim thereon. He also places a bow and a bamboo arrow there, and recites certain spells, and calls on the gods. The victim is said to die in a couple of days. But, if he understands that the ejjugadu has thus invoked the gods, he may inform another ejjugadu, who will carry out similar operations under another tree. His bow and arrow will go to those of the first ejjugadu, and the two bows and arrows will fight as long as the spell remains. The man will then be safe. The second ejjugadu can give the name of the first, though he has never known him.

Writing concerning the Yerukalas, Mr. Fawcett says that the warlock takes the possessed one by night to the outskirts of the village, and makes a figure on the ground with powdered rice, powders of various colours, and powdered charcoal. Balls of the powders, half cocoanut shells, betel, four-anna pieces, and oil lamps are placed on the hands, legs and abdomen. A little heap of boiled rice is placed near the feet, and curds and vegetables are set on the top of it, with limes placed here and there. The subject of the incantation sits near the head, while the magician mutters mantrams. A he-goat is then sacrificed. Its head is placed near the feet of the figure, and benzoin and camphor are waved. A little grain is scattered about the figure, to appease the evil spirits. Some arrack is poured into a cup, which is placed on the body of the figure, and the bottle which contained it is left at the head. The limes are cut in two, and two cocoanuts are broken. The patient then walks by the left side of the figure to its legs, takes one step to the right towards the head and one step to the left towards the feet, and walks straight home without looking back.*

In a field outside a village in South Canara, Mr. Walhouse noticed a large square marked in lines with whitewash on the ground, with magic symbols in the corners and the outline of a human figure rudely drawn in the middle. Flowers and boiled rice had been laid on leaves round the figure. He was informed that a house was to be built on the site marked out, and the figure was intended to represent the earth-spirit supposed to be dwelling in the ground. Without this ceremony being

* Journ. Anth. Soc., Bombay, II.

performed before the earth had been dug up, it was believed there would be no luck about the house.*

The following form of sorcery used, in Malabar, in compassing the discomfiture of enemies, is recorded by Mr. Walhouse.† Make an image of wax in the form of your enemy; take it in your right hand at night, and hold your chain of beads in your left hand. Then burn the image with due rites, and it shall slay your enemy in a fortnight. Or a figure representing an enemy, with his name and date of his birth inscribed on it, is carved out of *Strychnos Nux-vomica* wood. A mantram is recited, a fowl offered up, and the figure buried in glowing rice-husk embers. Or, again, some earth from a spot where an enemy has urinated, saliva expectorated by him, and a small tuft of hair, are placed inside a tender cocoanut, and enclosed in a piece of *Strychnos Nux-vomica.* The cocoanut is pierced with twenty-one nails and buried, and a fowl sacrificed. In 1903 a life-size nude female human figure (plate XIX) with feet everted and directed backwards, carved out of the wood of *Alstonia scholaris,* was washed ashore at Calicut. Long nails had been driven in all over the head, body and limbs, and a large square hole cut out above the navel Inscriptions in Arabic characters were scrawled over it. By a coincidence the corpse of a man was washed ashore close to the figure. It probably represented the figure of a woman who was possessed by an evil spirit, which was nailed to it before it was cast into the sea, and was made on the Laccadive

* Ind. Ant., X, 1881.

† Ind. Ant., V, 1879.

Plate XIX.

Sorcery Figure.

islands, some of the residents on which are famous as necromancers. In obstinate cases of possession by an evil spirit, the only remedy is to bind the spirit by shutting it up in a jar, and throw it into the sea. The Kodangallūr (cock-feast) Bhagavāthi was rescued from the sea by a fisherman. It was shut up in a jar, and thrown into the sea by a great magician. The story is repeated in the Arabian Nights. The spirit of a deceased Brāhman (man or woman) is the most difficult of all to propitiate. A timber merchant at Calicut some time ago spent more than a thousand rupees for this purpose. He had built a new house, and on the morning after the kutti pūja (house-warming) ceremony his wife and children were coming to occupy it. Just as they entered the grounds, a cow ran against one of the children, and knocked it down. This augured evil, and, in a few days, the child was attacked with small-pox. One child after another caught the disease, and at last the man's wife also got it. They all recovered, but the wife was laid up with some uterine disorder. The astrologers said that the house was once a Brāhman's, whose spirit still haunted it. It had been disturbed, and must be propitiated. Very expensive ceremonies were performed by Brāhmans for a fortnight. The house was sold to the Brāhman priest for a nominal price. An image of the deceased Brāhman was made of gold, and, after the purification ceremonies, taken to Rāmēsvaram, where arrangements were made to have daily worship performed to it. The house, in its purified state, was sold back by the Brāhman priest. The woman was taken to the maternity hospital. The astrologer had predicted that the displeasure of the spirit would be exhibited on the way by the breaking of dishes and by furniture catching fire—a very strange prediction, because the bed on which the woman was lying in the train caught fire by a spark from the engine. After the spirit had been thus propitiated, there was peace in the house.

The native servant of a friend of mine in Madras found buried in a corner of his master's garden the image of a human figure, which had been deposited there by an enemy who wished to injure him. The figure was made of flour mixed with "walking foot earth," *i.e.*, earth from ground which the servant had walked over. Nails, fourteen in number, had been driven into the head, neck, and each shoulder, elbow, wrist, hip, knee, and ankle. And buried with the figure were fourteen eggs, limes, and balls of camphor, and a scrap of paper bearing the age of the servant, and the names of his father and mother. A Muhammadan fortune-teller advised the servant to burn the effigy, so at midnight he made an offering of a sheep, camphor, betel-nuts, and cocoanuts, and performed the cremation ceremony.

In a recent note,* it is started that curious phenomena take place in connection with persons who are possessed. "The victim suddenly takes fire; lamps are as suddenly extinguished in his presence, even when there is not the slightest breath of air stirring. Stones are hurled at him by unseen agencies, and nauseating substances foul his food when he is at meals. For hours

* Madras Mail, November 1905.

on end he lies stretched on the ground to all appearances dead, or madly whirls round and round in a frightful manner. After the fit passes away, the worn-out victim eats an incredibly large quantity of food. If the victim is a women, her children die of strange diseases, and frequent abortions take place. Should the spirit of a learned Brāhman who has committed suicide, or come to other untimely end, enter even the most illiterate person, the possessed one chants Vēdic hymns, and incantations with an enunciation that a Ghanapathi might envy. The counter-art of devil driving offers a fairly profitable living to a large class of people. The spirit itself not infrequently gives information through the victim as to its identity, and stipulates to vacate possession, if a sacrifice of a specified number of sheep or fowls is made to it. Sometimes it asks for other lodgings, as in the New Testament story, and the exorciser, taking it at its word, drives a nail into the nearest tree, and adjures it to live thereon like an honest devil. The Lingadars of the Kistna district have made a speciality of bottling the spirit, literally, within a very narrow compass, the bottles being cast away in a place where no one can come across them, and liberate the imprisoned devils. One favourite tantra of the South Indian sorcerer consists of what is popularly known in Tamil as a pavai, that is to say, a doll made of some plastic substance, such as clay or wheat flour. A crude representation of the intended victim is obtained by moulding a quantity of this material, and a nail or pin driven into it at a spot corresponding to the limb or organ that is intended to be affected. For instance, if there is to be paralysis of the right arm, the pin is stuck into the right arm of the image; if madness is to result, it is driven into the head, and so on, appropriate mantras being chanted over the image, which is buried at midnight in a neighbouring cremation ground. So long as the pavai is underground, the victim will grow from bad to worse, and may finally succumb to the disease, if steps are not taken in time. Sometimes, instead of a doll being used, the corpse of a child recently buried is dug out from the ground, and re-interred after being similarly treated. The only remedy consists in another sorcerer being called in for the purpose of digging out the pavai. Various are the methods he adopts for discovering the place where the doll is buried, one of them being very similar to what is known as crystal-gazing. A small quantity of a specially prepared thick black fluid or ointment is placed on the palm of a third person, and the magician professes to find out every circumstance connected with the case of his client's mental or physical affliction by attentively looking at it. The place of the doll's burial is spotted with remarkable precision, the nail extracted, and the patient is restored to his normal condition as by a miracle."

In Malabar, a wooden figure or image is sometimes made, and a tuft of a woman's hair tied on its head. It is fixed to a tree, and nails are driven into the neck and breast to inflict hurt on an enemy. The following form of sorcery is resorted to in Malabar.* A mantram is written

* F. Fawcett, Madras Museum Bull., III, 3, 1901.

on the stem of the kaitha plant, on which is also drawn a figure representing the person to be injured. A hole is bored to represent the navel. The mantram is repeated, and at each repetition a certain thorn (kāramullu) is stuck into the limbs of the figure. The name of the person, and of the star under which he was born, are written on a piece of cadjan, which is stuck into the navel. The thorns are removed, and replaced twenty-one times. Two magic circles are drawn below the nipples of the figure. The stem is then hung up in the smoke of the kitchen. A pot of toddy and some other accessories are procured, and with them the warlock performs certain rites. He then moves three steps backwards, shouts aloud thrice, fixing in the thorns again, and thinking all the while of the particular mischief with which he will afflict the person to be injured. When all this has been done, the person whose figure has been drawn on the stem, and pricked with thorns, feels pain as if he was being pricked. By the Thanda Pulayans of the west coast a ceremony called urasikotukkuka is performed with the object of getting rid of a devil, with which a person is possessed. At a place far distant from the hut, a leaf, on which the blood of a fowl has been made to fall, is spread on the ground. On a smaller leaf, chunām and turmeric are placed. The person who first sets eyes on these becomes possessed of the devil, and sets free the individual, who was previously under its influence. The Thanda Pulayans also practice maranakriyas, or sacrifices to demons, to help them in bringing about the death of an enemy. Sometimes affliction is supposed to be brought about by the enmity of those who have got incantations written on a palm-leaf, and buried in the ground near a house by the side of a well. A sorcerer is called in to counteract the evil charm, which he digs up, and destroys.* "When," Mr. Govinda Nambiar writes,† "a village doctor attending a sick person finds that the malady is unknown to him, or will not yield to his remedies, he calls in the astrologer, and subsequently an exorcist, to expel the demon or demons which have possessed the sick man. If the devils will not yield to ordinary remedies administered by his disciples, the mantravādi himself comes, and a devil dance is appointed to be held on a certain day. Thereat various figures of mystic device are traced on the ground, and in their midst a huge and frightful form representing the demon. Sometimes an effigy is constructed out of cooked and coloured rice. The patient is seated near the head of the figure, and opposite her sits the magician adorned with bundles of sticks tied over the joints of his body, tails and skins of animals, etc. Verses are chanted, and sometimes cocks are sacrificed, and the blood is sprinkled on the demon's effigy. Amidst the beating of drums and blowing of pipes the magician enters upon his diabolical dance, and, in the midst of his paroxysm, may even bite live cocks, and suck with ferocity the hot blood."

Some time ago an old woman, hearing that her only son was lying dangerously ill, sought the aid of a

* L. K. Anantha Krishna Aiyer. Monograph Eth. Survey, Cochin.

† Indian Review, 1900.

magician, who proceeded to utter mantrams, to counteract the evil influences which were at work. While this was being done, an accomplice of the magician turned up, and, declaring that he was a policeman, threatened to charge the two with sorcery if they did not pay a certain sum of money. The old woman paid up, but discovered later on that she had been hoaxed.

The two following quaint beliefs are recorded by Mr. Gopal Panikkar.* (1) In the regions above the earth are supposed to exist huge monsters, to whom is assigned the responsibility of supplying the earth with water. They possess enormous physical strength, and have two huge horns and large flashing eyes. All the summer they are engaged in drawing up water from the earth through their mouths, which they spit out as rain in the wet season. A still ruder imagination ascribes rain to the periodical discharge of urine by these monsters. Hence, in some places, there exists an aversion to the use of rain water for human consumption. Thunder is produced by their horns coming into violent collision as they work together; lightning by the friction of the horns. (2) The appearance of what is usually known as jack-o'-lantern in marshy places is believed, in Malabar, to be caused by light and sparks emitted from the mouths of peculiar devils, who make fishing their profession, which they practise especially on rainy and foggy nights. When they have caught fish, they cook them by putting then in their mouths, which are hot furnaces.

* Madras Christ. Coll. Magazine, 1896.

A few years ago, a zamindar in the Godāvari district engaged a Muhammadan to exorcise a devil which haunted his house. The latter, explaining that the devil was a female and fond of jewellery, induced the zamindar to leave a large quantity of jewels in a locked receptacle in a certain room, to which only the exorcist, and of course the devil, had access. The latter, it was supposed, would be gratified by the loan of the jewels, and would cease to annoy. The exorcist managed to open the receptacle and steal the jewels, and, such was the faith of his employer, that the offence was not suspected until a Police Inspector seized Rs. 27,000 worth of the jewels in Vizagapatam on suspicion, and they were with difficulty traced to their source.*

Quite recently a native servant was charged with beating with a cane a woman who was suffering from malarial fever two months after her confinement, in order to drive out a devil, said to be the spirit of a woman who was drowned some time previously, with which she believed herself to be possessed. The woman died three days after the beating, and various abrasions were found on the body and head. The Sub-Magistrate held that the hurt was part of the ceremony, to which the husband and mother of the woman, and the woman herself gave their consent. But, as the hurt was needlessly severe, the servant was fined twenty-five rupees, or in default, five weeks' rigorous imprisonment. The District Magistrate submitted the case to the High Court for

* Police Report, 1903.

Plate XX.

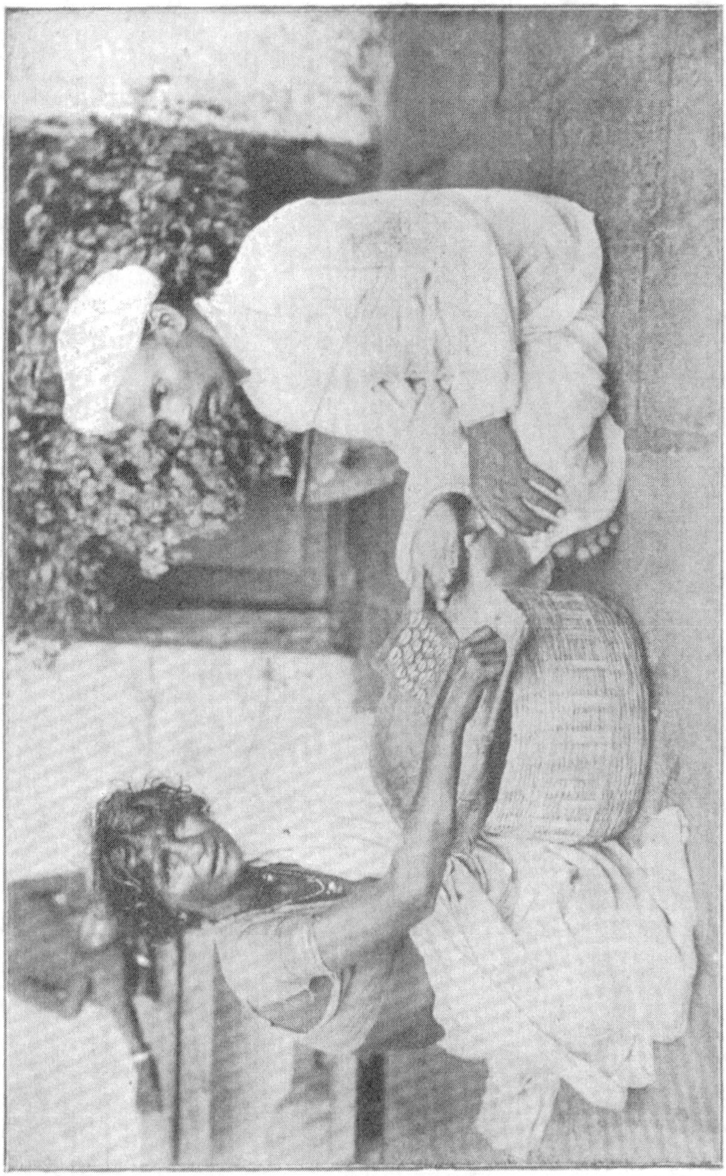

Fortune-telling with Cowry Shells.

enhancement of the sentence. The medical evidence showed that the death of the woman was not in any way due to the strokes received from the cane, and the Judge saw no reason for enhancement.

In conclusion I may quote a few examples of sorcery culled from the ever entertaining annual reports of the Chemical Examiner to Government :—

(*a*) A wizard came to a village in order to exorcise the devil which possessed a certain woman. He was treated like a prince, and was given the only room in the house, while the family turned out into the hall. He lived there for several days, and then commenced his ceremonies. He drew the figure of a lotus on the floor, made the woman sit there, and commenced to twist her hair with his wizard's wand. When she cried out, he sent her out of the room, saying she was unworthy to sit on the lotus figure, but promising nevertheless to exorcise the devil without her being present. He found a half-witted man in the village, drugged him with ganja, brought him to the house, and performed his ceremonials on this man, who, on becoming intoxicated with the drug, began to get boisterous. The wizard tied him up with a rope because he had become possessed of the devil that had possessed the woman. The man was subsequently traced by his relatives, found in an unconscious state, and taken to hospital. The wizard got rigorous imprisonment.

(*b*) Some jewels were lost, and the mantrakāra was called in to detect the thief. The magician erected a screen, behind which he lit a lamp, and did other things to impress the crowd with the importance of his mantrams. To the assembly he distributed betel-leaf patties containing a white powder, said to be holy ashes, and the effect of it on the suspected individuals, who formed part of the crowd, is said to have been instantaneous. So magical was the effect of this powder in detecting the thief that the unfortunate man ultimately vomited blood. When the people remonstrated with the magician for the severity of his magic, he administered to the sufferer an antidote of solution of cow-dung and the juice of some leaf. The holy ashes were found to contain corrosive sublimate, and the magician got eighteen months' rigorous imprisonment.

(*c*) A barber had been poaching on the local limits within which another barber and his family claimed the right to shave, and he had been diverting some of the latter's income into his own pockets. A third barber, a mutual friend, had been learning "sorcery and medicine" from barber No. 2, and, while these two were in a liquor shop, barber No. 1, who happened to be passing, was invited by the mutual friend to join them in a drink. He refused, but consented when the latter promised to add some sugar to the toddy to keep down its deletérious effects. The sugar was stirred into No. 1's cup, and the three drank to each other. Barber No. 2 had been educating the mutual friend to aid and abet him in an attempt on his opponent's life by stirring a mixture of arsenic and mercury compounds in the toddy. The victim recovered under prompt treatment in the hospital.

Votive offerings (*Ex votos*).—In addition to the observance of penances and fasting, Hindus of all castes, high and low, make various kinds of offerings to the gods, with the object of securing their good-will or appeasing their anger. By the lower castes offerings of animals—fowls, sheep, goats, or buffaloes—are made, and the gods whom they seek to propitiate are minor deities, *e.g.*, Ellamma or Muneswara, known as Kshudra Dēvatas (blood-thirsty gods), to whom animal sacrifices are acceptable. The higher castes usually perform vows to Venkateswara of Tirupati, Subramanya of Palni, Virarāghava of Tiruvallūr, Tirunārayana of Melkote, and other celebrated gods. But they may, if afflicted with serious disease, at times, as at the leaf festival at Periyapalayam, seek the good offices of minor deities. On the last day of the Gangajatra festival at Tirupati, a figure is made of clay and straw, and placed in the tope (grove), where crowds of all classes, including Paraiyans, present food to it. Buffaloes, goats, sheep, and fowls are sacrificed, and it is said that Brāhmans, though they will not be present, send animals to be slaughtered. At the conclusion of the festivity, the image is burned. During the feast, which continues over ten days, the lower orders of the people paint themselves, and indulge in much boisterous merriment. Those who have made a vow to Ganga fast for some days before the festival begins. They wear a structure made of bamboo in the form of a car, which is decorated with paper of different colours, and supported by iron nails pressed into the belly and back, and, with this structure on their heads, they go about. Those who have been attacked by cholera or other serious disease make a vow to Ganga, and perform this ceremonial.

The simplest and commonest votive offerings are fruit, such as plantains and cocoanuts. Without an offering of fruit no orthodox Hindu would think of entering a temple, or the presence of a native of position. The procession of native servants and retainers, each bringing a gift of a lime, on New Year's Day is familiar to Anglo-Indians. By the rules of Government, the prohibition of the receipt of presents from Native Chiefs and others does not extend to the receipt of a few flowers or fruits, and articles of inappreciable value, although even such trifling presents should be discouraged.

Between the Madras museum and the Government maternity hospital a small municipal boundary stone has been set up by the side of the road. To this stone supernatural powers are attributed, and it is alleged that in a banyan tree in a private garden close by a Mūni lives, who presides over the welfare of the hospital, and must be propitiated if the pregnant woman is to get over her confinement without complications. Women, coming to the hospital for their confinement, vow that they will, if all goes well, give a present of a cocoanut, betel, or flowers when they leave. Discharged patients can be seen daily, going to the stone and making offerings. On the day of their discharge, their friends bring camphor and other articles, and the whole family goes to the stone, where the camphor is burnt, a cocoanut broken, and perhaps some turmeric or flowers placed on it. The new-born child is placed on the bare ground in front of the stone, and the mother, kneeling down, bows before it. The foreheads of both mother and child are marked with the soots from the burning camphor. If her friends do not bring the requisite articles, the woman goes home, and returns with them to do pūja to the stone, or it is celebrated at a temple or her house. The offerings are removed by those who present them, or by passers-by on the road. Women, after delivery, keep iron in some form, for example a knife, in their room, and carry it about with them when they go out. The Rev. S. Nicholson informs me that when a Māla woman is in labour, a sickle and some nīm leaves are always kept on the cot. In Malabar it is customary for those who have to pass by burning-grounds or other haunted places to carry with them iron in some form, *e.g.*, a knife, or an iron rod used as a walking-stick. When pregnant women go on a journey, they carry with them a few twigs or leaves of the nīm tree, or iron in some form, to scare evil spirits lurking in groves or burial-grounds, which they may pass.

The forms which votive offerings take are very multifarious. Sometimes, for example, they assume the form of bells, lamps, brass pots, articles made in wood or clay, images of various deities, cradles, leather shoes, coins, the hair of a new-born child, lumps of jaggery, salt and other things. When people are prevented from going to a temple at the proper time, hair is sometimes removed from their children's head, sealed up in a vessel, and put into the receptacle for offerings when the visit to the temple is made. In cases of dangerous sickness, the hair is sometimes cut off, and offered to a deity. "The sacrifice of locks," Mr. A. Srinivasan writes, "is meant to propitiate deceased relations, and the deity which presides over life's little joys and sorrows. It is a similar intention that has dictated the ugly disfigurement of widows. We meet with the identical fact and purpose in the habit of Telugu Brāhmins, and all non-Brāhmins in general, sacrificing their whole locks of hair to the goddess Ganga at Prayaga, to the god Venkatēsa of Tirupati, and other local gods. The Brāhmin ladies of the south have more recently managed to please Ganga and other gods with just one or two locks of hair."

Marching, on one occasion, towards Hampi, where an outbreak of cholera had recently occurred, I came across two wooden gods on wheels by the roadside, to whom had been offered baskets of fruit, vegetables, earthen pots, bead necklets and bangles, which were piled up in front of them. By the sides of the roads in the Bellary district, Mr. W. Francis writes,* "often stands a wooden-frame-work mounted on little wheels, and bearing three wooden images. This is the car of Māriamma, the goddess of small pox and cholera, and her son and daughter. When disease breaks out, the car bearing her and her children is taken round the village with music and other due ceremony, and dragged to the eastern boundary. By this means the malignant essence of the goddess is removed from the village. The adjoining villagers hasten to prevent this from settling

* Manual of the Bellary district.

on them, by taking the car on with musical honours as before. The car is thus often wheeled through a whole series of villages." The Khonds prevent the approach of the goddess of small-pox by barricading the paths with thorns and ditches, and boiling caldrons of stinking oil.*

"A palmyra palm in the jungle near Ramnād with seven distinct trunks, each bearing a goodly head of fan-shaped leaves is", General Burton writes,† "attributed to the action of a deity, and stones smeared with oil and vermilion, and broken cocoanuts, and fowl's feathers lying about, testified that pūja and sacrifice were performed here."

Outside the temple of the village goddess at Ojini in the Bellary district, Mr. Fawcett tells us "are hung numbers of miniature cradles and bangles presented by women who have borne children, or been cured of sickness through the intervention of the goddess. Miniature cows are presented by persons, whose cows have been cured of sickness, and doll-like figures for children. One swāmi (god) there is, known by a tree hung with iron chains, hooks—anything iron; another by rags, and so on. The ingenious dhōbi (washerman), whose function is to provide torches on occasions, sometimes practices on the credulity of his countrymen by tying a few rags to a tree, which by-and-by is covered with rags, for the passers-by are not so stiff-necked as to ask for a sign other than a rag; and, under cover of the darkness, the dhōbi makes his torch of the offerings."

* Macpherson. Memorials of Service in India. † An Indian Olio.

On the road to Tirupati, the goddess Gauthala Gangamma has her abode in a margosa or āvaram tree, surrounded by a white-ant hill. Passers by tear off a piece of their clothing, and tie it to the branches, and place a small stone at the base of the ant-hill. Occasionally cooked rice is offered, and fowls are sacrificed, and their head and legs tied to the tree. It is recorded by Mr. Walhouse * that, when going from the Coimbatore plain to the Mysore frontier, he has seen a thorn-bush rising out of a heap of stones piled round it, and bearing bits of rag tied to its branches. These rags are placed there by nomad Lambādis, who are said to fasten rags torn from their garments to a bush in honour of Kampalamma (kampa=a thicket). In the Telugu country, rags are offered to a god called Pathalayya (Mr. Rags). On the trunk-roads in the Nellore district, rags may be seen hanging on the bābūl (*Acacia arabica*) trees. These are offerings made to Pathalayya by travellers who tear off pieces of their clothing, with a vague idea that the offering thereof will render their journey free from accidents, such as upsetting of their carts, or meeting with robbers.

It is narrated by Moor † that "he passed a tree, on which were hanging several hundred bells. This was a superstitious sacrifice by the Bandjarrahs (Lambādis), who, passing this tree, are in the habit of hanging a bell or bells upon it, which they take from the necks of their sick cattle, expecting to leave behind them the complaint also. Our servants particularly cautioned us

* Ind. Ant. IX, 1880. † Narrative of Little's Detachment.

against touching these diabolical bells; but, as a few were taken for our own cattle, several accidents that happened were imputed to the anger of the deity, to whom these offerings were made; who, they say, inflicts the same disorder on the unhappy bullock who carries a bell from this tree as he relieved the donor from." At Diguvemetta in the Kurnool district, I came across a number of bells, both large and small, tied to the branches of a tamarind tree, beneath which were an image of Malalamma and a stone bull (Nandi). Suspended from a branch of the same tree was a thick rope, to which were attached heads, skulls, mandibles, thigh bones, and feet of fowls, and the foot of a goat.

The god of the Aligiri Dēvastanam temple at Tirupati appears annually to four persons in different directions, east, west, south and north, and informs them that he requires a shoe from each of them. They whitewash their houses, worship the god, and spread rice-flour thickly on the floor of a room, which is locked for the night. Next morning the mark of a huge foot is found on the floor, and the shoe has to be made to fit this. When ready, it is taken in procession through the streets of the village, conveyed to Tirupati, and presented at the temple. Though the makers of the shoes have worked in ignorance of each other's work, the shoes brought from the north and south, and those from the east and west are believed to match and make a pair. Though the worship of these shoes is chiefly meant for Paraiyans, who are prohibited from ascending the Tirupati hill, as a matter of fact all, without distinction of caste, worship them. The shoes are placed in front of the image of the god near the foot of the hill, and are said to gradually wear away by the end of the year. "At Bēlur in the Mysore Province," Mr. Rice writes,* "the god of the temple is under the necessity of making an occasional trip to the Baba Budan hills to visit the goddess. On these occasions he is said to make use of a large pair of slippers kept for the purpose in the temple. When they are worn out, it devolves upon the chucklers (leather-workers) of Channagiri and Bisvapatna, to whom the fact is revealed in a dream, to provide new ones." In order to present the slippers, they are allowed to enter the court-yard of the temple.

Mr. Walhouse informs us † that the champak and other trees round the ancient shrine of the Trimurti at the foot of the Ānaimalai mountains are thickly hung with sandals and shoes, many of huge size, evidently made for the purpose, and suspended by pilgrims as votive offerings.

"At Timmancherla," Mr. Francis writes,‡ "there is the tomb of a holy Muhammadan named Masthan Ali, in whose honour an urus (religious ceremony) is held annually in April, which is attended by followers of the Prophet from many villages around. Hindus make vows at the tomb, which has a special reputation for granting offspring to the childless, and take part in the urus along with the Mussulmans. The Reddi (head-man) of the village, who is a Hindu, brings the first offerings in

* Mysore. † Ind. Ant. IX, 1880.

‡ Gazetteer of the Anantapur district.

procession with much ceremony to the Mussulman priests who preside at the function." Carved wooden figurines, male and female, represented in a state of nudity, are manufactured at Tirupati and sold to Hindus. Those who are childless perform on them the ear-boring ceremony, in the belief that, as the result thereof, issue will be born to them. Or, if there are grown-up boys or girls in a family who remain unmarried, the parents celebrate the marriage ceremony between a pair of the dolls, in the hope that the marriage of their children will speedily follow. They dress up the dolls in clothes and jewellery, and go through the ceremonial of a real marriage. Some there are who have spent as much money on a doll's wedding as on a wedding in real life.

Among the Billavas of South Canara, in the case of grown-up boys and girls who die before marriage, a form of marriage of the dead is celebrated. The spirit of the deceased boy takes possession of one of his relatives, and expresses a desire that his marriage should be performed. The relatives make enquiries, and try to discover the spirit of a girl of a suitable bari (marriage division) which is, in like manner, troubling her relatives. When the search has been successful, two clay figures, or figures in rice flour representing the deceased boy and girl, are made, and the marriage ceremony is performed as in the case of living persons.

A Brāhmini bull, Mr. A. Srinivasan writes, "is dedicated to god Venkateswara of Tirupati for the benefit of the living in fulfilment of vows. The act of dedication and release is preceded by elaborate rituals of marriage, as among men and women. The bride, which should be a heifer that has not calved, is furnished by the father-in-law of the donor. The heifer is united in holy wedlock to the bullock, after formal chanting of mantrams, by the tying of the tāli and toe-rings to the neck. In this sham marriage, the profuse ornamentation of the couple with saffron and red powder, the pouring of rice on their heads, and the procession in the streets with music, are conspicuous features." I am told that, if the devotee cannot afford a live animal, a mimic representative is made in rice.

At the Uchāral festival in the Malabar district, representations of cattle in straw are taken in procession to the temple of Bhagāvati. At a harvest festival in Malabar, representations of cattle are made from the leaves of the jāk tree, and placed in an old winnowing basket. The materials for a feast are placed in a pot, and toy agricultural articles (cattle-shed, plough, yoke, etc.) made of plantain leaf ribs, and the pot are carried round each house three times, while the children call out "Kālia, Kālia, monster, monster, receive our offering, and give us plenty of seed and wages, protect our cattle, and support our fences." The various articles are then placed under a jāk tree on the eastern side of the house.*

Painted hollow clay images are made by special families of Kusavans (potters) known as pūjāri, who, for the privilege of making them, have to pay an annual

* C. Karunakara Menon, Madras Mus. Bull. v. 3, 1906.

fee to the headman, who spends it on a festival at the caste temple. When a married couple are anxious to have female offspring, they take a vow to offer figures of the seven virgins, who are represented all seated in a row. If a male or female recovers from cholera, small-pox, or other severe illness, a figure of the corresponding sex is offered. A childless woman makes a vow to offer up the figure of a baby, when she brings forth offspring. Figures of animals—cattle, sheep, horses, etc.—are offered at the temple when they recover from sickness, or are recovered after they have been stolen. The pupils of the eyes of the figures are not painted in till they are taken to the temple, where offerings of fruit, rice, etc., are first made, as it is the painting of the pupils which endows the figure with life. Even the pupils of a series of these images, which were specially made for me, were not painted at the potter's house, but in the verandah of the travellers' bungalow where I was staying. Horses made of clay, hollow and painted red and other colours, are set up in the fields to drive away demons, or as a thank offering for recovery from sickness or any piece of good luck. The villagers erect these horses in honour of the popular deity Ayanār, the guardian deity of the fields, who is a renowned huntsman, and is believed, when, with his two wives Purna and Pushkala, he visits the village at night, to mount the horses, and ride down the demons.

I have recently received a collection of clay figures, such as are worshipped by fishermen on the Ganjam coast, concerning which Mr. H. D'A. C. Reilly writes to me as follows: "I am sending you specimens of the chief gods worshipped by the fishermen. The Tahsildar of Berhampur got them made by the potter and carpenter who usually make such figures for the Gopalpur fishermen. I have found fishermen's shrines at several places. Separate families appear to have separate shrines, some consisting of large chatties (earthen pots), occasionally ornamented, and turned upside down, with an opening on one side. Others are made of bricks and chunām (lime). All that I have seen had their opening towards the sea. Two classes of figures are placed in these shrines, viz., clay figures of gods, which are worshipped before fishing expeditions, and when there is danger from a particular disease which they prevent; and wooden figures of deceased relations, which are quite as imaginative as the clay figures. Figures of gods and relations are placed in the same family shrine. There are hundreds of gods to choose from, and the selection appears to be a matter of family taste and tradition. The figures, which I have sent, were made by a potter at Venkatarayapalle, and painted by a carpenter at Uppulapathi, both villages near Gopalpur. The Tahsildar tells me that, when he was inspecting them at the Gopalpur travellers' bungalow, sixty or seventy fisher people came and worshipped them, and at first objected to their gods being taken away. He pacified them by telling them that it was because the Government had heard of their devotion to their gods that they wanted to have some of them in Madras." The collection of clay figures includes the following:—

Rajamma, a female figure, with a sword in her right hand, riding on a black elephant. She blesses barren women with children, and favours her devotees with big catches when they go out fishing.

Yerenamma, riding on a white horse, with a sword in her right hand. She protects fishermen from drowning, and from being caught by big fish.

Bhagirathamma, riding on an elephant, and having eight or twelve hands. She helps fishermen when fishing at night, and protects them against cholera, dysentery, diarrhœa, and other intestinal disorders.

Nookalamma wears a red jacket and green skirt, and protects the fishing community against small-pox.

Orosondi Ammavaru prevents the boats from being sunk or damaged.

Bhāgadevi rides on a tiger, and protects the community from cholera.

Veyyi Kannula Ammavaru, or goddess of a thousand eyes, represented by a pot pierced with holes, in which a gingelly (*Sesamum*) oil light is burnt. She attends to the general welfare of the fisher folk.

Pre-historic stone celts, found in the bed of a river, and believed to be the thunderbolts of Vishnu, are stacked as votive offerings by the Malaiālis of the Shevaroy hills in their shrines dedicated to Vignesvara, the elephant god who averts evil. The Burmese believe that, when the powers above quarrel, they throw celts at one another, and that, when one misses, it falls to the earth. They attach considerable importance to them for medicinal purposes, and powdered celt is said to be equally good for a pain in the stomach or an inflamed eye.

Lumps of jaggery are thrown into temple tanks by those who are suffering from boils or abscesses, in the belief that they will be resolved as quickly as the molasses are dissolved in the water. For the cure of warts, salt tied up in bundles is sometimes offered.

Should sickness be attributed to a god or goddess, a vow is made, in token whereof a copper or silver coin is wrapped up in a piece of cloth dipped in turmeric paste, and kept in the house or tied to the neck or arm of the sick person. A cock may be waved round the patient's head, and afterwards reared in the house, to be eventually offered up at the shrine of the deity. Some families keep in their homes small pots called thelkodukku undi (scorpion sting vessels), and occasionally drop therein a copper coin, which is supposed to secure immunity against scorpion sting. In some families the money thus offered is limited to two annas monthly. Putting money into an undi as an offering to a particular deity is a very common custom. In the case of a popular god, such as the one at Tirupati, the earthen pot is sometimes replaced by a copper money box or iron safe. In south Canara there was a well-to-do family, the members of which kept on depositing coins in the family undi, which were set apart for the Tirupati god during a number of generations. Not only in cases of sickness, but even when a member of the family went to a neighbouring village and returned safely, a few coins were put into the undi. For some reason the opening of the undi and offering of its contents at Tirupati was postponed, and when it was finally opened, it was found to contain a miscellaneous collection of coins, current and uncurrent,

Plate XXI.

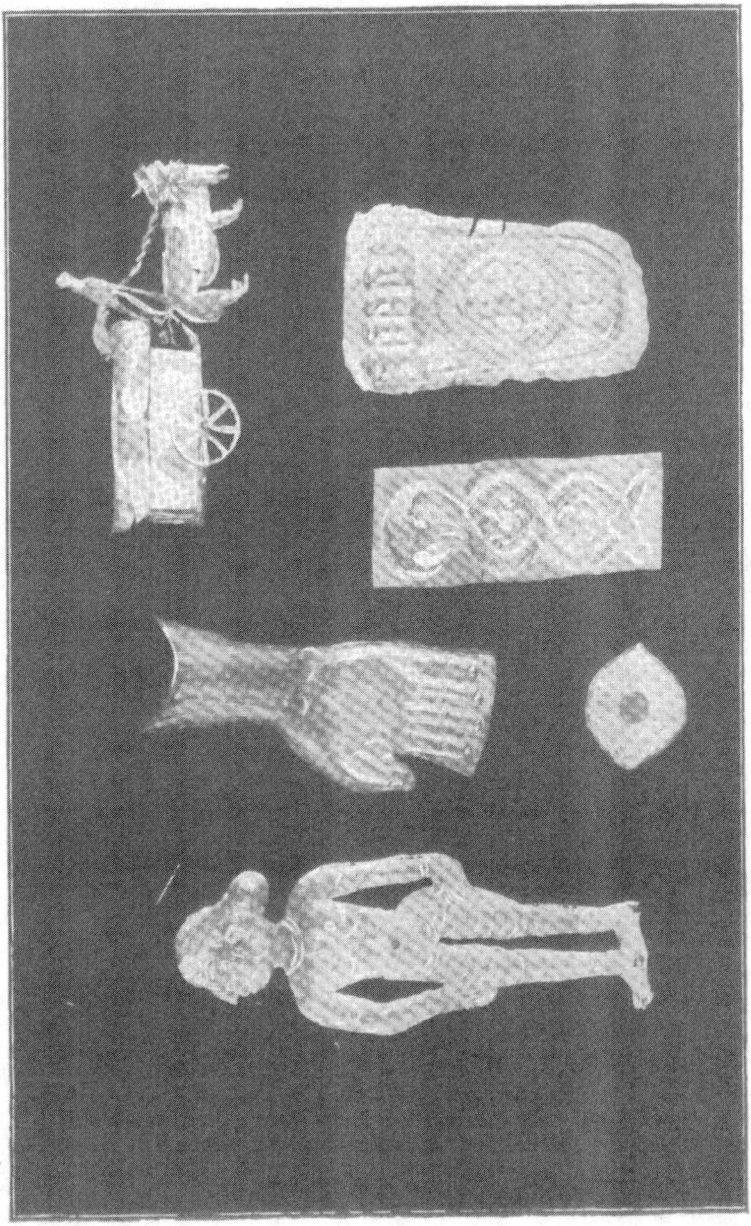

Votive Offerings.

On one occasion, a man who had been presented with two annas as the fee for lending his body to me for measurement offered it, with flowers and a cocoanut, at the shrine of the village goddess, and dedicated to her another coin of his own as a peace-offering, and to get rid of the pollution caused by my money. During a recent tour, a gang of Yerukalas absolutely refused to sit on a chair, and I had to measure their heads while they squatted on the ground. To get rid of my evil influence, they subsequently went through the ceremony of waving red coloured water (arati) and sacrificing fowls.

As a thanksgiving for recovery from illness, the offerings take the form of silver or gold representations of the part of the body affected, which are deposited in a vessel kept for the purpose at the temple. Such *ex votos* are kept for sale in the vicinity of the temple, and must be offered by the person who has taken the vow, or on whose behalf it has been taken. Children have, in addition to the silver articles, to place in the vessel one or two handfuls of coins.

Of silver *ex votos* collected from temples in the Tamil country (plate XXI), the Madras museum possesses an extensive collection, in which are included the face, hands, feet, buttocks, tongue, larynx, navel, nose, ears, eyes, mammæ, genitalia, etc.; snakes offered to propitiate the anger of serpents; snakes coiled *in coitu*; sandals, umbrellas, and cocoanuts strung on a pole. When a person has been ill all over, a silver human figure, or thin silver wire of the same length as himself, and representing him is sometimes offered. Silver umbrellas and flags are also offered at temples. At Pyka in South Canara, brass or clay figures of the tiger, leopard, elephant, wild boar, and bandicoot rat are presented at the shrine of a female bhūtha named Poomanikunhoomani, to protect the crops and cattle from the ravages of these animals. A brass figure of Sarabha (plate XXII), a mythological eight-legged animal, supposed to be the vehicle of the god Virabhadra is presented as an offering at some Sīva temples in South Canara, in cases where a person is attacked with a form of ulcer known as Sīva punnu, (Sīva's sore or ulcer). These brass and clay figures must be solid, as the bhūthas would be very angry if they were hollow.

In Malabar a Brāhman magician transfers the spirits of those who have died an unnatural death to images made of gold, silver, or wood, which are placed in a temple, or special building erected for them.

When litigation arises in Malabar in connection with the title to a house and compound (grounds) in which it stands, a vow is made to offer a silver model representing the property, if a favourable decree is obtained. Some time ago, a rich landlord gave to the temple a silver model representing the exact number of trees, house, well, etc., and costing several hundreds of rupees, when a suit was decided in his favour. In cases of domestic calamities, supposed to be due to the wrath of serpents, images of snakes are offered to Sīva or Vishnu. Such images are also presented by Brāhmans on days of eclipse by those on whose star-day the eclipse falls, to appease the wrath of the terrible Rāhu. The lizard, associated

Plate XXII.

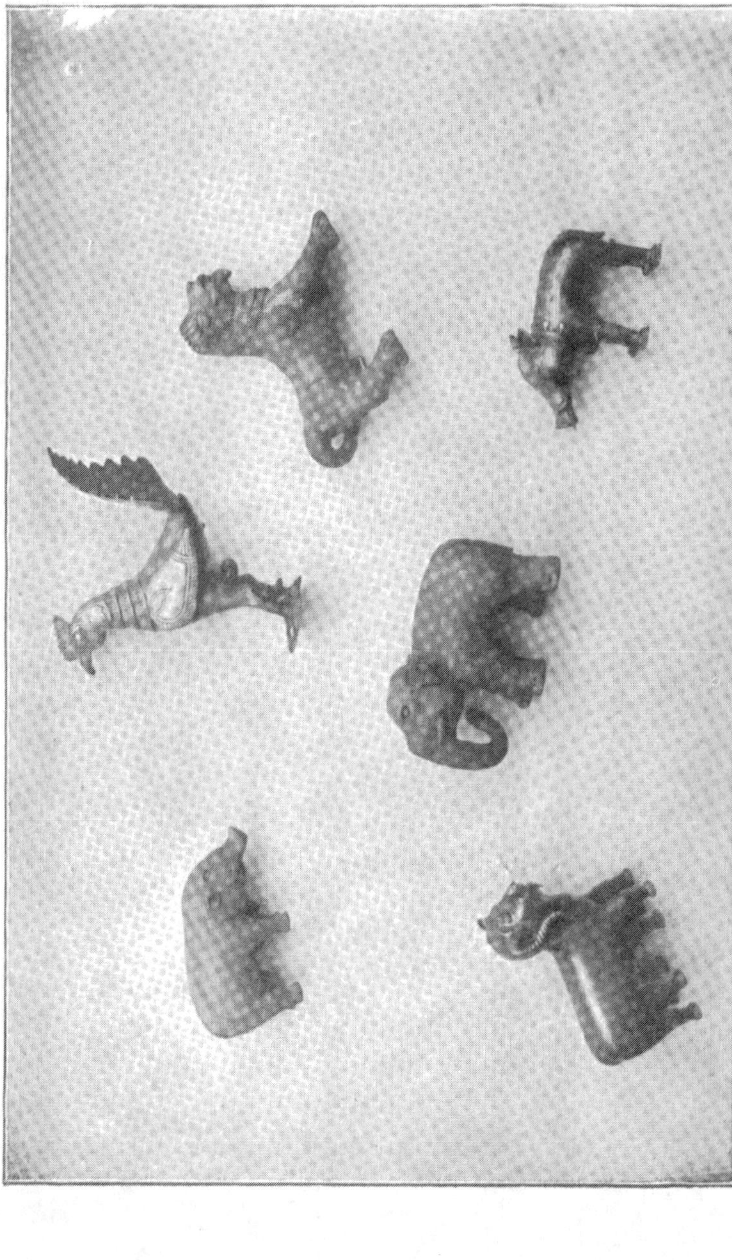

Votive Offerings.

with the name of Sīva, is regarded as sacred. It is never intentionally killed, and, if accidentally hurt or killed, an image of it in gold or silver is presented by high-caste Hindus to a Sīva temple*. In Malabar a silver tortoise is offered in certain cases of severe abdominal pain. Among the Coorgs, figures roughly beaten in silver plates, bronze images, or figures on a slab of pot-stone, representing their ancestors, are placed, together with sticks surmounted with silver, knives, etc., in a small building or niche near the house. Or a sort of bank is made for them under a tree in the fields where the family's first house has stood.† A pilgrim to the shrine of Subramaniya at Palni in the Madura district carries with him a kāvadi, (portable shrine). Of kāvadis there are two kinds, one containing milk in a pot, the other containing fish. When the time comes for the pilgrim to start from his home, he dresses in reddish orange clothes, shoulders his kāvadi and proceeds on his journey. Together with a man ringing a bell, and perhaps one with a tom-tom, with ashes on his face, he assumes the rôle of a beggar. The well-to-do are inclined to reduce the beggar period to a minimum, but a beggar every votary must be, and as such he goes to Palni, and there fulfills his vow, and leaves his kāvadi, a small sum of money, and his hair if it has been allowed to grow long after his father's death.‡ Miniature silver kāvadis are carried by females and young persons to Palni, and miniature silver crowns are given by pilgrims as a votive offering to the god.

* Cochin Census report, 1901. † Rev. F. Kittel, Ind. Ant. II, 1873.

‡ F. Fawcett, Madras Museum Bull., III, 3, 1901.

Pilgrims on the west coast smoke a pipe made of the green leaf-stalk of the plantain. A piece about eighteen inches in length is cut off, and a hole bored at the thicker end, through which a thin stick (usually the mid-rib of a cocoanut leaf) is passed through the stalk for about twelve inches. This forms the tube of the pipe, and communicates with a notch cut in the middle of the leaf-stalk. A funnel, made of the leaf of the jāk tree, is placed in the terminal pole, and filled with tobacco or ganja. The material to be smoked is lighted with a piece of burning charcoal, and the pipe drawn by applying the lips to the notch. Such a pipe is only used once or twice, and then thrown away.

By the Savaras of Vizagapatam, rudely carved and grotesque wooden representations of lizards, parrots, peacocks, human beings, guns, pick-axes, daggers, swords, musical horns, etc., are dedicated to the tribal deity. They would not sell them to the district officer who acquired them on my behalf, but parted with them on the understanding that they would be worshipped by the sirkar (Government).

During the annual festival of the Kotas of the Nilgiris, vows and offerings are made in the temples, and, on the day of the full moon, after a feast, the blacksmith, goldsmith, and silversmith constructing separately a forge and furnace within the temple, each makes something in the way of his avocation—a chopper or axe, ring, or other kind of ornament.*

* Harkness. Aboriginal Race of the Nilagiris, 1832.

Plate XXIII.

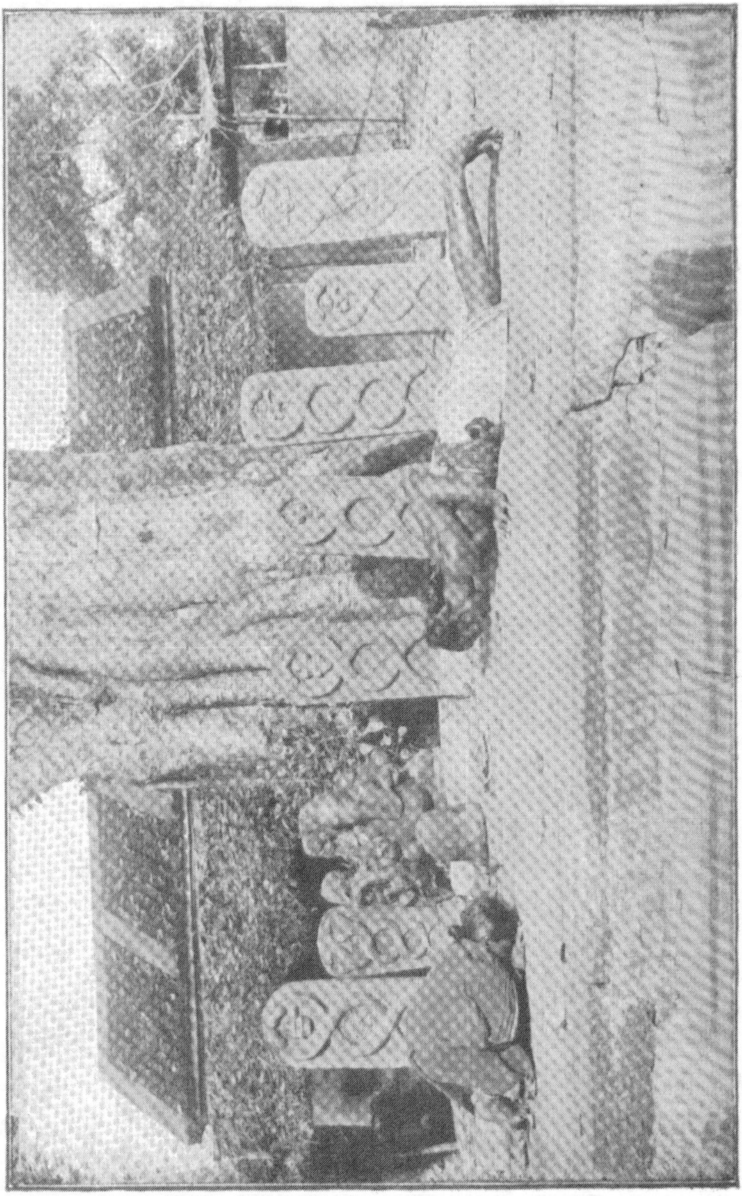

Snake Worship.

On the way leading up to the hill temple at Tirupati, small stones heaped up in the form of a hearth, and knots tied in the leaves of the young date palms (*Phœnix*) may be seen. These are the work of virgins who accompany the parties of pilgrims. The knots are tied to ensure the tying of the marriage tāli string on their necks, and the heaping up of stones is done with a view of ensuring the birth of children to them. If the girls revisit the hill after marriage and the birth of offspring, they untie the knot on a leaf, and disarrange one of the hearths. Men cause their name to be cut on rocks by the wayside, or on the stones with which the path leading to the temple is paved, in the belief that good luck will result if their name is trodden on.

On the side of the roads leading from Bustar, the Rev. J. Cain noticed several large heaps of stones, which the Lambādis had piled up in honour of the goddess Guttalamma. Every Lambādi who passes the heaps is bound to add one stone thereto, and make a salaam to it.*

Mixed-metal bowls, engraved both on the outside and inside with texts from the Qurān, are taken or sent by Muhammadans to Mecca, where they are placed at the head of the tomb of the prophet, and blessed. They are much-valued articles, and used in cases of sickness for the administration of medicine or nourishment.

When a temple is far away, and persons who wish to make offerings thereat cannot, owing to the expense of

* Ind. Ant., VIII, 1879.

the journey or other reason, go there themselves, the votive offerings are taken by a substitute. If the god to whom the offering is made is Srinivāsa of Tirupati, a small sum of money must be offered as compensation for not taking it in person. The Tirupati god is sometimes called Vaddi Kāsulu Varu in allusion to the money (kāsu) or interest. In some large towns, in the months of July and August, parties of devotees may be seen wandering about the streets and collecting offerings to the god, which will be presented to him in due course.

The following quaint custom, which is observed at the village of Pullambadi in the Trichinopoly district, is described by Bishop Whitehead.* "The goddess Kulanthal-Amman has established for herself a useful reputation as a settler of debts. When a creditor cannot recover a debt, he writes down his claim on a scroll of palmyra leaves, and offers the goddess a part of the debt, if it is paid. The palmyra scroll is hung up on an iron spear in the compound of the temple before the shrine. If the claim is just, and the debtor does not pay, it is believed that he will be afflicted with sickness and bad dreams. In his dreams he will be told to pay the debt at once, if he wishes to be freed from his misfortunes. If, however, the debtor disputes the claim, he draws up a counter-statement, and hangs it on the same spear. Then the deity decides which claim is true, and afflicts with sickness and bad dreams the man whose claim is false. When a claim is acknowledged, the

* Madras Diocesan Record, October, 1905.

debtor brings the money, and gives it to the pūjāri, who places it before the image of Kulanthal-Amman, and sends word to the creditor. The whole amount is then handed over to the creditor, who pays the sum vowed to the goddess into the temple coffers in April or May. So great is the reputation of the goddess, that Hindus come from about ten miles round to seek her aid in recovering their debts. The goddess may sometimes make mistakes, but, at any rate, it is cheaper than an appeal to an ordinary court of law, and probably almost as effective as a means of securing justice. In former times no written statements were presented: people simply came and represented their claims by word of mouth to the deity, promising to give her a share. The custom of presenting written claims sprang up about thirty years ago, doubtless through the influence of the Civil Courts. Apparently more debts have been collected since this was done, and more money gathered into the treasury."

"The Hindus," the Rev. A. (now Canon) Margöschis writes,* "observe a special day at the commencement of the palmyra season, when the jaggery (palm-juice sugar) season begins. Bishop Caldwell adopted the custom, and a solemn service in church was held, when one set of all the implements used in the occupation of palmyra-climbing was brought to the church, and presented at the altar. Only the day was changed from that observed by the Hindus. The perils of the palmyra-climber are great, and there are many fatal accidents by falling from

* Christianity and Caste, 1893.

trees forty to sixty feet high, so that a religious service of the kind was particularly acceptable and peculiarly appropriate to our people." The conversion of a Hindu into a Christian ceremonial rite is not devoid of interest.

A few years ago, a shrine was erected at Cochin for a picture of the Virgin and child, which attained to great celebrity for its power of working miracles. "Many stories," Mr. Fawcett writes,* "of the power of the picture are current. A fisherman, who had lost his nets, vowed to give a little net, if they were found. The votive offerings, which are sometimes of copper or brass, take strange forms. There are fishes, prawns, rice, plants, cocoanut trees, cows, etc. A little silver model of a bridge was given by a contractor, who vowed, when he found his foundations were shaky, to give it if his work should pass muster. The power of the picture is such that the votaries are not confined to the Christian community. There are among them many Hindus and Mahomedans."

The festival of Ayudha Pūja (worship of tools or implements) is observed by all Hindu castes during the last three days of the Dasara or Navarathri in the month of Purattasi (September–October). It is a universal holiday for all Hindu workmen. Even the Brāhman takes part in this pūja. His tools, however, being only books, it is called Saraswati pūja, or pūja to the goddess or god of learning, who is either Saraswati or Hayagriva. For the worship of the latter, young culms of the grass *Cynodon Dactylon* are specially secured, and used. Reading books and repetition of Vēdas must be

* Calcutta Review, 1889. The making of a shrine.

done; and, for the purpose of worship, all the books in a house are piled up in a heap. Other castes all clean the various implements used by them in their daily work, and worship them. The Kammālan (artisan) cleans his hammers, pincers, anvil, blow-pipe, wire-plate, etc.; the Chettis (merchants) clean their scales and weights, and the box into which they throw their money.

The racket marker at the Madras Club decorates the entrance to the scoring box, in which his rackets are kept, with a festoon of mango leaves. The weaving and agricultural classes will be seen to be busy with their looms and agricultural implements. The Sembadavan, Pattanāvan, and Bestha fishermen pile up their nets for worship. As every implement is being worshipped, no work can be done during the festival. Even the bandy-wala (cart-driver) paints red and white strips on the wheels and axles, and enjoys a holiday. Not so the bullocks, for the cart-driver's idea of a holiday is to drive his cart recklessly in all directions. I have myself been profusely garlanded when present as a guest at the elaborate tool-worshipping ceremony at our local School of Arts, where, in 1905, pūja was done to a bust of the late Bishop Gell set up on an improvised altar, with a cast of Saraswati above, and various members of the Hindu Pantheon around.

A festival, which is attended by huge crowds of Hindus of all classes, takes place annually in the month of Audi (July–August) at the village of Periyapalayam, where the goddess Māriamma is worshipped under the name of Periyapalayaththamman. According to the legend, as narrated by the Rev. A. C. Clayton,* "there was once a rishi who lived on the banks of the Periya-palayam river with his wife Bavāni. Every morning she used to bathe in the river, and bring back water for the use of the household. But she never took any vessel with her in which to bring the water home, for she was so chaste that she had acquired power to form a water-pot out of the dry river sand, and carry the water home in it. But one day, while bathing, she saw the reflection of the face of the sky-god Indra in the water, and could not help admiring it When she returned to the bank of the river and tried to form her water-pot out of sand as usual, she could not do so, for her admiration of Indra had ruined her power, and she went home sadly to fetch a brass water-vessel. Her husband saw her carrying this to the river, and at once suspected her of unchastity, and, calling his son, ordered him to strike off her head with a sword. It was in vain that the son tried to avoid matricide. He had to obey, but he was so agitated by his feelings that, when at last he struck at his mother, he cut off not only her head but that of a leather-dresser's wife who was standing near. The two bodies lay side by side. The rishi was so pleased with his son's obedience that he promised him any favour that he should ask, but he was very angry when the son at once begged that his mother might be restored to life. Being compelled to keep his word, he told the son that, if he put his mother's head on her trunk, she would again live. The son tried to do so, but in his

* Madras Mus. Bull., V, 2, 1906.

haste took up the head of the leather-dresser's wife by mistake, and put it on Bavāni's body. Leather-dressers are flesh eaters, and so it comes about that on the days when her festival is celebrated, Bavāni—now a goddess—longs for meat, and thousands of sheep, goats and fowls must be slain at her shrine."

The vows, which are performed at the festival, are as follows:—

(1) Wearing a garment of margosa leaves, or wearing an ordinary garment, and carrying a lighted lamp made of rice-flour on the head.

(2) Carrying a pot, decorated with flowers and margosa leaves, round the temple.

(3) Going round the temple, rolling on the ground.

(4) Throwing a live fowl on to the top of the temple.

(5) Throwing a cocoanut in front, prostrating on the ground in salutation, going forward several paces and again throwing the cocoanut, and repeating the procedure till three circuits of the temple have been made.

(6) Giving votive offerings of the idol Parasurama, cradle with baby made of clay or wood, etc., to bring offspring to the childless, success in a law suit or business transaction, and other good luck. In addition a pongal (boiling rice) has to be offered, and by some a sheep or goat is sacrificed.

If a vow has been made on behalf of a sick cow, the animal is bathed in the river, clad in margosa leaves, and led round the temple. The leaf-wearing vow is resorted to by the large majority of the devotees, and performed by men, women, and children. Those belonging to the more respectable classes go through it in the early morning, before the crowd has collected in its tens of thousands. The leafy garments are purchased from hawkers, who do a brisk trade in the sale thereof. The devotees have to pay a very modest fee for admission to the temple precincts, and go round the shrine three or more times. Concerning the Periyapalayam festival a recent writer observes that "the distinctive feature is that the worshippers are clad in leaves, instead of wearing ordinary clothing. The devotees are bound to wear a garment made of fresh margosa twigs with their leaves. This garment is called vēpansilai. It consists of a string three or four yards long, from which depend, at intervals of two to three inches apart, twigs measuring about two feet in length, and forming a fringe of foliage. This string being wound several times round the waist, the fringe of leaves forms a kilt or short petticoat, which not only covers the body suitably, but also looks picturesque in its sylvan style. Men are content to wear the kilt, but women wear also around their neck, a similar garment, which forms a short cloak reaching to the waist. To impress on devotees the imperative obligation imposed on them to wear the leaf garment in worshipping the goddess, it is said that a young married woman, being without chldren, made a vow to the goddess that, on obtaining a son, she would go on a pilgrimage to Periyapalayam, and worship her in accordance with the ancient rite. Her prayer having been answered, she gave birth to a son, and went to Periyapalayam to fulfil her vow. When, however, it was time to undress and put on the vēpansilai, her modesty revolted. Unobserved by her party, she secretly tied a small cloth around her waist, before putting on the vēpansilai. So attired, she went up to the pagoda to worship. On seeing her coming, the terrible goddess detected her deceit, and, waxing wroth, set the woman's leaf dress all ablaze, and burnt her so severely that she died." At a festival to the village goddess at Kudligi in the Bellary district, the procession is, Mr. Fawcett tells us, headed by a Mādiga naked save for a few margosa leaves. The wearing of these leaves on the occasion of festivals in honour of Māriamma is a very general custom throughout Southern India.

DEFORMITY AND MUTILATION.

In his little book* on fashions in deformity, or alteration of some part of the body from its natural form, Sir W. Flower says that "some of them have been associated with religious or superstitious observances; some have been vaguely thought to be hygienic in motive; most have some relation to conventional standards of improved personal appearance." As simple examples of the last in Southern India may be incidentally noted the beauty spots daubed on the foreheads of villagers on the occasion of a festival with sandal-paste or bright anilin powders, or with the purple juice of the fruit of *Eugenia Arnottiana* by the Toda women of the Nīlgiris. Among some classes, the females cut discs out of the shining green elytra of a buprestid beetle, and stick them on their foreheads as beauty marks instead of the more usual kunkam (turmeric, or starch coloured with anilin dyes) or santhu (black paste made of charred rāgi or other millet). The use of black antimony (surma) or lamp black as a cosmetic for the eyelids, and improving the complexion by smearing the face with turmeric, are very widespread among females. So, too, among Muhammadan men, is dyeing the nails and hair red with henna leaves (*Lawsonia alba*).

Thinking that it will give their husbands increase of years, women freely bathe themselves in turmeric water,

* Fashion in Deformity (Nature series), 1881.

which is matchless in beneficial effects. The use of water in which turmeric has been infused, by which they give to the whole body a bright yellow or gold colour, is prescribed to wives as a mark of the conjugal state, and forbidden to widows.* Some Canarese women (Vakkaliga, Kuruba, Holeya, etc.), like the Malays, consider blackened teeth to be more beautiful than white. The staining process is carried out before puberty is reached. The girl, whose teeth are to be coloured, softens the gums, and removes the tartar, by sucking lime-juice. The paste, which consists of a mixture of myrabolams (fruit of *Terminalia*), sulphate of iron, cutch, pods of *Acacia arabica*, and areca nut, is then applied. Its application is said to produce intense pain, and the girl may have to lie low for several days. Sometimes women of the higher classes stain their teeth in the same manner, when they get loose, or when they suffer from tooth-ache. The wearing of heavy brass armlets sometimes gives rise to extensive sores and cicatrices. Boring the nostrils and helix of the ear for the insertion of precious jewels set in gold, brass and bead ornaments, simple brass rings, and hoops or pieces of stick like matches, is widely resorted to. The cartilage of the ear of a Khond girl is pierced, and, until she is officially married, she wears in the holes long pieces of grass. After marriage, brass rings are substituted. In Coorg the carpenter has the exclusive privilege of piercing the ears for ornaments. At the ceremony of investiture of

* Ellis, Kural.

a Mysore Holeya with the musical instrument which is the badge of priestly rank in his caste, the officiating Bairāgi bores a hole in his right ear with a needle, and from the punctured wound two drops of blood fall on the ground.

The custom of calling a newly-born child, after the parent has lost a first born or more in succession, by an opprobrious name is common amongst many castes in Southern India, including even Muhammadans. Kuppuswāmi (= Sir dungheap) is one of the commonest names for such children, and they have the distinguishing mark of a pierced nostril and ear (on the right side) with a knob of gold in it.* Sometimes a woman, who has lost a child, when she is again pregnant, makes a vow that the child, when born, shall be named after the god or goddess (Srinivāsa or Alamēlu) at Tirupati. The infant is accordingly taken to the Tirupati temple, where its hair is removed, and the lobe of the ear pierced. Some of the members of the Kiriattil clan of Nāyars, who call themselves Padināyirattil (one of ten thousand) pierce the ears, but never wear earrings.† A Nāyar was noticed by Mr. Fawcett, whose right nostril was slit vertically, as if for the insertion of a jewel. His mother had miscarried in her first pregnancy, so, according to custom, he, the child of her second pregnancy, had had his nose slit. In the Mysore province, the custom of boring the right side of the nostrils of children, whose elder brother or sister died

* B.R.B. Ind. Ant., IX., 1880.

† F. Fawcett, Madras Mus. Bull. III, 1901.

Plate XXIV.

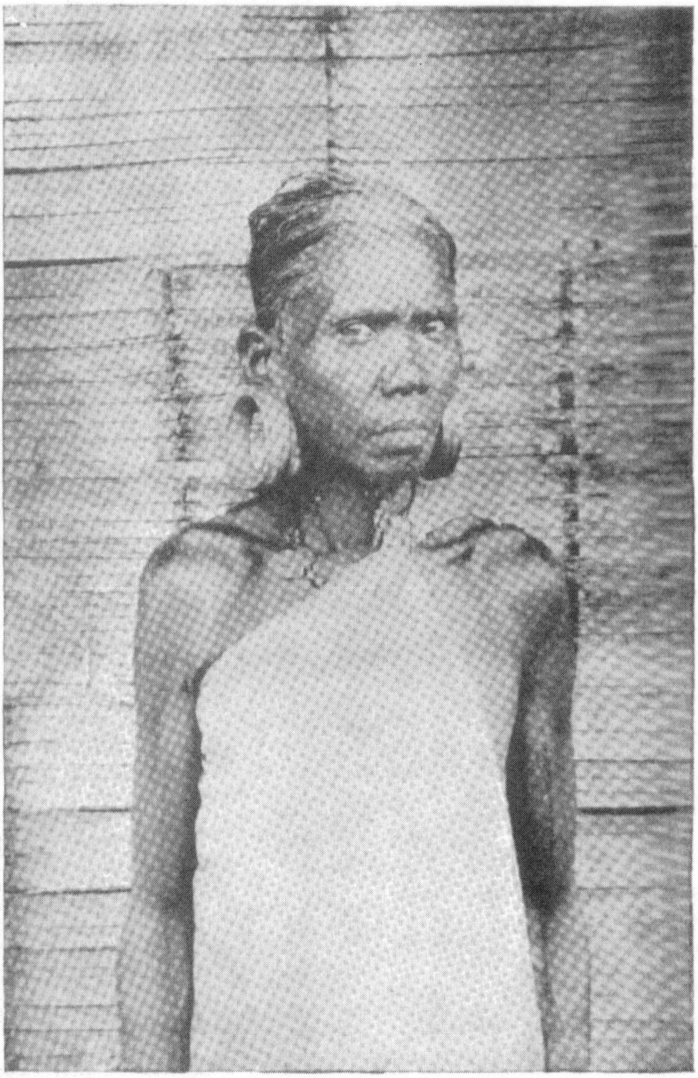

Kădir, dilated Ear-lobes.

soon after their birth, prevails. Such children are called gunda (rock), kalla (stone), hucha (lunatic), tippa (dung-hill). The last name is given after some rubbish from a dung-hill has been brought in a sieve, and the child placed in it.*

Mutilation as a means of "improving" personal appearance reaches its highest point in dilatation of the lobes of the ears, which, it has been suggested, was originally adopted in India for the purpose of receiving a solar disc. For the following note I am indebted to Canon A. Margöschis, of the S.P.G. Mission, Tinnevelly, who is a practical authority on the subject. "To produce this artificial deformity," he writes, "is the work of men of the Koravar caste, whose occupations are bird-catching and basket-making. On or about the third day after birth, the troubles of a female begin, for the child's ears must be operated on, and for this purpose a knife with a triangular blade is used. Sometimes the ceremony is postponed until the child is sixteen days old. Among the Hindus a 'good day' is selected, and Christians choose Sunday. The point of the knife is run through the lobe of the ear until the blade has penetrated for half an inch of its length. Both ears are cut, and a piece of cotton-wool is placed in the wounds, to keep the cut portions dilated. Every other day the Koravar must change the wool, and increase the quantity introduced. If the sores fester, a dressing is used of castor-oil and human milk in equal parts, and, if there is much suppuration, an astringent, such as tamarind juice

* Narayan Aiyangar, Ind. Ant. IX, 1880.

lotion, is used. The cut lobes will take not less than a month to heal, and for the whole of that time the process of dilatation is continued by passing through the lobes pledgets of cotton-wool, increasing gradually in size. After the wounds have healed, pieces of cotton cloth are rolled up (plate XXV), and placed in the lobes instead of the cotton-wool; and this is done for a few days only, when leaden rings are substituted, which are added to in number until as many as six or eight rings are in each ear. These drag the lobes down more and more, and, by the time the infant is a year old, the process of elongating the lobes is complete in so far as the acute stage is concerned, and all that is necessary afterwards is to leave the leaden rings in the ears, and to let the elongated lobes grow as the child grows. Instead of keeping a large number of rings in the ears, they are melted down into two heavy, thick rings, which are kept in the ears until the girl is twelve or thirteen years old, and by that time the acme of beauty will have been attained so far as the ears are concerned, because the lobes will reach down to the shoulders on each side. This is perfection, and reminds one of the man on one of the islands near New Guinea, the lobes of whose ears had been converted into great pendent rings of skin, through which it was possible to pass the arms.* The fees for the operation are 10 annas to Rs. 1–1–6. The custom described prevails among the following castes: Vellālas, Shānars, Maravans, Paravans, shepherds, dyers, tailors, oilmongers, Pallas, and Pariahs. The females of the

* Flower, *Op cit.*

Plate XXV.

Dilated Ear-lobes.

Paravar caste (Roman Catholic fisher caste) are famous for the longest ears, and for wearing the heaviest and most expensive golden ear jewels made of sovereigns. Ordinary ear jewels cost Rs. 200, but heavy jewels are worth Rs. 1,000 and even more. The longer the ears, the more jewels can be used, and this appears to be the rationale of elongated ears. In former days men also had long ears, but it is now reserved for the men who play the bow and bells at demon dances. With regard to the prevalence of this custom of mangling the human body, and the possibility of its gradual removal, the missionaries, especially in Tinnevelly, have all along been the sternest foes of the barbarity. In one boarding school alone, consisting of 224 girls, there are 165 with short ears, so that only 59 have them elongated. And, of the 165, no less than 51 have had their long ears operated on and cut short at the mission hospital, and this they have consented to as a voluntary act. As it was once the fashion to have long ears, and a mark of respectability, so now the converse is true. Until the last twenty years, if a woman had short ears, she was asked if she was a dancing girl (dēva-dāsi) because that class kept their ears natural. Now, with the change of customs all round, even dancing girls are found with long ears. Muhammadan women have their ears pierced all round the outer edges, and as many as twenty or twenty-five rings, of iron or gold, are inserted in the holes; but the lobes are not elongated. The artificial deforming of the body assumes various phases in different parts of the world, and we have but to refer to the small feet of the

Chinese, the flattening of the skull of infants among the North American Indians, and the piercing and elongation of the upper lip amongst certain tribes in Central Africa. In all cases these are attempts to improve upon nature, and the results are as revolting as they are often ghastly and cruel. The torture inflicted upon helpless Tamil babes is so cruel that it would be humane and righteous for Government to interfere, and abolish long ears. The number of persons suffering from deafness and chronic discharges from the ear is very considerably increased in consequence of the barbarity described above."

In connection with the practice of dilating the lobes of the ears among the Kallans of the Madura district, Mr. J. H. Nelson writes * that "both males and females are accustomed to stretch to the utmost possible limit the lobes of their ears. The unpleasant disfigurement is effected by the mother boring the ears of her baby, and inserting heavy pieces of metal, generally lead, into the apertures. The effect so produced is very wonderful, and it is not at all uncommon to see the ears of a Kallan hanging on his shoulders. When violently angry, a Kallan will sometimes tear in two the attenuated strips of flesh, which constitute his ears, expecting thereby to compel his adversary to do likewise as a sort of an *amende honorable*: and altercations between women constantly lead to one or both parties having the ears violently pulled asunder. And formerly, where a Kalla girl was deputed, as frequently happened, to guide a stranger in safety through a Kalla tract, if any of her caste-people

* Manual of the Madura district.

attempted to offer violence to her charge in spite of her protestations, she would immediately tear open one of her ears, and run off at full speed to her home to complain of what had been done. And the result of her complaint was invariably a sentence to the effect that the culprits should have both their ears torn in expiation of their breach of the by-laws of the forest."

The following rules, which were formerly drawn up by Kallans, under compulsion by their servants, are distinctly quaint.

(1) If a Kallan lost a tooth through a blow given by his master, the latter was to be fined ten Kāli chakrams (coin).

(2) If a Kallan had his ear torn under punishment, his master must pay a fine of six chakrams.

(3) If a Kallan had his skull fractured, his master must pay thirty chakrams, or in default have his own skull fractured.

(4) If a Kallan had his arm or leg broken, his master must pay a fine of twenty chakrams, give the injured man a certain amount of grain, cloths, etc., and likewise grant him in fee-simple as much nanjey (wet cultivation) land as could be sown with a kalam of seed, and two kurukkams of punjey (dry cultivation) land.

(5) If a Kallan were killed, his master must pay a fine of one hundred chakrams, or in default be put at the mercy of the murdered man's relatives.

It is recorded in the Cuddapah Manual that a Yerukala came to a certain village, and, under the pretence of begging, ascertained which women wore valuable jewels, and whether the husbands of any such were employed at night in the fields. In the night he returned, and, going to the house he had previously marked, suddenly snatched up the sleeping woman by the gold ear-ring she wore with such violence as to lift up the woman, and in such a way as to wrench off the lobe of the ear. In a case of assault with robbery committed in 1901 in the outskirts of Salem town by some Koravars on an old man, the lobe of his ear was cut off in order to remove his ear-ring. A new form of house-robbery has been recently started by the Koravas. They mark down the residence of a woman, whose jewels are worth stealing, and lurk outside the house before dawn. Then, when the woman comes out, as is the custom, before the men are stirring, they snatch her ear-rings and other ornaments, and are gone before an alarm can be raised. Recently, in a fight between two women in Madras, one bit off the lobe of the ear of the other. In a report on the Coimbatore dispensary, 1852, Mr. Porteous mentions that he treated within the year "lacerated wounds on eight out- and nine in-patients, all these formed cases of criminal process, and were all inflicted by tearing off the ear ornaments forcibly." *

Mr. (now Sir) F. A. Nicholson, who was some years ago stationed at Ramnād in the Madura district, tells me that the young Maravan princesses used to come and play in his garden, and, as they ran races, hung on to their ears, lest the heavy ornaments should rend asunder the filamentous ear lobes.

* Chevers. Manual of Medical Jurisprudence for India.

Among the female Tiyans of Malabar the practice of dilating the lobes of the ears prevails, though the deformity is not carried to such an extreme length as in Madura and Tinnevelly. The operation is performed, when the child is a few months or a year old, either by goldsmiths or by astrologers called Pannikar in South and Kanisan in North Malabar. The lobe is pierced with a gold pin or thorn, and a thread inserted to prevent the wound from closing up. The ear is dressed daily with butter. After a week or two the thread is replaced by a thin plug of wood, and subsequently gradual dilatation is effected by means of pith soaked in water to make it swell. Further dilatation is effected by means of solid wooden ornaments, or rolls of lead or cadjan.

Writing in the sixteenth century concerning the Nāyars of the west coast, Cæsar Frederick states* that "the Nairi and their wives use for a braverie to make great holes in their eares, and so bigge and wide that it is incredible, holding this opinion, that the greater the holes bee, the more noble they esteeme themselves. I had leave of one of them to measure the circumference of one of them with a thread, and within that circumference I put my arme up to the shoulder, clothed as it was, so that in effect they are monstrous great. Thus they doe make them when they be litel, for then they open the eare and hang a piece of gold or lead thereat, and within the opening, in the hole they put a certain leafe that they have for that purpose, which maketh the hole so great." Further, Ralph Fitch, writing about the

* Hakluyt's Voyages. Glasgow Edition, 1904.

inhabitants of Cochin, states * that "the men be of a reasonable stature; the women litle; all black, with a cloth bound about their middle hanging down to their hammes; all the rest of their bodies be naked: they have horrible great eares with many rings set with pearles and stones."

Allusion may next be made to the widespread custom of tattooing the skin. In a paper on tattooing (or tatuing) read at the Anthropological Institute in January 1888, Miss Buckland refers to the practice of tattooing among the Nāgas of Assam, and to the tattooing of breeches, reaching from the waist to the knee, with which the male Burman is adorned. But, in the map illustrating the paper, Peninsular India, south of 20°, is left a perfect and absolute blank. And, in the discussion which followed the reading of the paper, Colonel Kincaird, recognising the hiatus, remarked that "his observation led him to believe that this custom is wide spread on the arms and legs among the women of the lower castes of the Tamil, etc., races in the south and south-east of the peninsula."

Of tattooing an admirable detailed account is given in the Mysore census report, 1901. The following note on the practice of tattooing, as carried on in the city of Madras, is mainly based on information extracted in the course of interviews with professional female tattooers, of whom the first arrived in a condition of maudlin intoxication. These women belong to the class of Koravas, or Yerukalas, "a vagrant tribe found

* Hakluyt's Voyages. Glasgow Edition, 1904.

throughout the Madras Presidency, who wander about the country in gangs, selling baskets, carrying salt, telling fortunes, and pilfering and robbing whenever an opportunity occurs. As house-breakers they are especially expert, and burglary is their favourite crime." * The men are also employed in hunting, bird-snaring, and as actors of native plays, which they perform on the road-side. Sometimes they masquerade as mendicants, and go about, beating a drum, and begging from house to house in the bazār. From the Police records I gather that a gang of this thief class camped in a certain spot in the Vizagapatam district for more than two months. The women went about begging, and effecting an entrance into respectable houses by tattooing girls. The gang then suddenly disappeared. "Both men and women of the Korava class wear tattoo marks of circular or semi-circular form on their foreheads and forearms. When they are once convicted, they enlarge or alter in some other way the tattoo marks on their forearms, so that they may differ from the previous descriptive marks of identification entered by the Police in their search books and other records." †

The female tattooers leave Madras during the harvest season, and pay professional visits to the neighbouring districts, travelling as far as Pondicherry in the south and Cuddapah in the north. By these women Brāhmans, Sūdras of all classes, Paraiyans, and Tamil-speaking Muhammadans (Labbais) are operated on. The patterns

* Madras Census Report, 1891.

† P. Paupa Rao Naidu, History of Railway Thieves, 1900.

range from a dot or straight line to complex geometrical or conventional designs. Figures of wild animals are not met with, but scorpions, birds, fishes, flowers and the Vaishnava sect mark are common. So, too, are the initials or name in Tamil characters on the forearm. Sometimes Hindu males are tattooed, as an amusement, when boys, or, in some cases among the lower classes, when grown up. For example, many Pulayan men in Travancore are tattooed on the forehead with a crescent and circular spot, and the Irulas of Chingleput with a vertical stripe along the middle of the forehead. The Chakkiliyan men of Madras are very freely tattooed, not only on the forehead, but, also with their name, conventional devices, dancing girls, etc., on the chest and upper extremities. The following information was supplied by a Tamil man, with a European ballet-girl tattooed on his upper arm, who was engaged in varnishing cases in one of the museum galleries. "Some years ago I went to Ceylon with a native theatrical company. While in Colombo I made the acquaintance of a Sinhalese who was a professional tattooer. He had an album of patterns. I was attracted by their beauty, and subjected myself to the operation. It was an easy and painless operation as compared with that of the Madras tattooer. The Sinhalese man had the needles tied together in a different way, *e.g.*, for pricking straight lines five or six needles are tied together in a row; for pricking curves the needles are arranged in a curve. The Madras tattooer has the needles arranged in a bundle, and the operation, as performed with them, is painful, and sometimes followed by swelling and ulceration." Asked whether he was glad he had been tattooed, he replied that, when he got married he was ashamed of it, and kept it hidden by his cloth. One result of emigration to Burma is that Tamil men sometimes return from that country tattooed with elaborate devices worthy of the tattooed nobleman in a booth at a race-meeting. The Eurasian body being enveloped in clothes, it was not till they stripped before me for the purposes of anthropometry that I became aware how prevalent the practice of tattooing is among the male members of the community. Nearly all the hundred and thirty men whom I examined were, in fact, tattooed on the chest, upper arms, forearms, wrists, back of the hands, or shoulders. The following are a few of the devices in blue, with occasional red, recorded in my notes :—

Queen Alexandra.	Watteau shepherdess.
Steam-boat.	Burmese lady.
Ballet-girl.	Elephant.
Flowers in a pot.	Sailing boat.
The word 'Mercy'.	Initials of inamorata.
Royal arms.	Scorpion.
Crown and flags.	Crossed swords.
Cross and anchor.	Bracelets.
Dancing girl.	Lizard.
Heart and cross.	Bugles.

Many of the Roman Catholic Eurasians of Malabar have a bird tattooed on their forearms as the emblem of the Holy Ghost. And, in like manner, some Syrian Christians are tattooed with the sign of the cross

Among native females the parts of the body selected for the operation are the arm, fore-leg, forehead, cheeks, and chin. But sometimes, in cases of muscular pain or other disorder, the operation is performed as a remedial agent over the shoulder joint, or on the thigh, or other parts of the body. A legend runs to the effect that, many years ago, a Paraiyan woman wished her upper arms and chest to be tattooed in the form of a bodice. The operation was successfully performed until the region of the heart was reached, and then a vulnerable part was punctured by the needles, with the result that the woman died. Whence has arisen a superstitious objection to tattooing of the breasts. Tattooing is sometimes a sign that puberty has been reached.

The Tamil equivalent of tattooing is pachai-kuthu-kirathu, or pricking with green. The marking ink is prepared in the following manner. Turmeric (kappa manja) powder and agathikirai (leaves of *Sesbania grandiflora*) are rubbed together in a mortar or on a grinding stone. The mixture is spread on a thin cloth, and rolled up in the form of a wick, which is placed in an open lamp charged with castor-oil. The wick is lighted, and the lamp covered with a new earthen pot, on the inside of which the lamp black is deposited. This is scraped off, and mixed with human milk or water. Instead of agathi-kirai, arugampillu (green parts of *Cynodon Dactylon*) or karisirangkani (*Eclipta alba*) may be used in the preparation of the wick. As a pricking instrument, three or more sewing needles are fastened together with thread. In the performance of the operation, the pattern, selected from the dirty bundle of drawings on paper, is first traced on the skin with a blunt stick dipped in the prepared ink, which is pricked in with the needles. The part is then washed with cold water, and a coat of ink rubbed over the surface. To allay the pain, oil is applied, and a small quantity of turmeric powder is rubbed in, to brighten the colour and prevent swelling. The Korava women, being illiterate, are unable to tattoo initials or names unless they are first drawn for them. They are able to execute the complicated patterns, with which they are, from long practice, familiar, with considerable dexterity, and will tattoo any pattern which is new to them, provided that it is first drawn. The woman who described the tattooing process to me traced out very elaborate patterns with great rapidity with the blunt stick which she was accustomed to use, but could make no way at all with a pencil. The Burmese patterns are, as already indicated, far more artistic, varied, and complicated than those executed by Koravas; and some of these patterns are now being copied by the Madras tattooers. The tattooer's fee is said to range from a quarter-anna for a dot or line to twelve annas for a complex design. And in up-country villages payment appears to be made in kind, and a present of rice to be the usual remuneration.

A Kuncha Korava tattooer woman, whom I interviewed, kept her needles and drawing stick in a hollow bamboo, and the marking mixture in the scooped out fruits of the bael (*Ægle Marmelos*) and palmyra palm (*Borassus flabellifer*). The hot weather, she said, is more favourable than the cold season for the operation, as the swelling is less. To check which she applied a mixture of lamp-oil, turmeric, and avarai (*Dolichos Lablab*) leaves.

Tattooing does not find any favour with North Travancore Nāyars. It is only in the case of Nāyar women living to the south of Quilon that the custom seems to prevail. Some accounts trace it to the influence of a Moghul Sirdar, who invaded Travancore in 1680 A.D.

In a recent article * Mr. Risley identifies the tattooed designs of the Dōmbs of Jeypore as being related to the religion and mythology of the tribe; totems; and having reference to their traditional avocations.

Among the Todas of the Nīlgiris, the operation is performed by an elderly woman. Women only are tattooed, and, it is said, they must have borne one or more children. Girls are, however, occasionally tattooed after reaching puberty, but before giving birth to children. And I have seen several multiparæ, in whom the absence of tattoo marks was explained on the ground that they were too poor to afford the expense of the operation, or that they were always suckling or pregnant—conditions in which the operation would not, it was said, be free from danger. The dots and circles on the chest, back, arms, and legs, of which the simple devices are made up, are marked out with lamp-black made into a paste with water, and the pattern is picked in with the spines of the common mountain barberry (*Berberis aristata*). The Badaga women of the Nīlgiris use the spines of *Carissa spinarum* for the same purpose.

* Man. July, 1902.

I have seen a Bēdar of the Bellary district, who had dislocated his shoulder when a lad, and been tattooed over the deltoid with the figure of Hanumān (the monkey god) to relieve the pain.

In the Bellary district the Lingayats have one Basivi (dedicated prostitute) of their caste in every large village. Her initiation is carried out in the following way. "The headmen of the caste meet, and perform a ceremony wedding her to her caste. A tāli, on which is figured a bull (Nandi, Siva's bull) is tied by the village Jangam or priest, who draws a lingam on a betel leaf, and tattooes the figure on her upper arm, over the deltoid, with juice of the cashew-nut (*Anacardium occidentale*). This is often omitted, and she is not marked in this way."*

An interesting custom, which prevails among the Kādirs and Mala Vēdars of the Anaimalai hills and Travancore, and among them alone, so far as I know, of the entire population of the Indian peninsula, is that of chipping all or some of the incisor teeth, both upper and lower, into the form of a sharp-pointed, but not serrated cone. The operation, which is performed with a chisel or bill-hook and file by members of the tribe skilled thereat on Kādir boys at the age of eighteen, and girls at the age of ten or thereabouts, has been thus described. The girl to be operated on lies down, and places her head against a female friend, who holds it tightly. A third woman takes a sharpened bill-hook, and chips away the teeth till they are shaded to a point, the girl operated on writhing and groaning with the pain. After the

* F. Fawcett, Journ. Anth. Soc., Bombay, II, 1881.

operation she looks dazed, and in a very few hours the face begins to swell. Pain and swelling last for a day or two, accompanied by severe headache. The Kādirs say that chipped teeth make an ugly person look handsome, and that one whose teeth have not been chipped has teeth like, and looks like a cow. An ugly old Mala Vēdar man, who had his teeth very slightly filed, on being asked why he had not conformed to the tribal fashion, grinned and said "What beauty I was born with is good enough for me." Probably the operation had proved more than he could bear; or, may be, he could not afford to pay the betel-nut and leaves which are the customary fee of the filer. The operation is performed with a curved bill-hook with a serrated edge.* The fact is worthy of record, as a link between the inhabitants of Southern India and Ceylon, that deformity of the teeth exists as a tribal custom among the Rhodias, of whom M. Deschamps writes as follows.† "J'ai parcouru deux centres importants de Rhodias: dans l'un j'ai remarqué la pratique de la mutilation des dents, complètement ignorée par l'autre. Dans le premier, sur cinq ou six sujets observés, hommes et femmes, avaient les incisives supérieures limées, non point sur la tranche ou les bords inférieurs, ainsi que le font beaucoup de peuples primitifs, mais sur la face extérieure et sur toute la longueur d'une, deux ou trois incisives. Quelquefois la partie inférieure de la dent offre, en outre, un véritable sillon horizontal d'un demi à un millimètre de creux.

* Mrs. Evans: Madras Museum Bull. II, No. 3, 1899.
† E. Deschamps: Au Pays des Veddas, Ceylon, 1890.

L'époque à laquelle se fait cette mutilation est indifférente, mais je l'ai observée sur une petite fille de treize ans. La raison qu'ils me donnèrent de cette coutume, pour diminuer la longuer de la face, est non moins curieuse."

Turning now to fashion associated with religious or superstitious observance. It is needless to dilate on the prevalent Hindu custom of painting religious marks, or smearing sacred ashes on the forehead and other parts of the body. Nor is it necessary to enlarge on circumcision as practised by the Muhammadan community. In connection, however, with circumcision, in the troublous times of the Muhammadan usurpation of Mysore and at the present day, some interesting facts are worthy of notice. It is recorded * that "the prisoners taken by the French in the *Hannibal* to the number of nearly 500 were landed at Cuddalore in June, 1782. In August they were delivered over to Hyder Ally Khan, and marched to Bangalore. In October the youngest, to the number of 51, were sent to Seringapatam. Their heads were shaved, all their things were taken from them, and they were circumcised. All were bound on parade, and rings, the badge of slavery, were put into their ears. Several European boys were taught dancing in the country style and forced to dance in female dress before Tippoo." The operation was performed, when the victim of it was under the influence of a narcotic called majum, after, the hair had been cropped by a barber. It is narrated †

* Narrative of William Drake, midshipman of the *Hannibal*. Seton-Karr. Selections from Calcutta Gazettes.

† Narrative of the sufferings of James Bristow, 1794.

that some of Haidar's European prisoners, after they had been made what was termed Mussulman, neglected no opportunity of showing their contempt for the religion of their tormentors, and their cruelty, by catching dogs and bandicoot rats, and circumcising them publicly.

When Tippoo (or Tīpū) was at Calicut, the Pagans were deprived of the token of their nobility, a lock of hair called kudumi; and every Christian who appeared in the streets must either submit to be circumcised, or be hanged on the spot.* Among other acts of cruelty committed by Tippoo, it is stated that, seeing a Lingayat woman selling curds in the street without a bodice, he ordered the cutting off of her breasts. As a result of which act the wearing of long garments came into use among the whole female population of Mysore. It is recorded that, on one occasion, a Nāyar woman appeared before the Zamorin of Calicut's lady with her breasts concealed, and they were cut off as the wearing of a bodice was considered immodest. Of other forms of punishment by mutilation, two further examples may be cited. During one of the voyages of Vasco de Gama to Malabar, "the Captain-major ordered them to cut off the hands and noses of all the crews, and put all that into one of the small vessels, into which he ordered them to put the friar, also without ears, nose, or hands, which he ordered to be strung round his neck, with a palm-leaf for the king of Calicut, on which he told him to have a curry made, to eat of what his friar brought

* Bartolomeo. Voyage to the East Indies, 1776-89.

him."* In the Vizagapatam Manual (1869) Mr. Carmichael states that "in cases of rape (in Jeypore) the procedure was to cut the woman's nose off, and, after beating the man well, to turn him out of the caste by stuffing his mouth with beef In cases of murder, the Rājah generally had the man's hands, nose, and ears cut off, but, after all that, he seldom escaped the vengeance of the deceased's relatives. There is a man now living in the village of Bassoonee, whose hands were cut off by order of Rājah Chaitan Deo fourteen years ago. He was taken red-handed straight to the Rājah, and his hands were off within an hour of the commission of the deed. He has been supported by the Rājah ever since."

At the Parlakimedi rebellion in the last century, the rebels wounded the peasants, or cut off their noses, and sent them into Mr. Russell, who had been sent to Ganjam with a special commission by Government, saying that the blood was upon his head.† It is recorded by Moor‡ that, during the operations against Tippoo Sultan, "the enemy one day caught a fine young woman belonging to our line, and, to their indelible disgrace, cut off her nose, and in that condition the poor creature came back to camp." Haidar and Tippoo were in the habit of cutting off the noses and ears of those of their English prisoners who were caught when attempting to escape. One was afterwards led round the fort on a jackass, with his face to the tail. Tippoo, when before Mangalore, cut off

* Correa. Three Voyages of Vasco de Gama.

† S. P. Rice. Occasional Essays on Native South Indian Life, 1902

‡ Narrative of the Operation of Little's Detachment.

the noses and ears of a whole sepoy brigade, which attempted to prevent an execution.* In the days of Tirumala Nayakar, the Mysoreans had been cutting off noses, and sending them by sackfuls back to Mysore. So the troops of the Naykar scattered through Mysore for noses to cut off in retaliation. They succeeded even to the extent of cutting off the nose of the king himself. This was called the chase after noses.†

To revert to circumcision. It is a curious fact that many of the Kallans of the Madura district practise this rite. The origin thereof is uncertain, though it has been suggested that it is a survival of a forcible conversion to Muhammadanism of a section of the Kurumbas who fled northwards on the downfall of their kingdom.‡ At the time appointed for the initiatory ceremony, the Kallan youth is carried on the shoulders of his maternal uncle to a grove or plain outside the village, where betel is distributed among those who have assembled, and the operation is performed by a barber-surgeon. *En route* to the selected site, and throughout the ceremony, the conch shell (musical instrument) is blown. The youth is presented with new cloths. It is noted in the Kurnool Manual (1886) that the Katikavandlu, who sell mutton, are either Mahārattas or Mussulmans. Some are called Sultāni butchers, or Hindus forcibly circumcised by the late Nawāb of Kurnool. From the Mysore Census Report, 1891, I learn in connection with the Myāsa

* Chevers. *Op. cit.*

† J. S. Chandler, Calcutta Review, 1903.

‡ Nelson, Madura Manual.

Bēdars (hunters) that "the rite of circumcision is performed on boys of ten or twelve years of age. The custom seems to have been imbibed when the members of this sub-caste were included in the hordes of Haidar Ali. It also points to a possible conversion, more or less complete, to Islam in those periods of disorder, and a subsequent relapse to Hinduism. For, simultaneously with the circumcision, other rites, such as the panchagavyam, the burning of the tongue with a nīm stick, etc. pre-eminently Brāhmanical, are likewise practised prior to the youth being received into communion." "The Myāsas," Mr. Francis writes,* "seem quite proud of the custom, and scout with scorn the idea of marrying into any family, in which circumcision is not the rule. A very small piece of the skin is cut off by a man of the caste, and the boy is then kept for eleven days in a separate hut, and touched by no one. His food is given him on a piece of stone. On the twelfth day he is bathed, given a new cloth, and brought back to the house, and his old cloth and stone are thrown away. His relations in a body then take him to a tangēdu (*Cassia auriculata*) tree, to which are offered cocoanuts, flowers, and so forth." Of conversion to Muhammadanism at the present time, a good example is afforded by the Cherumans of Malabar, concerning whom the Census Superintendent, 1881, writes as follows. "Conspicuous for their degraded and humiliating disabilities are the Cherumars. This caste numbered 99,009 in Malabar at the Census of 1871, and, in 1881, is returned as only 64,725. There are 40,000

* Manual of the Bellary district, 1904.

fewer Cherumans than there would have been but for some disturbing influence, and this is very well known to be conversion to Muhammadanism. This honour of Islam once conferred on the Cheruman, he moves at one spring several places higher than that which he originally occupied, and the figures show that nearly 50,000 Cherumans and others have availed themselves of the opening. The conversion of a Pariah, or low-caste Hindu to Muhammadanism raises him distinctly in the social scale, and he is treated with more respect by Hindus." Among the Mukkuvan fishermen of Malabar conversion to Islam is common. The converts are called Pu-Islam or Putiya Islam (new Islam).* During the disturbance in Tinnevelly in 1899, some of the Shānars, men, women, and children, are said to have gone into the Muhammadan fold, their places of worship being converted into improvised mosques. The men shaved their heads, and grew beards; and the women had to make sundry changes in their dress. And, in the case of boys, the operation of circumcision was performed. When an adult Hindu joins the sect of Daira or Māhadēv Muhammadans in Mysore as a convert, an interesting mock rite of circumcision is gone through, as a substitute for the real operation. A betel leaf is wrapped round the penis, so that it projects beyond the glans, and is snipped instead of the prepuce.

As in Africa, and among the American Indians, Australians, and Polynesians, so in Southern India artificial deformity of the hand is produced by chopping off some

* Madras Census Report, 1891.

of the fingers. Writing in 1815, Buchanan (Hamilton) * says that "near Deonella or Deonhully, a town in Mysore, is a sect or sub-division of the Murressoo Wocal caste, every woman of which, previous to piercing the ears of her eldest daughter, preparatory to her being betrothed in marriage, must undergo the amputation of the first joints of the third and fourth fingers of her right hand. The amputation is performed by the blacksmith of the village, who, having placed the finger in a block, performs the operation with a chisel. If the girl to be betrothed is motherless, and the mother of the boy has not before been subjected to the amputation, it is incumbent on her to suffer the operation." Of the same ceremony among the Morsa-Okkala-Makkalu of Mysore the Abbé Dubois says † that, if the bride's mother be dead, the bridegroom's mother, or in default of her the mother of the nearest relative, must submit to the cruel ordeal. In an editorial footnote it is stated that this custom is no longer observed. Instead of the two fingers being amputated, they are now merely bound together, and thus rendered unfit for use. In the Census Report, 1891, it is recorded that this type of deformity is found among the Morasas, chiefly in Cuddapah, North Arcot, and Salem. "There is a sub-section of them, called Veralu icche Kāpulu, or Kāpulu who give the fingers, from a curious custom which requires that, when a grandchild is born in a family, the wife of the eldest son of the grandfather must have the last two joints of the third and

* East India Gazetteer.

† Hindu Manners, Customs, and Ceremonies. Ed. 1897.

fourth fingers of her right hand amputated at a temple of Bhairava." Further, it is stated in the Manual of the Salem district (1883) that "the practice now observed in this district is that, when a grandchild is born in a family, the eldest son of the grandfather, with his wife, appears at the temple for the ceremony of boring the child's ear, and there the woman has the last two joints of the third and fourth fingers chopped off. It does not signify whether the father of the first grandchild born be the eldest son or not, as in any case it is the wife of the eldest son who has to undergo the mutilation. After this, when children are born to other sons, their wives in succession undergo the operation. When a child is adopted, the same course is pursued."

The origin of the custom is narrated by Wilks,* and is briefly this. Mahadeo or Sīva, who was in great peril, after hiding successively in a castor-oil and jawāri plantation, concealed himself in a linga-tonde shrub from a rākshasa who was pursuing him, to whom a Marasa Vakkaliga cultivator indicated, with the little finger of his right hand, the hiding-place of Sīva. The god was only rescued from his peril by the interposition of Vishnu in the form of a lovely maiden meretriciously dressed, whom the lusty rākshasa, forgetting all about Sīva, attempted to ravish, and was consumed to ashes. On emerging from his hiding-place, Sīva decreed that the cultivator should forfeit the offending finger. The culprit's wife, who had just arrived at the field with food for her husband, hearing this dreadful sentence, threw

* History of Mysore.

herself at Sīva's feet, and represented the certain ruin of her family if her hushand should be disabled for some months from performing the labours of the farm, and besought the deity to accept two of her fingers instead of one from her husband. Sīva, pleased with so sincere a proof of conjugal affection, accepted the exchange, and ordered that her family posterity in all future generations should sacrifice two fingers at his temple as a memorial of the transaction, and of their exclusive devotion to the god of the lingam. For the following account of the performance of the rite, as carried out by the Morasa Vakkaligaru of Mysore I am indebted to an article by Mr. V. N. Narasimmiyengar.* These people are roughly classed under three heads, viz.: "(1) those whose women offer the sacrifice; (2) those who substitute for the fingers a piece of gold wire, twisted round the fingers in the shape of rings. Instead of cutting the fingers off, the carpenter removes and appropriates the rings; (3) those who do not perform the rite. The *modus operandi* is as nearly as possible the following. About the time of the new moon in Chaitra, a propitious day is fixed by the village astrologer, and the woman who is to offer the sacrifice performs certain ceremonies or pūja in honour of Sīva, taking food only once a day. For three days before the operation she has to support herself with milk, sugar, fruits, etc., all substantial food being eschewed. On the day appointed, a common cart is brought out, painted in alternate stripes with white and red ochre, and adorned with gay flags, flowers, etc.,

* Ind. Ant. II., 1873.

in imitation of a car. Sheep or pigs are slaughtered before it, their number being generally governed by the number of children borne by the sacrificing woman. The cart is then dragged by bullocks, preceded by music, the woman and her husband following, with new pots filled with water and small pieces of silver money, borne on their heads, and accompanied by a retinue of friends and relatives. The village washerman has to spread clean cloths along the path of the procession, which stops near the boundary of the village, where a leafy bower is prepared, with three pieces of stone installed in it, symbolising the god Sīva. Flowers, fruits, cocoanuts, incense, etc., are then offered, varied occasionally by an additional sheep or pig. A wooden seat is placed before the image, and the sacrificing woman places upon it her right hand with the fingers spread out. A man holds her hand firmly, and the village carpenter, placing his chisel on the first joints of her ring and little fingers, chops them off with a single stroke. The pieces lopped off are throw into an ant-hill, and the tips of the mutilated fingers, round which rags are bound, are dipped into a vessel containing boiling gingily oil. A good skin eventually forms over the stump, which looks like a congenital malformation. The fee of the carpenter is one kanthirāya fanam (four annas eight pies) for each maimed finger, besides presents in kind. The woman undergoes the barbarous and painful ceremony without a murmur, and it is an article of the popular belief that, were it neglected, or if nails grow on the stump, dire ruin and misfortune will overtake the recusant family.

Staid matrons, who have had their fingers maimed for life in the above manner, exhibit their stumps with a pride worthy of a better cause. At the termination of the sacrifice, the woman is presented with cloths, flowers, etc., by her friends and relations, to whom a feast is given. Her children are placed on an adorned seat, and, after receiving presents of flowers, fruits, etc., their ears are pierced in the usual way. It is said that to do so before would be sacrilege." In a very full account of deformation of the hand by the Berulu Kodo sub-sect of the Vakkaliga caste in Mysore, Mr. F. Fawcett says,* that it was regularly practised until the Commissioner of Mysore put a stop to it about twenty years ago. "At present some take gold or silver pieces, stick them on to the finger's ends with flour paste, and either cut or pull them off. Others simply substitute an offering of small pieces of gold or silver for the amputation. Others, again, tie flowers round the fingers that used to be cut, and go through a pantomime of cutting by putting the chisel on the joint, and taking it away again. All the rest of the ceremony is just as it used to be." The introduction of the decorated cart, which has been referred to, is connected by Mr. Fawcett with a legend concerning a zamindar, who sought the daughters of seven brothers in marriage with three youths of his family. As carts were used in the flight from the zamindar, the ceremony is, to commemorate the event, called bandi dēvuru, or god of cars. As by throwing ear-rings into a river the fugitives passed through it, while the zamindar was

* Journ. Anth. Soc., Bombay, I, 1889.

drowned, the caste people insist on their women's ears being bored for earrings. And, in honour of the girls who cared more for the honour of their caste than for the distinction of marriage into a great family, the amputation of part of two fingers of women of the caste was instituted. Since the prohibition to cut off fingers, Mr. Rice says * that the women content themselves with putting on a gold or silver finger-stall or thimble, which is pulled off instead of the end of the finger itself.

I pass on to the subject of the manufacture of eunuchs by castration, for the following account of which I have to indent on an article on the Kojahs by Dr. J. Shortt.† "The Kojahs," he writes, "are the artificially created eunuchs, in contradistinction to the Higras (impotents) or natural eunuchs. Some years ago there were three Kojahs at the head of the State prison or royal mahāl at Vellore, in charge of some of the wives, descendants, and other female connections of Tippu Sultan. These men were highly respected, held charges of considerable trust, and were Muhammadans by birth. Tales were often repeated that the zenāna women (slaves and adopted girls) were in the habit of stripping them naked, and poking fun at their helplessness. There were two Kojahs in the employ of the late Nabob of the Carnatic. They were both Africans. On the death of the Nabob the Government allowed one of them a pension of fifteen rupees a month. Sometimes Hindus, Sūdras, and Brāhmins subject themselves to the operation (of castration) of their own accord

* Mysore.

† Journ. Anth. Inst., II, 1873.

from a religious impression. Others, finding themselves naturally impotent, consider it necessary to undergo the operation, to avoid being born again at a future birth in the same helpless state. The operation is generally performed by a class of barbers, sometime by some of the more intelligent of the eunuchs themselves, in the following manner. The patient is made to sit on an upturned new earthen pot, being previously well drugged with opium or bhang. The entire genitals being seized by the left hand, an assistant, who has a bamboo lath slit in the centre, runs it down quick close to the pubis, the slit firmly embracing the whole of the genitals at the root, when the operator, with a sharp razor, runs it down along the face of the lath, and removes penis, testicles, and scrotum in one swoop, leaving a large clean open wound behind, in which boiling gingily oil is poured to staunch the bleeding, and the wound covered over with a soft rag steeped in warm oil. This is the only dressing applied to the wound, which is renewed daily, while the patient is confined in a supine position to his bed, and lightly fed with conjee (rice gruel), milk, etc. During the operation the patient is urged to cry out 'Din' (the faith in Mahomed) three times." A local eunuch, whom I interviewed, informed me that castration used to be performed in Hyderabad at about the age of sixteen. A pit, 3½ feet deep, was dug in the ground, and filled with ashes. And, after the operation, the patient had to sit on the ashes, with crossed legs, for three days. The operation was performed under the influence of narcotics by a Pir—the head of the Kojah community.

Of branding as a form of mutilation many examples are afforded in Southern India. The Kota men of the Nīlgiris have the cicatrix of a burn made as a tribal mark with a burning cloth across the lower end of the back of the forearm when they are more than eight years old. Many of the Toda men have one or more raised cicatrices forming nodulous growths (keloids) on the right shoulder. These scars are produced by burning the skin with red-hot sticks of *Litsæa* (the sacred fire-sticks); and the Todas believe that the branding enables them to milk the buffaloes with perfect ease. When the birth of a first child is expected in a Toda family, on the first new moon day a ceremony called ur vot pimmi takes place, during which an elderly woman rolls up a rag to the size of a small wick, dips it in oil, lights it, and with the burning end brands the pregnant woman's hands in four places, one at each end of the lowest joints of the right and left thumbs, and one dot on each wrist. Sometimes branding is resorted to as a curative agent, and, when sick people are in a state of collapse from high fever, they are branded between the eyebrows, on the toes, or nape of the neck, with a piece of bangle glass, leather, nīm stick, or piece of turmeric.

Flat, round cicatrices on the forehead, chest, and nape of the neck, are said to be found in every caste in some parts of the Kistna district. They are caused by branding with turmeric or a cheroot for infantile convulsions, which are believed to be caused by the babies inhaling tobacco smoke in ill-ventilated rooms. I have seen men of the Māla and other castes branded with a circle round the navel as a cure for colic, and a Kaikōlan man branded with a series of large and small discs on the chest and abdomen for illness when he was a baby. The Rev. S. Nicholson informs me that, after a new-born Māla child has been washed, it is branded with a hot needle in twenty vital parts and handed back, roaring lustily, to its mother. Some Lingayat children are branded with a hot needle on the stomach, under the idea that disease is hereby warded off. Children who suffer from fits are branded with a heated twig of margosa or a glass bangle. Some Shānāns, at Nazareth, were branded on the forehead to cure sore-eyes during childhood. The Kathira vandlu (scissors people), and other nomadic tribes, are branded under the following conditions. As the gangs move on, exposed to changes of weather, the children sometimes get a disease called sandukatlu or palakurkura. The symptoms are similar to those which children sometimes have when they are teething. As a curative agent, they are branded on the face between the eyebrows, or the outer corners of the eyes, and sometimes on the abdomen. The brand-marks on the face and corners of the eyes are circular, and those on the abdomen generally horizontal. The circular marks are made with a long piece of saffron, one end of which is burnt for the purpose, or with an indigo-dyed cloth rolled like a pencil, and burnt at one end. The horizontal marks are made with a hot needle. Similar brand-marks are made by some caste Hindus on their children. In some parts of the Mysore province and Salem district, when a child is born, it is at once branded on various parts of the body, *e.g.*, near the navel, on the foot, back of the hands, face, nape of the neck, and sides of the abdomen. The Bestas of North Arcot are divided into Telugu Bestas and Parikiti Bestas, the difference between whom is chiefly one of religious observance, the former being in the habit of getting themselves branded on the shoulders with the Vaishnavite emblems, the chank and chakra,* and the latter never undergoing this ceremony † At the ceremony of dedication of a girl as a Basivi (dedicated prostitute) in the Bellary district, " a tāli, on which is depicted the nāmam of Vishnu, fastened to a necklace of black beads, is tied round her neck. She is given, by way of insignia, a cane as a wand, carried in the right hand, and a gopālam or begging basket, which is slung on the left arm. She is then branded with a heated brass instrument with a chakra on the right shoulder, a chank on the left shoulder, and a chakra over the right breast. The mark over the breast is never done, if there is any suspicion that the girl is not a virgin. The branding in Vishnu temples is sometimes merely a pretence, when the girl under dedication is very young, sandalwood paste being interposed between her skin and the heated instrument. Among the castes (Boyas, Kurubas, etc.), who make Basivis of their girls, a few men are branded on both shoulders with the chank and chakra, in order to obtain a closer communication with the deity, and to ensure their salvation. They are somewhat honoured among

* The chank is the shell of the mollusc *Turbinella rapa*, of which the right-handed variety is held very sacred. The chakra is the wheel of the law.

† Manual of the North Arcot district.

their fellows, and, at a marriage, receive the first betel leaf and other tokens of respect. Men who are branded are buried face downwards. Curiously, there are men of these castes who are dedicated to goddesses. They are generally beggars and wear female attire. They are not celibates, and may be branded at any time." * A recent petition to a European Magistrate in the Bellary district runs as follows. Petition of —, aged about 17 or 18. I have agreed to become a Basivi, and get myself stamped by my guru (priest) according to the custom of my caste. I request that my proper age, which entitles me to be stamped, may be ascertained personally, and permission granted to be stamped. A case, in which branding was resorted to as a means of extorting a confession, is recorded by Mr. M. Lewin.† Two prisoners appeared before him with their bodies branded, while the arms of one of them were swollen from the effects of a tight ligature. It is noted in the diary of Ananda Ranga Pillai ‡ that, in 1738, the Governor of Pondicherry decided that "those who brought into the town pagoda coins having a fineness of less than eight touches would not only render themselves liable to a fine of 1,000 pagodas, but would be treated with ignominy by being branded with the figure of a dog, and being severely dealt with in other ways." The Oriya Haddis are said to admit to their ranks persons from all castes, except the Rellis and Mēdaras, after first branding their tongues with a

* F. Fawcett. Journ. Anth. Soc., Bombay, 1891.
† Torture in Madras, 1851.
‡ Edited by Sir J. F. Price, Vol. I, 1904.

piece of gold wire.* When an outsider is received into the fraternity of the Donga (thieving) Dāsaris, they take him "to the side of a river, make him bathe in oil, give him a new cloth, hold a council, and give a feast. They burn a twig of the sami (*Prosopis spicigera*) or margosa tree, and slightly burn the tongue of the party who has joined them, to make him a Donga-Dāsari. This is their way of purification and acceptance of every new member, who, soon after the tongue-burning ceremony, is given a seat in the general company, and made to partake of a common feast."† When an excommunicated Badaga of the Nīlgiris is received back into the tribe, his tongue is burnt with sandal wood.

When proceeding on a pilgrimage to the temple of Subramaniya Swāmi at Palni, some devotees pierce their cheeks with a long silver needle, which traverses the mouth cavity; pierce the tongue with a silver arrow which is passed vertically through the protruded organ; and place a silver shield in front of the mouth, so that it may not be opened except when they are drinking milk. Some Dāsaris (Vaishnavite mendicants) have permanent holes in their cheeks, into which they insert the needles when they go about the country in pursuit of their profession. Writing concerning pilgrims, Mr. Fawcett says ‡ that "one had his tongue protruding outside his teeth, and kept in position by a silver skewer through it. The skewer was to be left in for forty days. Several of the

* Madras Census Report, 1901.

† T. M. Natesa Sastri, Calcutta Review, October 1905.

‡ Journ. Anth. Soc., Bombay, II, 1890.

pilgrims wore a handkerchief tied over the mouth, they being under a vow of silence. One poor man wore the regular instrument of silence, the mouth-lock (a wide silver band over the mouth, the ends reaching over the cheeks) a skewer through both cheeks keeping the ends together, and of course the mouth open. People fed him, as he sat patiently in a nice tent-like affair, with rice, etc."

For the following note on branding as a religious ceremonial I am indebted to Mr. K. Rangachari. Branding for religious purposes is confined to the two sections—Sri Vaishnavas and Mādhvas—of the Hindu community. Sri Vaishnava Brāhmans are expected to undergo this ordeal at least once during their life-time, whereas Mādhva Brāhmans have to submit to it as often as they visit their guru (head of a mutt or religious institution). Of men of other castes, those who become followers of a Vaishnava or Mādhva Achārya (guru) or mutt, are expected to present themselves before the guru for the purpose of being branded. But the ceremony is optional, and not compulsory as in the case of the Brāhmans. Among Sri Vaishnavites the privilege of branding is confined to the elder members of a family, Sanyāsis (ascetics), and the heads of the various mutts. All individuals, male and female, must be branded, after the upanayanam ceremony (thread marriage) in the case of males, and after marriage in the case of women. The disciples after a purificatory bath, and the usual worship to their god, proceed to the residence of the Achārya or to the mutt, where they are initiated into their religion, and branded with the chakra on the right shoulder and chank on the left. The initiation consists in imparting to the disciple, in a very low tone, the mula munthra, the words namonarayanaya, the sacred syllable Om, and a few mantrams from the Brāhma Rahasyam (secrets about god). A person who has not been initiated thus is regarded as unfit to take part in the ceremonies which have to be performed by Brāhmans. Even close relations, if orthodox, will refuse to take food prepared or touched by the uninitiated.

Concerning Mādhvas, Monier Williams writes as follows.* "They firmly believe that it is a duty of Vaishnavas to carry throughout life a memorial of their god on their persons, and that such a lasting outward and visible sign of his presence helps them to obtain salvation through him. 'On his right arm let the Brāhman wear the discus, on his left the conch-shell.' When I was at Tanjore, I found that one of the successors of Mādhva had recently arrived on his branding visitation. He was engaged throughout the entire day in stamping his disciples, and receiving fees from all according to their means."

Mādhvas have four mutts to which they repair for the branding ceremony, viz.: Vyasaraya, Sumathendra and Mulabagal in Mysore, and Uttarāja in South Canara. The followers of the Uttarāja mutt are branded in five places in the case of male adults, and boys after the thread marriage. The situations and emblems selected are the chakra on the right upper arm, right side of the

* Brahmanism and Hinduism.

Plate XXVI.

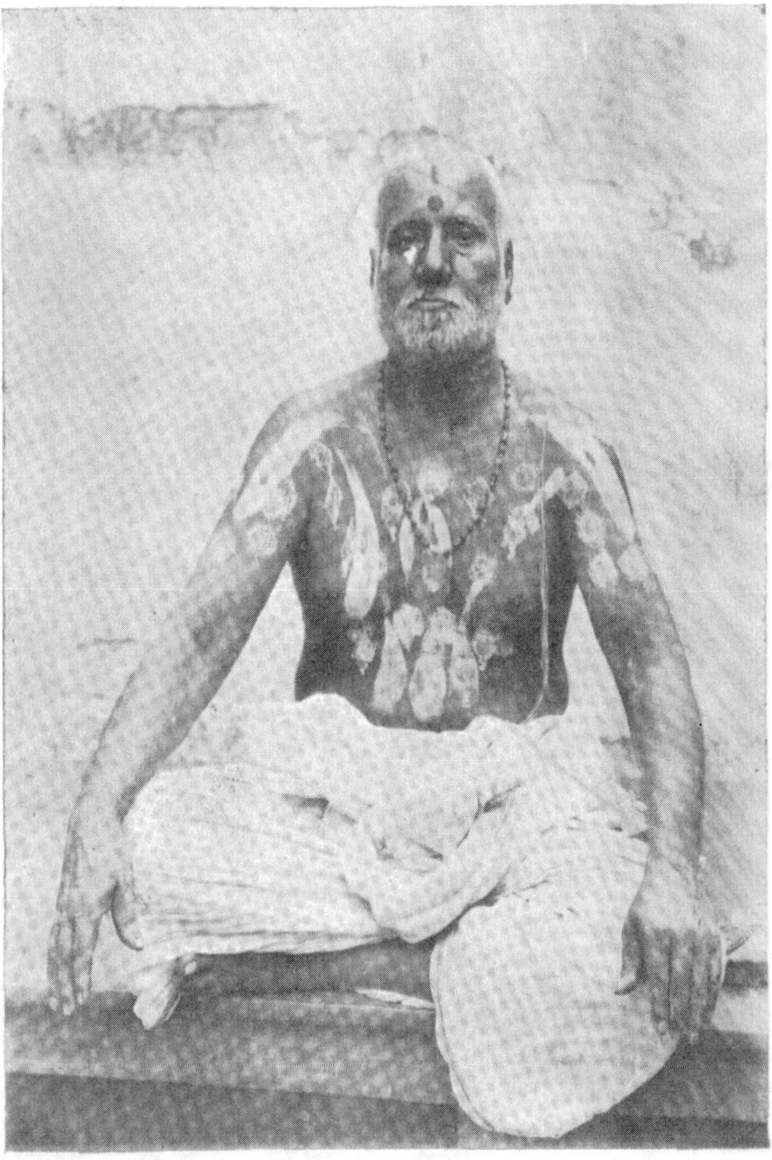

Mādhva Brāhman.

chest, and above the navel; the chank on the left shoulder and left side of the chest. Women, and girls after marriage, are branded with the chakra on the right forearm and the chank on the left. In the case of widows, the marks are impressed on the shoulders as in the case of males. The disciples of the three other mutts are generally branded with the chakra on the right upper arm, and chank on the left. As the branding is supposed to remove sins committed during the interval, they get it done every time they see their guru. There is with Mādhvas no restriction as to the age at which the ceremony should be performed. Even a new-born babe, after the pollution period of ten days, must receive the mark of the chakra, if the guru should turn up. Boys before the upanayanam, and girls before marriage, are branded with the chakra on the abdomen just above the navel. The copper or brass branding instruments (muthras) are not heated to a very high temperature, but sufficient to singe the skin, and leave a deep black mark in the case of adults, and a light mark in that of young people and babies. In some cases, disciples, who are afraid of being hurt, bribe the person who heats the instruments; but, as a rule, the guru regulates the temperature so as to suit the individual. If, for example, the disciple is a strong, well-built man, the instruments are well heated, and, if he is a weakling, allowed to cool somewhat before their application. If the operator has to deal with babies, he presses the instrument against a wet rag before applying it to the infant's skin. Some matathipathis (head priests of the mutt) are, it is said, inclined to be vindictive, and to make a very hot application of the instruments, if the disciple has not paid the fee (gurukānika) to his satisfaction. The fee is not fixed in the case of Sri Vaishnavas, whereas Mādhvas are expected to pay from one to three months' income for being branded. Failure to pay is punished with excommunication on some pretext or other. The area of skin branded generally peels off within a week, leaving a pale mark of the muthra, which either disappears in a few months, or persists throughout life. Mādhvas should smear daily with gopi paste (white kaolin) five muthras on the following places: forehead, outer corners of the eyes, three places on the neck, the upper arms, chest, and three places on the abdomen. The names of these muthras are: chakra, chank or shanka, gātha (weapon of war used by Bhīma, one of the Pāndavas), padma (lotus), and Narayana.

TORTURE IN BYGONE DAYS AND A FEW STRAY SURVIVALS.

In 1855 a Commission was appointed by the Government of Madras to investigate all cases, which might be brought before the Commissioners, either of torture inflicted by instruments or other means, or of punishment of any kind illegally administered. In their report the Commissioners stated that to those to whom the word torture necessarily and immediately conveys ideas of the inquisition, thumb-screws, rack and wheel, such a term would probably appear inapplicable, as expressive of the degree of violence which their enquiries brought to light. On the other hand, if the word be used in the ordinary acceptation assigned to it by Dr. Johnson, "pain by which guilt is punished, or confession (and we may add money) extorted, then we think that it may with perfect propriety be applied to designate the practices prevalent in Madras." The very plays of the populace are said to have often excited the laughter of many a rural audience by the exhibition of revenue squeezed out of defaulters coin by coin, through the application of familiar "provocatives" under the superintendence of a caricatured Tahsildar (native magistrate). It is recorded that, on one occasion, a Tahsildar naively remarked that, had he not buried some suspected parties up to their necks in mud, and dipped others at the end of a picottah pole into a well within an inch of their lives, he would never have got the evidence which led to the conviction of a pack of villains. A picottah is the old-fashioned form of machine still used for raising water, and consists of a long lever or yard pivotted on an upright post, weighted on the short arm, and bearing a line and bucket on the long arm. The Commissioners, in their report, incidentally refer to one Ali Khān, who became Nawāb of Bengal in 1718, and used to oblige defaulters to wear leather long-drawers filled with live cats. And one of his people ordered a pond to be filled with everything disgusting, to which, in scorn of the Hindus, he gave the name of 'Bickoont' (Paradise), and through this detestable pool the defaulters were dragged by a rope tied under their arms.

The following forms of torture and coercion, mainly culled from the report of the Commissioners, with additions, have been proved, or reported to have been inflicted for non-payment of Government tax or the elucidation of confession :—

1. Preventing an individual from going to his meals or other calls of nature, bringing water for cooking food, and sleeping; and preventing cattle from going to pasture by confining them in the house with its occupants.

2. Confinement in the stocks. In connection with this "penal and pedal machine" (Dean Hole) it was exacted by Regulation XI, 1816, that heads of villages have, in cases of a trivial nature such as abusive language and inconsiderable assaults or affrays, power to confine the offending parties in the village choultry (lock-up) for a time not exceeding twelve hours; or, if the offending parties are of the lower castes of the people, on whom it

may not be improper to inflict so degrading a punishment, to order them to be put in the stocks for a time not exceeding six hours. Some years ago a case was tried on appeal before the High Court of Madras,* in which a Muhammadan dealer in miscellaneous wares was convicted by a native petty magistrate in the Trichinopoly district of theft of an iron measure and eight annas worth of copper coin, and sentenced to be put in the stocks for three hours. The High Court, on appeal, ruled that a Muhammadan cannot be said to belong to the lower castes of the people, and that it is probable that the framers of the regulation had in view those castes which, prior to the introduction of British rule, were regarded as servile. In another case which was argued before the High Court of Madras, a Mâla, who was a convert to Christianity, was sentenced to confinement in the stocks for using abusive language. The Judge, in summing up, stated that "the test seems to be not what is the offender's creed, whether Muhammadan, Christian, or Hindu, but what is his caste. If he belongs to one of the lower castes, a change of creed would not, of itself, in my judgment, make any difference, provided he continues to belong to the caste. If he continues to accept the rules of the caste in social and moral matters, acknowledges the authority of the headmen, takes part in caste meetings and ceremonies, and, in fact, generally continues to belong to the caste, then, in my judgment, he would be within the purview of the regulation. If, on the other hand, he adopts the

* Indian Law Reports, Madras Series, 1883.

moral standards of Christianity instead of those in his caste, if he accepts the authority of his pastors and teachers in place of that of the headman of the caste, if he no longer takes part in the distinctive meetings and ceremonies of the caste . . . . then he can no longer be said 'to belong to one of the lower castes of the people,' and his punishment by confinement in the stocks is no longer legal.' *

More recently (1903) it was ruled by the High Court that the Shānāns belong to the lower classes, who may be punished by confinement in the stocks.

Some years ago a Brāhman was employed as the custodian of a village god and his appurtenances. A festival was coming on, and an inventory was taken. Some jewels, valued at about three hundred rupees, were missing. The Brāhman was suspected and questioned, but naturally made no confession. He was confined in the village stocks for a whole night under the order of the village munsif (magistrate) sitting in council with the kurnam (village accountant), and was subjected to various indignities. As morning broke, he confessed, and promised to point out where he had hidden the spoil. On his being released, he managed to put a pen-knife, which he had concealed, into the village munsif, and then cut his throat. The case was enquired into, and the police officer was satisfied that the man had suffered torture, but not at the hands of the police. The stocks were *en evidence* in a recent dispute between the Nāttukōttai Chettis landlords and their tenants in the Madura district.

* *Ibid.* 1901.

3. Flogging with an instrument composed of four or five plaited thongs of leather, three or four feet long. The thongs were attached to a ring, with another ring to serve as a handle. This form of scourge was known by Muhammadans as zīrbund (a martingale).

4. Beating with slippers.

5. Beating the legs, and other parts of the body, with a leather strap or tamarind switch.

6. Sembadavans (Tamil fishermen) are punished, by the village council, by being bound with ropes. Twigs of the tamarind tree are kept near them, to indicate flogging, and a knife to denote cutting of the tongue. Women are, as a punishment, made to carry a basket of rubbish and a broom round the village. It is on record * that some European prisoners, serving under Haidar Ali, who had been circumcised, and made officers of a battalion of Chaylahs, were brought in front of their men, with their hands tied behind, and received three lashes with a bunch of tamarind twigs from each of the Chaylahs, which amounted to fifteen hundred lashes.

7. The kittie or cheerata.—Defined as a simple machine, consisting merely of two sticks tied together at one end, between which the fingers were placed as in a lemon squeezer. By means of this instrument the fingers were gradually bent backwards towards the back of the hand, until the sufferer, no longer able to endure the excruciating pain, yielded to the demands made on him. One case of squeezing the breast of a woman with the "kitty" was reported. If no kitties were ready at

* Narrative of the Sufferings of James Bristow, 1794.

hand, an order for them was given to the village carpenter. Strings of them, ready for application, are said to have been commonly and openly hung up in some zamindar's cutcherries (court-houses). In 1832 a European Judge gave evidence to the effect that he had seen a man with a finger double the usual thickness from injury by a kittie, consisting of two pieces of stick, like a vice, tied together at the end, on which the foot was stamped.

8. Placing the wrists between two pieces of wood, which were repeatedly squeezed together with great force, and binding very tightly round the arm a rough rope, charged with powdered chillies and mustard seed, and moistened with a solution of salt, which sometimes gave rise to extensive ulceration.

9. Beating the joints of the arms and legs with a wooden mallet.

10. Application of smart blows on the ankle bones with a short thick stick.

11. Compelling an individual to interlace his fingers, of which the ends were squeezed by the hands of peons (orderlies), who occasionally introduced the use of sand to secure a firmer grip.

12. Placing the hand flat on the ground, and then pressing downward at either end a stick placed horizontally over the back of the fingers.

13. A common form of extracting information is said to be entwining a wet string round the first joints of the fingers, bringing the end between the middle fingers, and tying the hand tightly back towards the elbow. The string is then beaten with a stick, as if it was a cotton-

carding machine. The vibration causes sufficient pain to make the most obdurate person speak out. Or cotton-wicks, saturated with oil, are wrapped round the fingers, and lighted in succession.

14. Tying by the hands to a tree, and beating with tamarind switches.

15. Tying in a stooping position to the wheel of a bandy (country cart).

16. Hanging up head downwards.

17. Suspension by the arms tied behind the back.

18. Striking two defaulters' heads against each other, or tying them together by the back hair.

19. Annānthāl.—Placing an individual in a stooping position, fastening a string to each great toe, passing the bight over the back of the neck, and putting a stone on his back. The angavastram or handkerchief of the defaulter was sometimes used as a substitute for the rope. Or the rope was made of a creeper, or straw, which could always be obtained in a village. In reporting on this form of ordeal, an officer commanding a regiment expressed his opinion as follows. "The stooping posture enforced by the leg and neck being held in proximity no doubt must be highly inconvenient, and to a plethoric Englishman might almost amount to torture, but to the supple cool-blooded native I should hesitate in describing the enforced attitude as one of torture."

20. Standing exposed to the sun, with a heavy stone on the head, on the back between the shoulders, or on the nape of the neck, with one foot on the ground, and the other leg raised by means of a string passed round the neck and big toe.

21. Placing a person in the sun with a stone on his head, and the trigger of a matchlock shut upon his ear.

22. If a Jōgi pleads inability to pay the fine inflicted for committing adultery, he has to walk a furlong with a mill-stone on his head.

23. Squatting with the gluteal region touching the ground. The arms were then placed under and inside the thighs, and the individual was made to take hold of his ears, one with each hand. If he attempted to move, he was struck with a cane.

24. Passing an individual's turban or a wisp of grass over his neck, fastening it under the knees so as to put him in a bending posture, and placing a heavy stone on the back. In lieu of stones, lumps of mud were sometimes applied. And, in one case, a portion of a mud wall is specified.

25. Sitting in the sun, during the hottest part of the day, with the head of the hair all loose, and executing a curious operation of turning the head in a whirling manner, which was known as extracting the devil, the driving out of which was assisted by flagellation.

26. Sitting down with a stone in each hand, the palms upwards in line with the shoulder.

27. A large slab of stone, such as is used for building purposes, is placed on a man's chest and abdomen, with turbans between it and the skin, so that no mark of the stone is left thereon. Another man sits astride the stone, and brings pressure to bear.

28. Keeping an individual in a stooping posture by holding him down by the back-hair, while others were placed astride on his back.

29. Standing in water or mud, exposed to the heat or inclemency of the weather.

30. Standing upon one leg, with a large log of wood on the head.

31. One of a man's legs was pulled and tied to a tree, in the heat of the sun, as high as possible, while his body was secured to another tree, thereby compelling him to support himself only on one leg.

32. Suspension by the feet to the bough of a tree, or fastening an individual to a tree, under which a fire had been kindled for the purpose of suffocating him with the smoke. A woman, with a view to extorting a confession of theft (which she had not committed), was tied up by one arm to the branch of a tree, and, while suspended above the ground, her cloth having partly fallen off, she was whipped with tamarind switches on her private parts.

33. Binding the arms backwards very tightly with cords, to act as a tourniquet, and impede the circulation.

34. A man was reported to have swung a young girl by her hands and hair to the beam of his house, beaten her, and branded her face and arm with a hot knife, because she had taken nine pice (small coin) from his room.

35. Placing sharp-pointed stones in the hollows of the knees, and making the individual sit for hours together on his haunches.

36. Muskets were turned down by making a man support them with the muzzles resting on his great toes, in which position he continued for hours together in the heat of the mid-day sun.

37. A man was made to support another, exposed to the heat of the sun, in the position of horse and rider for a few hours, when the rider dismounted and was ridden by the other for the same length of time.

38. Twisting the ears, or the application of ear-twitchers.

39. Pounding the back with the fists.

40. Pinching the fleshy parts with sand.

41. Compression of small portions of the skin of the inner part of the thighs and other sensitive spots between the points of iron pincers.

42. Application of hot oil to the skin.

43. A man, having lost some small article from his house, proceeded, as a matter of ordinary routine, to dip the hands of his three wives into boiling cow dung, to induce them to confess.

44. Application of the end of a lighted cigar to various parts of the body.

45. Confinement in a small room, with a rat-snake for company.

46. Searing with hot irons, or branding with a hot sickle.

47. Driving thorns under the nails.

48. Putting a person into a room or cage, the floor of which is thickly studded with sharp nails, or into a closed room full of smoke. In the days of the Portuguese in Malabar, criminals are said to have been put into a barrel with the points of nails projecting into its interior, and rolled about.

49. Tightening a strong tape applied round the waist.

50. Making a man run up and down, while he was held by the ears, or pulled by the back-hair.

51. Pulling out, singeing, or lifting by the hairs of the moustache, which, besides inflicting physical pain, were considered a mark of disgrace.

52. Tying a scratching and burrowing beetle called the carpenter or potter's beetle or poollay insect, within a half cocoanut shell or cloth over the navel or scrotum. A European Police Officer tells me that he has tried the burrowing beetle on himself, and writes to me as follows. "My experiences were so dreadful that I should have willingly confessed to any crime to the District Magistrate, who was with me at the time. The subject's arms have to be tied behind his back, and he must lie flat on his back. The sensation is at first rather amusing, it then becomes annoying, and in a very few minutes positive agony. It is just as if the insects are getting into your vitals in swarms. A cold sweat, and an 'all gone,' feeling was the result. When the shell is removed, all unpleasant symptoms disappear, and no mark of any description in the region of the navel can be seen. This is, of course, very important in torture cases. I believe it is a common practice in the southern districts, and not confined to the police, but resorted to by village councils in the settlement of disputes."

53. Introduction of live blood-suckers (lizards with sharp claws) within the clothes. In recent years, a woman who was convicted of murder stated, in her appeal,

that she confessed because the police suspended her head downwards, beat her, stripped off her clothes, and threatened to let a live blood-sucker into her " body." In cases where confession by a woman is sought for, the following treatment is said to be resorted to. She is put into a pair of baggy Muhammadan trousers, which are tightly tied round the knees and waist. Within the trousers a large blood-sucker is let loose. The sharp claws and spines of the dorsal crest are said to be excessively irritating, as the animal wanders about in search of a haven between the legs or under the gluteal region from the prodding which it receives to keep it on the move. Two men who were living in concubinage with a widow could not get her to disgorge money wherewith they might indulge in cock-fighting and other local sports. They, accordingly, tied her knees into her arm-pits, and threatened to torture her with a blood-sucker. The threat was most effective, as they went off with some thing like twelve hundred rupees, leaving the widow trussed.

54. Application to the eyes of the acrid juice of the cashew-nut (*Anacardium occidentale*). The oil is at the present day used medicinally as a powerful rubefacient and vesicant. The Judge of Mangalore, many years ago, met with a case in which a person who found a boy stealing his cashew-nuts, rubbed the acrid juice into his eyes.*

55. Beating the soles of the feet with twigs of the milk-hedge plant (*Euphorbia Tirucalli*), the juice of which

* Chevers. *Op. cit.*

produces severe blistering. In a false charge of torture, the juice of this plant was used to produce the appearance of branding.

56. In the Vizagapatam hill tracts, a species of nettle grows, which causes excruciating irritation of the skin, but leaves no mark. A person, tied down, and gently stroked with the nettle on the most sensitive portions of his external anatomy, will, it is reported, say whatever is required of him.

57. Squeezing the testicles.

58. Inserting chillies into the eyes, nostrils, or urethra. For the purpose of extracting confessions from women, a disgusting application of chillies was sometimes resorted to. A clergyman, many years ago, informed the Collector of Tanjore that, having missed a cheque from his table, he made enquiry among his servants concerning it. In order to ascertain whether it had been taken by the only child on the establishment, his eyes were filled with red chillies by the other servants.*

59. Insertion of iron wire, a heated bougie, or straw into the urethra. A few years ago, a man who was admitted into hospital made a statement that he had been attacked three weeks previously by robbers, who thought he had some money concealed in a field. They threw him on his back, forced a piece of stiff spikey grass (spear-grass) into his urethra, and worked it up and down till it broke off short. The piece of grass, which was seven inches long, was removed by urethral incision. In a parallel case, a narrow strip of bamboo, and the midrib

* Chevers. *Op. cit.*

of the leaflet of a cocoanut tree smeared with powdered chillies, were used instead of a blade of grass.

60. A young girl was dropped down a well by a rope fastened round her neck, with a view to extorting a confession of theft.

61. Ducking in a pond on a cold morning, and then having the subject punkahed vigorously (presumably with a hand fan).

62. Dipping in wells and rivers, till the individual was half suffocated.

63. Putting a person into a nest of red ants is said to have been an effective method of extracting a confession. This, with the recollection of an encounter with red ants before me, I can readily believe.

64. A Urāli woman of the Coimbatore hills, who, after marriage, refuses to live with her husband, is punished thus. She is tied to a tree, and the Kolkāran (assistant to the head-man) empties the contents of a hornet or wasp's nest at her feet. After a few minutes the woman is questioned, and, if she agrees to live with her husband, she must, in token of assent, lick a mark made on his back by the Kolkāran with fowl's excrement, saying "You are my husband. In future I shall not quarrel with you, and will obey you" Even after this ordeal has been gone through, a woman may, on payment of a fine, leave her husband in favour of another man of the tribe.

65. Another form of punishment for a woman found guilty of adultery is to tie a mortar in front, and a cat on her back, and drag her through the streets, while the mortar drags her towards the ground, and the cat scratches her in its struggles to get free.

66. If a Malaiāli woman of the Javādi hills commits adultery, the young men of the tribe are set loose on her to work their wicked way, after which she is put in a pit filled with cow-dung and other filth. An old man naively remarked that adultery was very rare.

67. When a man of the Baidya (Billava) caste in South Canara had criminal intercourse with a Paraiyan woman, a form of punishment, known as gudi shudda, was resorted to in former days. Seven huts were erected, and set on fire. The delinquent was then made to pass through the fiery furnace.

68. Compelling a person to eat human excrement.

69. Tying bullock bones, and other degrading articles, round the neck.

70. Putting a low-caste man on the back of a man of higher caste.

71. Bringing a man's wife, sisters, or daughters, removing their clothing by force, and making them appear naked before himself and other men.

72. Tying the hair of the head to a donkey or buffalo's tail, and parading through the streets of the village.

73. Of trial by ordeal with boiling lead and oil, the following cases are recorded in the Tellicherry Factory diary, 1762. "The king regent of Colastria's minister being arrived, the Moorman accused by the Tivity this day dipped his fingers three times into boiling lead, scooping out some every time, after which his hand was sealed up in a bag as customary, to be opened on the third day. Three days later it is recorded that,

the Moorman's hand being this day unsealed, no burn or blister appeared upon it, whereon he was released, and the Tivity, his accuser, sentenced to pay him the sum of . . fanams as a retaliation. A Nair, being accused by a Moor of intending to kill him with a musquet offered to clear himself by dipping his hand in boiling oil, which the Moor was at first willing to abide by. But an entry in the diary states that the Moor, having declined to abide by the decision of the Tryal of boiling oil, the Nair is released, and the Moor and two witnesses produced by him fined the sum of fifty fanams each, being esteemed agreeable to the custom of the country to have falsely accused him."

74. Among the Jōgis, as a proof of chastity, the ordeal of drinking a potful of cow-dung or chilly water has to be undergone. In former days, a person accused of adultery in Travancore was permitted to submit to the ordeal of dipping the hands in boiling ghī at the temple of Suchindram. This temple derives its name from Indra, who according to the legend, had illicit intercourse with Ahalya, the wife of Gautama Rishi, and had to undergo this form of ordeal.*

From a collection of reports (1793) from Rājas and other native chiefs in Malabar relative to the system and usages observed by them and their ancestors in the administration of justice, I gather that, if any Brāhman was suspected of theft or cohabitation with a woman of low caste, the Rāja sent him, together with the four principal people of the country, with a letter to the

* S. Appadorai Iyer, M.S.

pagodà of Sujindrah, where they were to inform the heads of the pagoda of all particulars. After the usual custom had been paid to them, a pot of cocoanut oil was boiled on a fire; and, when it was properly boiled, the suspected person dipped his hand into it. If the hand blistered, he was pronounced guilty. If a Nāyar was, in like manner, suspected, he had to submit to the ordeal in the fort of Baliapatnam.

75. To test the chastity of a Tangalān Paraiyan bride, the following ordeal had to be undergone on the wedding day, immediately after the tāli-tying ceremony. Some cakes were placed in boiling oil in an earthen or iron receptacle. The bride, after a bath and clad in wet clothes, had to pick out the cakes with her hand, after an examination of her hair, nails, and cloth, to see if she had about her any charm or magical drug. Immediately after taking out the cakes from the oil, she had to husk a small quantity of rice. And, if she did this successfully, her chastity was established. One form of punishment inflicted on Paraiyans by their head-man is making a man crawl on his hands and knees between the legs of a Paraiyan woman.

76. The following form of ordeal among the Koravans is described by Mr. F. S. Mullaly.* "Should a Koravan suspect another of having committed a crime, and he denies it, several persons take new pots, put rice and water in them, and place them on the fire. Whosoever's rice boils first has not committed the offence, but the owner of the second pot which boils is deemed the

* Criminal Classes of the Madras Presidency.

guilty one, and he has to pay all the expenses. If two pots boil at the same time, they resort to trial by ordeal. A new pot is filled with boiling ghī with a four-anna piece in it, and the suspected person is told to take it out. If he is innocent, he will at once offer to do so; but, if guilty, so great is their superstition, he will at once confess."

77. In Travancore there was a judicial ordeal by snake bite. The accused thrust his hand into a mantle, in which a cobra was wrapped up. If it bit him, he was guilty; if not, he was innocent. "That we have here," Frazer writes,* "a relic of totemism appears not only from the worship of snakes in the district, but also from the fact that, if a dead cobra was found by the people, it was burned with the same ceremonies as the body of a man of high caste."

78. The crocodile ordeal, in which a man swam across a sheet of water swarming with these beasts, was in vogue in Malabar, to determine the guilt or innocence of criminals. "The accused," Visscher writes,† "is compelled, after a solemn profession of innocence in the presence of the Brāhmins and nobles, and of a great concourse of people to swim across this (Cranganoor) river and back; or, if he cannot do this, he must be dragged through, holding on with his hands to a boat. If the crocodile pulls him under, it is a sign of his guilt; if otherwise, he is released as innocent."

79. The following method of discovering theft or any kind of concealment by chewing rice is described by

* Totemism, 1887. † Letters from Malabar.

Daniel Johnson.* "A Brāhmin is sent for, who writes down all the names of the people in the house, or who are suspected. Next day he consecrates a piece of ground by covering it with cow-dung and water, over which he says a long prayer. The people then assemble on this spot in a line facing the Brāhmin, who has with him some dry rice, of which he delivers to each person the weight of a four-cornered rupee, or that quantity weighed with the sacred stone called salagram, which is deposited in a leaf of the pippal or banyan tree. At the time of delivering it, the Brāhmin puts his right hand on each person's head, and repeats a short prayer; and, when finished, he directs them all to chew the rice, which at a given time must be produced on the leaves masticated. The person or persons, whose rice is not thoroughly masticated, or exhibits any blood with it, is considered guilty. The faith they all have of the power of the Brāhmin, and a guilty conscience operating at the same time, suppresses the natural flow of saliva to the mouth, without which the hard particles of the rice bruise and cut the gums, causing them to bleed, which they themselves are sensible of, and in most instances confess the crime." The same writer gives the three following modes of ascertaining the persons guilty of practising witchcraft :—

First.—Branches of the saul (*Shorea robusta*) tree, marked with the names of all the females in the village, whether married or unmarried, who have attained the age of twelve years, are planted in the water in the morning

* Sketches of Field Sports as followed by the Natives of India, 1822.

for the space of four hours and-a-half; and the withering of any of these branches is proof of witchcraft against the person whose name is annexed to it.

Second.—Small portions of rice enveloped in cloths, marked as above, are placed in a nest of white ants. The consumption of the rice in any of the bags establishes sorcery against the woman whose name it bears.

Third.—Lamps are lighted at night. Water is placed in cups made of leaves, and mustard-seed and oil are poured, drop by drop, into the water, whilst the name of each woman in the village is pronounced. The appearance of the shadow of any woman on the water, during the ceremony, proves her a witch.

80. A queer form of punishment is sometimes inflicted by the caste council when a Rāvelo (Oriya temple servant) ill-treats and deserts his wife. He is made to sit under one of the bamboo coops with which fish are caught, and his wife sits on the top of it. Five pots of water are then poured over the pair of them, in imitation of the caste custom of pouring five pots of water over a dead body before it is taken to the burning ground, the ceremony taking place in the part of the house where the corpse would be washed. The wife then throws away a ladle, and breaks a cooking-pot, just as she would have done had her husband really been dead, and further breaks her bangles, and tears off her necklace, as she would have done if she was really a widow. Having thus signified that her husband is dead to her, she goes straight off to her parents' house, and is free to marry again.*

* Madras Census Report, 1901.

81. A Koraga woman of South Canara, when found guilty of adultery, is said to be treated in the following extraordinary way. If her paramour is of low caste similar to herself, he has to marry her. But, in order to purify her for the ceremony, he has to build a hut, and put the woman inside. It is then set on fire, and the woman escapes as best she can to another place where the same performance is gone through, and so on until she has been burnt out seven times. She is then considered once more an honest woman, and fit to be again married.

82. "Sometimes," a recent writer states "a big chain hangs suspended from a tree, and the village panchayats (tribunals) are held in the Aiyanar (or Sangali Karuppan) temple. The accused is made to submit to an ordeal in proof of his innocence. The ordeal consists in his swearing on the chain, which he is made to touch. He has such a dread for this procedure that, as soon as he touches the chain, he comes out with the truth, failure to speak the truth being punished by some calamity, which he believes will overtake him within a week. These chains are also suspended to the trees near the temples of village goddesses, and used by village panchayats to swear the accused in any trial before the panchayat."

83. *Gallows.*—In the Bellary Manual (1872) it is recorded that "the hills through which the Otikanama ghāt passes, were till recently the haunt of some of the worst characters in the district, where they met to arrange their plans for gang robberies, and into the recesses of which they retreated with their plunder obtained from

the rich villages around. About thirty years ago, one of these gangs attacked a village on the Otikanama ghāt, and, having looted it, set fire to a large hut in which some seventy women and children had taken refuge. Some of the ring-leaders were captured, and, after being executed, were hung up in chains near the scene of their crime, where their bones are still to be seen in the iron cages, in which they were suspended." In the jungles of Anantapur, about 3½ miles from the village of Bukkapatnam, is a gallows,* said to have been erected by order of Sir Thomas Munro. The cross-beams and supports are made of teak, and the two iron cages suspended to the cross-beam by big iron hooks. Local people say that it was used only once, when the two ring-leaders of a band of dacoits, the terror of the neighbourhood, were bound, put alive into the cages, each of which is only just big enough to hold a man, and starved to death. The mode of torture had such an excellent effect on the rest that no more was heard of dacoity. On a stone near one of the gallows, an inscription in Telugu records that Hoosain Sahib and Badē Ibrahim Jemadar, were hung near Pasikallu, by order of the Foujdari Court, on September 8th, 1837, for killing a man by throwing a noose.

84. The manner of carrying out capital punishment in Malabar, in days gone by, was sometimes barbarous in the extreme. "Criminals," Mr. Logan writes,† "were cut in half and exposed on a cross-bar, in the manner still adopted with tigers and panthers slain in hunting

* Recently transferred to the Madras Museum.

† Malabar Manual, 1887.

expeditions, and offered as a sacrifice to local deities. Thieves were similarly cut in two and impaled on a stake, which probably had a cross-bar, as the word for it and that for an eagle or vulture are identical. But impaling alive was also known, and, in 1795, two Māppilas were thus treated after a pretended trial for alleged robbery in a Nayar's house. Finally, great criminals were at times wrapped up in green palm leaves, and torn asunder, probably by elephants."

85. The Civil Surgeon of Coimbatore, many years ago, mentions a case in which a subordinate official, to extort a confession, enveloped the limbs of a person in cotton soaked in oil, which he set fire to.* Professional burglars, who wish to find out where valuables are concealed, even nowadays pour kerosine oil over those from whom they wish to extract the information, and threaten to set fire to it if they do not reveal their secret. A successful method of extorting a confession, which is still resorted to, is to keep on talking by relays to the suspect, and continue to ply him with the same question without ceasing both by day and night. Some years ago, in Malabar, a man was accused, and, being strongly suspected, was taken into nominal custody for the purpose of investigation. He gave several rambling and contradictory statements, so the police officer kept him on the march, with orders that he was not to be allowed to sleep until he revealed the truth. He was kept going from station to station for nearly four days, and finally gave a full confession.

* Chevers. *Op. cit.*

From the collection of reports already referred to, I have gathered the following information relating to punishment and ordeal in bygone days in Malabar:—

1. If any Kurian detected another at night in an apartment with his wife or mistress, he was permitted to kill him, and cut off the woman's hair and repudiate her.

2. If any Kurian robbed the treasury, or anything else belonging to the Rāja, he was first to repay the value of what he had stolen, and sometimes had his hand or a finger cut off, or was put to death.

3. For various forms of petty larceny, the offender was confined and received corporal punishment. If proved guilty a second time, he was deprived of a member, and put to death with a sword for a further offence.

4. If a person committed theft, he was kept in confinement for six months or a year, and a little of his flesh or nose cut off.

5. If a Tīyan, Māppila, or other Kurian was accused of robbery or illicit cohabitation, and the charge was not clearly proved, those learned in the shāstras assembled with a court, and an iron hatchet was made red-hot. The accused, after declaring his innocence, had to take the hatchet in his hand, and, if the hand was burnt, he was pronounced guilty, and punished by amputation of a hand or finger, or with death.

6. If anyone was convicted of a serious theft, he was put to death, unless he was a Brāhman, in which case he was excommunicated.

7. If the Rāja's Protikars levied more than their just dues, and extorted money from or otherwise oppressed

the people, the Rāja caused the offender to be seized and exposed to the public gaze on the high-road with his hands and feet in irons.

8. In the event of a personal quarrel between two persons, when the wounds were equal, the parties had to pay their own expenses until they were cured. But if only one of the parties was wounded, the other was ordered to pay the expenses of the wounded man till his wounds healed.

9. For adultery between a man of low caste and a woman of high caste, the man was put on the cahu, and the woman given by the Rāja as a slave to whom he pleased.

10. When a person committed murder, he was, before the death sentence was carried out, given rice or betel, or whatever he desired to eat. He was then put to death by "having his skull taken off by a scalping knife, the body to be fixed on the cahu, a pole fixed in the ground for the purpose." If the criminal escaped, and endeavours to catch him were ineffectual, his effects were secured, and the corpse of the deceased was burnt in his house. The practice of hanging criminals is said not to have been introduced till the time of Haidar Ali.

11. Sometimes criminals were put to death by shooting. It is noted, for example, that, if a woman was caught by anyone in fornication, she was put to death with a sword or musket.

12. If a difference arose between two people meeting of the principal men of the thirty thousand was convened, and they sometimes decreed that the plantain trees, betel vines, betel-nut and cocoanut trees in the garden of the

guilty person should be cut down, other plants destroyed with a sword, and his house unroofed.

13. If, in a dispute, one man killed another, the principal men of the thirty thousand met at the fort of Valachereecota, and on entering the first house thereof turned their targets and sat thereon while they awaited the sentence of the oracle Paradēvada.

14. Any person wounding a Brāhman or a cow was, if blood was seen to issue from the wound, punished with death.

15. If a Brāhman killed a cow, he was excommunicated, or subjected to the expiation required by the shāstras.

16. If a Brāhman woman was ruined in character, she was excommunicated, and, the ceremonies of her obsequies having been performed, she was made over as a part of the property of Government.

CORPORAL PUNISHMENT IN VERNACULAR SCHOOLS.

THE following account is based on notes supplied by native correspondents who have in their early youth witnessed some of the punitive methods here described. Many of the forms of punishment have been demonstrated to me, when in camp, by young and old, who were evidently giving a graphic description of what they had themselves seen or undergone. It is worthy of notice that, in many cases, the school-mates of the culprit took part in the administration of the punishment, as, in former days, every soldier of a regiment was made a public executioner in the punishment of running the gauntlet (or gantlope).

1. The teacher in vernacular schools, like members of his calling in other parts of the world, uses the rod, which is a rattan about a quarter of an inch thick and three feet in length, sometimes ornamented with a silver ferrule at each end. This, and the style used for writing on palm leaves, are the insignia of his profession. There is no restriction as to the parts of the body to which the rod is applied, but the palms of the hands, buttocks, and back are the most favourite spots. Caning is sometimes resorted to in lieu of a fine for bad conduct. Sometimes boys had to keep their buttocks uncovered during the whole time they were in school, so that they were ready for caning if they were naughty.

In addition to caning, the following forms of punishment are, or were, formerly inflicted.

2. Pulling and screwing the lobe or helix of the ears, or boxing the ears.

3. Hitting the head with the knuckles.

4. Slapping the cheeks, which may be done by the teacher, another boy in the class, or the culprit himself, if his previous conduct has been good.

5. Two naughty boys slap each other on the cheeks.

6. Pinching the fleshy parts of the body, more especially the thigh.

7. Putting some sand or powdered granite dust on the bare thigh, and pinching the part. In village schools the children are seated on the floor with sand spread out in front of them. They learn the alphabet by writing with the forefinger in the sand, which is always at hand as a punitive medium.

8. The boy stands with his feet together, and, crossing his arms in front, holds the lobe of his right ear with the left hand, and of his left ear with the right hand. He is then made to stoop down, and touch the ground with his elbows from ten to a hundred times according to the gravity of the offence.

9. Passing one hand under the leg, catching hold of the nose, and rising and sinking alternately.

10. A stick, four or five feet long, is passed under the knees, and the boy places his elbows beneath it. The thumbs and big toes are tied together by separate strings. Thus trussed, he is rolled away into a corner of the school-room, there to meditate on his fault.

11. The boy is converted into a horse, and made to carry about another boy seated on his back, with frequent turnings.

12. The arms are crossed so that the fingers of the right hand grasp the tip of the left ear, and *vice versâ*. The boy then has to sit down and stand up alternately a number of times proportionate to the gravity of his offence.

13. There are some plants (nettles), the leaves of which, when rubbed into the skin, cause a burning and pricking sensation. The hands of the boy are tied in front, and the leaves applied to the back. The effect lasts for several hours, at the end of which time cocoanut oil is rubbed in to prevent swelling.

14. The boy is made to stoop, with only the big toe and forefinger of the right side touching the ground, and the whole weight of the body is thrown on the toe and forefinger. If the other toes and fingers touch the ground, they are rapped with the cane. This punishment is called standing on needles.

15. The right ankle being crossed over the left thigh, the boy has to stoop with the tip of the right forefinger touching the ground.

16. The boy stoops down with his legs stretched apart, and his right hand on the ground about three feet in front of him, while he reads a book held in the left hand.

17. Kneeling alternately on the right and left knee, while the ears are clutched with the hands of the crossed arms.

18. Standing or hopping on one leg.

19. Another form of punishment is known as sitting like a chair. In this the boy, with his hands tied or crossed in front, or stretched out at right angles to the trunk, is made to squat with his back touching a wall, and the buttocks on a level with the knees. Sometimes spiny fruits are placed in the hollow of the bent knee-joints. A line is drawn on the wall above his head, which must not be raised above the line. The steel style used for writing is fixed into the ground with its sharp-pointed end towards the buttocks. In a modified form of this subtle punishment, the school slates are piled up on the boy's lap or head.

20. The feet being several feet from a wall, the forehead is made to touch the wall, and, in this uncomfortable attitude, a book held in the hands is read.

21. The legs being stretched wide apart, the boy has to sit alternately on the right and left buttock.

22. The boy sits on the floor, with his clothes removed, and hands and feet tied. His face, body, and limbs, and the ground around him, are smeared with jaggery water. Ants and other insects are attracted by this, and the skin becomes covered with them.

23. He is made to stand up with the arms crossed in front. His feet are then dragged apart, and he has to stand with the legs widely separated.

24. He has to crawl between the outstretched legs of the other pupils.

25. He is made to stoop down. A loop of string is passed round his neck and one of the big toes, or the

thumbs are tied to the toes. The punishment may be increased by placing a heavy stone or another boy on his back.

25A. As a punishment for bad handwriting, the boy is made to hold his right arm horizontally, bent as in the act of writing. Then any article which is at hand, such as a slate, piece of paper, or strip of palm-leaf (olei) is placed over the elbow-joint, and the boy has to write without letting the article fall off. If it does, he is caned, and the performance is repeated.

26. There is a species of red ant, which builds its nest in trees, and whose bite produces severe pain. A boy may be punished by scattering the live occupants of a nest over his body.

27. Hanging by the hands, or punishment of the bow. A rope or bar, which is sometimes bow-shaped, strong enough to bear the weight of the boy, is suspended like a trapeze from the roof, and clutched with interlocked or tied fingers. Burning paddy husk or chillies, sharp stones, thorns, or prickly-pear, are spread on the floor beneath him, so that he is afraid to let go his hold. To make this punishment more severe, it was sometimes combined with number 26.

28. If a boy wants to relieve nature, he is made to spit on a tile heated by exposure to the sun, and must return before the saliva, which takes the part of a sand-glass, has dried up.

29. The boy is made to masticate straw, like donkeys or bullocks.

30. He has to spit on the joints of the fingers, dip them in the sand, and strike them forcibly on a bench or stone.

31. If a boy refuses to do his lessons, another lad tells him that he will bring butter out of his thumb, the back of which he rubs with dry earth or sand till it begins to abrade the skin.

32. The boy is ordered to stand in the blazing sun with a weight, *e.g.*, a stone, on his head or in his hands; and, if he refuses to obey, receives a caning, or is pushed out of the room by the other boys. It may be noted that, as punishment for adultery, an unfaithful Yānādi woman is made to stand, with her legs tied, for a whole day in the sun, with a basket full of sand on her head.

33. Two naughty boys are made to seize each other by the ears, and stand up and sink down alternately, while they sing "You and I are shameless fellows."

34. The boy kneels down, and heavy stones are placed on his calves.

35. He is rolled in the sand during the hottest part of the day.

36. The block and chain (a variant of the bilboes). This consists of a block of heavy wood, sometimes shaped like an Indian club, to which is attached a strong iron chain four or five feet in length. The log may be placed on the back of the naughty boy, who has to read a book while in a stooping attitude; or the free end of the chain is fastened by a padlock to the leg of the boy, who has to drag or carry the block about with him, it may be for several days. This form of punishment is still practised

in the city of Madras, where a carpenter's apprentice was recently seen dragging after him a block, to which he was chained. It is resorted to by rural schoolmasters, carpenters and blacksmiths, parents and guardians. Some years ago a native of Madura, whose young wife was fond of gadding about, punished her by making her drag about a log chained and padlocked round her leg.

37. In the case of boys who shirk attendance at school, the teacher, accompanied by his pupils, proceeds to the house of the truant, and puts on his head a fool's-cap made of paper, bamboo, palm-leaf, or grass matting. He is then marched off, or carried by his fellow students to school amid the clapping of hands and beating of drums.

38. Two boys, who are guilty of chatting or quarrelling in the school-room, are made to stand face to face. They get a good grip of each other's ears, and tug thereat till their foreheads come in painful contact. If they are slow, the teacher seizes hold of their heads, and brings them forcibly together. As a variant, they may, while hanging on to the ears, be made to sit down and stand up alternately.

39. Boys are made to kneel down on the hard ground, sometimes with arms outstretched and a heavy stone in the hands, till they have learnt their lesson.

40. The introduction of benches into school-rooms has created a novel form of punishment. The boy lies flat on the bench, back upwards, and is tied to it by strings round the neck, waist, and legs. While he is thus captive, his arms are stretched out by two other boys, and he receives a caning.

41. The naughty boy is made to do menial services for the schoolmaster, such as drawing water from the well, etc.

42. The boy's parents, sister or other near relations, are spoken of, in his presence, in vulgar and abusive language.

Since the introduction of the Grant-in-aid Code the punishment of the young idea has undergone considerable modification. The old schoolmaster is, like Dominie Dobiensis, often loved and respected by his pupils, and there is a Tamil proverb that "the schoolmaster will attain the abode of Vishnu (*i.e.*, bliss), and the doctor will go to hell."

SLAVERY.

In a note on slavery, the Madras Census Commissioner, 1871, writes as follows. "In times prior to British rule, the whole of the Pariah community, without exception, were the slaves of the superior castes. The Pariahs were not the only slaves in these times, for almost all the inferior agricultural tribes were in a similar position. The Hindu law recognised five descriptions of service, four of which might be performed by any one without loss of dignity or caste, but the fifth order of service was to be performed by slaves only, styled Dass, from their Dasyan or aboriginal descent. The 'undue service' to be exacted of the latter class included the sweeping and cleaning of the house, the doorway, the necessary and other impure places, and, in times of sickness, attendance upon the patient after the natural evacuations, and to take away the excrement, and rub the feet." There were fifteen species of slavery recognised:—

(1) Those born of female slaves.
(2) Those purchased for a price.
(3) Those found by chance.
(4) Slaves by descent.
(5) Those fed and kept alive in famine times.
(6) Those given up as a pledge for money borrowed.
(7) Those binding themselves for money borrowed.
(8) Those captured in battle.

(9) Those unable to pay gambling debts.
(10) Those becoming slaves of their own wish.
(11) Apostates from a religious life.
(12) Slaves for a limited period.
(13) Slaves for subsistence.
(14) Those who for love of slave women became slaves,
(15) By voluntary sale of liberty.

Of these fifteen descriptions of slaves, the first four could never obtain their liberty without the consent of their owners. The other kinds of slaves might obtain their freedom under stipulated conditions. Slave women, however, bearing sons to their masters, became free. People of any caste might sell themselves into slavery, or be made slaves by conquest, etc., but "the Brāhmin alone can never be a slave." "The Pallans," it is stated in the Tanjore Manual, "are prædial labourers, and are employed exclusively in the cultivation of lands. They have everywhere a separate spot allotted to them for residence, which is called Pallachēri, in distinction from that occupied by the Pareiya class, which is called Paracchēri. The Palla women expose their body above the waist—a distinctive mark of their primitive condition of slavery, of which, however, no trace now exists."

Of the history of slavery in Malabar, the following admirable account is given * by Mr. W. Logan, who was for many years Collector of that district. "The question of slavery and the slave trade attracted the

* Malabar Manual.

early attention of the Honourable Company's Government. In 1792, the year in which British rule commenced, a proclamation was issued against dealing in slaves. A person offering a slave for sale was considered to be a thief. The slave was to be forfeited, and the person offering him for sale was to be fined five times his value. The purchaser was to be similarly treated. The houses of suspected slave traders were to be well watched, and the traders caught *in flagrante delicto* were to be handed over to the Rājas to be dealt with. Fishermen and Māppillas conveying slaves were to be severely flogged, and fined at the rate of ten rupees each slave. Vessels used in trade (except fisher-boats) were to be confiscated. But the proclamation was not to prevent the privileged superior castes from purchasing the children of famine-stricken parents, on condition that the parents might re-purchase their children on the advent of better times. This proclamation was chiefly directed against the prevalent practice of robbers carrying off by force the children of the most useful inhabitants, the Tiyars and other cultivators. This practice was kept alive by the facility with which the slaves could be sold on the coast to the agents of vessels engaged in the trade, sailing from the French settlement at Mahē and the Dutch settlement at Cochin. These ships in general carried the slaves to the French islands. In 1819 the Principal Collector wrote a report on the condition of the Cherumar, and received orders that the practice of selling slaves for arrears of revenue be immediately discontinued. In 1821, the Court of Directors expressed considerable dissatisfaction at the lack of precise information which had been vouchsafed to them, and said 'We are told that part of the cultivators are held as slaves: that they are attached to the soil and marketable property.' In 1836 the Government ordered the remission in the Collector's accounts of Rs. 927–13–0, which was the 'annual revenue' from slaves on the Government lands in Malabar, and the Government was at the same time 'pleased to accede to the recommendation in favour of emancipating the slaves on the Government lands in Malabar.' This freedom was not, however, to be proclaimed, and the measure was to be carried out in such a manner 'as not to create any unnecessary alarm or aversion to it on the part of other proprietors, or premature hopes of emancipation on that of other slaves.' This was a wise step on the part of Government, for it strengthened their hands in future years in recommending others to do as they had already done. But, at the same time, they need have been under no apprehension as to the effects of such an emancipation on the minds of other slaves. It is only people with *initial* ideas of liberty who fret under a system of compulsory customary employments. In 1841 Mr. E. B. Thomas, the Judge at Calicut, wrote in strong terms a letter to the Sadr Adālat, in which he pointed out that women in some talūks (divisions) fetched higher prices, in order to breed slaves; that the average cost of a young male under ten years was about Rs. 3–8–0, of a female somewhat less; that an infant ten months old was sold in a court auction for Rs. 1–10–6 independent of the price of its mother; and that, in a recent suit, the right to twenty-seven slaves was the 'sole matter of litigation, and was disposed of on its merits.' In a further letter Mr. Thomas pointed out that the slaves had increased in numbers from 144,000 in the census 1835 to 159,000 in the census 1842. It was apparently these letters which decided the Board of Directors to send out orders to legislate. And the Government of India passed Act V of 1843, of which the provisions were widely published throughout Malabar. The Collector explained to the Cherumar that it was in their interest, as well as their duty, to remain with their masters, if treated kindly. He proclaimed that 'the Government will not order a slave who is in the employ of an individual to forsake him and go to the service of another claimant; nor will the Government interfere with the slave's inclination as to where he wishes to work.' And again, 'Any person claiming a slave as janmam, kānam or panayam, the right of such claim or claims will not be investigated into at any one of the public offices or courts.' These measures received the cordial approval of the Court of Directors, who, in 1845, wrote as follows. 'It would defeat the very object in view to create any estrangement between them and their masters, and moreover would be an act of injustice and bad faith, of which the masters would be entitled to complain.' In 1852, and again in 1855, the fact that traffic in slaves still continued was brought to the notice of Government, but on full consideration no further measures for the emancipation of the Cherumar were deemed to be necessary. The Cherumar even yet have not realised what public opinion in England would probably have forced down their throats fifty years ago, and there is reason to think that they are still, even now, with their full consent, bought and sold and hired out, although, of course, the transaction must be kept secret for fear of the penalties of the Penal Code, which came into force in 1862, and was the real final blow at slavery in India. The slaves, however, as a caste will never understand what real freedom means, until measures are adopted to give them indefeasible rights in the small orchards occupied by them as house sites."

Writing to me concerning Malabar at the present day, a correspondent states that "in almost every talūk we have jungle tribes, who call themselves the 'men' of Jenmis.* In the old days, when forests were sold' the inhabitants were actually entered in the contract as part of the effects, as, in former times, the landlord sold the *adscripti* or *ascripti glebæ* with the land. Now that is not done. However, the relationship exists to the following extent, according to what a Tahsildar (revenue official) tells me. The tribesmen roam about the forests at will, and each year select a place, which has lain fallow for five years or more for all kinds of cultivation. Sometimes they inform the Jenmi that they have done so, sometimes they do not. Then, at harvest time, the Jenmi, or his agent, goes up and takes his share of the produce. They never try to deceive the Jenmi. He is asked to settle their disputes, but these are rare. They never go

* Jenmi or Janmi. Proprietor or landlord.

to law. The Jenmi can call on them for labour, and they give it willingly. If badly treated, as they have been at times by encroaching plainsmen, they run off to another forest, and serve another Jenmi. At the Onam festival they come with gifts for the Jenmi, who stands them a feast. The relation between the jungle folk and the Jenmi shows the instinct in a primitive people to have a lord. There seems to be no gain in having a Jenmi. His protection is not needed, and he is hardly ever called in to interfere. If they refused to pay the Jenmi his dues, he would find it very hard to get them. Still they keep to him."

"Conversion to Muhammadanism," Mr. Logan writes, "has had a marked effect in freeing the slave caste in Malabar from their former burthens. By conversion a Cheruman obtains a distinct rise in the social scale, and, if he is in consequence bullied or beaten, the influence of the whole Muhammadan community comes to his aid." The same applies to the Nayādis, of whom some have escaped from their degraded position by conversion to Islam. In the scale of pollution the Nayādi holds the lowest place, and consequently labours under the greatest disadvantage, which is removed with his change of religion.

In the middle of the last century, when planters first began to settle in the Wynād (in Malabar), they purchased the land with the Paniyans living on it, who were practically slaves of the land-owners. In some localities, where the Janmis have sold the bulk of the land, and have consequently ceased to find regular employment for them, the Paniyans have taken kindly to working on coffee estates under European control.

In Wigram's 'Malabar Law and Custom,'* the word adima is defined as "feudal dependency of a Nayar upon his patron: slavery." And the terms adima and kūdima are said to mean "a slave or one subject to the landlord, the grant (of land) being generally made to such persons. A nominal fee of about two fanams a year is payable to the landlord, to show that he still retains the proprietary title."

In his report on the forest administration in Coorg, 1902–03, Mr. C. McCarthy writes as follows concerning the jungle Kurumbas, who now work for the forest department. "We experienced, in connection with the Kurubas, one of those apparent aberrations of sense and intellect, the occurrence of which amongst this peculiar race was foreshadowed in the last report. The Chief Commissioner is aware that, in the interests of the Kurubas themselves, we substitute for a single cash payment distributions of the same value of food-grains, clothes and cash in equal proportions of each. Now, seventy years ago, before the annexation of Coorg, the Kurubas and similar castes were prædial slaves of the dominant Coorgs, receiving no other remuneration for service than food and clothing. In fact, this institution, nothing less than real slavery, was not entirely broken up until the great demand for local labour created by the opening up of the country for coffee cultivation so late as 1860–70, so that

* 2nd Ed. By L. Moore, 1900.

the existing generation are still cognisant of the old state of affairs. Last year, during the distribution of rewards for the successful protection of the reserves that season from fire, it seems that the idea was put into the heads of these people that our system of remuneration, which includes the distribution of food and clothing, was an attempt to create again at their expense a system of, as it were, forest slavery; with the result that for a time nothing would induce many of them to accept any form of remuneration for the work already performed, much less to undertake the same duties for the approaching season. It was some time, and after no little trouble, that the wherefore of this strange conduct was discovered, and the suspicions aroused put at rest."

In an article on the hill tribes of Travancore,* Mr. Conner states that "in earlier times the murder of a slave was scarcely considered a crime. The deed of transfer goes to say 'You may sell or kill him or her.' The latter privilege has now of course ceased."

Of slavery on the west coast, an excellent account is given by the Rev. S. Mateer,† from which the following extracts are taken. "Every wealthy man, and even individuals of inferior caste, had a number of bondsmen born in slavery. The number of persons originally reduced to a state of slavery were increased by the sale of children in times of famine and distress, which has occurred even in our own day. Other additions have been made, from time to time, by petty princes

* Madras Journ. Lit. Science, I, 1833.

† Native Life in Travancore, 1883.

carrying away captives in their wars, by the fraud or violence of kidnappers, as a judgment on criminals, as a punishment on females of the higher classes who have fallen, and are cast out to associate with the lowest of the population. Muhammadans and Roman Catholics of property also purchased slaves, in order to proselytise them to their own religion. On account of the law of caste pollution, these slaves have all been engaged solely in prædial or field work, not domestic service, as they could not enter the houses of their masters, nor be used for personal attendance. Even in the fields, their work must be superintended from a certain distance. A curious custom existed, which is said to have added to the numbers of the enslaved. The various castes met at fighting grounds at Pallam, Ochira, etc., and at this season it was supposed that low-caste men were at liberty to seize high-caste women if they could manage it, and to retain them. A certain woman at Mundakayam, with fair Syrian features, is said to have been carried off thus. Hence arose a popular error that, during the months of February and March, if a Pulayan meets a Sūdra woman alone, he may seize her, unless she is accompanied by a Shānar boy. Gundert says that this time was in the month Karkadam (15th July to 15th August), during which high caste women may lose caste if a slave happens to throw a stone at them after sunset. The Pariahs in North Travancore formerly kidnapped females of high caste, whom they were said to treat afterwards in a brutal manner. Their custom was to turn robbers in the month of February, just after the ingathering of the harvest, when they were free from field work, and at the same time excited by demon worship, dancing, and drink. They broke into the houses of Brāhmans and Nāyars, carrying away their children and property, in excuse for which they pretended motives of revenge, urging a tradition that they were once a division of the Brāhmans, but entrapped into a breach of caste rules by their enemies making them eat beef."

Concerning the Paraiyans of Travancore, the Rev. S. Mateer writes further * that "during the war with Tippu, proclamation was made that every Parayan in this district must have a Nāyar or master, and belong to someone or other. All who were not private property would be made slaves of the sirkar (Government), which was greatly dreaded on account of the merciless oppression, and obliged to cut grass for the troops, and do other services. Many, therefore, became nominally slaves to some respectable man, asking it as a kindness to free them from Government slavery. This reminds us of the Roman clients and patrons. Several respectable families begged the Nambūri high priest, visiting Suchindram and other temples, to call them his slaves for which they paid him one fanam a head per annum. This payment is still kept up. This priest conferred upon them additional benefits, for in their troubles and oppressions he wrote to the Government, requiring for them justice and proper treatment. The slaves of a Nambūri would also be treated with consideration on account of his sacred position and rank. These families,

* Journ. Roy. As. Soc. XVI.

'pōtty slaves,' still intermarry only among themselves, as in this case the wife could not be claimed by a different owner from the husband's."

The following account of the social status of the leaf weaving Thanda Pulayans of Cochin is given by Mr. L. K. Anantha Krishna Aiyer.* "The Thanda Pulayans appear to have been the slaves of the soil till 1854, when they were emancipated. Even now their condition has not undergone any material improvement. Though they are left more to themselves, they still work for farmers or landlords for a daily wage of paddy. If they run away, they are brought back, and punished. There is even now a custom that, when a farmer or landlord wants a few Pulayans to work in the fields, he obtains their services on payment of fifteen to twenty rupees to them, or to their master. When a Pulayan's services are thus obtained, he works for his new master for two edangalis of paddy a day. They can obtain their liberation on the return of the purchase money, which they can never hope to earn. Having no property which they can claim as their own, and conscious perhaps that their lot will be the same wherever they go, they remain cheerful and contented, drudging on from day to day, and have no inclination to emigrate to places where they can get higher wages. The Cherumans of Palghāt, on the contrary, enjoy more freedom. Many go to the Wynād, and some to the Kolar gold-fields, where they receive a good money-wage. The Thanda Pulayans, as has been said, work for some landlord, who allows them small bits of

* Monograph. Eth. Survey of Cochin.

land. The trees thereon belong to the master, but they are allowed to enjoy their produce during their residence there. When not required by the master, they can work where they like. They have to work for him for six months, and sometimes throughout the year. They have little to do after the crop has been garnered. They work in the rice-fields, pumping water, erecting bunds (mud embankments), weeding, transplanting, and reaping. Men, women, and children may be seen working together. After a day's hard work in the sun or rain, they receive their wages, which they take to the nearest shop, called mattupitica (exchange shop), where they receive salt, chillies, etc., in exchange for a portion of the paddy, of which the remainder is cooked. The master's field must be guarded at night against the encroachment of cattle, and the depredations of thieves and wild beasts. They keep awake by shouting aloud, singing in a dull monotone, or beating a drum. Given a drink of toddy, the Pulayan will work for any length of time. It is not uncommon to see them thrashed for slight offences. If a man is thrashed with a thanda or leafy woman's garment, he is so much disgraced in the eyes of his fellowmen that he is not admitted into their society. Some improve their condition by becoming converts to Christianity. Others believe that the spirits of the departed would be displeased if they became Christians."

In a note on the Koragas and Holeyas of South Canara,* Mr. Ullal Raghavendra Rao writes as follows. "The destined slave is washed and anointed with oil, and

* Ind. Ant. III, 1874.

new clothes are given him. The master takes a plate, pours some water into it, and drops in a piece of gold. The slave drinks the water, takes some earth from his future master's estate, and throws it on such spot as he chooses for his use, which is then given over to him, with the trees thereon. Although these slaves are in a degraded condition, yet they appear to be by no means dejected or unhappy. A male slave gets three hanis of paddy or a hani and-a-half of rice daily, besides a small quantity of salt. The female slave gets two hanis of paddy or one hani of rice, and, if they be man and wife, they may easily sell a portion of their rice, and procure other necessaries. They are also allowed one cloth each every year, and besides, when transferred from one master to another, they get a cocoanut, a jack-tree and a spot in which they can sow a quarter or half a mura of paddy. The greater number of slaves belong to the aliya santānam* castes, and, among these people, a male slave is sold for three Bhaudri pagodas,† and a female slave for five pagodas; whereas the few slaves who follow the makkala santānam ‡ custom fetch five pagodas for the man, and only three pagodas for the woman. This is because the children of the latter go to the husband's master, while those of the aliya santānam slaves go to the mother's master, who also has the benefit of the husband's services. He has, however, to pay the expenses of their marriage, which amount to a pagoda and-a-half; and, in like manner, the master of the

* Aliya santānam. Inheritance in the female line.

† Pagoda. A gold coin, worth Rs. 3-8-0.

‡ Makkala santanam. Inheritance in the male line.

makkala santānam slave pays two pagodas for his marriage, and gets possession of the female slave and children The master has the power of hiring out his slaves, for whose services he receives annually one mura of rice. They are also mortgaged for three or four pagodas."

The following account of slavery among the Holeyas of Mysore is taken from the Census report, 1891, where it is stated that "in the malnād the Holaya degenerated into the agrestic slave, and till a few decades ago under the British rule, not only as regards his property but also with regard to his body, he was not his own master. The vargdār, or land-holder, owned him as a hereditary slave. The genius of British rule has emancipated him, and his enfranchisement has been emphasised by the allurements of the coffee industry with its free labour and higher wages . . . . The Holaya in the far west of the province still continues in many respects the bondsman of the local land holder of influence, and some of the social customs now prevailing among the Holayas fully bear out this fact. In most of the purely malnād or hilly talūks, each vargdār owns a set of servants styled Huttālu or Huttu-Alu and Mannālu or Mannu-Alu. The former is the hereditary servitor of the family, born in servitude, and performing agricultural work for the land-holder from father to son. The latter is a serf attached to the soil, and changes hands with it. These are usually of the Holaya class. In order to rivet the ties which bind these hereditary labourers to the soil, it is alleged that the local capitalists have improvised a kind of Gretna Green marriage among them. A legal marriage of the orthodox type contains the risk of a female servant being lost to the family in case the husband happened not to be a Huttālu or Mannālu. So, in order to obviate the possible loss, a custom prevails, according to which a female Huttālu or Mannālu is espoused in what is locally known as the manikattu form, which is neither more nor less than licensed concubinage. She may be given up after a time, subject to a small fine to the caste, and anybody else may then espouse her on like conditions. Not only does she thus remain in the family, but her children will also become the landlord's servants."

Until recent years the Kottai Vellālas, who live within a mud fort at Srivaiguntam in the Tinnevelly district, housed within the fort certain prædial slaves (kottar or smiths) of inferior social status. "These slaves," Mr. Boyle writes,* "partly from the changed social atmosphere of the time, and partly from want of sufficient space within the fort, have within the last generation been turned out to live beyond the enclosure, but they still work for their hereditary masters at rates fixed far more by custom than the competition of the market."

In a note on the privileges of servile castes Mr. M. J. Walhouse writes † that "it is well known that the servile castes in Southern India once held far higher positions, and were indeed masters of the land on the arrival of the Brāhmanical race. Many curious vestiges of

* Ind. Ant. III, 1874.

† *Ibid.*

their ancient power still survive in the shape of certain privileges, which are jealously cherished, and, their origin being forgotten, are much misunderstood. These privileges are remarkable instances of survivals from an extinct state of society—shadows of long-departed supremacy, bearing witness to a period when the present haughty high-caste races were suppliants before the ancestors of degraded classes, whose touch is now regarded as pollution. At the bull-games (jellikattu) at Dindigul in the Madura district, which have some resemblance to Spanish bull-fights, and are very solemn celebrations, the Kallar, or robber caste, can alone officiate as priests, and consult the presiding deity. On this occasion they hold quite a Saturnalia of lordship and arrogance over the Brāhmans. In the great festival of Sīva at Trivalūr in Tanjore, the head-man of the Parēyars is mounted on the elephant with the god, and carries his chauri. In Madras, at the annual festival of the goddess of the Black Town, when a tāli is tied round the neck of the idol in the name of the entire community, a Parēyan is chosen to represent the bridegroom. In Madras, too, the mercantile caste (Kōmatis), and in Vizagapatam the Brāhmans, had to go through the form of asking the consent of the lowest castes to their marriage, though the custom has now died out. At Mēlkote in Mysore, the chief seat of the followers of Rāmanuja Achārya, and at the Brāhman temple at Bēlur, the Holeyas or Parēyars have the right of entering the temple on three days in the year, specially set apart for them." At Mēlkote the Holeyas and Mādigas are said to have been granted the privilege of entering the *sanctum sanctorum* along with Brāhmans and others on three days by Rāmanuja. In 1799, however, the right to enter the temple was stopped at the dhvaja-stambham, or consecrated monolithic column. Besides the privilege of entering the temple, the Holeyas and Mādigas have the right to drag the car At both Bēlur and Mēlkote, as soon as the festival is over, the temples are ceremonially purified. It is said that the Brāhmans in Mysore consider that great luck will wait upon them, if they can manage to pass through the Holeya quarter of a village unmolested, and that, should a Brāhman attempt to enter their quarters, they turn out in a body and slipper him, in former times, it is said to death.*

Should a Brāhman venture into a paracheri (Paraiyan quarter), water with which cow-dung has been mixed, is thrown over his head, and he is driven out. Some Brāhmans consider an abandoned paracheri an auspicious site for an agrahāra (Brāhman quarter). At the festival of Gangamma at Palmanēr † a Paraiyan assists the Tsākali (washerman) pūjāri, and, during the period of the ceremonies, he is allowed to wear the sacred thread of the twice-born † "Paraiyans," the Rev. A. C. Clayton writes, ‡ "are allowed to take part in pulling the cars of the idols in the great festivals of Conjeevaram, Kumbakonam and Srīvilliputtūr. Their touch is not reckoned to defile the ropes used, so that other Hindus will also pull with them. With this may be compared the fact that the Telugu Mālas are custodians of the

* J. S. F. Mackenzie, Ind. Ant., II, 1873.

† Manual of the North Arcot district.

‡ Madras Museum Bull. V., 2, 1906.

goddess Gauri, the bull Nandi, and Ganēsa, the chief gods of the Saiva Kāpus and Balijas." The Mālas of the Bellary district are considered to be the servants of the Banajigas (traders) for whom they act as caste messengers on the occasion of marriages and funerals. At marriages, six Mālas, selected from certain families, lead the procession carrying flags, etc., and sit in the verandah of the marriage house. At funerals a Māla carries the brass ladle bearing the insignia of the right hand section, which is the emblem of the authority of the Dēsai (head man of the section). At a Kamma funeral, when the corpse reaches a spot which is made to represent the temple of Arichandra, the bier is set down, and a Paraiyan or Māla repeats the following formula. "I am the first born (*i.e.*, the representative of the oldest caste). I wore the sacred thread at the outset. I am Sangu Paraiyan (or Reddi Māla). I was the patron of Arichandra. Lift the corpse, and turn it round with its head towards the smāsanam (burning-ground), and feet towards the house."

During the celebration of village festivals in some places, an unmarried Mādiga woman, called for the occasion Mātangi (a favourite deity), abuses and spits upon the people assembled, and they do not take this as an insult, because they think that her spittle removes the pollution. The woman is, indeed, regarded as the incarnation of the goddess herself. Similarly, the Mālas use very obscene language when the god is taken in procession to the streets of the caste people.* In an exceedingly interesting account of the festival of the

* Madras Census report, 1891.

village goddess Uramma, at Kudligi in the Bellary district, Mr. F. Fawcett writes as follows. "The Mādiga Basivis (dedicated prostitutes) are given alms, and join in the procession. A quantity of rice and rāgi (grain: *Eleusine Coracana*) flour is poured into a basket, over which one of the village servants cuts the throat of a small black ram. The carcase is laid on the bloody flour, and the whole covered with old cloths, and placed on the head of a Mādiga, who stands for some time in front of the goddess. The goddess is then carried a few yards, the Mādiga walking in front, while a hole is dug close to her, and the basket of bloody flour and the ram's carcase are buried. After some dancing by the Mādiga Basivis to the music of the tom-tom, the Mādigas bring five new pots, and worship them. A buffalo, devoted to the goddess after the last festival, is then driven or dragged through the village with shouting and tom-toming, walked round the temple, and beheaded by the Mādiga in front of the goddess. The head is placed in front of her, with the right foreleg in the mouth, and a lamp, lighted eight days previously, is placed on top. All then start in procession round the village, a Mādiga naked but for a few margosa leaves, and held by two others, leading the way. Behind him are all the other Mādigas, carrying six hundred seers of cholam (millet: *Sorghum*), which they scatter; and, following them, all the other villagers. . . . . The Mādiga is said to be in mortal terror while leading the procession, for the spirit or influence of the goddess comes over him. He swoons before the procession is completed. At noon the people collect again at Uramma's temple, where a purchased buffalo is sacrificed. The head is placed in front of the goddess as before, and removed at once for food. Then those of the lower Sūdra castes, and Mādigas who are under vows, come dressed in margosa leaves, with lamps on their heads, and sacrifice buffaloes, sheep, and goats to the goddess."

In an account of a village festival in the Cuddapah district, Bishop Whitehead informs us * that two buffaloes are brought by the Mādigas and Mālas One of the Mālas, called the Asādi, chants the praises of the goddess during the ceremony. The animals are killed by a Mādiga, by cutting their throats with a knife, one being offered to Peddamma, and the other to Chinnamma. Some of the cholam is then taken in baskets, and put under the throats of the buffaloes till it is soaked with blood, and then put aside. A Mādiga then cuts off the heads of the buffaloes with a sword, and puts them before the idol. He also cuts off one of the forelegs of each, and puts it crosswise in the mouth. Some of the cholam is then put on the two heads, and two small earthen saucers put upon it. The stomachs are then cut open, and some of the fat taken out, melted, and put in each saucer with a lighted wick. A layer of fat is spread over the eyes and mouths of the two heads, some of the refuse of the stomach is mixed with the cholam soaked in blood, and a quantity of margosa leaves put over the cholam. The Asādi then takes some of the mixture, and sprinkles it round the shrine three times, saying Kō bāli, *i.e.*, accept the sacrifice. Then the basket is given to another Māla, who asks permission from the village officials and ryots to sprinkle the cholam. He also asks that a lamb may be

* Madras Diocesan Record, April, 1905.

killed. The lamb is killed by a washerman, and the blood allowed to flow on to the cholam in the basket. The bowels of the lamb are taken out, and tied round the wrist of the Māla." A procession is formed, and other lambs are sacrificed during the course of it. Part of the flesh of one of the buffaloes, which have been sacrificed, is given to five Māla children, called Siddhulu, *i.e.*, holy or sinless; the rest is eaten by the Mālas.

At the chāl (furrow) ceremony in Malabar, "the master of the house, the cultivation agent, and Cherumars (agrestic slaves), assemble in the barn. A portion of the yard in front of the building is painted with rice-water, and a lighted bell-lamp is placed near at hand with some paddy and rice, and several cups made of the leaves of the kanniram (*Strychnos Nux vomica*) as many cups as there are varieties of seed in the barn. Then, placing implicit faith in his gods and deceased ancestors, the master of the house opens the barn-door, followed by the Cheruman with a new painted basket containing the leaf-cups. The master then takes a handful of seed from a seed-basket, and fills one of the cups, and the cultivating agent, head Cheruman, and others who are interested in a good harvest, fill the cups till the seeds are exhausted. The basket, with the cups, is next taken to the decorated portion of the yard. A new ploughshare is fastened to a new plough, and a pair of cattle brought on to the scene. Plough, cattle, and basket are all painted with rice-water. A procession proceeds to the fields, on reaching which the head Cheruman lays down the basket, and makes a mound of earth with the spade. To this a little manure is added, and the master throws a handful of seed into it.

The cattle are then yoked, and one turn is ploughed by the head Cheruman. Inside this at least seven furrows are made, and the plough is dropped to the right. An offering is made to Ganapathi, and the master throws some seed into a furrow. Next the head Cheruman calls out "May the gods on high, and the deceased ancestors bless the seed which has been thrown broadcast, and the cattle which are let loose; the mother and children of the house, the master, and the slaves, may they also vouchsafe to us a good crop, good sunshine, and good harvest."* At the ceremony in Malabar, when the transplantation of rice is completed, during which a goat is sacrificed to Mūni, the protector of cattle and field labourers, the officiating priest is generally the cultivation agent of the family, who is a Nāyar, or sometimes a Cheruman.†

By the Penal Code it is enacted that—

Whoever imports, exports, removes, buys, sells, or disposes of any person as a slave, or accepts, receives, or detains against his will any person as a slave, shall be punished with imprisonment for a term which may extend to seven years, and shall also be liable to a fine.

Whoever habitually imports, exports, removes, buys, sells, traffics or deals in slaves, shall be punished with transportation for life, or with imprisonment for a term not exceeding ten years, and shall be liable to a fine.

Whoever unlawfully compels any person to labour against the will of that person, shall be punished with imprisonment for a term which may extend to one year, or with a fine, or with both.

* C. Karunakara Menon, Madras Mus. Bull., V, 2, 1905.
† *Ibid.*

MAKING FIRE BY FRICTION, FLINT AND STEEL.

The making of fire by friction with two pieces of wood is still extensively practised by the hill and jungle tribes, who live remote from weekly markets where lucifer matches are sold.

At the Meriah sacrifice in Ganjam, the flesh of the sacrificed victim, cut off by the villagers, was buried, and the bowels, lungs, liver, and other internal organs were cremated in a fire kindled with fire made by friction. Among the Nambūtiri Brāhmans, the sacred fire for sacrifices should be produced by the friction of two pieces of wood. And, during their marriage rites, fire is made with pieces of the wood of the jāk tree and pīpal (*Ficus religiosa*).*

Fire is, in these advanced days, obtained by the Todas in their dwelling huts for domestic purposes from matches. The men who came to be operated on with my measuring instruments had no hesitation in asking for a match, and lighting the cheroots which were distributed among them, before they left the bungalow dining-room. Within the precincts of the dairy-temple the use of matches is strictly forbidden, and fire is kindled with the aid of two dry sticks of *Litsæa Wightiana*. Of these one, terminating in a blunt convex extremity is about 2′ 3″ long ; the other, with a hemispherical cavity scooped

* F. Fawcett. Madras Mus. Bull., III, 1, 1900.

out close to one end, about $2\frac{1}{2}''$ in length. A little nick or slot is cut on the edge of the shorter stick, and connected with the hole in which the spindle stick is made to revolve. "In this slot the dust collects, and, remaining in an undisturbed heap, seemingly acts as a muffle to retain the friction-heat until it reaches a sufficiently high temperature, when the wood-powder becomes incandescent."* Into the cavity in the short stick the end of the longer sticks fits, so as to allow of easy play. The smaller stick is placed on the ground, and held tight by firm pressure of the great toe applied to the end furthest from the cavity, into which a little finely powdered charcoal is inserted. The larger stick is then twisted vigorously, "like a chocolate muller" (Tylor), between the palms of the hands by two men, turn and turn about, until the charcoal begins to glow. Fire, thus made, is said to be used at the tiriēri (sacred mand or dwelling place), the dairy-houses of ordinary mands, and at the cremation of males. In an account of a Toda green funeral,† Mr. Walhouse notes that, "when the pile was completed, fire was obtained by rubbing two dry sticks together. This was done mysteriously and apart, for such a mode of obtaining fire is looked upon as something secret and sacred." At a Toda funeral (of a female), I provided a box of tändstickers for lighting the pyre. A fire-stick, which was in current use in a dairy, was polluted, and rendered useless, by the touch of my Brāhman assistant! It is recorded by Harkness that a Brāhman was not only

* R. Bache. Royal Magazine, Aug. 1901. † Ind. Ant. III, 1874.

refused admission to a Toda dairy, but actually driven away by some boys, who rushed out of it when they heard him approach. Like the Todas, the Nāyādis of Malabar produce fire with two sticks of *Litsæa sebifera*, in the shorter of which a cavity is scooped out. They do not, like the Todas, put powdered charcoal into the cavity, but ignite a cotton rag by means of the red-hot wood dust produced by the friction. A very similar method is in vogue among the Yānādis of Nellore (plate XXVII). The cavity scooped out in the smaller stick is square instead of round. No charcoal powder is used, but a rag or dried leaves are set fire to. The sticks are obtained from the following trees:—*Protium caudatum*, *Bauhinia racemosa*, *Ficus, sp.*, *Stereospermum suberifolium*, and a tree belonging to the order Laurineæ. The Yānādis of Sriharikota make fire with dried twigs of the female *Cordia monoica*. The twigs of the male tree are said not to answer the purpose so well. I have seen a Kānikar of Travancore use as an impromptu twirling stick the blunt end of an arrow (plate XXVIII).

In making fire by friction, the Kotas of the Nīlgiris employ three forms of apparatus:—(1) a vertical and horizontal stick with sockets and grooves, both made of twigs of *Rhodomyrtus tomentosus*; (2) a small piece of the root of *Salix tetrasperma* is spliced into a stick, which is rotated in a socket in a piece of the root of the same tree. (3) a small piece of the root of this tree, made tapering at each end with a knife or fragment of bottle glass, is firmly fixed in the wooden handle of a drill. A shallow cavity and groove are made in a block of the same wood,

Plate XXVII.

Yānādis making Fire.

Plate XXVIII.

Kānikars making Fire.

and a few crystalline particles from the ground are dropped into the cavity. The block is placed on several layers of cotton cloth, on which chips of wood, broken up small by crushing them in the palm of the hand, are piled up round the block in the vicinity of the groove. The handle is, by means of a half cocoanut shell, pressed firmly down, and twisted between the palms, or rotated by means of a cord. The incandescent particles, falling on to the chips, ignite them. The Kota pūjāri must for all purposes, domestic or ceremonial, use fire made by friction, and he keeps a broken pot, in which fire should be constantly kept up. The other priest, called tērkāran or dēvādi, when he requires fire, takes it from the pūjāri.

By the Badagas of the Nīlgiris fire is made by friction (niligolu or upright stick) at the annual fire-walking ceremony. The vertical stick is made of a twig of *Rhodomyrtus tomentosus*, which is rotated in a socket in a long thick piece of a branch of *Debregeasia velutina*, in which a row of sockets has been made. The rotation is produced by a cord passed several times round the vertical stick, of which each end is pulled alternately. The horizontal block is pressed firmly on the ground by the toes of a man, who presses a half cocoanut shell down on the top of the vertical stick, so as to force it down into the cavity (plate XXVIIIa). A Badaga, who failed in an attempt to demonstrate the making of fire by this method, gave as an excuse that he was under worldly pollution, from which he would be free at the time of the fire-walking rite. Though the Badagas make fire by friction, reference is made, in their folk legends, not to this method of obtaining fire, but to chakkamukki (flint and steel,) which is repeatedly mentioned in connection with cremation.

Concerning the making of fire by the Kurumbas of the Mysore forests, Mr. Theobald writes as follows. "They follow the same method as the Todas, but never use powdered charcoal in the cavity of the horizontal stick, which is held down by their feet or by a companion. The fine brown powder formed during the rotation of the longer vertical stick gives sufficient tinder, which soon ignites, and is placed on a small piece of cotton rag rolled loosely, and blown gently until it catches fire. The vertical stick is held between the palms, and has a reciprocal motion by the palms being moved in opposite directions, at the same time using a strong downward pressure, which naturally brings the palms to the bottom. They are then at once raised to their original position, and the operation is continued till the naturally formed tinder ignites."

The following description, by a native correspondent, of fire-making by the Pulayans of Travancore may be quoted as an example of the difficulties with which a Superintendent of Ethnography in India has to struggle. "They know how to make fire, *i.e.*, by friction of wood as well as stone, etc. They take a triangular cut of stone & 1 flat oblong size flat. They hit one another with the maintenance of coir or cotton, then fire sets immediately, & also by rubbing the 2 barks frequently with each other they make fire."

The Paniyans, who dwell at the base of the western ghāts in Malabar, make fire by what is known as the Malay or sawing method (plate XXIX). A portion of a

Plate XXVIII-A.

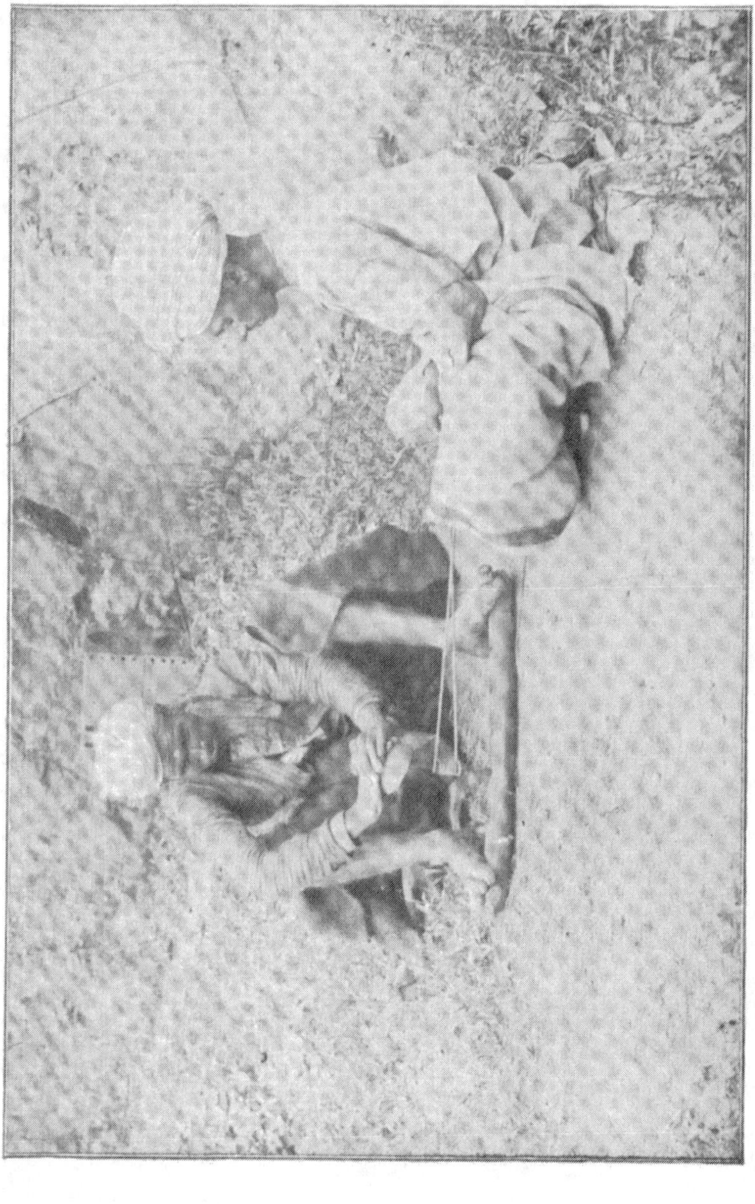

Badagas making Fire.

Plate XXIX.

bamboo stem, about one foot in length, in which two nodes are included, is split longitudinally into two equal parts. On one half a sharp edge is cut with a knife. In the other a longitudinal slit is made through about two-thirds of its length, which is stuffed with a piece of cotton cloth. The latter is held firmly on the ground with its convex surface upwards, and the cutting edge drawn, with a gradually quickening sawing motion, rapidly to and fro across it by two men, until the cloth is ignited by the incandescent particles of wood in the groove cut by the sharp edge. The cloth is then blown with the lips into a blaze, and the tobacco or cooking fire can be lighted.

The following account of the sawing method of making fire, as carried out by a hill-man in Vizagapatam, is given by a correspondent of the Indian Antiquary. * "He took a piece of dry bamboo, split it lengthways, and cut a notch on the convex side. He then tore a bit of rag from his cloth, and placed it on the ground under the notched bamboo, which he held tightly between his toes. He then got a bit of dry tamarind wood, and, cutting a knife-edge on it, shaped it to fit into the notch. He then rubbed this stick violently to and fro in the notch, until dust began to drop on the cloth. By and by the dust-laden cloth began to smoke, and, after perhaps two minutes, he took it up and blew the cloth into a flame."

By some tribes the fire-sticks are collected during the hot dry season, and stacked above the kitchen fire, so that, when the rainy season ensues, a stock of dry wood

* Vol. III, 1879.

for making fire is available. Everyone familiar with life in India during the rains knows the state of temper produced by effects to light a cheroot from a box of matches made with red phosphorus. And the jungle man, with his more primitive but effective method, has the advantage over the cultured European.

Turning now to the use of the flint and steel. The Kādirs of the Ánaimalai hills make fire by means of an iron bar, a piece of quartz as a strike-a-light, and the floss of the silk-cotton tree (*Bombax malabaricum*), over which powdered charcoal has been rubbed. The Irulas of Chingleput employ for this purpose a piece of the pithy stem of *Æschynomene aspera*, in the upper surface of which a small cavity is scooped out. Against the pith an angular fragment of quartz is held firmly, and, by means of a smart and dexterous blow thereon from a flat iron instrument hollowed out on one side to support the thumb, a spark is made to fall on the pith, which is blown into a blaze. A rather more elaborate apparatus is used by one of the jungle tribes of Travancore. The man carries in his tobacco and betel bag a little box made from a bamboo stem with a node as its bottom, which is stuffed with silk floss (*Bombax ?*), and also holds a piece of quartz, and a flat piece of iron. Fire is obtained, as in the previous case, by igniting the floss with a spark from the quartz. I could not but admire the skill of the expert tribesmen, who were amused at my efforts to strike a light, which only produced a maimed thumb. By the Chenchus of the Nallamalai hills the floss of *Eriodendron anfractuosum* is used instead of that of *Bombax*.

FIRE-WALKING.

> Moxque per ardentes stipulæ crepitantis acervos,
> Trajicias celeri strenua membra pede.
>
> OVID. FASTI.

THE ceremonial observance of walking through hot ashes (fête de feu) is very widespread throughout Southern India. As a typical example thereof, an account* may be given of the ceremony as it took place at St. Thomas' Mount, near the city of Madras, in 1901. The festival took place in connection with a small temple dedicated to the goddess Draupati, the polyandrous wife of the five Pāndavas, who, to prove her chastity during their absence in exile, submitted to the trial by ordeal of walking through fire. The celebration of the festival, it is believed, secures to the villagers their cattle and crops, and protection from dangers of all kinds. An individual who suffers from any chronic complaint makes a vow in the name of the goddess that, if he is cured, he will walk over fire. If he who takes the vow is poor, he must wait till a celebration takes place. But, if he is a man of means, he brings about the festival at his own cost. For ten days before the fire-walking special worship of the goddess was performed thrice daily. In the temple was recited the Māhābarata

* H. K. Beauchamp. Wide World Magazine; and Madras Mail, 1901.

in Tamil to hundreds of people gathered about the premises by a pūjāri (priest). And, every night, portions of the Māhābarata were acted in primitive village fashion to several hundred spectators. A day or two before the last day of the festival the vow-taker, after bathing, goes to the temple dressed in a saffron-dyed cloth, and gets the priest to tie a piece of saffron-dyed thread, with a bit of saffron attached to it, to his right hand (to the left in a woman). He sleeps in the temple at night, and is denied access to the interior of his house. The devotee observes a fast on the day of the fire-walking, and, early in the morning, goes to the temple, and worships the goddess along with others who have taken similar vows. They then bathe in a tank, to secure perfect cleanness of the body. Meanwhile, about midday, the temple servants heaped fuel on a permanent platform on an open space of ground. In this instance the fuel was a ton of jungle wood, and two cart-loads of charcoal. The vow-takers returned from their bathing, and set fire to the fuel heaped on the platform. At the end of the platform a shallow trench had been dug, in which the wood and charcoal were burnt, until the whole was a mass of glowing embers. These were then racked out of the trench, and spread evenly to a depth of three or four inches over a space, some five yards square, marked out in the centre of the platform. The trench, when cleared of the embers, was partially filled with water, and all round the area of red-hot cinders water was freely sprinkled. An hour before the fire-walking, the vow-takers assembled near the platform with the priest, who, to satisfy himself that all was right with the devotees, performed three tests, the first of which consisted of balancing a sword on its tip on the rim of an earthen pot. In the second test the priest put a few pieces of burning charcoal in a towel dipped in saffron-water, without the cloth being affected. The third and last test was that a few flowers and limes, thrown into the lap of the idol a few days before, had kept fresh. [In some villages round Madras the pūjāri used to place a few red hot cinders in the lap of the idol, and it was regarded as a bad sign if the cloth on which they were deposited became burnt. The falling of a flower from the wreath of the idol to the right was regarded as a good sign]. The procession of the goddess Draupati, followed by images of Krishna and Arjuna, started from the temple a little after 6 P.M. and wended its way through the dense crowd to the scene of the fire-walking ceremony. The idols were placed in front of the platform, and, after worship had been offered, the priest, decked with garlands and clad in a yellow cloth, walked over the embers with measured steps and quite calmly. The other devotees then rushed on to the platform, and walked over the glowing cinders to the other side, where they cooled their feet in a puddle of water (the pāl-kuli or milk pit). The glowing embers were loose, not beaten down or flattened in any way, and the feet of the fire-walkers, as they passed through, actually sank into the loose bed of fire. This was particularly noticeable in the case of the pūjāri during his calm and deliberate passage. Neither he, nor the devotees, lifted their feet high. They seemed rather to wade through the embers, as through shallow water. The relations of the performers were waiting on the other side to receive them. These covered them with new cloths, gave them something to drink, and conducted them home. An interesting feature of the ceremony was that a boy about eight years old walked over the embers, while a still smaller child was hurried over, hanging on to its father's hand. A few performers, too, carried children across on their shoulders. One young man, who went through the ordeal, carrying a decorated pot on his head, took part in a cricket match on the following day. A few of those who took part in the ceremony were questioned whether they felt any pain, or whether they protected their feet by rubbing them with the juice of some plant. The suggestion was received with resentment, and considered profane. The most common explanation of the immunity from burning is that a decoction of the *Aloe indica* is used. It is said that the fleshy part of the leaves is bruised, and squeezed through flannel. A glutinous juice is thus extracted, not unlike castor-oil in consistency. This is rubbed into the skin of the feet, and palms of the hands. The hair, beard, and eyebrows are also thoroughly saturated with it. After a careful and thorough anointing, the devotee is able to pass over glowing embers without hurt. He is, it is said, even able to drag a red-hot chain through his hands, and to comb his hair and beard with a red-hot metal comb. Many of those assembled at the ceremony took away with them some of the sacred ashes, to be used as a charm to drive away devils and demons.

As showing the simple faith in the ceremony, the sad evidence, given at the inquest by the mother of a young man who died as the result of tumbling into the fire-pit, may be cited.* "Pakkiri, who is lying here a corpse, is my son. He was attacked with jaundice, and I made a vow of treading fire for it. He got well. So he trod the fire last year and the year before. But this year his fate came upon him. I am blind of both eyes. I did not go with Pakkiri to the fire-treading. I went when I heard news that he had fallen into the fire and been burnt. I and my daughter carried him home. He died last night." In commenting on this case, Mr. Andrew Lang, says † that "Mr. Stokes explains that 'the fire would hardly injure the tough skin of the sole of a labourer's feet.' Yet it killed a boy"! But it must be borne in mind that, both in this case and the one from Tinnevelly quoted hereafter (p. 485), the individuals died as the result of severe burns on a part of the body where the skin is less thick than on the sole of the foot.

At a fire-walking ceremony in Mysore a few years ago, the devotees were clad in wet garments. The god having been carried thrice round the pit, the female devotees were conducted thereto, and several shovelfuls of the glowing embers thrown over their heads. The men walked over the ashes, and a quantity of ghī and milk was then poured over them. The priest then proclaimed that nobody could walk over the ashes without receiving hurt. The Abbé Dubois notes ‡ that those, whose weak

* H. J. Stokes. Ind. Ant. II, 1873. † Magic and Religion, 1901.

‡ Hindu Manners, Customs and Ceremonies.

limbs do not permit of their running over the hot embers, cover the upper part of the body with a wet cloth, and, holding a chafing dish filled with burning coals, pour the contents over their heads. This feat is called the fire-bath.

Some Dombs in Vizagapatam are reputed to have been able to pour blazing oil over their bodies. And a Domb man is said to have had a miraculous power of hardening his skin, so that any one could have a free shot at him without hurting him. Some Dāsaris (religious mendicants) exhibit the Panda sērvai performance, which consists in affecting to be possessed by the spirit of a deity, and beating themselves all over the body with a flaming torch, after covering it probably with some protecting substance.*

In Malabar a class of pseudo-Brāhmans derive their name of Tīyāttunni or Tīyādi (fire-play) from the ceremony of jumping through fire before temples. And, on the west coast, when celebrations are held in honour of Chāmundi, a much dreaded female divinity, the dancer who represents, and is supposed to be possessed by her, dances and rolls upon a pile of burning embers without any injury.†

At the annual fire-walking ceremony of the Badagas of the Nīlgiris, the local deity, in token of a vow to whom a long plait of hair is worn, is propitiated with a four-anna piece, a cocoanut, camphor, incense, and flowers. Prior to walking through the ashes, jasmine

* Manual of the N. Arcot district.

† M. J. Walhouse. Ind. Ant., VII, 1878.

or rhododendron flowers are thrown thereon, and, if the omens are favourable, is said not to be singed. So too, milk poured on the ashes is said not to produce a hissing noise. Fortified by their belief, in the goodwill of the god, they go through the ceremonial. And, if any one suffers hurt therefrom, he takes it as a proof of the displeasure of the deity. The Harava (jumper) sept of the Badagas is said to be so called from the rite, in which they leap over fire. It was noted by an eye-witness that "no preparation, or application of any anti-fire lotion was in evidence. The only suspicious fluid about was the cocoanut milk flooding the floor, in which all fire-walkers, as well as non-fire-walkers, trampled alike. I examined the feet of one of the men, and one of the women, who went through the ceremony, but, beyond black impressions on the soles, there was no marked injury." Sometimes the Badagas drive their cattle, which have recovered from sickness, over the burning embers in performance of a vow.

In a picturesque account of a ceremony of walking through fire at Nuagada (or Nuvagōde) in Ganjam, Mr. S. P. Rice writes as follows.* "A holy man comes forth, a fire is kindled—no small fire of twigs, but a blaze of jungle faggots, the flames leaping up breast-high. Through this the inspired one walks unharmed, and proceeds to take his seat on a pile of sharp, strong thorns, raised about two feet from the ground, and woven in the form of a stool about two feet square.

* Occasional Notes on Native South Indian Life, 1901.

This is the crucial test. So lightly clad as to be almost naked, he takes his seat on the forbidding throne. If he is truly inspired, the thorns will break beneath him, or will be turned aside, powerless to pierce his divinely protected skin. But woe unto that man, into whom the true god has not entered! Not for him will the thorns fall away harmless: he shall taste to the full the bitterness of his presumption." To Mr. J. G. D. Partridge I am indebted for the following account of the Ganjam ceremony, at which he was present as an eye-witness. "In the village of Nuvagōde, situated in the Surangi zamindary, a fire-walking ceremony is performed once a year, during the Dassara festival, by the priest of the temple of a village goddess. I arrived at this village on the morning of the 6th October, 1902, and saw the preparations that had been made for the ceremony, which was to take place that night. A pit, six to nine inches deep, and about nine feet long and four feet broad, had been dug in a field close to the temple, and was filled with the ashes of a wood fire, which had been burning during the day. Alongside this pit, and separated by about six inches, was another of the same size filled with embers. At 9 P.M. the Zamindar of Surangi sent word that the priest was about to begin, and that, before walking over the fire, he would sit on a seat of thorns, during which time he was endowed with prophetic powers. A most fantastic spectacle, which no European had perhaps ever been fortunate enough to witness, presented itself before me. The villagers, with several hundred people from the neighbourhood, all Uriyas filled the street, and in the middle, to the sound of twenty drums and many horns, danced the priest of the goddess, a young man, with a bare sword in his right hand. He was dressed as a woman, with rows of silver bells round his waist, and a large head-dress covered with feathers. I had seen him in the morning in the little temple of the goddess called Koraisani, and should not have recognised him in the peculiar dress he now wore. He seemed perfectly frenzied, and leapt about. But he was well aware of everything that went on, as, in addition to his dancing, he acted as master of the ceremonies, rushing about in the crowd, talking to the Zamindar, and telling me when all was ready for his performances. The thorn seat was hanging like a swing from a small upright stand. The sticks were closely interlaced, and the thorns projected two or three inches from them. He placed a small cloth on the thorns, and then jumped into the seat, holding on to ropes at the sides, but allowing his whole weight to rest on the seat. When he had done this for several minutes, I found that the thorns had pierced the small cloth, but, as far as I could see, had not hurt the priest. His clothes were thin, and afforded no protection from the thorns. He constantly stupified himself by inhaling incense from a small censer, and I presume that he felt no pain in consequence of this. There were no signs of blood, however, on his body. He claimed no special powers, though his sensations must have been in some way deadened when he sat on the thorns. He did not invite any of the spectators to follow his example; and he would certainly not have found any one anxious to imitate him. About this time he thought he could inform me of the contents of my pocket, but unfortunately his prophetic powers failed. He said I had one rupee and some gold, but I had five rupees and no gold. No other attempt was made to test his powers in this line. He next went to the fire-pits, which were a mass of red-hot ashes; sprinkled not more than a handful of incense on to them; dipped his feet in a mixture of rice-water and milk; and walked across one pit, leading another man. He then dipped his feet again in the fluid mixture, and returned by the other pit. The time he took in walking across one pit was not more than four seconds, and he took about four steps on the ashes. At least fifty persons in the crowd walked over the pits afterwards, but they went a little faster than the priest, and some of them only took two steps on the ashes. Their feet were not hurt, and they did not wash them in any mixture before or after they went over the ashes. I infer from the way in which the performance was conducted that any one can easily walk rapidly over the ashes, but that, if he goes like the priest, he must dip his feet in the mixture both before and after walking across them. The priest tried to convince a gentleman near me, who was rather sceptical, that it would not hurt him, if he walked over the ashes, but this person was quite satisfied with seeing others perform. The priest only walked once across the two pits, and he afterwards danced for an hour, when I thought it time to depart. The performance takes place every year."

An observant friend, who witnessed a fire-walking ceremony some years ago in one of the southern districts, informs me that nine-tenths of the performers were youngsters, who evidently did it for a lark.

In a note on a fire-walking festival in Travancore Mr. G. F. D'Penha writes as follows.* "We could not see how hot the cinders were. But, judging from the look of them when we first arrived on the scene, and the length of time that elapsed before the ceremony took place, I should not think that the walking over the pathway was such a very hazardous operation after all. The previous market day we met a young man who was to go through the ceremony, and asked him why he did it. He told me he had been ill, and had promised the god that he would go through this performance if he recovered. He got better, and so was carrying out his part of the contract. This was, he said, the third year that he had done it."

To Mr. G. H. Bernays I am indebted for the following account of a fire-walking ceremony, which he witnessed at Sivakāsi in the Tinnevelly district. "During the evening I saw a great glow in the sky, and thought that a fire must have occurred in Sivakāsi. About 9 P.M., I had to go to the bazār, to preserve order, as the Mohurrum happened to be running concurrently with a Hindu procession. After the close of the latter I went round to the mosque about 11 P.M. In front of the mosque was a circular pit with a slightly raised wall about a foot high all round, and with an opening on the east and west.

* Ind. Ant., XXXI, 1902.

The pit, I should say, was roughly speaking about 1 foot or 1½ feet deep, and about 8 feet in diameter. In it a huge wood fire was blazing. It was the light of this, which I had seen from my bungalow some hours before. The flames were now allowed to die down until the pit was simply a mass of glowing red-hot ashes, the heat of which was so intense as to prevent one from going within three or four yards of the pit. Soon after a procession came out from the mosque, led by a venerable old man. They formed themselves round the pit, and the old priest, standing at the east end, recited various prayers, to which the others responded. Finally a man came out of the crowd, and, entering at the east end of the pit, walked through the glowing ashes. On arriving at the centre of the pit he halted, stooped down, and, gathering some of the ashes in his hands, threw them up in the air, and allowed them to fall in a red rain upon his naked body. He then walked slowly out at the other side. He was followed by several others, who all did the same with varying degrees of pace. Meantime the crowd kept up a continuous cry of "Dīn, Dīn." Finally a gōsha woman, with a child wrapped up, was brought forward and seated near the east end of the pit, while someone (I think it was the old priest) picked up handfuls of the glowing ashes, and poured them over her, and a man near by brushed them off the woman at once, to prevent her cloth from catching fire. After this ceremony the usual Mohurrum 'tamāsha' took place. It is difficult to note what struck me most, but it was perhaps a sense of mystic weirdness which was given by the dull glow of the fire, the serried ring of faces lit only by a few torches, and the figure of the old priest chanting his prayers. I felt a sense of powerlessness in the presence of a rite which I did not understand, and I think, as I looked at the faces, I began to understand a little of the meaning of 'fanaticism.' As far as I saw, no preparation was applied to the feet or body of the fire-walkers, though it may have been done inside the mosque. None of them showed any signs of hurt afterwards." I have often, in former days, wondered at the casual manner in which road coolies walk, with bare feet, over the sharp angular fragments of crystalline rock, when making a macadam road; and experience in measuring native feet has taught me how non-ticklish their soles are.

At Gūgūdu in the Anantapur district, Mr. Francis writes,* the Mohurrum is, strange to relate, entirely managed by the Hindus of the village, the Muhammadans taking but a small part in it. Hindus, to the number of several thousands, also come in for the ceremony from the adjoining villages. At the real Mohurrum, a pit is dug, and a bonfire made in it, round which lamentations over the death of Hussain and Hasan are made. In the Hindu's version of the ceremony, as at Gūgūdu, this item is developed into a regular fire-walking ceremony, which takes place twice, during the course of the Mohurrum, on the ninth and eleventh days. "First the musicians, who are Mangalas (barbers) by caste, walk through the fire, and then follow all sorts and

* Gazetter of the Anantapur district.

conditions of others, both Hindus and Muhammadans. The same thing on a smaller scale is done at the Mohurrum at Mālyavantam. The Muhammadan Pīrs at Gūgūdu are held in great veneration, and all castes, even Brāhmans it is said, make their vows to them, and distribute sugar to the poor if they are successful in obtaining the object of their desires."

It was noted some years ago, as a happy reform, by the Collector of Tanjore that, since Government set its face against the ancient practice, the people use flowers instead of fire, and tread on them devoutly in honour of the goddess.

As bearing on the subject of walking through fire, I may quote extracts from the selections from the records of the Madras Government, * which show, *inter alia*, that the ceremony is not confined to the Hindu community. In summing up the reports received from the officials of the various districts, the Government expressed its opinion that "the ceremony of walking through fire is only of partial occurrence, and can scarcely be called a religious observance, being performed for the most part in fulfilment of vows voluntarily made. The practice does not appear to be acceptable to the higher classes."

Madras.—The observance is confined to the lowest orders of the people, and the same individuals exhibit annually, like any other class of jugglers; though there are some few, who go through the supposed ordeal in fulfilment of vows.

* Reports on the swinging festival and the ceremony of walking through fire, 1854.

Ganjam.—It has been customary at Chicacole to perform this ceremony immediately after the hook-swinging festival, the same parties performing in both. The Muhammadans also, during the Mohurrum, are in the habit of passing through the fire.

North Arcot.—On the last day of the festival, a shallow pit, half a foot deep, and several yards broad and long, is filled with firewood fully ignited. The only classes who take any part in the proceedings are some of the Sūdra classes, and, for the most part, those of the least consideration and of the least range of intelligence. The Brāhmans have no concern with them.

Salem.—The Hindus observe the ceremony on the last day of some of their festivals, and it is not unusual during the Mohurrum for Muhammadans, in fulfilment of a vow, to leap in and out of the pits, in which they kindle bonfires opposite their ashoorkhānas (ten-day houses), while the embers are still burning.

Tinnevelly.—During the celebration of the Mohurrum in 1850, a Muhammadan fell accidentally into a fire-pit prepared for the ceremony of walking through, and died three days afterwards. It was reported that the accident occurred from the individual being under the influence of liquor. Since the occurrence of the accident the practice of lighting fires in pits during the Mohurrum festival has been discontinued in that village.

Godāvari.—There is one class, viz., the Lingadharloo, by whom the fire treading is regarded as an efficacious observance for recovering their sanctity if by any chance they lose their lingam (the symbol of Sīva, which they wear); but, even amongst them, it is not considered an essential ceremony.

Nellore.—In the month Madur (Jamad-ul-aval) the fakirs (Muhammadan) walk on, and roll in fires at two places at Nellore. This custom does not appear to be enjoined by their religion, but has been observed a long time in memory of their priest named Bundashaw Madar.

Kistna.—The devotee or devotees proceed to the temple or spot fixed upon with all the pomp and parade they can muster. They are excited by noisy music, and the recitation of stanzas descriptive of the attributes and miracles of the deity. Religious enthusiasm is roused to the highest pitch by the time the spot is reached, and the devotees run or hop over the coals as quickly as possible. It is said by some that the feet and legs are anointed with a preparation, which prevents the embers from affecting them. Sometimes the performers, or some of their followers, by way of making the ceremony more attractive and imposing, pierce their eyelids, tongues, the fleshy parts of their arms, etc., with narrow nails, to one or both ends of which cotton wicks are attached and ignited. Among the Muhammadans, the ceremony is sometimes observed, at the Mohurrum, before the astanam or hall where the Pīrs are installed and exhibited.

HOOK-SWINGING.

In summing up a series of reports on the swinging festival, the Government of Madras, in 1854, expressed the opinion that it "is on the whole less frequently observed now than formerly. In some few districts the practice is as prevalent as ever; in the majority, however, it is on the decline, while in none can it be called general. Further it does not seem to be in any way connected with the religion of the observers, but to be performed in fulfilment of vows. In some cases it would appear that the observance has led to loss of life. This would, of course, justify the interference of the magistracy, and, in future, any occurrence of this nature should lead to the prohibition of the ceremony of the village where it happened. The best method of discouraging this objectionable practice must be left to the discretion of the different magistrates, but the Governor in Council feels confident that, if it be properly explained that the object of Government is not to interfere with any religious observance of its subjects, but to abolish a cruel and revolting practice, the efforts of the magistracy will be willingly seconded by the influence of the great mass of the community, and more particularly of the wealthy and intelligent classes who do not seem to countenance or support the swinging ceremony."

From the Government records (1854) the following details are culled.*

* Reports on the swinging festival, and ceremony of walking through fire, 1854.

In 1852 two men were killed during the celebration of the festival in the Salem district, in consequence of the pole from which they were suspended having accidentally snapped. In the Tanjore district the festival was known to have been practised in former years in a hundred and twenty-five towns and villages, and still took place occasionally in seventy-eight places. In the Nellore district swinging festival of the following nature were observed either annually or at intervals of two to thirty years:—

(1) Gaulaupooseedy, *i.e.*, a man hung to the end of a cross beam fixed on a post by the skin, etc., of his back with iron hooks.

(2) Gumpaseedy, *i.e.*, a man sitting in a basket, or on a plank hung to the end of the iron beam thereof.

(3) Pucaseedy, *i.e.*, iron hooks fixed in the sides of a man, who has to walk round a pagoda.

(4) Tallaseedy, *i.e.*, a man hung to a post by a rope tied to his waist.

In the Kistna district there had been no swinging for several years, but the custom was reintroduced by an old pensioned Hindu Subadar. It appeared that his father's sister performed sutti 70 or 80 years since, and a temple was erected to her memory on the site of her immolation, and in commemoration of the event a swinging festival was held annually. This had ceased for many years until the return of the old subadar, when, out of respect to the memory of his relative, he restored the temple, and re-established the swinging festival at his own expense. The Paraiyans were, it is stated, the principal performers at the village swinging ceremonials, and they received from one to four rupees from a general fund subscribed by the villagers, or granted for the purpose by some public-spirited individual. In one report it is mentioned that, on the party who had been accustomed to pay the swingers having left, the villagers, afraid lest a discontinuance of the practice should be productive of calamity, took to swinging sheep and pumpkins, a much more reasonable exhibition of devotion. In cases of famine, cholera, or other calamity, a swinging festival was held for the purpose of propitiating the deity, and, at the same time, a slaughter of goats, sheep, pigs, fowls, and even male buffaloes took place. In the Canara district, on the occasion of a very extensive celebration, the swinging was combined with an extensive slaughter of animals. The pole was erected in the close vicinity of a high heap of reeking heads. All the men, women and children were in holiday attire, and hundreds of the latter were brought close to the heap of heads, and showed intense excitement and enjoyment in witnessing the struggles of the dying animals, or in hearing their shrieks.

In front of the Māriamma temple at Mūdabiduri in South Canara stands a quadrangular stone, which is hollowed out at the top. It was formerly used as a receptacle for a wooden beam, on which another beam was made to revolve at the hook-swinging festival. The necessary wooden implements are still preserved near the temple.* The apparatus for hook-swinging still lies outside the Periyapalayam temple near Madras.

* E. Hultzsch, Government Epigraphist. Annual Report, 1900–01.

Of this barbarous ceremony, as carried out at the latter end of the eighteenth century, an interesting account is given by Sonnerat, * who thus describes it. "Those who imagine they have received great benefits from Mariatale, or wish to obtain them, make a vow to suspend themselves in the air. This ceremony consists in passing two iron tenter-hooks, tied to the end of a very long lever, through the skin of the votary's back. This lever is placed at the top of a mast twenty feet high. As soon as the votary is hung on the hooks, they press the other end of the lever, and lift him up in the air. In this state they turn him round as often as he chooses. He commonly has a sword and shield in his hands, and makes the motions of a man who is fighting. He must appear cheerful, whatever pain he may feel: for, if tears escape him, he is driven from his caste, but this seldom happens. The votary who is to be hung up drinks some intoxicating liquor, which makes him almost insensible, and looks upon this dangerous preparation as a pastime. After turning him several times round, they take him off, and he is soon cured of his wounds. The quickness of the cure passes for a miracle in the eyes of the zealots of this goddess. The Brāhmans do not assist at this ceremony, which they despise. The worshippers of Mariatale are of the lowest castes."

In the early part of the last century Mr. Elijah Hoole was present as an eye-witness of a hook-swinging ceremony at Royapettah in the city of Madras, of which he

* Voyage to the East Indies and China, 1774 and 1781.

gave the following graphic description.* "A pole, thirty or forty feet high, was planted in the ground perpendicularly, having an iron pivot on the top, on which rested the middle of an horizontal yard or cross pole, which might also be about forty feet in length. This latter was managed by a rope attached to one end, reaching down to the ground, by means of which it could be made to turn upon the centre as fast as the people could run. Near the other end of the cross-pole, attached to a short rope, were two bright iron hooks, and at the extreme end was a short rope, about the length of that to which the hooks were attached. By slackening the rope for the management of the cross pole, the other end, to which the hooks were attached, was lowered to a platform higher than the heads of the assembled multitude, from whence, when it was raised, was borne into the mid-air a man, with no other dress than a waist cloth, and supported only by the muscles and flesh of the middle of the back, into which were thrust the iron hooks. When the cross pole, thus laden, had regained its horizontal position, it was turned quickly on the pivot, by the persons holding the rope at the other end moving round with it at a good pace. It was impossible to look at the deluded votary of superstition thus painfully suspended without a sickening horror, not merely from an idea of the agonies endured by him, but also from a fear lest the flesh should tear by his weight, and that, falling from a height which would ensure his destruction, he should, by death, complete the sacrifice thus offered to the infernal gods.

* Personal narrative of a mission to the South of India, 1820 to 1828.

The rising of the flesh taken up by the hooks seemed to threaten such a catastrophe, and the short rope at the extremity of the pole, being within reach of the person suspended, was perhaps intended to afford, in such a case, some chance of safety. Some of the persons thus suspended appeared fearful of falling, and held constantly by the rope, as, by this means, they perhaps hoped to relieve themselves of some degree of the pain which must be endured. Others, more bold and hardy, made no use of the rope, and, as though happy as well as fearless, thrust their hands into their cloth, and, taking out a profusion of flowers, provided for the occasion, showered them abroad amongst the people, who struggled to catch and preserve them as though they had been blessings from heaven. One fellow, by way of additional bravado, fired a pistol, which he had stuck in his waist for the purpose.* I never pressed through the assembled crowds near enough to see the hooks put into the flesh, but was told that the only means used to deaden the pain was a smart blow, given with the open hand, on that side of the back into which the hook was to be inserted. From the indifference with which they mingled with the crowd after the ceremony, and the smallness of the streams of blood I have seen trickling from the wounds, I should suppose that a less quantity of blood than would be imagined is lost by the devotees. I think I have seen five or six persons swing in one day. Swinging is neither practised nor sanctioned by the Brāhmans; at least they have disavowed it to me; and

* Sometimes the suspended man would blow a trumpet, or sing a song.

Plate XXX.

Hook-swinging.

I never observed any besides the lower classes of the Hindus conducting or participating in the ceremony. It is said to be observed in consequence of vows made in time of sickness or danger, in expiation of an offence, or for the obtaining of children or some other desired object."

"Hook-swinging," the Rev. Mr. Phillips writes, * "is performed after the consent of the goddess is obtained. If a lizard is heard chirping at the right side, it is regarded as a sign of her consent." It is believed that the man who is swung suffers no pain if the cause is a good one, but excruciating agony if it is a bad one.

It was, Moor tells us,† customary for a man to swing in performance of a vow, if he married a certain girl within a certain time. And a person might swing by proxy. He was told of a venerable dame, who came on behalf of her daughter, who had vowed to swing if the child, with which she was pregnant, was a boy. The damsel had been delivered only a short time before the arrival of swinging day, and the old lady went through the ceremony for the young woman in the straw with great resolution, and to the satisfaction of the assembled throng.

In a recent note ‡ on the Izhuvas of the Cochin State, Mr. L. K. Anantha Krishna Iyer states that "there are two kinds of hook-swinging, namely Garuda (Brāhminy kite swinging) and thoni tukkam (boat swinging). [The Brāhminy kite, *Haliastur indus*, is the vehicle of Vishnu,

* Evolution of Hinduism, 1903.

† Narrative of Little's Detachment, 1794.

‡ Monograph Eth. Survey of Cochin.

who is represented in temples as a winged human being]. The ceremony is performed in fulfilment of a vow, to obtain some favour from the deity Kāli. In the fight between Kāli and the demon Darika, the latter was completely defeated, and the former, biting him on the back, drank his blood to gratify her feelings of animosity. Hook-swinging symbolises this incident, and the blood shed by the insertion of the hook through the flesh is intended as an offering to the goddess. The performer of the ceremony should bathe early in the morning, and be in a state of preparation for a year or forty-one days by worshipping Bhagavāti. He should strictly abstain from meat, intoxicating liquors, and association with women. During the morning hours he dresses himself in a garment tucked into the waist band, rubs his body with oil, and is shampooed particularly on the back, into which the hooks will be inserted. He is also taught by his instructor to perform various feats and gesticulations called payitta. This he continues till the festival. In kite-swinging, a kind of car resting on two axles with four wheels is used. On it there is a horizontal beam resting on two vertical supports. A strong rope tied to a ring attached to the beam is connected with the hook, which passes through the flesh of the back. Over the beam there is a kutaram (tent) tastefully decorated, inside which two or three persons can swing at a time. In some places there is a different arrangement, and, instead of the beam and supports, there is a small pole, on which rests a horizontal beam provided with a metal ring at one end. The beam acts as a lever, so that one end of it can be lowered to give some rest to the swinger.

Plate XXXI.

Hook-swinging

The rope tied to the ring is connected with the hook and the waist-band. For boat-swinging the same kind of vehicle, but without wheels, is in use. For kite-swinging the performer has his face painted green, and he puts on an artificial beak and wings like those of the kite. He wears long locks of hair like those of an actor in a kathakali (Malabar drama). Various feats are performed to the accompaniment of musical instruments, and, as he swings, the car is dragged three, five, seven, nine, or eleven times round the temple. In boat-swinging the performer puts on the same kind of dress, without the beak and wings. Sometimes pillayeduthu thukkam, or swinging with a child in performance of a vow, is performed. The child is handed over to the swinger, who carries it as he swings. The swinging ceremony is performed by Nāyars, Kammālars, Kuruppans, and Izhuvas.

Of the ceremony as performed in recent years at the Kollangodu temple in Travancore, an excellent account is given by the Rev. T. Knowles,* from which the following précis has been compiled. In front of the temple was a booth containing the image of the goddess Bhadra Kāli, a cruel deity, who is supposed to delight in blood. At a little distance was the car. The bottom part of this was very much like a lorry used when transporting large logs of timber by means of elephants. There were four solid wheels of thick timber, with a framework, like a railway waggon on a small scale. To this were attached two thick cable ropes. Joined to the sides of the car

---

* Wide World Magazine, September, 1899.

were two upright posts, about 15 feet high, strengthened with stays and cross-pieces. On the top was a piece of thick timber with a hole in it, and the bottom rounded, which fitted into a cross-piece, and allowed the long beam on which the men were swung to move up or down. This beam was some 35 or 40 feet long, and about 9 inches in diameter. It was placed through the hole in the piece of timber on the top of the upright frame, and balanced in the middle like a huge see-saw. At one end of the pole was a covered canopy, and at the other long ropes were fastened, which trailed on the ground. The whole arrangement of the car was such that, by lowering one end of the long beam to the ground, and fastening a man to it, and then pulling down the other end by the ropes, the man could be raised into the air a height of some 40 feet or more. The whole car could then be dragged by the thick cable ropes round the temple. While the subject was being prepared for swinging, a mat was stretched above his head, partly to do him honour, partly to protect him from the sun. .His head and neck were richly ornamented, and below he was bedecked with peacock's feathers, and clad in a loin-cloth, which would bear some, if not all the weight of his body. Amid the firing of mortars, beating of tom-toms, the screeching of flutes, and the shouts of the crowd, the canopied end of the long beam was lowered, and the devotee, lying prone on the ground, was fastened to the beam by means of ropes passing under his arms and around his chest. To some of the ropes hooks were fastened. The priests took hold of the fleshy part of the man's back, squeezed up the flesh, and put some four hooks at least through it. A rudely fashioned sword and shield were then given to the man, and he was swung up into the air, waving the sword and shield, and making convulsive movements. Slowly the people dragged the car round the temple, a distance not quite as far as round St. Paul's cathedral. Some of the men were suspended while the car was dragged round three or four times. The next devotee was fastened in the same way to the beam, but, instead of a sword and shield, the priests gave him an infant in his arms, and devotee and infant were swung up in the air, and the car dragged round the temple as before. Some children were brought forward, whose parents had made vows about them. The little ones were made to prostrate themselves before the image of Kāli. Then the fleshy parts of their sides were pinched up, and some wires put through. This done, the wires were placed in the hands of the relatives, and the children were led round and round the temple, as though in leading strings. It is on record that, when the devotee has been specially zealous, the whole machine has been moved to a considerable distance while he was suspended from it, to the admiration of the gaping multitudes."

At Madura, Mr. Knowles states, on the occasion of a hook-swinging festival a few years ago, the devotee was swung by hooks alone, and not by ropes and hooks. The pole was longer than that used at Kollangōdu, and decorated with coloured cloth something like a barber's pole, and garlanded with flowers. Instead of it being fixed on a car, a large platform was used. The fleshy part of the man's back was first beaten to cause it to swell, and two large hooks were fastened into the flesh.

The Abbé Dubois,* in describing the hook-swinging ceremony, says that "a priest beats the fleshy part of the back until it is quite benumbed. While suspended, the devotee is careful not to show any sign of pain; indeed he continues to laugh, jest, and gesticulate, like a buffoon in order to amuse the spectators, who applaud and shout with laughter. After swinging in the air for the prescribed time, the victim is let down, and, as soon as his wounds are dressed, he returns home in triumph."

Some years ago, a man in a village, north of the Godāvari river, who had four holes in his loins from previous swingings, complained to the Deputy Commissioner that his occupation was gone, as he was no longer allowed to be swung. Quite recently the Governor of Madras was approached by a ryot (agriculturist), on behalf of the community, with a request for permission to revive the practice of hook-swinging in a certain village of the Madura district. He represented, with all earnestness, that, since this ceremony had been stopped, the rainfall had been deficient and the crops scanty; cholera had been prevalent; and in families where there were five or six children ten years ago, there were now only two or three.

A variant of the form of hook-swinging dealt with above is described by Tavernier, who, writing in the seventeenth century, narrates how devotees "go out of the city and fasten iron hooks to the boughs of several trees. Then come a great number of poor people, and hang themselves, some by the sides, some by the brawn

* Hindu Manners, Customs, and Ceremonies.

Plate XXXII.

Sidi Viranna.

of their backs, upon these hooks, until, the weight of their body tearing away the flesh, they fall of themselves. T'is a wonderful thing to see that not so much as one drop of blood should issue from the wounded flesh, nor that any of the flesh should be left upon the hooks; besides that in two days they are perfectly cured by such plasters as their Brāhmans give them."

A ceremony which is closely allied to hook-swinging is the tūkkam (lifting), which takes place during the kumbhum kodum or pot festival in Travancore, for the following account of which I am indebted to the Madras Mail, 1902. On a wooden platform is an upright frame, on which is a transverse bar, both ends of which can be raised or lowered at will. Facing the temple there were three such platforms, and each of them was occupied by a man who performed the tūkkam ceremony. He was fitted with a head gear resembling an old poke-bonnet. From the rim were suspended slender threads of coloured beads and tinsel. On his shoulders rested a pair of wooden epaulettes, which looked gilded. His costume was turkey red and black, and from the waist downwards he was covered with a skirt of peacock's feathers. Under his arms ran a leather band, by which, when the transverse bar was raised, he hung in mid-air. Behind the band were two steel hooks, which pierced the skin very slightly. In his hands each man held a bow and what seemed to be an arrow, and from time to time he shouted and gesticulated in an alarming manner. There was a distinct military air about the dress and demeanour of the men.

As human hook-swinging is forbidden, a pseudo-ceremony has been subsituted for it, and was recently performed for my special edification at Chennapatna in the Mysore province The nature of the apparatus which is erected for the occasion, and decorated with coloured cloths, flags, and leafy twigs of the mango tree, is rendered clear by reference to plate XXXIII, which shows Sidi Vīranna suspended on high, and Māriamma in her shrine carried above its bearer's head. To the top of the framework a brass umbrella and kalasam (brass pot) are affixed. The end of the beam to which the figure of Sidi Vīranna (plate XXXII) is suspended, is adorned with a canopy with mango leaves tied to it. The goddess Māriamma in her shrine, borne by a pūjāri, and Sidi Vīranna carried by a boy, are conducted to a tank where they are worshipped, and brought in procession to the scene of the swinging ceremony. To a long beam, which is lowered to the ground, Sidi Vīranna, carrying in his hands a sword and shield, and dressed up in a gaudy turban and silk-bordered cloth, is secured by means of a rope made of human hair, which is tied to a hook in the middle of his back. The beam is then hoisted on high, and Sidi Vīranna rotated round and round, accompanied by the goddess Māriamma, and Holeya musicians playing weird music with fife and drum. Sometimes a cradle is tied to the beam beneath the canopy, and children are placed in it. And occasionally men, tied to the beam by ropes passed round the waist, are hoisted. The festival usually commences on a Tuesday, and lasts for three days. On the first day the

Plate XXXIII.

Pseudc-Hook-swinging.

goddess Māriamma is worshipped by Brāhmans only, and on the following day by other castes, who make offerings of fowls and sheep. The swinging of the god is carried on for several hours. At its conclusion, the goddess is taken in procession through the streets, and, when the temple is reached, a fire-walking ceremony, called konda, takes place. Over the hot embers strewn in front of the temple, the pūjāri, with the goddess, walks three times, and enters the temple. It is said that he receives no injury to his feet, if he fasts and keeps himself pure on the day of the ordeal.

At a roadside hamlet near Kumulam in the South Arcot district, my assistant saw a pseudo-hook-swinging ceremony being performed. The beam had a sheep tied to it, as a substitute for a human being. One family had taken a vow to tie their child to the beam for one revolution thereof, but the police intervened, and the child's clothes and a sheep were swung instead. At a pseudo-hook-swinging ceremony in the Bellary district, as carried out at the present day, a Bēdar is suspended by a cloth passing under his arms. The Mādigas always swing him, and have to provide the hide ropes which are used.*

I am indebted to Messrs. Wiele & Klein for the photographs illustrating the human hook-swinging ceremony.

* Manual of the Bellary district.

INFANTICIDE.

THE sacrifice of infant life may, so far as Southern India is concerned, be classified under two heads: (*a*) criminal offence as a means of getting rid of inconvenient offspring, or as an act of revenge; (*b*) tribal custom. The Abbé Dubois * notes that parents used to abandon on a high road innocent babies, who happened to be born on a certain day, which the prognostications of the professional astrologer had signified to be unlucky. And there were even unnatural parents who went the length of strangling or drowning these tiny victims of stupid and atrocious superstition. A few years ago a newly-born baby was found dead in a ditch, and one of a gang of Basavis (dedicated prostitutes), working at a neighbouring factory, was suspected of being the mother. The police officer announced his intention of examining all the Basavis, and she who was in a state of lactation, with no baby to account for her condition, would be charged with knowledge of the infant's death. Of infanticide as an unauthorised act of mercy by the Irulas of the Nīlgiris, the following account is given by Harkness.† During the winter, or while they are wandering about the forests in search of food, driven by hunger, the families or parties separate one from another. On these occasions

* Hindu Manners, Customs, and Ceremonies.

† Description of a singular Aboriginal Race inhabiting the summit of the Neilgherry hills, 1832.

the women and young children are often left alone, and the mother, having no longer any nourishment for her infant, anticipates its final misery by burying it alive. The account was given and corroborated in such a manner as to leave no doubt of its correctness.

It is stated by Orme, on the authority of the Jesuit Father Martin, that the fury of revenge operates so strongly among the 'Colleries' (Kallans) that a man, for a slight affront, has been known to murder his wife and all his children, merely to have the atrocious satisfaction of compelling his adversary to commit like murders in his own family. The former practice of infanticide by the Kallans is dealt with at greater length in the Manual of the Madura district, where it is stated, on the authority of the survey account, that "a horrible custom exists among the females of the Colleries. When a quarrel or dissension arises between them, the insulted woman brings her child to the house of the aggressor, and kills it at her door to avenge herself, although her vengeance is attended with the most cruel barbarity. She immediately thereafter proceeds to a neighbouring village with all her goods. In this attempt she is opposed by her neighbours, which gives rise to clamour and outrage. The complaint is then carried to the head Ambalacaur, who lays it before thè elders of the village, and solicits their interference to terminate the quarrel. In the course of this investigation, if the husband finds that sufficient evidence has been brought against his wife that she had given cause for provocation and aggression, he proceeds unobserved by the assembly to his house, and brings one of his children, and, in the presence of witnesses, kills his child at the door of the woman, who had first killed her child at his. By this mode of proceeding he considers that he has saved himself much trouble and expense, which would otherwise have devolved on him. This circumstance is soon brought to the notice of the tribunal, who proclaim that the offence committed is sufficiently avenged. But, should this voluntary retribution of revenge not be executed by the convicted person, the tribunal is prolonged to a limited period, generally fifteen days. Before the expiration of that period one of the children of the convicted person must be killed. At the same time he is to bear all expenses for providing food, etc., for the assembly during three days." Such atrocities are not permitted under British rule.

In the Manual of the Vizagapatam district it is stated that female infanticide used to be very common all over the Jeypore country, and the Rājah is said to have made money out of it in one large talūk (division). The custom was to consult the Dāsari (priest) when a female child was born as to its fate. If it was to be killed, the parents had to pay the Amīn of the talūk a fee for the privilege of killing it; and the Amīn used to pay the Rājah three hundred rupees a year for renting the privilege of giving the license and pocketing the fees.

The practice of female infanticide was formerly very prevalent among the Khonds of Ganjam, and, in 1841, Lieutenant Macpherson was deputed to carry into effect the measures which had been proposed by Lord Elphinstone for the suppression of the Meriah (human) sacrifice and infanticide. The crime was ascribed to various beliefs, viz.: (1) that it was an injunction by god, as one woman made the whole world suffer; (2) that it conduces to male offspring; (3) that woman, being a mischief-maker, is better out of the world than in it; (4) that the difficulty, owing to poverty, in providing marriage portions was an objection to rearing females. From Macpherson's well-known report * the following extracts are taken. "The portion of the Khond country in which the practice of female infanticide is known to prevail is roughly estimated at 2,400 square miles, its population at 60,000, and the number of infants destroyed annually at 1,200 to 1,500. The tribes (who practice infanticide) belong to the division of the Khond people which does not offer human sacrifices. The usage of infanticide has existed amongst them from time immemorial. It owes its origin and its maintenance partly to religious opinions, partly to ideas from which certain very important features of Khond manners arise. The Khonds believe that the supreme deity, the sun god, created all things good; that the earth goddess introduced evil into the world; and that these two powers have since conflicted. The non-sacrificing tribes makes the supreme deity the great object of their adoration, neglecting the earth goddess. The sacrificing tribes, on the other hand, believe the propitiation of the latter power to be the most necessary worship. Now the tribes which practice female infanticide hold that the sun god, in contemplating the

* Selections from the Records of the Government of India (Home Department), No. V. 1854.

deplorable effects produced by the creation of feminine nature, charged men to bring up only as many females as they could restrain from producing evil to society. This is the first idea upon which the usage is founded. Again, the Khonds believe that souls almost invariably return to animate human forms in the families in which they have been first born and received. But the reception of the soul of an infant into a family is completed only on the performance of the ceremony of naming upon the seventh day after its birth. The death of a female infant, therefore, before that ceremonial of reception, is believed to exclude its soul from the circle of family spirits, diminishing by one the chance of future female births in the family. And, as the first aspiration of every Khond is to have male children, this belief is a powerful incentive to infanticide." Macpherson, during his campaign, came across many villages of about a hundred houses, in which there was not a single female child. In his arguments with the people, he asserted that inquiry would prove that the opinion that male births are increased by the destruction of female infants is unfounded. And, with respect to the justification which is laid on the ground that the destruction of infants is a less evil than that which must arise from the contests attendant on the capricious dissolution of their marriages, he held it to be obvious that the practice of infanticide, and the cause of those contests re-act upon each other, alternately as cause and effect. Infanticide produces a scarcity of women, which raises marriage payments so high that tribes are easily induced to contest their adjustments when dissolutions of the tie occur, while these dissolutions are plainly prompted by that scarcity which prevents every man from having a wife. On the cessation of infanticide women would become abundant, and the marriage payment would become small. Every man would have a wife as elsewhere. Women would have less power to change, and, when they did, there would be no difficulty in making the requisite adjustment of property.

In 1855, Captain Frye found many Baro Bori Khond villages without a single female child in them.

In former times, the Lambādis, before setting out on a journey, used to procure a little child, and bury it in the ground up to its shoulders, and then drive their loaded bullocks over the unfortunate victim. In proportion to the bullocks thoroughly trampling the child to death, so their belief in a successful journey increased.*

The practice of infanticide, as it prevailed among the Todas of the Nīlgiris, is best summed up in the words of an aged Toda, during an interview with Colonel Marshall.† "I was a little boy when Mr. Sullivan (the first English pioneer of the Nīlgiris) visited these mountains. In those days it was the custom to kill children, but the practice has long died out, and now one never hears of it. I don't know whether it was wrong or not to kill them, but we were very poor, and could not support our children. Now everyone has a mantle (putkūli), but formerly there was only one for the whole family. We did not kill them

* Rev. J. Cain, Ind. Ant., VIII, 1879.

† A Phrenologist amongst the Todas, 1873.

to please any god, but because it was our custom. The mother never nursed the child, and the parents did not kill it. Do you think we could kill it ourselves? Those tell lies who say we laid it down before the opening of the buffalo-pen, so that it might be run over and killed by the animals. We never did such things, and it is all nonsense that we drowned it in buffalo's milk. Boys were never killed—only girls; not those who were sickly and deformed—that would be a sin; but, when we had one girl, or in some families two girls, those that followed were killed. An old woman (kelachi) used to take the child immediately it was born, and close its nostrils, ears, and mouth with a cloth thus—here pantomimic action. It would shortly droop its head, and go to sleep. We then buried it in the ground. The kelachi got a present of four annas for the deed." The old man's remark about the cattle-pen refers to the Malagasy custom of placing a new-born child at the entrance to a cattle-pen, and then driving the cattle over it, to see whether they would trample on it or not.* The Missionary Metz † bears out the statement that the Toda babies were killed by suffocation.

In a recent note on the proportion of the sexes among the Todas, ‡ which brings out very clearly the great excess of male over females, Mr. R. C. Punnett states that "all who have studied the Todas are agreed upon the frequency of the practice in earlier times. Marshall,

* Ellis, History of Madagascar.

† Tribes inhabiting the Neilgherry hills. By a German Missionary, 1856.

‡ Proc. Cambridge Philosoph. Soc., XII, 1904.

writing in 1872, refers to the large amount of female infanticide in former years, but expresses his conviction that the practice had by that time died out. Marshall's evidence is that of native assurance only. Dr. Rivers, who received the same assurance, is disinclined to place much confidence in native veracity with reference to this point, and, in view of the lack of encouragement which the practice receives from the Indian Government, this is not altogether surprising. The supposition of female infanticide, by accounting for the great disproportion in the numbers of the sexes, brings the Todas into harmony with what is known of the rest of mankind." In summarising his conclusions, Mr. Punnett, notes that—

(1) Among the Todas, males preponderate greatly over females.

(2) This preponderance is doubtless due to the practice of female infanticide, which is probably still to some extent prevalent.

(3) The numerical preponderance of the males has been steadily sinking during recent years, owing probably to the check which foreign intercourse has imposed upon female infanticide.

MERIAH SACRIFICE.

The ethnological section of the Madras Museum received a few years ago a very interesting relic in the shape of a human (Meriah) sacrifice post from Baligudu in Ganjam (plate XXXIV). This post, which was fast being reduced to a mere shell by 'white-ants,' is, I believe, the only one now in existence. It was brought by Colonel Pickance, who was Assistant Superintendent of Police, to Baligudu from some place in the south-west of the Chinna Kimedi Maliahs, and set up in the ground near the gate of the reserve Police barracks.

"The best known case," Mr. Frazer writes,* of human sacrifices systematically offered to ensure good crops is supplied by the Khonds or Kandhs, a Dravidian race in Bengal and Madras. Our knowledge of them is derived from the accounts written by British officers, who, forty or fifty years ago, were engaged in putting them down. The sacrifices were offered to the earth goddess, Tari Pennu or Bera Pennu, and were believed to ensure good crops, and immunity from all diseases and accidents. In particular, they were considered necessary in the cultivation of turmeric, the Khonds arguing that the turmeric could not have a deep red colour without the shedding of blood. The victim, a Meriah, was acceptable to the goddess only if he had been purchased, or had been born

* The Golden Bough.

Plate XXXIV.

Meriah Sacrifice Post.

a victim, that is the son of a victim father, or had been devoted as a child by his father or guardian."

In 1837, Mr. Russell, in a report on the districts entrusted to his control, wrote as follows.* "The ceremonies attending the barbarous rite, and still more the mode of destroying life, vary in different parts of the country. In the Māliahs of Goomsur, the sacrifice is offered annually to Thadha Pennoo (the earth) under the effigy of a bird intended to represent a peacock, with the view of propitiating the deity to grant favourable seasons and crops. The ceremony is performed at the expense of, and in rotation by certain mootahs (districts) composing a community, and connected together from local circumstances. Besides these periodical sacrifices, others are made by single mootahs, and even by individuals, to avert any threatening calamity from sickness, murrain, or other cause. Grown men are the most esteemed (as victims) because the most costly. Children are purchased, and reared for years with the family of the person who ultimately devotes them to a cruel death, when circumstances are supposed to demand a sacrifice at his hands. They seem to be treated with kindness, and, if young, are kept under no constraint; but, when old enough to be sensible of the fate that awaits them, they are placed in fetters and guarded. Most of those who were rescued had been sold by their parents or nearest relations, a practice which, from all we could learn, is very common. Persons of riper age are kidnapped by

* Selections from the Records, Government of India, No. V, Human Sacrifice and Infanticide, 1154.

wretches who trade in human flesh. The victim must always be purchased. Criminals, or prisoners captured in war, are not considered fitting subjects. The price is paid indifferently in brass utensils, cattle, or corn. The zanee (or priest), who may be of any caste, officiates at the sacrifice, but he performs the poojah (offering of flowers, incense, etc.) to the idol through the medium of the Toomba, who must be a Khond child under seven years of age. This child is fed and clothed at the public expense, eats with no other person, and is subjected to no act deemed impure. For a month prior to the sacrifice there is much feasting and intoxication, and dancing round the Meriah who is adorned with garlands, etc., and, on the day before the performance of the barbarous rite, is stupefied with toddy, and made to sit, or, if necessary, is bound at the bottom of a post, bearing the effigy above described. The assembled multitude then dance around to music, and, addressing the earth, say: 'O God, we offer the sacrifice to you. Give us good crops, seasons, and health.' After which they address the victim 'We bought you with a price, and did not seize you. Now we sacrifice you according to custom, and no sin rests with us.' On the following day, the victim, being again intoxicated and anointed with oil, each individual present touches the anointed part, and wipes the oil on his own head. All then proceed in procession around the village and its boundaries, preceded by music, bearing the victim and a pole, to the top of which is attached a tuft of peacock's feathers. On returning to the post, which is always placed near the village deity called Zakaree

Pennoo, and represented by three stones, near which the brass effigy in the shape of the peacock is buried, they kill a hog in sacrifice, and, having allowed the blood to flow into a pit prepared for the purpose, the victim who, if it has been found possible, has been previously made senseless from intoxication, is seized and thrown in, and his face pressed down until he is suffocated in the bloody mire amid the noise of instruments. The Zanee then cuts a piece of flesh from the body, and buries it with ceremony near the effigy and village idol, as an offering to the earth. All the rest afterwards go through the same form, and carry the bloody prize to their villages, where the same rites are performed, part being interred near the village idol, and little bits on the boundaries. The head and face remain untouched, and the bones, when bare, are buried with them in the pit. After this horrid ceremony has been completed, a buffalo calf is brought in front of the post, and, his fore feet having been cut off, is left there till the following day. Women, dressed in male attire and armed as men, then drink, dance and sing round the spot, the calf is killed and eaten, and the Zanee (priest) is dismissed with a present of rice and a hog or calf."

In the same year, Mr. Arbuthnot, Collector of Vizagapatam, reported as follows. "Of the hill tribe, Codooloo, there are said to be two distinct classes, the Cotia Codooloo and Jathapoo Codooloo. The former class is that which is in the habit of offering human sacrifices to the god called Jenkery, with a view to secure good crops. This ceremony is generally performed on the Sunday preceding or following the Pongal feast. The victim is seldom carried by force, but procured by purchase, and there is a fixed price for each person, which consists of forty articles such as a bullock, a male buffalo, a cow, a goat, a piece of cloth, a silk cloth, a brass pot, a large plate, a bunch of plantains, etc. The man who is destined for the sacrifice is immediately carried before the god, and a small quantity of rice coloured with saffron is put upon his head. The influence of this is said to prevent his attempting to escape, even though set at liberty. It would appear, however, that, from the moment of his seizure till he is sacrificed, he is kept in a continued state of stupefaction or intoxication He is allowed to wander about the village, to eat and drink anything he may take a fancy to, and even to have connection with any of the women whom he may meet. On the morning set apart for the sacrifice, he is carried before the idol in a state of intoxication. One of the villagers officiates as priest, who cuts a small hole in the stomach of the victim, and with the blood that flows from the wound the idol is besmeared. Then the crowds from the neighbouring villages rush forward, and he is literally cut into pieces. Each person who is so fortunate as to procure it carries away a morsel of the flesh, and presents it to the idol of his own village."

Concerning a method of sacrifice, which is illustrated by the post preserved in the museum, Colonel Campbell records * that " one of the most common ways of offering the sacrifice in Chinna Kimedi is to the effigy of an elephant (hatti mundo or elephant's head) rudely carved

* Personal Narrative of Service among the Wild Tribes of Khondistan.

in wood, fixed on the top of a stout post, on which it is made to revolve. After the performance of the usual ceremonies, the intended victim is fastened to the proboscis of the elephant, and, amidst the shouts and yells of the excited multitude of Khonds, is rapidly whirled round, when, at a given signal by the officiating Zanee or priest, the crowd rush in, seize the Meriah, and with their knives cut the flesh off the shrieking wretch as long as life remains. He is then cut down, the skeleton burnt, and the horrid orgies are over. In several villages I counted as many as fourteen effigies of elephants, which had been used in former sacrifices. These I caused to be overthrown by the baggage elephants attached to my camp in the presence of the assembled Khonds, to show them that these venerated objects had no power against the living animal, and to remove all vestiges of their bloody superstition." In another report Colonel Campbell describes how the miserable victim is dragged along the fields, surrounded by a crowd of half intoxicated Khonds who, shouting and screaming, rush upon him, and with their knives cut the flesh piecemeal from the bones, avoiding the head and bowels, till the living skeleton, dying from loss of blood, is relieved from torture, when its remains are burnt, and the ashes mixed with the new grain to preserve it from insects. Yet again he describes a sacrifice which was peculiar to the Khonds of Jeypore. "It is", he says, "always succeeded by the sacrifice of three human beings, two to the sun to the east and west of the village, and one in the centre, with the usual barbarities of the Meriah. A stout wooden post about six feet long is firmly fixed in the ground, at the foot of it a narrow grave is dug, and to the top of the post the victim is firmly fastened by the long hair of his head. Four assistants hold his outstretched arms and legs, the body being suspended horizontally over the grave, with the face towards the earth. The officiating Junna or priest, standing on the right side, repeats the following invocation, at intervals hacking with his sacrificing knife the back part of the shrieking victim's neck. 'O Mighty Manicksoro, this is your festal day. To the Khonds the offering is Meriah, to kings Junna. On account of this sacrifice you have given to kings kingdoms, guns, and swords. The sacrifice we now offer you must eat, and we pray that our battle-axes may be converted into swords, our bows and arrows into gun powder and balls; and, if we have any quarrels with other tribes, give us the victory. Preserve us from the tyranny of kings and their officers.' Then, addressing the victim, 'That we may enjoy prosperity, we offer you a sacrifice to our god Manicksoro, who will immediately eat you, so be not grieved at our slaying you. Your parents were aware, when we purchased you from them for sixty rupees, that we did so with intent to sacrifice you. There is, therefore, no sin on our heads, but on your parents. After you are dead, we shall perform your obsequies.' The victim is then decapitated, the body thrown into the grave, and the head left suspended from the post till devoured by wild beasts. The knife remains fastened to the post till the three sacrifices have been performed, when it is removed with much ceremony." In an account by Captain Mac Viccar of the sacrifice as carried out at Maji Deso, it is stated that "on the day of sacrifice the Meriah is surrounded by the Khonds, who beat him violently on the head with the heavy metal bangles, which they purchase at the fairs, and wear on these occasions. If this inhuman smashing does not immediately destroy the victim's life, an end is put to his sufferings by strangulation, a slit bamboo being used for the purpose. Strips of flesh are then cut off the back, and each recipient of the precious treasure carries his portion to the stream which waters his fields, and there suspends it on a pole. The remains of the mangled carcase are then buried, and funeral obsequies are performed seven days subsequently, and repeated one year afterwards."

The Khonds of Bara Mootah promised to relinquish the rite on condition, *inter alia*, that they should be at liberty to sacrifice buffaloes, monkeys, goats, etc., to their deities with all the solemnities observed on occasions of human sacrifice; and that they should be at liberty, upon all occasions, to denounce to their gods, the Government, and some of its servants in particular, as the cause of their having relinquished the great rite.

The last recorded Meriah sacrifice in the Ganjam Māliahs occurred in 1852, and there are still Khonds alive, who were present at it. Twenty-five descendants of persons who were reserved for sacrifice, but were rescued by Government officers, returned themselves as Meriah at the Census, 1901. The Khonds have now substituted a buffalo for a human being. The animal is hewn to pieces while alive, and the villagers rush home to their villages, to bury the flesh in the soil, and so secure prosperous crops. The sacrifice is not unaccompanied by risk to the performers, as the buffalo, before dying, frequently kills one or more of its tormentors. This was the case near Balliguda in 1899, when a buffalo killed the sacrificer. In the previous year, the desire of a village to intercept the bearer of the flesh for a neighbouring village led to a fight, in which two men were killed.

It was the practice, a few years ago, at every Dassara festival in Jeypore, Vizagapatam, to select a specially fine ram, wash it, shave its head, affix thereto red and white bottu and nāmam (sect marks) between the eyes and down the nose, and gird it with a new white cloth after the manner of a human being. The animal being then fastened in a sitting posture, certain pūja was performed by the Brāhman priest, and it was decapitated. The supplanting of human victims by animals is indicated by various religious legends. Thus a hind was substituted for Iphigenia, and a ram for Isaac.

It was stated by the officers of the Meriah Agency that there was reason to believe that the Rāja of Jeypore, when he was installed at his father's decease in 1860–61, sacrificed a girl thirteen years of age at the shrine of the goddess Durga in the town of Jeypore.* The last attempted human sacrifice (which was nearly successful) in the Vizagapatam district, among the Kutia Khonds, was, I believe, in 1880. But the memory of the abandoned practice is kept green by one of the Khond songs, for a translation of which we are indebted to Mr. J. E. Friend-Pereira.†

* Vizagapatam Manual. † Journ., As. Soc., Bengal, 1898.

At the time of the great Kiabon (Campbell) Saheb's coming, the country was in darkness; it was enveloped in mist.

Having sent paiks to collect the people of the land, they, having surrounded them, caught the meria sacrificers.

Having caught the meria sacrificers, they brought them; and again they went and seized the evil councillors.

Having seen the chains and shackles, the people were afraid; murder and bloodshed were quelled.

Then the land became beautiful; and a certain Mokodella (MacPherson) Saheb came.

He destroyed the lairs of the tigers and bears in the hills and rocks, and taught wisdom to the people.

After the lapse of a month he built bungalows and schools; and he advised them to learn reading and law.

They learnt wisdom and reading; they acquired silver and gold. Then all the people became wealthy.

Human sacrifice was not practised in the Kurtilli muttah of the Ganjam Maliahs. The reason of this is assigned to the fact that the first attempt was made with a crooked knife, and the sacrificers made such a bad business of it that they gave it up. Colonel Campbell gives another tradition, that through humanity one of the Kurtilli Patros (head of a group of villages) threatened to leave the muttah if the practice was carried out.

ON DRESS.

As in Europe, so in Southern India, fashion plays an important rôle in connection with native dress, both male and female. The assumption of the turban by the autochthonous Todas of the Nīlgiris; the replacement of the tribal turban of the Badagas by knitted night cap of bright red or orange hue; the pork-pie cap, beloved of native student, and offtimes decorated with monstrous knitted flower pattern; the unstarched white shirt, patent leather boots, and white socks of the Bengāli Bābu clerk; the adoption by native cricketers of machine-made coloured blazers, as evil in colour contrast as those of many a house eleven at an English public school, are but a few examples of change for the worse in native male attire. Sometime ago I was shocked by the appearance of a member of my staff in a new patch-work white shirt adorned with no less than six individual and distinct trade-marks, representing the King Emperor, Britannia, an elephant, etc. A native of the labouring classes is, to my mind, far better dressed when clad in plain white loin cloth stained with indigenous seruver-dye, and white or seruver-red turban, than when his turban is dyed with Turkey-red, and the loin cloth is of white imported fabric with the much-prized trade-mark, or replaced by unseemly pantaloons made of some gaudy imported piece-good. No longer does the jungle tribesman, who has emerged from his uncivilised condition to work for regular wages on planters' estates, rest content with a simple country-made cloth around his loins, but appears, on high days and holidays, clad in turban or cap, and woven coat of English cut. And, on the occasion of a visit to the village of a hill tribe, I found the entire male community dressing in gorgeous apparel for a sacred festival in a neighbouring grove, and painting their faces with various marks with the aid of miniature looking-glasses and coal-tar dyes, which, with imported fabrics, are exposed for sale at the weekly shandy (market).

Between fashion in female dress in England and Southern India there is this marked difference, that, whereas in England change in form (with the bloomer and bicycle costumes as extreme examples in modern times) is the most conspicuous feature, in Southern India, while the shape of the sāri, jacket, and petticoat have remained unaltered, a radical change has taken place in recent years in both design and colour owing to the widespread introduction of imported printed fabrics (piece-goods), which now constitute a conspicuous feature of bazārs throughout the Madras Presidency. And it is curious to look back, and reflect that the term piece-goods was originally applied in trade to the Indian cotton fabrics exported to England.

Three primary factors are mainly responsible for guiding fashion so far as native female dress in Southern India is concerned, viz., novelty, the quaint or grotesque, and artistic beauty. And the least concerned, in these days of the decline and fall of South Indian industrial arts, is artistic beauty. The love of the grotesque, which prevails among the natives of Southern India, is best illustrated by the carvings on Hindu temples and mythological paintings, and is responsible for the demand for the eccentric devices on female dress, with which the bazārs are now stocked, and which are disseminated, through the medium of weekly fairs or markets, to remote places, which do not rejoice in the equivalent of milliner's shops.

In addition to new and showy design, which will captivate the native eye, the ticket or label on each piece is an important element of attraction, and as much ingenuity is displayed in the production of the grotesque on the ticket as on the fabric. And I have before me, as I write, a glazed label depicting a group composed of a native lady with turmeric complexion, clad in a pink sāri, seated on a maroon cushion, and engaged in conversation with a naked little boy blue, while a chubby pink child looks on round the corner of a violet purdah (curtain). We are nowadays familiar with litigation in connection with trade-marks in their commercial aspect. Not long ago an incident occurred, which related to these marks in their religious aspect. A public meeting of Muhammadans assembled in the mosque at Ootacamund with a view to taking steps to present a petition to the Governor to stop the importation of a certain brand of cigarettes made in Germany, as the trade-mark represented a bird of paradise with the kalīma (the Muhammadan confession of faith) round its neck, as being an insult to Muhammadans.

The *raison d'être* of the gaudy eccentricities of design in female apparel, men's shawls and turbans, which are now endemic in the bazārs of Southern India, is the endeavour on the part of the merchant to secure a fabric which will be attractive, and command an extensive sale combined with a large profit. For example, some time ago a fabric, intended for making up into female petticoats, arrived in the Madras market, with a flower and bird device and a wondrous border composed of an endless procession of white bicycles of ancient pattern with green gearing and treadles, separated from each other by upright stems with green and yellow fronds growing out of a conventional border. In another importation, the same bicycles appeared on a cloth with designs of flowers and fishes. The whole attraction of these fabrics laid in the representation of the bicycle, which is now established as a 'common object of the sea-shore' in Madras.

The native scale of colour differs from the British colour-scale, as represented by dyers, and mainly in this, that the English colours tend to be crude, while the native colours are of more subdued or compound tints. For example, the beautiful vegetable reds of Madura and Conjeeveram are not what we should call a true red like the imported Turkey-red, but, as can readily be seen in some of the beautiful woven cloths in the industrial section of the Madras museum, red with a slight admixture of blue. I do not for a moment contend that the imported fabrics, which form so conspicuous a feature of the female attire of the middle and lower classes of the native community, should possess the artistic merit, either in colour or design, of the lovely sāris manufactured at Adoni, Arni, Madura, Tanjore and other places, or the beautiful satins of Ayyampet. But I do condemn both colour and design of many of the imported colour-printed fabrics, which, in a native throng, offend the eye, when brought in contrast with the more subdued colouring of the woven cloths made by native weavers with country-dyed yarn. "It should," Ruskin writes,* "be one of the first objects of all manufacturers to produce stuffs not only beautiful and quaint in design, but also adapted for every-day service, and decorous in humble and secluded life. And your duty as manufacturers is to form the market as much as to supply it. And it rests with the manufacturer to determine whether he will make his wares educational instruments, or mere drugs of the market." With which quotation I close my brief lay sermon on modern dress, and return to ethnography.

Some tribes in Southern India have only recently advanced beyond what has been termed the fig-leaf state of society. Thus, writing in 1874, Mr. Ullal Raghavendra Rao states † that the Koragas of South Canara wear "leaves of the forest interwoven together. The story goes that, at the time when the Koragas reigned, one of these black-legged (the usual expression by which they are referred to during the night) demanded a girl of high birth in marriage. Being enraged at this, the upper class of the people withheld, after the overthrow of the Koraga empire, every kind of dress from Koraga

* The two Paths.

† Ind. Ant., III, 1874.

women, who, to protect themselves from disgrace, have since had recourse to the leaves of the forest, conceiving that god has decreed them this kind of covering." A few years later (1881) Mr. Walhouse tells us * that the Koragas wore an "apron of twigs and leaves over the buttocks. Once this was the only covering allowed them, and a mark of their deep degradation. But now, when no longer compulsory, and of no use, as it is worn over the clothes, the women still retain it, believing its disuse would be unlucky. I am told that the Koragas, when they come into a town, for marketing or other purpose, walk in Indian file, concealing their nakedness by means of a series of cloths stitched together, spread out between them, and extending down the line. A small piece of dry areca palm leaf sewed together covers the head of the Koraga, and forms a hat for him. This hat, at their feasts, he uses as a drinking-cup, which will hold a considerable quantity of liquor.

In a note on the Irulas, Mackenzie writes as follows.† "After the Yuga Pralayam (deluge, or change from one Yuga to another), the Villars or Irulans, Malayans, and Vēdans, supposed to be descendants of a Rishi under the influence of a malignant curse, were living in a state of nature, though they have now taken to wearing some kind of covering, males putting on skins and females stitched leaves."

The Thanda Pulayan women of the west coast wear a primitive dress, made of the leaves of a sedge (thanda), cut into lengths, and tied round the waist in such a

* Ind. Ant., X, 1881. † Tamil Manuscripts, Vol. III.

fashion that the unwoven strings hang in a bushy tail behind, and present the same appearance in front, reaching below the knees (plate XXXV). When a Thanda Pulayan girl first assumes this garment, to replace the strip of areca palm bark worn in early childhood, a ceremony called thanda kalyānam, or thanda marriage, is celebrated, which is the occasion of a feast of curry and rice, fish, and toddy. The garment is generally made by a female relative. It is fast going out of fashion, as Māppillas and others who own the Pulayans compel them to wear cotton cloths. The weaving of this garment is accounted for by a tradition that "a certain high-caste man had been sowing grain, and planting vegetables in his fields, but found that his daily work was in some unknown way frustrated. For, whatever he planted or sowed in the day, was carefully picked up and taken when men slept. So he set a watch, and one night he saw coming out of a hole hitherto unknown to him certain beings like men, but quite naked, who set to work destroying his hopes of a crop. Pursuing them, he succeeded in catching a man and woman, and he was so ashamed of their condition that he gave the man his own upper cloth, and made him put it on; but, not having one to spare for the woman, she (following mother Eve's example) made herself an apron of grass." *

The jungle Vettuvans of Malabar wear clusters of long leaves, suspended from the waist. The origin of this gear is said to be that, when the god Parameswara

* Rev. W. J. Richards, Ind. Ant., IX, 1880.

Plate XXXV.

Thanda Pulayan.

was distributing gifts of clothing to the various peoples of the earth, he asked the Vettuvan women whether they would prefer a daily or yearly change of apparel. They decided in favour of the former, and the god, to punish them for their ambition, decreed that their daily dress should consist of leaves. They change their foliage every noon, and sleep in it.

In a note on the Bhondas of Jaipūr, Mr. J. A. May informs us * that the female attire "consists of just a piece of cloth, either made of kerong bark and manufactured by themselves, or purchased from the weavers, about a foot square, and only sufficient to cover a part of one hip. It is attached to their waists by a string, on which it runs, and can be shifted round to any side. A most ludicrous sight has often been presented to me by a stampede among a number of these women, when I have happened to enter a village unexpectedly. On my approach, one and all hurried to their respective dwellings, and, as they ran in all directions, endeavoured to shift this rag round to the part most likely to be exposed to me. The peculiar dress originated in the following legend. The goddess Sita happened to travel through this part of the country, and, when she halted on one occasion, while superintending the preparation of her midday repast, found herself surrounded by a large number of naked women. She blushed to behold such indecency, and forthwith presented them with a piece of tusser silk cloth, which was eagerly accepted, but, when

* Ind. Ant., II, 1873.

divided, was found to supply each one with only just enough to cover one hip. The goddess, whose travelling wardrobe evidently did not allow of greater liberality, then commanded that they should always in future cover themselves thus much, death being the penalty of their disobedience. My informant gave me to understand that one of the Government Agents some years ago insisted on a young woman being properly clothed. The result was she survived the change only three days."

According to the Vizagapatam Manual, the small strip of hempen cloth worn by the Bonda or Nanga (naked) Porojas is so adjusted as to leave the left thigh, both in front and behind, entirely uncovered. They are required, moreover, to shave their heads. Any relaxation of either custom would lead, it is believed, to the destruction of the tribe by tigers.

The bustle or dress-improver, made of tadamāra fibre, and worn by the Gadaba women of Vizagapatam outside the loin-cloth, is said to have been copied from that of Sīta, the wife of Rāma, when she followed her banished lord to the wilds of Dandakāranyam. Each division of the Gadabas has a distinctive dress for females, manufactured out of the karenga fibre. Thus, the cloth of the Boda Gadaba women consists of black or blue and white stripes; the Parengi Gadabas wear white with a thin red border; the Allaru Gadabas wear red, blue, and white.*

* H. D. Taylor, Madras Census Report, 1891.

Plate XXXVI.

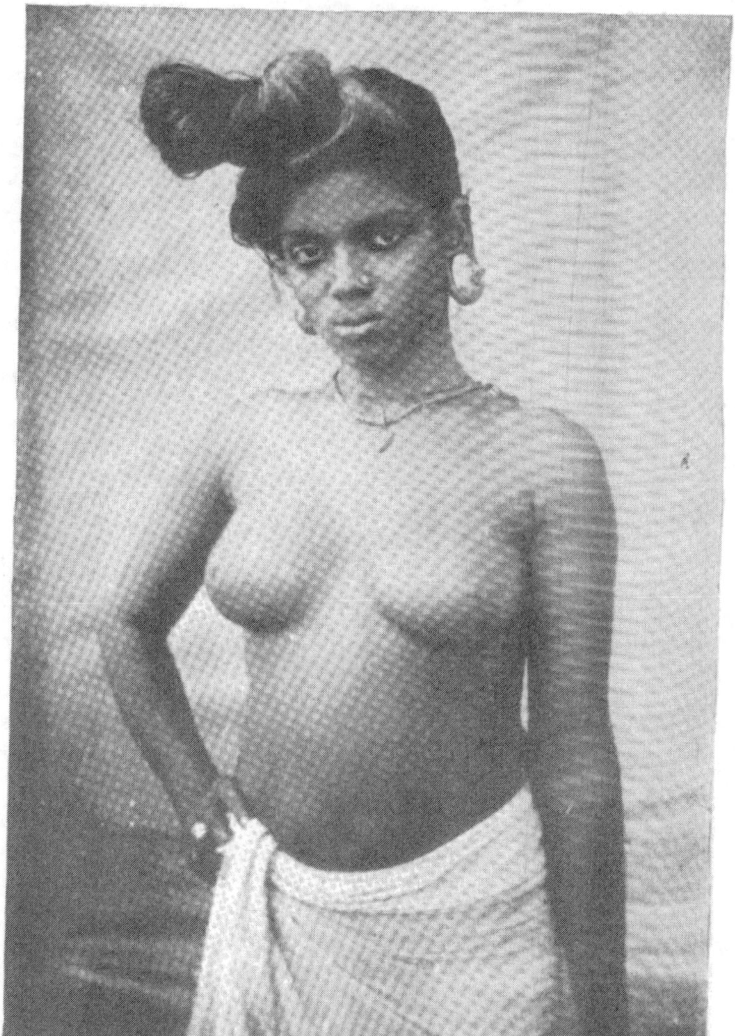

Tiyan Woman.

"In the first quarter of the nineteenth century," Mr. G. T. Mackenzie writes,* "the female converts to Christianity, in the extreme south, ventured, contrary to the old rules for the lower castes, to clothe themselves above the waist. This innovation was made the occasion for threats, violence, and a series of disturbances. Similar disturbances arose from the same cause nearly thirty years later, and, in 1859, Sir Charles Trevelyan, Governor of Madras, interfered, and granted permission to the women of the lower castes to wear a cloth over the breasts and shoulders."

Concerning the Tiyans of Malabar, Moor, writing towards the close of the eighteenth century, † narrates that "we were told that, many years ago, during the reign of a princess, the men were addicted to practices so vile that a distant hint of them can only be given; and, to wean their minds from such intercourse, and turn them to their proper object, she caused the upper part of the females' garments to be lain aside; supposing such a continual display of attractive charms could not but have the wished-for effect. Another authority informed us that a treasonable insurrection was nearly effected by the aid of the females, who carried arms under their garments, and supplied the men with them; and from this cause proceeds their present nakedness". By General Burton ‡ the adoption of a covering to the breasts on the west coast is naively attributed to the outspoken remarks of the British soldier.

* Christianity in Travancore, 1901.

† Narrative of Little's Detachment, 1794.

‡ An Indian Olio.

The jungle Kādir women of the Ánaimalai hills, when they meet a European on the road, with their body-cloths wrapped round them in such a way as to expose the upper halves of their breasts, manifest symptoms of shyness and modesty, and stand aside with face averted so that they cannot see the stranger, on the same principle which prompts some eastern women, if surprised when taking a bath, to turn the face, no further concealment being necessary. Ideas of modesty, it has been said, are altogether relative and conventional, and it is not the feeling of shame that has given rise to the covering of the body, but the covering that has provoked the feeling of shame. This is well illustrated by the difference in behaviour of the native females of Malabar and the Tamil women of the east coast. In Malabar the body-clothing of the Nāyar, Tiyan, Cheruman females, etc., above the loins is exceedingly scanty. As Mr. Logan says:* "The women clothe themselves in a single white cloth of fine texture, reaching from the waist to the knees, and occasionally, when abroad, they throw over the shoulder and bosom another similar cloth. But by custom the Nayar women go uncovered from the waist. Upper garments indicate lower caste, or sometimes, by a strange reversal of western notions, immodesty." According to ancient custom, Nāyar women in Travancore used to remove their body-cloth in the presence of the Royal Family. But, since 1856, this custom has been abolished, by a proclamation during the reign of H.H Vanchi Bala Rāma Varma Kulasakhara Perumal

* Manual of Malabar.

Bhagiodya Rāma Varma. In a critique on the Indian Census Report, 1901, Mr. J. D. Rees observes * that, "if the Census Commissioner had enjoyed the privilege of living among the Nāyars, he would not have accused them of an 'excess of females.' The most beautiful women in India, if numerous, could never be excessive." The observant Abbé Dubois noticed that, "of all the women in India, it is especially the conrtesans (dancing girls or Dēva-dāsis) who are the most decently clothed, as experience has no doubt taught them that for a woman to display her charms damps sensual ardour instead of exciting it, and that the imagination is more easily captivated than the eye."† A Tamil woman, young or old and wizened, going along the high road, with breasts partially uncovered by her ample body-cloth, will, when she sees a European coming, pull the cloth over them from a feeling of shame in the presence of the foreigner, which is absent in the presence of her fellow-countrymen. So, too, a Tamil or Toda woman, when undergoing the process of measurement at my hands, is most particular in arranging her upper garment so as to conceal her breasts, whereas a Malabar woman has no hesitation in appearing with breasts completely exposed, or in throwing off the slender wrapper which may cover her shoulders, and considers the exposure in no way immodest.

A friend, bartering for the two bead necklets, which constituted the full-dress of a jungle girl, had no difficulty in securing one, but no bribe would tempt her to part with the second, as, in its absence, she would be naked.

* Nineteenth Century, 1904.

† Hindu Manners, Customs and Ceremonies.

NAMES OF NATIVES.

An orthodox Brāhman, when asked his name, will not give it readily and in a direct manner, but will, after some hesitation, say "People call me" or "My name is said to be" so and so. On meeting a person, such as an elder, to whom respect is due, it is strict etiquette to prostrate oneself before him, and repeat his abhivathanam, which contains his sakha (Vēda), gōtra (house name), and name. This is only done by the very orthodox. Some Brāhmans believe that, if they mention their name or age, they run the risk of shortening their life. Moreover, from a Hindu point of view, self must always be kept in the background as a sign of modesty. Even in the Sanskrit grammar the third person comes first, and the first last. A slōka runs to the following effect:—

> Atma nāma gurornāma ;
> Namāthikripunasyacha ;
> Srēyaskāmo nagrinhiyāth ;
> Jyestāh pathya kalathryayoh.

Which, being translated, means that he who wishes for a prosperous life should not pronounce the name of his natural or spiritual father (guru), eldest son or wife, or a great miser. A Sanskrit stanza in the Sukranitisara runs to the effect that one may not make known the following nine things: one's age, wealth, family secrets, mode of acquiring knowledge of mantrams or medicine connection with the opposite sex, gifts to others, respect or disgrace to oneself.

Wives believe that to tell their husband's name, or pronounce it even in a dream, would bring him to an untimely end. Most Brāhman, and some non-Brāhman castes, name their children after their grandparents or great-grandparents, who are not living. In such cases, the parents call them by pet names, or abbreviated forms of their true names, of which the following are examples:—

Pet names.—Payyan, Mogu, Nayana, Doraswāmi, Chikkia, Doddappa, Appanna, Anappa, Swāmi (converted into Sami).

Abbreviated names.—Kittu or Kichchu (Krishna), Rāmu (Ramaswāmi), Rukku (Rukmani), Janu (Janaki), Chechu (Seshadri), Ecchi (Lakshmi), Mani (Subrahmanian), Nanu (Narayana), Rāju (Rājagopalan).

Some Lingayats name their children after their ancestors, especially after grandparents. So long as these are living, the children are named after the gods, but assume their names after their death.

Women may not call their parents, husband, father and mother-in-law, brother or sister-in-law by their name. The mother-in-law will be called amma, and the sister-in-law akka. A girl, when she enters into a new family on marriage, receives a new name. This name is given to her by her husband's relations, and signifies that she has *de facto*, not only *de jure*, become a member of her husband's family. So much importance is attached to the new name that it completely ousts the girl's former name. The old name is known as her mother's house name, the new one as her mother-in-law's name.

Victoria, or Rāni, after the late Queen-Empress, is the name given to pet daughters in many Hindu families.

And the title Empress is said to have been used as a surname by a well-known Dāsi (dancing-girl) in the city of Madras. Prince of Wales is sometimes the pet name given to an eldest son.

The custom of calling a newly-born child, after its parents have lost a first born or more in succession, by an opprobrious name, is common among many classes, including even Muhammadans. In the Mysore country the custom of boring the right nostril of a child, whose elder brothers or sisters have died, prevails. Such children are called Gunda (rock), Kalla (stone), Huccha (lunatic), Tippa (dung-hill). The last name is given after some rubbish from a dung-heap has been brought in a sieve, and the child placed on it.* "Other names of despised things," Mr. A. Srinivasan writes "are Pentayya (refuse), Siprayya and Dibbadu (broom and mound of earth); of distasteful objects Vembu (nīm tree); and of words that mean disrelish Rossayya (disgust). Chithabi (decayed leaf), a Muhammadan name, shows that the principle of self-abasement finds favour with the Moslem also. Some call themselves cats (Pillayya and Pillamma) in the hope that they may atone thereby for the sin of having caused the death of cats." Lingayat children, whose predecessors have died in their infancy, are named Sudugadavva (burial ground), Tippiah or Tippavva (rubbish heap), Tirakappa (mendicant), Gundappa (rock). These names signify humility, and are given in the belief that god will have pity on the parents, and give the children a long lease of life.

* Narayan Aiyangar. Ind. Ant., IX., 1880.

The custom of giving opprobrious names, to avert the jealousy of evil powers, is common in the Telugu country. For example, Pichchi (mad), Verri (idiot), Engili (spittle), are very potent for this purpose. Another device is to give a Hindu child a Muhammadan or English name, such as Badē Sahib or Rāpsan (corruption of Robertson).* Longly is used as a name for a maimed person in the district in which Mr. Longley of the Civil Service, who had a maimed limb, served. A robber, who was hung at Trichinopoly, became so popular as a demon that children were frequently named after him.†

It is a custom among some Hindu women, when they lose their first two children, to beg of three persons three rags as bedding for the third child. They also dig a grave, and fill it in, or roll the child in the dust, or in a tray filled with bran. Sometimes they beg for money instead of bran, and with the money collected have a silver ornament made, which they tie on to the neck of the child. This custom is very common among the Telugus. Sterile women believe that children will be born to them, if they place a newly-born infant in their lap, or perform for it the unlovely duties of a nurse.

Vows are sometimes made at a snake shrine with the object of procuring issue, and if a child is born, it is given an appropriate name, such as Nāgappa, Subbana, Nāgamma, etc.‡

Childless parents, to whom offspring is born after the performance of a vow, name it after the deity, whose aid

* H. G. Prendergast. *Ibid.*

† Monier Williams. Brahmanism and Hinduism.

‡ Manual of the Bellary district, 1905.

has been invoked, such as Srinivāsa at Tirupati, Lakshmi-narasimha at Sholingūr, or some other local god or goddess. At Negapatam, some Hindus make vows to the Mirān (Muhammadan saint) of Nagūr, and name the child after him. The name thus given is not, however, used in every-day life, but abandoned, like the ceremonial name given prior to the Hindu upanayanam ceremony.

The following nicknames, given on account of physical attributes or deformity, are selected from a long vocabulary, which has been mainly brought together during my tribal wanderings:—

Thief.	Blind.
Hunchback.	Crow.
Stout.	Left-handed.
Piles.	Treble-jointed.
Pot-bellied.	Snorer.
Black-bellied.	Lame.
Spleen.	Scarred.
Fond of honey.	Dwarf
Brought up on bran or buttermilk.	Protruding navel.
	Crook-necked.
Puffy-cheeked.	Bandy-legged.
Glutton.	Shaky-legged.
Drunkard.	Long-legged.
Hairy as a fox.	Itch-legged.
Bushy-haired.	Donkey-legged.
Bear.	Tall as a palmyra.
Crocodile.	Tremulous head.
Hairy like the tail of a mongoose.	Monkey-head.
	Bald-head.
Dirty.	Double-head.

Big-head.	Man who keeps on scratching his body.
Mango-shaped head.	Stammerer.
Stone-head.	With mouth like a Yāli (mythological beast common in temple carvings).
Cocoanut-shaped head.	Fakir (mendicant).
Blood-shot-eyed.	Short as a brinjal.
Elephant-eyed.	Old.
Cat-eyed.	Knees knocking together.
Squint-eyed.	Long-nosed like a crow.
Big nose.	Toothless.
Legless.	Broom.
Crooked mouthed.	Disgust.
Irregular toothed.	Nīm tree.
Tobacco.	Strong as a hammer.
Man who came back from the cremation ground.	
Man who revived after death.	

I am informed by Mr. Vincent that the Kādirs of the western mountains have a peculiar word āli, denoting apparently a fellow or thing, which they apply as a suffix to animate and inanimate objects, *e.g.*, Karaman āli, black fellow; pūv āli, flower. Among Kādir nicknames, the following occur:—

White hand.	Tiger.
White mother.	Pain.
White flower.	Fruit.
Long legs.	Milk.
Round man.	Virgin.
Stick.	Love.
Beauty.	Breasts.
Myna (a bird).	

A former Head Magistrate of a district was known as Vendikkai Dorai (Mr. Hibiscus esculentus)—a name, which is given in reference to the sticky nature of the mucilage in *Hibiscus* fruits, to those who try to smooth matters over between contending parties. The nickname Velakkennai (castor-oil) is given for a similar reason.

The name Kulla Katthirikkai, or short brinjal (fruits of *Solanum Melongena*) is given to people of dwarfish stature. The name Balegadde is derived from ancestors who had to subsist on the stem of the plantain (balegadde) during their flight before the advance of Tīpū Sultān. Rēpatikira Doragāru (Mr. Come To-morrow) is the name given by natives to Europeans who back out of interviews. Among one division of the Savaras, names are given to children after Government appointments, or officials who are held in esteem by the community. Such are Governor, Collector, Superintendent, Tahsildar (native revenue officer), Innes, Master, and Kolnol (colonel) The names Sirkar (Goverment) and Cutchery (court-house) occur among the Todas of the Nīlgiris.

In Ganjam, an individual was nicknamed Bojho Patro from his love of the tom-tom (native drum). An Urāli was named Kothē (a stone), because he was born on a rock near Kotagiri.

A petition from a native servant to his master refers, in English, to the relations between his wife and cock-eyed Virappan.

A Badaga was nicknamed Relly Hiriya because, like a certain Mr. Reilly, he had lost an eye. Among the Badagas Kūdan is a common pet name in memory of a monegar (head-man) of that name, who was very popular and famous some years ago. The Badagas give nicknames to those outside their own community, and a Revenue Inspector who had strabismus was called Oru Kanna Iyaru, or squint-eyed Iyar.

Names which have their counterpart in England are Black, White, Little, Short, Long and Green. To which may be added Red, Greenish-blue, and Brownish-black.

In the Bellary district, the names Munrol and Munrolappa, after Sir Thomas Munro, are common, and are given in hope that the boy may attain to the same celebrity as the former Governor of Madras. One of Sir Thomas Munro's good qualities was that, like Rāma and Rob Roy, his arms reached to his knees, or, in other words, he possessed the quality of an Ajanubahu, which is the heritage of kings, or those who have blue blood in them. This particular anatomical character I have myself met with only once—in a Tinnevelly Shānān, whose height was 173 cm. and span of arms 194 cm. Rob Roy, it will be remembered, could without stooping tie his garters, which were placed two inches below the knee. An old woman at Banganapalle, when asked her age, said that she was ten years old when Sir Thomas Munro visited Gūti. Instances of names of Anglo-Indians distinguished as soldiers, civilians, or merchants, are to be found in different parts of the Madras Presidency, with resultant hybrids such as Doveton Ranga Rao, Brodie Chengalraya Mudaliar, Crole Venkataswāmi Naidu, Dare-house * Venkataswāmi Naidu. In this way the name of Arthur Wellesley (afterwards Duke of Wellington) is perpetuated, and that of General Harris,

* Dare House=the Firm of Messrs. Parry & Co

the conqueror of Seringapatam, is connected with a shepherd family, one of whose ancestors was steward to the renowned Commander-in-chief.

It is stated in the Vizagapatam Manual that, during the reign of Chōla Chakravati, the Kamsalas (artisans) claimed to be equal to Brāhmans. This offended the sovereign, and he ordered their destruction. Some only escaped death by taking shelter with people of the "Ozu" caste. As an acknowledgment of their gratitude, many of the Kamsalas have Ozu affixed to their house-name, *e.g.*, Kattōzu, Lakkozu.

As examples of prenomens of Hindus and Muhammadans after well-known localities, the following may be quoted:—Madras Muhammad Hussain; Dindigul Alasingarachari; Trichinopoly Arumukkam Pillai; Arcot S. Babu Rao; Conjeeveram Dēvarajan; Madura S. Ramasubbha Aiyar. A Muhammadan in the Kurnool district had the name of the Lunjabunda Kasim Sahib. "In this district," a correspondent writes, "we have heap of villages, the names of which have Lunja (a prostitute) as a prefix. I believe that, in old times, the Muhammadan chieftains used to pension off their ladies, when the bloom was off them, and grant them a village site. The Muhammadan rule was not popular in these parts, and the folk of the country-side may have been responsible for names of villages such as Lunjalūr (prostitute's village), Lunjapoyalūr (village of the prostitute's standard), or Lunjabunda (prostitute's rock or fort)."

Native names are often the despair of Europeans when rapidly calling them out at a Levée or University convocation. The following are a few examples of tongue-twisters which, without rehearsal, it is difficult to produce *ore rotundo*: Bhogaraju Pattabhisitaramaiya; A. Minakshisundarasiva; Virupavajhula Mannarukrishnudu; N. Sarasvati Ardhanarisvara Aiyar; Tulisalamadattil N. Appu Aiyar; Singanallur Narayanachari Vadi Rajachar.

Among the Baidyas (Billavas) of South Canara, the names of males are derived from the day of the week on which they were born, such as Chome from Somavara (Monday), Thukra from Shukravara (Friday), and Thaniya from Shanivara (Saturday).

The Koragas of South Canara were, it is said, originally sun-worshippers, and they are still called after the days of the week Aita, Toma, Angara, Gurva, Tanya, and Tukra.* Writing concerning the Oriyas of Ganjam, Mr. S. P. Rice says† that "the lower classes of the Uriya people have a custom, from which De Foe has unconsciously borrowed. The names Sombaria (Monday), Sukria (Friday), are not at all uncommon, and Sunday and Thursday have also been requisitioned. Why Saturday should not be used is not inexplicable, for, from the time of the earliest Arcadian mythology, Saturday has been a day of evil omen, and many a Hindu has as superstitious a dread of beginning an undertaking on Saturday as some of us have of going a journey on Friday. Among the Uriyas, the appellations

* Ullal Raghavendra Rao, Ind. Ant., III, 1874.

† Occasional Essays on Native South Indian Life.

derived from the attributes of the gods are many and various. Syama-sundara means of a beautiful bluish colour, and was an attribute of Krishna. Brundavano means a forest of the sacred tulasi plant. Dasarathi is a good instance of the purely Sanskrit character of these names. It is derived from Dasaratha (ten cars)." Mr. Rice tells us further that "many are to be met with in the zamindaris who boast of three or even four names The additions are, for the most part, titles given by the various Zamindars, and they are often even more easily acquired than some knighthoods and many medals. A title, generally accompanied by more substantial recognition in the shape of land, is given for 'blessing' the Zamindar, for holding his umbrella, perhaps for handing him betel leaves. Thus titles, for the most part, denote some sort of compliment, such as Bhushano, an ornament; Ratno, a jewel; or Subuddhi, the wise."

Among the Khoduras, who manufacture bangles and rings worn by lower class Oriyas, a quaint custom exists, by which honorific titles, such as Sēnāpati, Māhāpatro, etc., are sold by the panchayat (council) to any man of the caste who covets them, and the proceeds are sent to Pūri and Pratābpur for the benefit of the temples.*

"A Nayar," Mr. Fawcett informs us, "addressing a Nambūtri, must speak of himself as a foot-servant. If he mentions his rice, he must call it gritty rice. Rupees must be called his copper coins. He must call his house his dung-pit, and so on."† A peculiarity with the

* Madras Census Report, 1901.

† Madras Mus. Bull., III, 1, 1900.

Nambūtiris is that they do not generally call themselves by their proper name, but only by the names of their illams (houses).

"One feature in Telugu names," Mr. A. Srinivasan writes, "is that they are sometimes not a safe index to the sex of the bearers. Males have names of the female deity, and, even where they bear those of the male deity, they often affix the termination amma. Thus Ankamma and Krishnamma come to be names of males, and illustrate the double source of confusion. Akasa Ramanna (Ramanna in the air, or man in the moon) is the usual subscription in anonymous petitions among the Telugus. Abrogation of one's class or caste name involves no inconsiderable sacrifice of self-love. Thus the name of Chenchayya among Brāhmans; Yānādi and Yerukala among other high castes; Chenchus, Yānādis, and Yerukalas being the aborigines. Not less significant is the adoption by non-Brāhmans of the names Brāhmanayya, Brāhmanna, or in vulgar form Bapanaiyya and Bapanamma."

Among the Nattamāns, the eldest son in each family has to be named after the village god, which gives its name to the kāni or sept to which the family belongs, and the child is usually taken to that village to be named.* In like manner, the first male child of the Kotas of the Nīlgiris at Kotagiri is always called Komuttan after the tribal god Kāmatarāya, and the numerous Komuttans are distinguished by the prefix big, little, carpenter, etc. After a birth among the Kois of the Godávari district,

* Madras Census Report, 1901.

the child is well washed on the seventh day, and all the neighbours and near relations assemble together to name it. Having placed the child on a cot, they put a leaf of the mhowa tree (*Bassia latifolia*) in the child's hand, and pronounce some name which they think suitable for it. If the child cries, they take it as a sign that they must choose another name, and so they throw the leaf away, and substitute another leaf and another name, until the child shows its approbation by ceasing to cry. Any public-spirited person in the village or neighbourhood, who is honoured by having his name bestowed upon it, ever after regards the child with some amount of interest.*

The Yerukala women are accustomed to honour their lords and masters with the dignified title of cocks.†

It has been noticed, at times of Census, that native Christians and Paraiyans, who masquerade in European clothes, return themselves as Eurasians, and it may be accepted that some benefit must be derived by the individual in return for the masking of his nationality. And it occasionally happens that pure-bred natives, with European name and costume, successfully pass themselves off as Eurasians, and are placed on a footing of equality with them in the matter of diet when they are in prison, being allowed the luxury of bread, butter, coffee, etc. ‡

The ingenious suggestion has been made that, when native Christians pose as Eurasians, the name Murugan

* J. Cain, Ind. Ant. V, 1876. † *Ibid.*

‡ Madras Census Report, 1901.

becomes Morgan, Ramaswāmi Ramsay, and Devadāsan Davidson. Equally ingenious is the suggestion that ancient Egyptian names have their Hindu counterparts, Rhamessamena becoming Ramasawmy, Ramases Rāma, Chryses Krishna, and so forth.

Native Christians, especially on the west coast, have Portuguese names such as Saldhana, Mascarenhas, Coelho, Sequeira, etc , derived from Portuguese sponsors when their ancestors were baptised after conversion. Others take the names of the priest who converts them to Christianity, *e.g.*, D'Monte, De Souza, etc. A telegram which was recently transmitted in the South Canara district, "Albuquerque, taluk sheristadar, on leave, Vasco de Gama acting involved in the arrangement," takes one back several centuries in Indian history.

"At Sadras," Bartolomeo writes,* "there is a Christian congregation. Most of the members are natural children of the Dutch and other Europeans. I baptised there some new-born infants ; and, I was inserting their names in the church register. I everywhere found in the book Filbo de fulano, Filbo de fulano. As I could not conceive it possible that a father should have so many children, I asked the sexton the meaning of the word fulano. He replied that it signified a person whose name was unknown, and that, when the father of a child could not be with certainty discovered, they put in the register Filbo de fulano."

* Voyage to the East Indies, 1800.

Among the Syrian Christians of the west coast, old and new testament names have become transformed as follows:—

Chacko; Yacob = Jacob.
Mani = Emanuel.
Yohan; Chona = John.
Thommen; Thommi; Thom = Thomas.
Chamuel = Samuel.
Cheriyan = Zachariah.
Mathan; Mathai; Mathoo = Mathew.
Chandi = Alexander.
Powlos = Paul.
Philippos = Philip.

Syrian Christians take the name of their father, their own name, and that of their residence. Whence names such as Edazayhikkal Mathoo Philip, or Kunnampuram Thommen Chandi result.

The honorific title Aiyar, which was formerly used exclusively as a title by Brāhmans, has now come to be used by every native clergyman working in the Church, and in the non-conformist missions of Southern India. The name which precedes the honorific title will enable us to discover whether the man is a Christian or Hindu. Thus, Yesudian Aiyar means the Aiyar who is the servant of Jesus.*

It has been said that every man in France is now Monsieur, *i.e.*, my feudal lord; and every man in Germany Mein Herr; and every man, in England Mr. *i.e.*, Master.† In like manner, the up-to-date Paraiyan butler of Europeans has the honorific title Avergal added as a suffix to his name on the envelopes of letters addressed to him.

* Rev. A. Margoschis. Christianity and Caste, 1893.
† Baring Gould, Strange Survivals, 1895.

COUVADE (HATCHING).

THE couvade, or custom in accordance with which the father takes to bed, and is doctored when a baby is born, is very widespread, and is described * by Sir John Lubbock (now Lord Avebury) in the sundry forms, which it assumes in Brazil, Borneo, Greenland, Spain, France, and other countries. To illustrate the quaint custom, an example from Guiana will suffice. "On the birth of a child, the ancient Indian etiquette requires the father to take to his hammock, where he remains some days as if he were sick, and receives the congratulations and condolence of his friends. An instance of this custom came under my own observation, where a man in robust health and excellent condition, without a single bodily ailment, was lying in his hammock in the most provoking manner, and carefully and respectfully attended by the women, while the mother of the new-born infant was cooking, none apparently regarding her." †

The couvade is referred to by Alberuni ‡ (about A.D. 1030), who says that, when a child is born, people show particular attention to the man, not to the woman. There is a Tamil proverb that, if a Korati is brought to bed, her husband takes the prescribed stimulant; and examples of the couvade in Southern India have been already recorded. Thus, writing about the Yerukalas,

* Origin of Civilisation and Primitive Condition of Man.

† Brett. Indian Tribes of Guiana.

‡ India. Trübner. Oriental Series.

the Rev. J. Cain tells us * that "directly the woman feels the birth pains, she informs her husband, who immediately takes some of her clothes, puts them on, places on his forehead the mark which the women usually place on theirs, retires into a dark room where there is only a very dim lamp, and lies down on the bed, covering himself up with a long cloth. When the child is born, it is washed and placed on the cot beside the father. Assafœtida, jaggery and other articles are then given, not to the mother, but to the father. He is not allowed to leave his bed, but has everything needful brought to him."

Among the Kuravars or basket-makers of Malabar, "as soon as the pains of delivery come upon a pregnant woman, she is taken to an outlying shed, and left alone to live or die as the event may turn out. No help is given to her for twenty-eight days. Even medicines are thrown to her from a distance; and the only assistance rendered is to place a jar of warm water close by her just before the child is born. Pollution from birth is held as worse than that from death. At the end of the twenty-eight days the hut in which she was confined is burnt down. The father, too, is polluted for fourteen days, and, at the end of that time, he is purified, not like other castes by the barber, but by holy water obtained from Brāhmans at temples or elsewhere." Among various other classes, it is customary for the husband to remove the pollution caused by his wife's confinement by means of ceremonial ablution.

* Ind. Ant., III., 1874.

To Mr. G. Krishna Rao, Superintendent of Police in the Shimoga district of Mysore, I am indebted for the following note on the couvade as practised among the Koramas. "Mr. Rice, in the Mysore Gazetteer, says that among the Koravars it is said that, when a woman is confined, her husband takes medicine for her. At the instance of the British Resident I made enquiries, and learned that the Kukke (basket-making) Koramas, living at Gopala village near Shimoga, had this custom among them. The husband learns from his wife the probable time of her confinement, and keeps at home awaiting the delivery. As soon as she is confined, he goes to bed for three days, and takes medicine consisting of chicken and mutton broth spiced with ginger, pepper, onions, garlic, etc. He drinks arrack, and eats as good food as he can afford, while his wife is given boiled rice with a very small quantity of salt, for fear that a larger quantity may induce thirst. There is generally a Koramar midwife to help the wife, and the husband does nothing but eat, drink, and sleep. The clothes of the husband, the wife, and the midwife are given to a washerman to be washed on the fourth day, and the persons themselves have a wash. After this purification the family gives a dinner to the caste-people, which finishes the ceremonial connected with child-birth. One of the men examined by me, who was more intelligent than the rest, explained that the man's life was more valuable than that of the woman, and that the husband, being a more important factor in the birth of the child than the wife, deserves to be better looked after."

The following legend is current among the Koramas, to explain the practice of the couvade among them. One day a donkey, belonging to a Korama camp pitched outside a village, wandered into a Brāhman's field, and did considerable damage to the crop. The Brāhman was naturally angry, and ordered his coolies to pull down the hut of the owner of the donkey. The Korama, outting himself at the feet of the Brāhman, for want of a better excuse, said that he was not aware of what his animal was doing, as at the time he was taking medicine for his wife, and could not look after it. It is suggested, in the Mysore Census Report, 1901, that the practice of the couvade has either long ceased to exist, or is a mere myth based upon a proverb evolved out of a Brāhman's gullibility in accepting the plea that a Korama was eating medicine because his wife was in childbed, as a conclusive proof of an alibi on his behalf.

It is noted by the Rev. S. Mateer * that, after the confinement of a Paraiyan woman in Travancore, the husband is starved for seven days, eating no cooked rice or other food, only roots and fruits; and drinking only arrack or toddy.

Possibly, as suggested by Reclus, the following Toda custom, described by Marshall, † is a survival of the couvade. After the child is born, the mother is removed to a shed, which has been erected in some sequestered spot, in anticipation of the approaching event. There she remains till the next new moon, and, for a month after her return home, she appears to have the house to

* Journ. Roy. As. Soc. XVI. † Phrenologist among the Todas, 1873.

herself, her husband remaining indebted to friends for shelter meanwhile.

The Nayādis of the Cochin State erect a special small hut, to which the woman retires when taken in labour. She is attended to by various female relations, and her husband all the while goes on shampooing his own abdomen, and praying to the mountain gods for the safe delivery of his wife. As soon as the child is born, he offers thanks to them for "having got the child out." *

I have been unable to obtain any confirmation of the practice of the couvade as recorded by Professor Tylor.† "The account," he writes, "for which I have to thank Mr. F. M. Jennings, describes it as usual among natives of the higher castes about Madras, Seringapatam, and on the Malabar coast. It is stated that a man, at the birth of his first son or daughter by the chief wife, or for any son afterwards, will retire to bed for a lunar month, living principally on a rice diet, abstaining from exciting food, and from smoking. At the end of the month he bathes, puts on a fresh dress, and gives his friends a feast." The evidence on which this account was based was that of a nurse born of English parents in India.

* K. Anantha Krishna Iyer.

† Introduction to the Study of Man and Civilisation.

EARTH-EATING.

THE practice of eating earth is widespread in many countries, and at Zanzibar there is a disease called safura induced thereby. It is on record that "the Bikanees of India eat a kind of unctuous clay, and Cutchee ladies are said to eat it, as in some other portions of the globe—Carinthia for example—the ladies eat arsenical earth, because they fancy it improves their complexions." *

From Mr. T. H. Welchman I received a sample of clay, which is eaten by the coolies, chiefly females, on the Cochin hills. "They roast it," he writes, "and eat it in large quantities, about 1 or 1½ lbs. They seem to be ashamed of the habit, and, if other people see them eating it, try to hide it. After about twelve months they swell up, especially the face and abdomen, and refuse all other food, drinking only water. Eventually they die. I am told that, to stop the practice, the natives administer castor-oil to the earth-eaters, but this does not prevent them from eating more, if they can get the chance. I have known several cases of death from this cause." A correspondent writes as follows from Mysore. "The habit of earth-eating appears to be common with the women of this province, and the adjacent talūk of Kollegal, but only when they are in a certain stage of pregnancy. It is only a certain kind of clay that is

* A. H. Japp. Indian Review, April, 1901.

eaten, either raw or baked. The latter process is said to give it a peculiar smell or flavour. I saw large quantities of this baked clay sold in the bazārs of Nanjengōd, and made wide enquiries from women who were in the habit of eating this clay as to any ill effects from the habit, and was invariably informed that they experience none whatever." Another correspondent writes: "I have known numerous instances of Mysoreans, reputed to be addicted to earth-eating, and of both sexes, while the habit once contracted by women is rarely, if ever, abandoned by them, and is invariably followed by fatal results. It is usually an easy matter to identify a confirmed clay or earth-eater, as their appearance suggests that they are suffering from pernicious anæmia, the face being unnaturally swollen or puffed and the abdomen distended, while the limbs are shrunk except at the joints, which appear enlarged, and are said to be painful. The particular kind of munnu, or earth, for which such an unnatural craving is gratified, is apparently to be found in every part of the Wynād that I have seen or resided in." Mr. G. Romilly, who has a tea-estate near Meppādi, Wynād, informs me that he has had several deaths on the estate of dropsical women who were mud-eaters, and that he has been told there are others, who have taken to the habit because they have struck a singularly luscious stratum of mud. They begin by eating it in secret, and, having once contracted the habit, cannot leave off. Men very rarely eat it, and the jungle tribes hardly ever. It is almost entirely Canarese women and children, and Coimbatore Tamils who indulge.

In a paper read before the Asiatic Society of Bengal (1905), Messrs. D. Hooper and H. H. Mann state that "in Mysore and many of the districts in Madras the habit is common. In the bazaars of Madras and Bangalore specially prepared clay is sold for consumption. Lower classes of Tamils, and Badagas, chiefly women, eat earth on the Nīlgiris. Muhammadans, or better class Tamils are not known to practise the custom. In Travancore and Cochin, earth-eaters are found largely among the imported labour on the tea estates. The coolies are Tamil-speaking people from Tinnevelly, Trichinopoly, and Nagercoil. The Kānis or hill tribesmen have not been observed to eat earth, and the Malayālis or natives of Travancore only occasionally indulge. Women, girls, and even crawling children contract the habit. In one estate in Travancore, the Medical Officer reports that 75 per cent. of the women and children are earth-eaters, men, as a rule, are not known to indulge."

BOOMERANG.

WRITING concerning this implement, Mr. Savile Kent states * that "according to Mr. Balfour two forms of this weapon are peculiar to India. One of these, of a simple curved shape and made of wood, is possessed by the Koli tribes of Guzerat. A second Indian form belongs to the Maravars of Madura, and differs in shape from both the above and the Australian type. The contour of this Maravan boomerang is almost crescentic, perfectly flat, but much broader at the more remote or distal extremity of the instrument as held in the hand. The narrower proximal or handle end is, moreover, fashioned into the form of a conveniently prehensile knob, which is usually roughly carved. Although commonly made of wood, it is not unfrequently constructed of steel, or even of ivory. This description of boomerang has been proved by General Pitt Rivers to belong to the category of those weapons which will return to the thrower when dexterously manipulated. From the multiplicity of evidence recorded (ancient Egyptians, Africa, Arizona, New Mexico, and Etruscan vases) the boomerang must evidently be regarded as a weapon that did not originate adventitiously with the Australian aborigines, or at any rate upon Australian soil, but was in all probability brought there with the earliest immigrants from the Asiatic continent." The South Indian boomerangs,

* The Naturalist in Australia, 1897.

Professor E. C. Stirling informs me, "lack the blade-like flatness and the spiral twist, which are always characters of the true Australian returning boomerang. The majority of boomerangs in Australia are not intended to return, and indeed it is now difficult to get the returning form."

In Egerton's 'Indian and Oriental Armour' boomerangs (katariya) used by the Kōls of Guzerat for throwing at hares, wild boars, and other animals, are described and figured. "These" Colonel Lane Fox says "conform to the natural curvature of the wood like the Australia boomerang, which they resemble in form." The Guzerat boomerang figured by Egerton resembles in shape that which is used by the Kallans and Maravans of Southern India, which are described by him, under the name of katari, as used by robbers in Tinnevelly.

"Boomerangs," Dr. G. Oppert writes,* "are used by the Tamil Maravans and Kallans when hunting deer. The Madras museum collection contains three (two ivory, one wooden) from the Tanjore armoury. (plate XXXVII). In the arsenal of the Pudukkōttai Rāja a stock of wooden boomerangs is always kept. Their name in Tamil is valai tadi (bent stick). When thrown, a whirling motion is imparted to the weapon, which causes it to return to the place from which it was thrown. The natives are well acquainted with this peculiar fact." The Dewān of Pudukkōtai writes to me as follows. "The valari (or valai tadi) is a short weapon, generally made of some hard-grained wood (vadathala, etc.). It is also sometimes

* Madras Journ. Lit. Science, Vol. XXV.

Plate XXXVII.

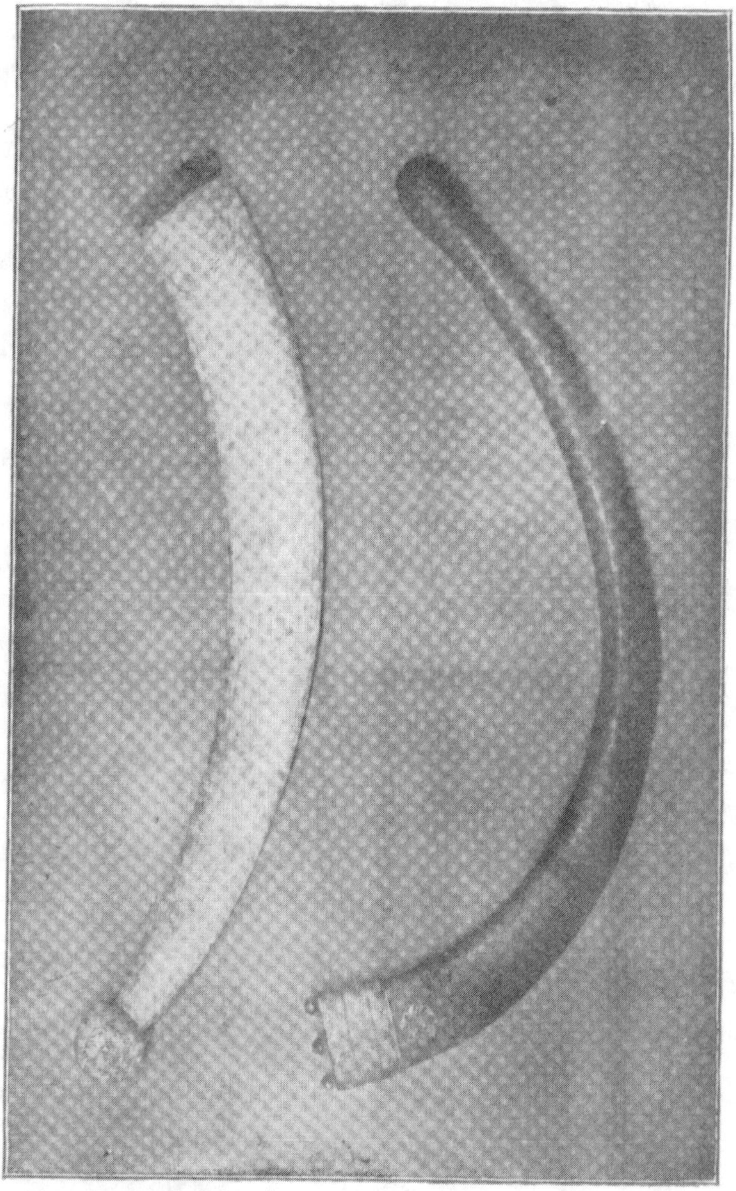

Boomerangs.

made of iron. It is crescent-shaped, one end being heavier than the other, and the outer edge is sharpened. Men trained in the use of the weapon hold it by the lighter end, whirl it a few times over their shoulders to give it impetus, and then hurl it with great force against the object aimed at. It is said that there were experts in the art of throwing the valari, who could at one stroke despatch small game, and even man. No such experts are now forthcoming in the State, though the instrument is reported to be occasionally employed in hunting hares, jungle fowl, etc. Its days, however, must be counted as past. Tradition states that the instrument played a considerable part in the Poligar wars of the last century, But it now reposes peacefully in the households of the descendants of the rude Kallan and Maravan warriors, who plied it with such deadly effect in the last century, preserved as a sacred relic of a chivalric past along with other old family weapons in their pūja room, brought out and scraped and cleaned on occasions like the Ayudha-pūja day (when worship is paid to weapons and implements of industry,) and restored to its place of rest immediately afterwards."

To Mr. R. Bruce Foote I am indebted for the following note on the use of the boomerang in the Madura district. "A very favourite weapon of the Madura country is a kind of curved throwing-stick, having a general likeness to the boomerang of the Australian aborigines. I have in my collection two of these Marávar weapons obtained from near Sivaganga. The larger measures $24\frac{1}{8}''$ along the outer curve, and the chord of the arc $17\frac{5}{8}''$. At the handle end is a rather ovate knob $2\frac{1}{4}$ long and $1\frac{1}{4}''$ in its maximum thickness. The thinnest and smallest part of the weapon is just beyond the knob, and measures $\frac{11}{16}''$ in diameter by $1\frac{1}{8}''$ in width. From that point onwards its width increases very gradually to the distal end, where it measures $2\frac{3}{8}''$ across, and is squarely truncated. The lateral diameter is greatest three or four inches before the truncated end, where it measures 1″. My second specimen is a little smaller than the above, and is also rather less curved. Both are made of hard heavy wood, dark reddish brown in colour as seen through the varnish covering the surface. The wood is said to be tamarind root. The workmanship is rather rude. I had an opportunity of seeing these boomerangs in use near Sivaganga in March 1883. In the morning I came across many parties, small and large, of men and big boys who were out hare-hunting with a few dogs. The parties straggled over the ground, which was sparsely covered with low scrub jungle. And, whenever an unlucky hare started out near enough to the hunters, it was greeted with a volley of the boomerangs, so strongly and dexterously thrown that poor puss had little chance of escape. I saw several knocked out of time. On making enquiries as to these hunting parties, I was told that they were in observance of a semi-religious duty, in which every Maravar male, not unfitted by age or ill-health, is bound to participate on a particular day in the year. I had never before come across such shikar (hunting) parties armed with boomerangs. Nor have I ever seen these weapons used in other parts of the peninsula, though

I have, in various other places, come across small parties furnished with short, straight throwing-sticks used to drive hares into hedged avenues leading up to nets. Whether a dexterous Maravar thrower could make his weapon return to him I could not find out. Certainly in none of the throws observed by me was any tendency to a return perceptible. But for simple straight shots these boomerangs answer admirably."

The story goes that some Kallans, belonging to the Vella (Vala ?) Nādu near Conjeeveram came down south with a number of dogs on a grand hunting expedition, armed with their peculiar weapons, pikes, bludgeons, and boomerangs. Somewhere in the neighbourhood of Mēlūr, whilst they were engaged in their sport, they observed a peacock showing fight to one of their dogs, and, thinking that the country must be a fortunate one, and favourable to bodily strength and courage, they determined to settle in it.* At a Kallan marriage the bride and bridegroom go to the house of the latter, where boomerangs are exchanged and a feast is held.† This custom appears to be fast becoming a tradition. But there is a common saying still current "send the boomerang (valari or valai-tadi), and bring the bride."

* Madura Manual. † G. F. D'Penha, Ind. Ant., XXV, 1896.

STEEL-YARDS, CLEPSYDRAS, KNUCKLE-DUSTERS, COCK-SPURS, TALLIES, DRY CUPPING.

The tūkkukol (weighing rod) is used in the Madras bazārs for weighing small quantities of vegetables, tamarinds, salt-fish, cotton, etc., by shop-keepers, and by hawkers who carry their goods for sale from door to door. But it is rapidly being replaced by English scales. It is practically a rough form of the Danish steel-yard. The beam consists of a bar of hard wood, *e.g.*, rosewood (*Dalbergia latifolia*) or tamarind, 19″ long, and tapering from 1½″ to 1″ in diameter. The scale-pan is a shallow cane basket, 9½ inches across, suspended by four strings from a point near the thin end of the bar. The fulcrum is simply a loop of string, which can be slid along the bar. The graduations are rough notches cut in the bar, and are not numbered, but, as there are only seven of them including the zero mark, they are probably well known to both purchaser and seller. The notches denote 5, 10, 15, 20, 30 and 40 palams, so that the machine can be used for weighing up to about 3 lb. (1 palam = 1¼ oz.). It will be seen from the description that the machine is not a very accurate one, but it is doubtless accurate enough for the purposes for which it is used.

In Malabar there is used for weighing an instrument fashioned on the principle of the Danish steel-yard. The yard, which is made of a hard wood, is about 4 feet long, and tapers from about $1\frac{1}{8}$ inch in the middle to $\frac{3}{4}$ inch at the ends. It is finished off at the heavy end with a loaded brass finial simply ornamented with concentric rings, and the hook end terminates in a piece of ornamental brass work, resembling the crook of a bishop's pastoral staff. The sliding fulcrum is simply a loop of coir (cocoanut fibre) string. The graduation marks, which are not numbered, are small brass pins let into the upper surface of the yard along the middle line, and flush with it. The principal graduations are each made of five pins disposed in the form of a small cross, and single pins serve for the intermediate graduations. Corresponding to each graduation mark on the upper surface of the yard there is a pair of brass pins on the middle line of each side, the pins of each pair being at a distance apart just sufficient to allow the string of the loop to lie between them. The object of these pins is to ensure that, when the instrument is in use, the loop may be accurately in a vertical plane through the graduation mark. The unit of weight employed is the palam of about 14 tolas, and the instrument is graduated from 1 to 100 palams (about 35 lb.). The last three graduations, representing 80, 90, and 100 palams, come upon the brass-work, and are marked by notches instead of pins. The graduation corresponding to 100 tolas has in addition a brass point about $\frac{1}{2}$ inch long, resembling the tongue of a small balance. The whole instrument is ornamental in design, and for a weighing machine of this class is fairly accurate, the sensibility being large on account of the considerable length of the yard. In a more simple form of weighing beam, used by native physicians and druggists in Malabar, the bar is divided into kazhiuchi (approximately tolas) and fractions thereof, and the pan is made of cocoanut shell.

For this account of weighing beams I am indebted to my friend Mr. E. W. Middlemast. The note may be supplemented by a quotation from 'Indo-Anglian Literature' which refers to an examination answer to the question, Graduate the Danish steel-yard. "This question is a downright violation of the laws of God, since we are not coolies neither petty shop-keepers that we will graduate a Danish steel-yard." Advantage was taken by the candidate of his high caste to cover his ignorance by assumed indignation.

Clepsydras.—The Madras museum possesses several specimens of a primitive form of horologe, or water-clock, which is thus referred to by Picart.* "The inhabitants of Mogul," he writes, "measure time by a water-clock, which, however, is very different from our clepsydras or hour-glass. The clepsydra used by the inhabitants of Mogul is in their language called gari or gadli, and has not so much work in it, but then it requires more attendance, a man being oblig'd to watch it continually. 'Tis a bason fill'd with water, in which they put a little copper dish with a very small hole in its bottom. The water comes by insensible degrees into this dish, which when full, and that the water contained in it begins to mix itself with that in the bason, it then sinks to the

* Religious Ceremonies and Customs of the several Nations of the World, 1731.

bottom. The time which it takes up in filling is by them called a gari, which, according to the observation I have made, amounts to twenty-two minutes thirty seconds of time; so that, when the day is exactly twelve hours in length, each part contains eight garies, that is 180 minutes, or three hours. As the days shorten, there are less garies in each part of the day, and more in those of the night; for we are always to add to the one what we subtract from the other, because the night and day together must regularly consist of 64 garies, that is 1,440 minutes, or 24 hours. As soon as one gari is ended, the person who watches the clock strikes as many blows upon a copper table as there are garies passed; after which he strikes others to show the part, whether of the day or night."

In Nepāl the measurement of time is regulated in the same manner. Each time the vessel sinks, a gong is struck, in progressive numbers from dawn to noon. After noon, the first ghari struck indicates the number of gharis which remain of the day till sunset. Day is considered to begin when the tiles on a house can be counted, or when the hairs on the back of a man's hand can be discerned against the sky.*

In Burma also a copper time-measurer, or nayi, was used. "As each nayi was measured off, a gong was beaten, and at every third hour the great drum-shaped gong was sounded from the pahōzin or timekeeper's tower within the inner precincts of the royal palace at

* Encyclopædia Britannica, 1884.

the eastern gate. From the pahō the beats were repeated on large bells by all the guards throughout the palace. To ensure attention to this matter in the olden days, the timekeeper could be carried off and sold in the public market, if he were negligent in the discharge of his duties, being then forced to pay a fine in the shape of ransom." *

In his account of the operations of the Maratha army against Tipū Sultān, Moor informs us † that "the manner of measuring time in Chittledroog and other forts is somewhat curious. It may be called a hydrostatic measure, being a small cup with a hole in its bottom, floated in a vessel of water; and, when a certain quantity of water is received into the cup, from its gravity it sinks, and points out the expiration of a particular portion of time. The water being kept unruffled, this may perhaps be a very accurate method of measuring time, as it is evident no other nicety is required but exactness in the hole of the cup, which may be easily determined. At each gurry, or half hour, the cup sinks, and the sentinel who has charge of the time measurer strikes the number upon a gong, and, emptying the cup, immediately sets it afloat. At the p'haurs, that is to say at three, six, nine, and twelve o'clock, he makes a clattering on the gong, and begins gurries again, similar to the bells on shipboard."

I gather from 'Asiatick Researches' (1798) that the hour-cup or kutoree was adjusted astronomically by an

* Burma under British Rule, and before. J. Nisbet, 1901.

† Narrative of Little's Detachment, 1794.

astrolabe, and that the cups were now and then "very scientifically marked in Sanscrit characters, and may have their uses for the more difficult and abstruse operations of the mathematician or astrologer. . . Six or eight people are required to attend the establishment of a ghuree, four through the day and as many at night, so that none but wealthy men or grandees can afford to support one; which is convenient enough for the other inhabitants, who would have nothing of this sort to consult, as (those being excepted which are attached to their armies), I imagine there are no other public (ghurees) clocks in all India."

This form of time-measurer, made of a half cocoanut or copper, is still in use among native physicians, astrologers, and others in Malabar. A cup of this nature was employed in the Civil Court at Mangalore in 1852, a peon being posted in charge of it, and beating on a gong the number of gadis every time that it sank. At the present day it is used on the occasion of marriage among the higher Hindu castes. The Brāhman priest brings the cup, and places the bridegroom in charge of it. It is the duty of the latter to count the gadis until the time fixed for his entrance into the wedding-booth. The apparatus is nowaday often replaced by a clock or watch, but the officiating priest insists on producing the cup, as he receives his fee for so doing.

The method of computing time by means of a water-clock, on which the gadiya, or nazhigai (24 minutes) and jām or jāmam (7 gadiyas) are indicated by nicks on the inside of the cup, is still in vogue at the huzur office and temple at Venkatagiri. The cup is in charge of a sepoy, who keeps the time, and makes it known to the public by beating a gong at the end of each gadiya or jām. To compensate for seasonal variations of day and night, correction is made in the length of the periods. The hole in the cup, after it has been in use for some time, becomes dilated, and to correct the error, it is contracted by beating the cup with a hammer. A standard cup is kept for the purpose of regulating the water-clock. The computation of time is reckoned by means of an hour-glass in some Brāhman (especially Mādhva) mutts. Mr. Percy Brown writes to me that Mr. J. L. Kipling introduced the water-clock for use by the Police at the Lahore Museum, as the clock was always getting out of order. The bowl is a copper one, floated in an earthen bowl, and takes an hour to sink. It is in charge of the policeman on duty, who strikes a gong each time that it sinks. Water-clocks are in use in many places in the Punjāb, and nearly always in connection with native sentry work.

Knuckle-dusters have for more than a century been used by a Telugu caste of professional wrestlers and gymnasts, called Jetti. The Jettis in Mysore are said to have been sometimes employed as executioners, and to have despatched their victim by a twist of the neck.* Thus, in the last campaign against Tīpū Sultān, General Matthews had his head wrung from his body by the "tiger fangs of the Jetties, a set of

* Rice, Mysore and Coorg Gazetteer.

slaves trained up to gratify their master with their infernal species of dexterity."* They are still considered skilful in setting dislocated joints. In a note regarding them in the last century, Wilks writes as follows.† "These persons constitute a distinct caste, trained from their infancy in daily exercises for the express purpose of exhibitions; and perhaps the whole world does not produce more perfect forms than those which are exhibited at these interesting, but cruel sports. The combatants, clad in a single garment of light orange-coloured drawers extending half way down the thigh, have their right arm furnished with a weapon, which, for want of a more appropriate term, we shall name a cæstus, although different from the Roman instruments of that name. It is composed of buffalo horn, fitted to the hand, and pointed with four knobs, resembling very sharp knuckles, and corresponding to their situation, with a fifth of greater prominence at the end nearest the little finger, and at right angles with the other four. This instrument, properly placed, would enable a man of ordinary strength to cleave open the head of his adversary at a blow; but, the fingers being introduced through the weapon, it is fastened across them at an equal distance between the first and second lower joints, in a situation, it will be observed, which does not admit of attempting a severe blow without the risk of dislocating the first joints of all the fingers. Thus armed, and adorned with garlands of flowers, the successive pairs of combatants, previously

* Narrative sketches of the conquest of Mysore, 1800.

† Historical sketches, Mysore, 1810-17.

matched by the masters of the feast, are led in to the arena; their names and abodes are proclaimed; and, after making their prostrations first to the Rāja seated on his ivory throne, and then to the lattices behind which the ladies of the court are seated, they proceed to the combat, first divesting themselves of the garlands, and strewing the flowers gracefully over the arena. The combat is a mixture of wrestling and boxing, if the latter may be so named. The head is the exclusive object permitted to be struck. Before the end of the contest, both of the combatants may frequently be observed streaming with blood from the crown of the head down to the sand of the arena. When victory seems to have declared itself, or the contest is too severely maintained, the moderators in attendance on the Rāja make a signal for its cessation by throwing down turbans and robes, to be presented to the combatants. The victor frequently goes off the arena in four or five somersaults, to denote that he retires fresh from the contest. The Jettis are divided into five classes, and the ordinary prize of victory is promotion to a higher class. There are distinct rewards for the first class, and in their old age they are promoted to be masters of the feast."

The Jettis of Mysore still have in their possession knuckle-dusters of the type described above, (plate XXXVIII) and take part annually in matches during the Dasara festival. A Jetti police constable, whom I saw at Chennapatna, had wrestled at Baroda, and at the Court of Nepāl, and narrated to me with pride how a wrestler came from Madras to Bangalore, and challenged

Plate XXXVIII.

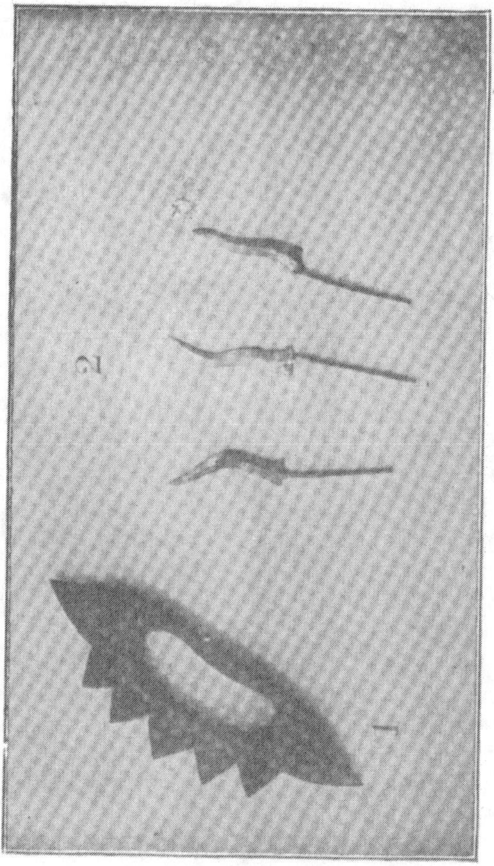

Knuckle-duster ; Cock-spurs.

any one to a match. A Jetti engaged to meet him in two matches for five hundred rupees a match, and, after going in for a short course of training, walked round him in each encounter, and won the money easily. The knuckle-duster, as used at the present day, is strapped over the knuckles with string passed through holes bored through the horn. It is believed that if, in a bout, a man loses an eye, it is a bad omen for the Government of Mysore.

Cock fighting, though said to have been introduced by Themistocles, to encourage bravery among the people who witnessed the contests, is a disgusting spectacle, and I agree with Colonel Newcome that it should be performed in secret. At Chennapatna, in Mysore, a fight was organised for my edification by Muhammadans, who laughingly said that they take more trouble over rearing their game-cocks than over their children. Steel spurs are not used, but the natural spurs are sharpened with a knife, so that they are as sharp as steel. For the purpose of the friendly combat, without money on the result, which I witnessed, the spurs were protected by linen bandages. A real good fight between two well-matched birds may last for several hours, or the combat may be over in a very few minutes. The top of the head, a spot behind the eye, and the chin were pointed out to me as the most fatal places for a stroke of the spur. If the fight is protracted, water may be administered three times, when one of the combatants collapses on the ground with its beak in the earth, and its eyes closed. When the bird is knocked silly, and cannot come up to the scratch, the fight is over. The seconds, between the rounds, bathe the bird's head and wounds with water, and pour water into the mouth, while rubbing the hand down the neck to assist the process of deglutition. The stray feathers collected in the beak are removed, and blood is extracted from the mouth with the fingers and a long feather picked up in the ring.

Cock-fighting is a very popular form of sport in South Canara among the Bants and other classes, and the birds are armed with cunningly devised steel spurs (plate XXXVIII) which constitute a battery of variously curved and sinuous weapons. The tail-feathers of a wounded bird are lifted up, and a palm fan waved to and fro over the cloacal orifice to revive it. The end of a fight at which I was present, recalled to mind Quiller-Couch's graphic description of a contest in 'The Ship of Stars.' "For a moment the birds seemed to touch to touch, and no more—and for a moment only—but in that moment the stroke was given. The home champion fluttered down, stood on his legs for a moment, as if nothing had happened, then toppled and lay twitching." The edges of the ghastly wound inflicted by the spur are brought together with needle and thread, and the bird may live to fight another day. Cock fighting is said* often to lead to gambling and quarrels, and is therefore actively discouraged by the police. It is, in consequence, generally managed unobtrusively.

Tallies, etc.—In the counting of areca-nuts, cocoanuts, etc., the tally is kept by making a score or notch on

* Gazetteer of the Anantapur district.

various substances, such as a piece of bamboo, leaf-stalk or fruit-stalk of the cocoanut. In Malabar I saw a Paniyan elephant mahout, who jealously guarded a bit of bamboo stick with notches cut in it, each of which represented a day for which he had to receive wages. The stick in question had six notches, representing six days' wages, or two rupees four annas. Sometimes knots are made in a piece of thick string or cocoanut fibre. Among the Khonds, Mr. J. E. Friend Pereira informs us,* "at the ceremonial for settling the preliminaries of marriage, a knotted string is put into the hands of the sēri dāh'pa gātāru (searchers for the bride), and a similar string is kept by the girl's people. The reckoning of the date of the betrothal ceremony is kept by undoing a knot in the string every morning. The Yānādis assist European sportsmen by marking down florikin, and those who are unable to count bring in a string with knots tied in it, to indicate the number of birds which they have marked.

In a note on an instrument used by Native mariners for finding their latitudinal position off the coast, Captain Congreve describes the following simple and ingenious instrument.† "A piece of thin board, oblong in shape, three inches long by one and a half wide, is furnished with a string suspended from its centre, eighteen inches long. A number of knots are made in this string, indicative of certain previously observed latitudes; in other words, coinciding with the positions of certain well-known

* Journ. As. Soc. Bengal, LXXI, 1902.

† Madras Journ. Lit. Science, XVI, 1850.

places on the coast. The position of these knots is obtained in the following manner. The observer elevates the board in his left hand, its longest side being upwards, and draws it backwards and forwards in front of his eye until its upright length exactly corresponds with, or covers the space included between the pole-star and the horizon. With his right hand he next catches hold of the string, and brings it to his nose. He makes a knot at the point where it touches that feature; and, if he at the time be abreast of Point Palmiras, an undeviating index is afforded, which will in future show him when he is off that point, the north star's elevation being always fixed, and therefore all the parts of the triangle formed by his line of sight, the string, and the distance between the polar star and the horizon, or the length of the board, equally as constant. To make the thing as clear as possible, suppose the observer finds, when out at sea, that the knot which measured the former coincidence of his position with Point Palmiras, again impinges on his nose, he is satisfied, on this occasion, he is in the same latitudinal line as he was on that, or that he is off Point Palmiras. He makes similar observations at, and the knot is fixed opposite each conspicuous place, on the length of the string, as far as Dondra head in Ceylon generally. Thus by a simple observation, at any future time the mariner is enabled to ascertain his position with sufficient accuracy for his purpose."

When weighing kopra (dried cocoanut kernels), it is customary to keep the tally by making holes in the kernel with the index needle of the weighing-beam. In the measurement of paddy a handful is taken from each measure, and kept apart on a board.

An illiterate milkman, who supplies milk daily to a customer, puts a few drops of milk on the cow-dung smeared floor, and, rubbing it in with the finger, makes therewith a dot on the wall. At the end of the month, the dots are counted, and the amount is settled. Dots are also made with charcoal, chunām (lime), or the juice of green leaves.

Dry-cupping.—A Dommara travelling medicine man, whom I interviewed at Coimbatore, was an expert at dry-cupping with a cow's horn. The apparatus consisted of the distal end of a cow's horn, with the tip removed, and surrounded by wax. Before the application of the horn to the skin of the patient, a hole is bored through the wax with a needle. The horn is then applied to the affected part. The air is exhausted from the horn by prolonged suction with the lips, and the hole in the wax stopped up. As the air is withdrawn from the cavity of the horn, the skin rises up within it. To remove the horn, it is only necessary to re-admit air by once more boring a hole through the wax. In cases of rheumatic pain in a joint, several horns are applied simultaneously.

The Pitt Rivers Museum at Oxford possesses dry-cupping apparatus, made of cow-horn from Mirzapur in North India and from Natal, and of antelope (black-buck) horn from an unrecorded locality in India.

INDEX.